THE GREAT INFIDEL

THE GREAT INFIDEL
A Life of David Hume

Roderick Graham

BIRLINN

First published in Great Britain in 2004 by Tuckwell Press Ltd

First published in paperback in 2005 by
John Donald, an imprint of Birlinn Ltd
This edition published in 2006 by Birlinn Ltd
West Newington House
10 Newington Road
Edinburgh
EH9 1QS

www.birlinn.co.uk

ISBN 10: 1 84158 520 3
ISBN 13: 978 1 84158 520 8

British Library Cataloguing-in-Publication Data
A catalogue record is available on request from
the British Library

Typeset by Hewer Text Ltd, Edinburgh
Printed and bound by Cox & Wyman, Reading

TO FIONA

There is another form of temptation, even more fraught with danger. This is the disease of curiosity . . . It is this which drives us to try and discover the secrets of nature, those secrets which are beyond our understanding, which can avail us nothing and which man should not wish to learn.

St Augustine of Hippo

Contents

Illustrations

Preface

This book is the story of the life of one of Scotland's greatest men. It is not an academic critique of his philosophy or an in-depth study of his political economy. Library shelves already groan under the weight of such works.

David Hume was born in Edinburgh on 26th April 1711 and christened as David Home. He died in the same city on 25th August 1776, his life having spanned the greater part of the eighteenth century.

Historians argue, as historians do, over the concept of a 'Long Eighteenth Century' and it is certainly true that the world did not change absolutely on 1st January 1700, nor were the changes complete by 31st December 1799. But the world and its thinking did change out of all recognition throughout that century and David Hume was not only a witness to, but one of the architects of, that change.

The world into which David Hume was born had already begun to witness the events that would separate the modern age from the last vestiges of the Anglo-Norman systems of government introduced over six hundred years before. Edinburgh in 1700 was still stricken by the financial collapse of the Darien Scheme – a lunatic attempt to found a colony in the swamps of Panama. This disaster, however, was of little or no interest to the farming communities which formed the greater part of the Scottish population, since they had already been coping with a drought which had lasted from 1696 and which would culminate in a severe famine in 1709. There were rumblings throughout Scotland about a parliamentary union with England and both countries were coming to terms with the installation of Dutch Protestants as monarchs in Britain.

Professor T.C. Smout has said that during the century 'practically all classes in Scottish society were conscious of a momentum which was carrying them towards a richer society'.[1] The new frontier for the richer society would move north from the English border to the Highland line. 'A harsh and unlovely type of poverty was the common fate; even among the upper classes it was but little tempered by more gracious ways of life.'[2]

The century would see the political importance of the monarchy decline through the dullness of Anne Stewart while the astuteness of Robert Walpole would transfer the real power to the Parliament in London. Britain solved the knotty problem of the royal succession by importing a German-speaking dynasty from Hanover, and by the turn of the nineteenth century the overall power of the Parliament had asserted itself.

This rational man, David Hume, would be at the heart of the Enlightenment – defined as that period when reason gained the ascendancy over faith – in Edinburgh as much as in Europe where conventional faith-based thought had already been revolutionised by the writings of Pierre Bayle in the seventeenth century. The American historian Barbara Tuchman said, 'Not God, but gravity, brought the apple down on Newton's head'.[3] The Enlightenment took time to shine its lamp in England and Scotland.

Hume was, in turn, law student, philosopher, merchant's clerk, tutor, judge-advocate to a general, librarian, historian (his own preferred description), essayist, diplomat and senior civil servant. He was also a reputed atheist, *bon viveur*, wit, key figure in the Scottish Enlightenment and darling of the Paris salons. No eighteenth-century novelist dared to give his hero a life of such bewildering variety.

In France he was *le bon David*, in Scotland James Boswell called him 'the Great Infidel'. The English thought him dangerously Scottish and the Scots found him bafflingly unorthodox. In a time of hypocritical morality his honesty appalled the establishment, and his writing was without fear or favour. At his funeral one man cried out, 'Ye ken he was an atheist!' To which another shouted, 'Aye, but he was honest!'

It was a spontaneous epitaph of which any man would be proud.

A NOTE ON CURRENCY VALUES. In 1750 one English pound had a buying power in contemporary terms of £81.05. Since most of Hume's transactions were in English pounds, readers wishing to convert the monetary amounts to contemporary values should multiply by eighty. I have modernised eighteenth-century punctuation and spelling where I felt clarity would be improved. I have also removed the capitalisation of nouns. Square brackets in the text mark my own interpolations. Any errors in translation from French are entirely mine.

Acknowledgements

T here are many people I would like to thank for help and encouragement while I was writing this book.

Firstly, my, now sadly late, agent at Curtis Brown, Giles Gordon, who
was the third person to think it was a good idea – my wife was the second –
and who firmly guided the first draft into readability.

It is impossible to undertake any research into David Hume without
reference to Ernest C. Mossner's *The Life of David Hume*. Writing over
fifty years ago, Professor Mossner cleared a lot of undergrowth and left
useful signposts for those who came after and, for this, I am grateful.

The research would also have been impossible without access to the
collections of Hume papers at the National Library of Scotland where I
was given unstinting help, especially by Dr Iain Gordon Brown who
provided an invaluable route map through the archive. Kenneth Dunn
gave enthusiastic help with Latin translations, and the book fetchers
walked miles to carry the heavy folio volumes of Hume's letters. Chris
Fleet of the Map Library in the National Library of Scotland sent staff
scurrying to provide me with eighteenth-century maps of Berwickshire,
London and Paris without a question as to why I might want to trace such
obscure locations.

Similarly, staff at the Special Collections department of the Edinburgh
University Library, at the British Library, at the National Archives of
Scotland, and at the Edinburgh Room of Edinburgh City Libraries
Information Services reacted with enthusiasm and pointed me in the
right direction, when, often, I was straying.

Dr Morrice McCrae, Dr Iain Milne and the librarians at the Royal
College of Physicians in Edinburgh re-diagnosed both Hume's final
illness and 'the Disease of the Learned' with medical enthusiasm.

At the Sir John Soane Museum in London, Stephen Astley, the
Assistant Curator of Drawings, displayed all of Adam's projections for
Hume's tomb while giving forth a fountain of information.

David K. Swan, J.P., Session Clerk at Chirnside Parish Church, kindly opened the church for me to witness the Victorian 'improvements' that had removed all traces of the Hume family's sojourn.

In France, Maryvonne LeBesecond, Frédéric Mongin, Delphine Quereux-Sbaï at the Bibliothèque Patrimoine of Reims all coped with my rudimentary French and were delighted that a Scotsman should wish to explore their city's past in their welcoming new building. Similarly, Henri Colluard, Librarian at the Prytanée National Militaire in La Flèche found documents I didn't know I needed.

Also at La Flèche, whatever god looks after researchers smiled on me when I arrived at the beautiful Relais Cicéro, since Henri Pascale, the owner of this hotel, is also the current owner of Yvandeau. When I told him of my purpose in the town, he smiled broadly and told me that David Hume had written his treatise in his bedroom! I was invited to visit his home to meet his charming wife and daughters while standing on the spot where, nearly two hundred and fifty years previously, European philosophy had changed for ever.

At L'Isle D'Adam, now a commuter suburb of Paris, M. Phelouzat gave the impression of having waited all his life for someone to enquire into the now, sadly, long-gone glory days of the château. His enthusiasm and information gave me an invaluable window on Hume's sojourn among the mighty in France.

Susanna Kerr at the Scottish National Portrait Gallery helped me find portrait illustrations while Alastair Chisholm fought his way through the picture libraries of the Louvre and Versailles to provide two obscure illustrations.

None of this would have been possible but for a generous travel grant from the Scottish Arts Council whom I also profoundly thank.

Charles Freeman, in his book *The Closing of the Western Mind* (Pimlico 2003), found the quotation from St Augustine and I thank him for making his research available to me.

ONE

The Ordinary Course of Education

On the morning of 26th April 1711 four prosperous-looking gentlemen entered a narrow alleyway, or close, on the north side of the Lawnmarket in Edinburgh's High Street. To their left the broad ground in front of the castle batteries swept down into the narrow approach of Castle Hill before widening again onto this market place. It was originally known as the 'Inland' market since it was where the local farmers could come to sell their goods much like the urban farmers' markets of today. There was a riot of colour as stalls were jammed against each other and the ear was assaulted with the loud and earnest negotiations between buyers and market traders. As the spring sun rose, so did the smell.

The buyers were largely the servants of the occupants of the 'lands' that bordered Edinburgh's High Street. Some of these buildings climbed to twelve stories with access to the individual lodgings or tenements by a common narrow stair which was steep, dark, and often slippery with filth of all sorts. On the lower floors lived the owners of the businesses below them at street level – dram-shops, jewellers, wig-makers, and other tradesmen's workshops of all sorts – while the most desirable lodgings were on the fourth and fifth floors, far enough away from the stink and din of the market but not too far to climb. Social class fell away as the climb increased with the very poorest on the top floors. Not the very poorest in Edinburgh, for they lived in disease-ridden misery wherever they could find shelter, but the poorest of those who could afford to rent property. Sadly the Inland market no longer operates here and today's shoppers are largely tired tourists being misdirected towards shops selling 'their' tartan.

The four men who were climbing the stair and keeping their Genoa velvet and French silk coats away from the slimy walls as they dodged the descending denizens of the human ant-hill were all lawyers: George, Master of Polwarth, Sir John Home of Blackadder, Sir Andrew Home, advocate, and Alexander Falconer, advocate. They were all related to each other and to the renter of the tenement, Joseph Home of Ninewells, advocate, and his wife Katherine, Lady Falconer. They had come to celebrate the birth of Joseph's second son. Not quite members of the nobility as such, but the heart of the solid country lairdry and professional classes of Scotland.

Now we would call them pillars of the Establishment, and if you stood outside the close today you would see no market, but the Establishment would still be well represented as members of the Scottish Parliament and civil servants go from their Assembly to their offices, and advocates coming from the courts brush past you.

Outside one of these courts is now a rather fanciful statue of the infant to whose future life these men were raising glasses of claret. He was christened David Home and in the left-hand margin of the civic register of births for that day a later hand has added 'The child here registered is the celebrated David Hume [sic] Historian and Philosopher'.[1] (He changed the spelling of his name from Home to Hume in 1734 when he grew bored with Englishmen being unable to pronounce it in the Scottish manner, but I shall continue with the original spelling until that time. His *History* was not published until 1754, so the marginalium was inserted forty years after his birth.)

Joseph Home's tenement had three or four rooms with waxed or polished uncarpeted floors, highly decorated ceilings, and wainscot or hangings on the walls, furnished with all the elegance that a middle-ranking advocate could afford. Silver and glass stood on mahogany and there was upholstered furniture in front of open fires. The bedroom furniture would be folded away during the day and there was no running water. All water would be fetched from a street well by the servants who slept wherever they could find space – the bottom of a wardrobe was a favourite spot – and each evening the waste material, solid or liquid, vegetable or human, was simply thrown out of the window with a cry of 'gardy-loo'. The cry originates from 'gardez l'eau', though why the good citizens of Edinburgh should resort to French while pouring their filth on unsuspecting passers-by is a mystery. In 1748 David Hume wrote, 'A chamber pot is a very formidable machine in Edinburgh'.[2] The High Street thus lay covered in ordure until early morning when it was more or less washed down, while the waste built up again in the houses. From time to time nature applied a severe remedy to this horror since the over-crowded houses were largely made of wood – a practice expressly for-bidden by law – and they frequently burned down.

But however risky his position in a fourth-floor tenement and however awful the smells that met his infant nostrils, the status of the witnesses to David Home's christening made it certain that his future as a lawyer was assured.

He already had a brother, John Home, elder by four years, as well as a sister Katherine. John would, of course, have first pick of the positions, but little David had an immediate passport into a profitable profession if he chose to use it. There would have been no reason for his parents to worry about anything except for the high rate of infant mortality, which then existed even in the upper middle class.

After more than a few glasses of Joseph Home's claret the witnesses would pick their careful, if unsteady way down the stair back into the bustling democracy of Edinburgh's High Street. David's brother and three-year-old sister were laid to bed and careful candles were lit. Joseph and Katherine themselves could relax after a successful day. The infant David, whose writings would underscore the thinking of the modern world and who would shine as the star of the Scottish Enlightenment, slept happily in his lace christening robe.

Although his father Joseph rented the tenement in Edinburgh, and would live there during the legal terms, the family home was in Berwickshire, at Ninewells, near the village of Chirnside, and it was here that David Home grew up. This was border country, and in the early eighteenth century peaceful farming was a comparatively new concept. Towards the end of the previous century David's grandfather, John, had kidnapped a neighbouring heiress, one Jean Home – and unsuccessfully attempted to sell her off to a kinsman. After being stabbed in a fight over a card game, he rose to be a Lieutenant of Militia before dying in his thirties. He married three times and left thirteen children, the eldest of whom was David's father who, in his turn, was accused of getting one of his uncle's servants pregnant and had to flee to Holland where he studied law. Pregnant village girls would also appear in David's life, so the Home blood still ran red and troublesome.

The village of Chirnside lies on the southernmost slope of the Lammermuir Hills and just to the north of the Whiteadder Water which runs south to join the Blackadder Water half a mile below the village and in turn it feeds the River Tweed at the English border. Ninewells house backed immediately on to a cliff fifty or so feet high sweeping down to the river and looking to the Cheviot Hills beyond in one of the loveliest situations in Scotland. The house Home knew has been altered, burnt down and rebuilt several times and in its place there now stands an elegant modern villa, but in David Home's day it was a prosperous farmhouse.

A. and M. Armstrong's map of 1771 shows it isolated from the village, but of sufficient importance to have its name, Ninewells, entered along with that of its owner. There were, presumably, nine springs on the estate. This meant that Joseph would be called 'Ninewells' locally. The Scottish idea of calling a man after his landholding was all too necessary here, for if you had merely called out 'Home!' fifty heads would have turned. The area was, and still is, infested with Homes, the most recent celebrated scion being the late Alec Douglas Home, the former conservative Prime Minister.

The house itself, according to the illustration in Drummond's *History*, was laid out facing a farmyard with the stables and stores to the left of the house, while there were three storeys of living accommodation in the house itself. With eleven chimney pots it was bigger than a farm steading, but by no means a stately home. Drummond, an outrageously snobbish Scotophobe, calls it 'a favourable specimen of the best Scotch laird's houses, by the possession of which they think themselves entitled to modify their family coat of arms, and establish coats of their own'.[3]

Given Joseph's station as laird and his wife's background – she was Lady Katherine Falconer in her own right – we can presume that the furnishings would be as fine as could be found. They would largely replicate those of the Edinburgh house, still a logistical problem for those with 'a place in the country', but straw and muddy footprints in the downstairs rooms would show the effects of being a house at the centre of a working farm, with the family rooms on the first floor. It would have been a warm, practical, and comfortable compromise between a farmhouse and a 'country house'. In his *My Own Life*, Hume says that he 'was seized very early with a passion for literature which has been the ruling passion of my life, and the great source of my enjoyments'.[4] So there were books.

The seventeenth century had seen a change in domestic Scottish rural architecture from building defensive castles to building baronial mansions, and this was a farmhouse belonging to a gentleman. David Home was raised in a stone house built to keep out the weather and to provide a centre for a working estate but the changes seen in his life to the culture of his country would mean that at his death his tomb would be designed by Robert Adam, the arbiter of Palladian elegance.

Although they were reasonably prosperous farmers, the family was not rich. Katherine had an inheritance of £24 annually, and Joseph received £227 in rents although he had debts of £1,738.[5] Joseph's legal earnings are unknown, although James Boswell, only a moderately successful advocate even when sober, earned 76 guineas in the summer session sixty years later in 1771.[6] Joseph Home probably earned half that amount. Given that £50 annually was a lavish rent for accommodation in Edinburgh and that Ninewells would be self-supporting, there was enough income for a comfortable way of life, education for the boys and the provision of a suitable 'tocher' or dowry for daughter Katherine. At least until John and David could start earning and Joseph could think of retiring.

For the present the boys would have had a carefree life around Ninewells. There were some of Britain's finest salmon waters to fish. Later, magpies and rooks fell to their musketry.[7] The remains of a Roman fort and a cave in the bank below the house could have been designed for small boys to play in, and the boys would have been taken under the wing of neighbouring farmers and gamekeepers to be introduced to the local wildlife. The port of Eyemouth was about ten miles distant and there they would watch the fishing fleet sailing and returning. Seagoing tales and the local stories of stealing English cattle, sheep or, indeed, anything else of value, were meat and drink for small boys, and even girls. But before the three children could have had much time to enjoy the world about them, disaster struck when in August 1713 Joseph Home died of an unknown cause.

In his *My Own Life* David Hume tells us:

> My father, who passed for a man of parts [a Scots phrase meaning possessed of many talents], died when I was an infant; leaving me with an elder brother and sister under the care of our mother, a woman of singular merit, who, though young and handsome, devoted herself entirely to the rearing and educating of her children.[8]

In other words, at the age of thirty-two and with sons of four and two and a daughter of three, Katherine chose not to remarry but to run the estate herself. David cannot have known much of his father, and John and Katherine would have had only the haziest of recollections. The children were now forced in on themselves. As the children from the laird's house they would not have found it easy to mix in games with the other local children, even in democratic Scotland. In the next year Katherine was authorised to collect the rents and incomes from the estate and on 23 October 1716 seven-year-old John Home became the official laird of Ninewells. With care and good husbandry the estate continued to flourish.

The family would have grown up in comparative, if somewhat frugal, comfort. John's clothes would serve for David, and the children's pleasures, compared to today's expensive imperatives, were cheaply provided. Fishing rods, and, in time, guns and horses, were part of the normal equipment of such a house. Provided young Katherine did not mind following her brothers in everything, her tomboyish behaviour would raise no eyebrows. In winter, or at night, there would be books by candlelight. In addition to the 'gentleman's' library his father would have possessed a considerable collection of legal and classical texts. Also, living in the manse only a mile or two from Ninewells was the Reverend George Home, who had married David's aunt. He was minister of Chirnside from 1704 to 1755, and it would be astonishing if he took no interest in his niece and nephews, especially if any one of them showed an inclination toward learning.

As minister George Home would also have had access to information about recently ordained clergymen as yet without a parish who could act as tutors to the boys. They were known as 'stickit ministers' and could be employed comparatively cheaply. If such a tutor existed he was 'of the household, but not of the family':

> Beside his religious functions he acted as tutor to the children and made himself generally useful to the family. When at a nobleman's table he knew his part, which was to rise when the table-cloth was removed, and, making obeisance, respectfully to remove himself as well.[9]

So the boys would have been taught the rudiments of grammar, mathematics and, of course, Latin. In the eighteenth century any education a girl received came from her mother, unless the family was very rich, in which case she may have been taught the gentler accomplishments of French and music. The austere severity of Latin grammar would surely damage those pretty, fragile little heads.

It may, of course, be that the Home boys spent part of their childhood in the village school where they would have mixed, albeit formally, with the local lads of the parish. David's uncle George, as minister, would have had a strong influence in the appointment of a 'dominie' or teacher and the provision of accommodation for him. In the democratic tradition that traces its roots back to John Knox, the boys of the village would have been guaranteed an education.[10] Though not all parishes provided schools, where they did, the sons of lairds sat, democratically if sometimes uneasily, with the sons of their father's ploughmen:

> In a few instances the sons of private gentlemen were bred at home by a tutor; but the far greater part went to the neighbouring schools every morning, foul day and fair day, carrying their little dinner with them.[11]

The church in Chirnside had been operating since 1176, although rebuilt in 1572, and the family, as local lairds, would have had their own pew. All four Homes would have sat in front of the family vault, at least with the appearance of attention, through two long services on each Sunday. The Rev George Home, although with a Covenanting background – his father, Alexander, had been hanged for his beliefs in 1682 – was not of the fire and brimstone persuasion, but cold food and a brisk uphill walk from Ninewells to an unheated church twice in the day would have made winter Sundays unwelcome. (In 1876 Victorian 'improvements' removed the Home family vault and almost all traces of the medieval church, although there is still a fine Norman doorway.)[12]

Since John, as the eldest son, would need to take charge of the estate as soon as was possible, he was no longer being prepared to study law with the intention of practising, but merely to gain enough education to equip him for the lairdly life for as long as the family could afford. But there was no such plan for David. John bent over his grammar knowing that one day he would need it in letters to agents, or knowing that mathematics would be essential for an estate manager, but David could gaze out of the window and wonder. He would know that extended leisure for a second son was not a realistic option, and was, in any case, unfair to his family. A career of some kind would have to be found and the law seemed the most obvious. The beauty of the countryside was enchanting, but as any farmer will tell you, a landscape, however beautiful, is not enough to provide an income. The dilemma of David's future would have to be faced one day.

Already during Home's life the last Stewart monarch, Anne, had died and George I had arrived from Hanover. An abortive attempt had been made to place James VIII, the Old Pretender, on the throne in 1715 and the maelstrom of Europe had come to a comparative peace with the death of Louis XIV. None of these events made any significant difference to life at Ninewells and the family may well have known little of them. Local news arrived by gossip or by itinerant packmen clattering through the countryside, selling small goods and bringing news of the outside world. They were unlikely to engage the lady of the house in discussions about the dynastic ambitions of the Stewart exiles. Nor would a ten-year-old boy pick up much news of Baltic or Dutch politics from the fishermen and merchants at Eyemouth.

The Homes were traditionally Whigs, in favour of Protestantism and Parliament, but Edinburgh and all talk of politics was a long way off, over bad roads around the coast, and even worse tracks over the Lammermuir Hills. The road from Haddington to Berwick over these hills is one of the most spectacular in Scotland, but today it bypasses Chirnside altogether. In Home's day it may have gone through the village but it was impassable in winter, and even in summer news would have come from Eyemouth or Berwick. Today, thanks to modern science, news of a far-off famine will have us reaching into our charitable pockets within twenty-four hours, but in the eighteenth century an invasion by a usurping king three hundred miles away was of no great concern while the price of ewes at Duns market was of vital interest. But with no father to bring news from the market, and no effective communication with Edinburgh, David Home's childhood was passed in a political vacuum.

All this changed abruptly, however, for on 27th February 1723 twelve-year-old David, followed by his brother John two days later, signed the matriculation book of Edinburgh University to become a student in the class of William Scott, the Professor of Greek. Beside both their names on the page is the figure '2' which seems to denote that they went immediately into the second year. First-year students spent their time almost entirely on the study of Latin, and the Home brothers were obviously thought to be fluent enough to be allowed to skip the year. Since most of the lectures were in Latin, such fluency was essential, even though the university was undergoing great changes. It was a characteristic of David Home's life that the upheavals of the eighteenth century paralleled the changes in his own life.

The greatest change in the university had occurred fifteen years earlier when Principal William Carstares had abandoned the medieval systems of 'regenting' whereby a student would be taught all subjects by a single individual throughout his entire studentship. The main thrust of the teaching then was ecclesiastical, theological and philosophical, and the regents were paid according to the numbers of their students who graduated. Obviously great care was taken to ensure high numbers of graduates, much as today students' pass rates are cosseted to massage the figures in the league tables which carry such weight in determining the future financing of a university. *Plus ça change.*

In 1723 Carstares, a Principal, according to John Ramsay of Ochtertyre, whose 'manly sense and knowledge of the world, joined to his worth and urbanity, enabled him to fill the Principal's chair with much dignity',[13] had introduced individual professorships and there were now over twenty members of the faculty including teachers of Law, Languages, Surgery and Botany. Edinburgh University was becoming a university recognisable to modern eyes, but, thanks to the universality of Latin, students from across the world attended, coming from Poland, Holland (where Leyden had provided a model for Carstares' modernisations) and even attracting students from America. One rich Virginian student managed to spend £120 on food and drink in a year – the equivalent of about £9,600 today.

The Scottish universities were internationally attractive since they did not demand the sworn adherence to Protestantism that was a prerequisite for attendance at Oxford or Cambridge. Possibly another part of the popularity of Scotland was that most students lived outwith the University in the town with its attendant pleasures of drink and female company. This is still true and Edinburgh's discos are probably as celebrated an attraction as, say, the University's Department of Informatics.

For more conservative students the faculty staff rented rooms to students, and we are told of George Stewart, Professor of Humanity, '. . . in his house many young people of fashion were boarded, who derived much benefit from his conversation, which was easy and dignified'.[14] There were also lodgings and study rooms in the main complex of buildings to the south of the High Street, between the Cowgate and the City walls. In college, the lodgings cost £2 per term with two students to a bed. The more affluent could have a bed to themselves for £4 per term. The lodgings that could be found in town varied according to the pockets of the individual students but the Home boys were lodged in the comparative luxury of a family house; while at the other end of the scale poorer students shivered in unheated garrets, living on what food they could bring from the country.

The university was a collegiate building, according to Gordon of

Rothiemay's bird's-eye-view of the city, published in 1646, comprising three large courtyards with the church of St Mary of the Fields in one of the gateways. The students would enter their own courtyard where their lodgings and study rooms were situated, and further east was a second courtyard with the library and offices. Adjacent to both of these to the south was a third, much larger, courtyard with the faculty accommodation and the Schools. Between this and the city wall were the archery butts. Beyond the church of St Mary of the Fields to the east was an elegant garden, for the professors only, with formal parterres and a small orchard. On Rothiemay's drawing the site looks grand enough but most contemporary commentators found it 'mean' and 'neither fit to accommodate, nor suited to the dignity of such an University'.[15] Senior students would defray their expenses by acting as unofficial tutors to the 'bejans' or first-year students.

Classes were from eight until twelve in the mornings and between two and four in the afternoons from Mondays to Fridays, with Saturday reserved for the public presentation of dissertations. Given the comparatively young age of the student body, much of the undergraduate learning must have been by rote, with essays that were simply regurgitations of lectures and set texts. Nowadays it is difficult to imagine that the brothers John and David were only respectively fourteen and twelve years of age but were already second-year undergraduates. However, in a different context, John had already been accepted as the official laird of Ninewells, authorised to collect the rents of the estate, when he was just seven years old, albeit with a mother's supervisory eye over his shoulder. For, in the eighteenth century, childhood was a temporary inconvenience. Richard 'Beau' Nash declared that children should be encouraged to dress and behave as adults as soon as they could and one has only to look at the miniature adults in contemporary portraits to see that this advice was followed enthusiastically.

Giving teenagers the freedom of life available in an eighteenth-century university meant that they would also wholeheartedly embrace the independence of thought which was now becoming accepted by their masters. And, after all, since the abolition of the 'regent' system the students did not suffer from the pressure to graduate at all costs. In the formal courses of the university Home would have been introduced to the works of John Locke and Samuel Clarke, if only by hearing of them in lectures or 'prelections'. The philosophies of both men – Locke especially

– were crucial to his later development. Since Clarke was celebrated for proving the existence of God by a logical argument, it must have seemed obvious to Home that a logical counter-argument could obtain. Clarke's argument was contained in the Boyle lectures he had delivered in Cambridge on *A Demonstration of the being and attributes of God*. This proceeded mathematically to prove the thesis that if something exists now it has existed from eternity. This must be true, otherwise nothing would exist now because from nothing nothing comes. What has existed from eternity is an independent being. That being is God.[16] Clarke realised that space and time are infinite, but then seems to fall into the trap of confusing infinity with God. Home would have objected vigorously to human thought being treated with what he saw as false logic. But he himself would have difficulty with the concept of infinity.

Locke had published his *Essay Concerning Human Understanding* in 1689 and in it he was enquiring into the very certainty of human knowledge. This was much more to Home's taste. His pursuit of philosophy must have started in undergraduate debate over these latest philosophical works, in one of which Clarke was a rational theist and in the other Locke was veering towards sceptical atheism.

Liberal cracks were beginning to show in the formal teaching, and philosophies which had no basis in the Christian tradition were being openly examined. Natural Philosophy and Mathematics were both heavily Newtonian in outlook with Stoicism putting human reason rather than religious faith at the forefront of thought. For most of this Home would have sat at the feet of Charles Mackie, who brought a European outlook to the university since he was himself an ex-student from Groeningen and Leyden. Mackie held the chair of Universal History and took the widest possible interpretation of the subject, lecturing on literature, Roman antiquities, and even a course on *The Rise and Progress of Papal Tyranny*! More conventional was the course in *Pneumatical and Ethical Philosophy* which was taught by William Law. This exotically named course was divided into four sections: first, metaphysical inquiry into such subtle and material substances as are imperceptible to the senses and known only through their operations, such as thought ('pneumatic' can be defined as pertaining to the air or gas; in other words, invisible); second, a logical proof of the immortality of the soul; third, the nature of immaterial beings not connected with matter; fourth, another proof of the existence of God. Most of this would have been received with total scepticism by Hume, while providing him with a series of arguments to refute. One can refute logic, but only deny faith.

The expansion of liberal thought flourishing throughout Europe had reached the learned teachers of whom many had studied abroad, principally at Leyden or Paris. What had very recently been heresy was now innovation.

This expansion spread beyond the formal limits of the university into clubs, both in Edinburgh and Glasgow. Most of the faculty in Edinburgh were members of the Rankenian Club:

> It is well known that the Rankenians were highly instrumental in disseminating through Scotland freedom of thought, boldness of disposition, liberality of sentiment, accuracy of reasoning, correctness of taste, and attention to composition.[17]

This club was one of the many – and there would be more – political, literary or philosophical clubs burgeoning in Edinburgh, and the faculty, still riding the wave of Carstares' innovations, joined them with enthusiasm. The club met in Ranken's tavern at six o'clock on Wednesdays on the west side of Hunter Square and debated new developments in all areas of intellectual endeavour. Primarily the topics were theological but discussion would spread to cover all subjects. Originally a social and dining club, its membership included most of the intellectuals in Edinburgh always keen for debate while emptying claret bottles.[18] The club members even corresponded extensively with that phenomenon of philosophy Bishop Berkeley and were unsurprised to be offered places in his scheme for a missionary college in Bermuda. Nobody accepted his offer.

The Rankenian Club was strictly for graduates only, so the teenage Hume, later an enthusiastic member and founder of clubs, could not have attended any meetings, but the atmosphere of innovative thought must have pervaded the student clubs of the university. It was now firmly in the European, rather than the English, mould and was conforming to some of Knox's ideals in *The Book of Discipline* in that it was providing a general education, rather than existing merely as a school of divinity. What was crucially important to Home's intellectual development was that he was living in a milieu where independent thought was starting to be tolerated and even encouraged.

Edinburgh had moved very far in less than the thirty years since 1696. In August of that year medieval morality still held power and struck at one

Thomas Aikenhead. He was a nineteen-year-old student of theology at Edinburgh University and, in company with three other undergraduates, was walking up Edinburgh's windy High Street at eight o'clock at night. The weather was bitterly cold for August – it had been wet and cold all summer – and the students were well wrapped up against the weather. They may well have warmed themselves at one of the many taverns in the area, but as the wind cut into Aikenhead, he turned to his companions and said, 'I wish right now I was in the place Ezra called Hell, to warm myself there'.[19] Later he would deeply regret the statement since one of his companions reported the remark to the ecclesiastical authorities who, with all the rigour of Orwell's 'thought police', began an investigation. Aikenhead had called the apostles 'a company of silly witless fishermen', and had referred to the Bible as 'Ezra's romances'. All this can be ascribed to tasteless undergraduate humour, but on 8 January 1697 Thomas Aikenhead climbed a ladder, had a noose placed around his neck, and was kicked into space to hang as a convicted blasphemer. With his last words he claimed simply to have followed reason where it led. It had led him to the gallows.

Only a few years later the atmosphere had changed completely and the universities in Glasgow and Edinburgh seethed with student clubs following these dangerous paths of reason. These clubs, of which Home would be a devoted member all his life, were now notorious for their encouragement of free thought. Edinburgh was clearly a hotbed of this ferment:

> It is well known that between 1723 and 1740 nothing was in more request with the Edinburgh *literati*, clerical and laical, than metaphysical disquisitions.[20]

Often these 'disquisitions' were being held in exclusive clubs such as the Rankenian but equally there were student clubs going hammer and tongs in debate:

> Their clubs and meetings seem to be no small fountain of the corruption of the youth . . . There has been a club at Edinburgh for some years who were of the opinion that we're in too narrow a way of thinking in this country, and that some of the younger students inclined to have greater freedom of thoughts; and a trial was to be made how notions of liberty and [theological] searching would go

down.[21]

And it was even worse in Glasgow:

> The students [in Glasgow] who affect to be persons of bright parts
> have a club called the Eleutherian Club . . . The clubs are likely to
> have very ill influence upon religion. People meet in them without
> any solid grave person to moderate, and give a fancy to their fancy
> and enquiries, without any stated rule of them or any solid
> principles. They declaim against reading and cry up thinking.[22]

Scotland had reeled with shock from the case of John Simson, Professor of
Divinity at Glasgow University, who had denied many of the accepted
precepts of Protestant faith. He taught what was not far removed from the
Arminian heresy that predestination was not inevitable since man was
endowed with free will. He also believed that the component members of
the Trinity were separate entities. His motto, *Ratio est principum et fundamentum theologiae*, could have been adopted by Home as his own. When
challenged over this apostasy in 1707, just twenty years after Aikenhead's
execution, 'John Simson treated his prosecutors with studied contempt,
endeavouring to turn them into ridicule'.[23] He was finally suspended from all
his duties and forbidden to preach.[24] Conventional theologians closed ranks
with a wholehearted detestation of reason and Hog of Carnock declared that
all God-fearing Christians should reject reason altogether in his wonderfully
named pamphlet *A letter to a gentleman detecting the gangrene of some errors
vented at this time*.[25] But the seeds were planted.

The students in Glasgow and Edinburgh would have followed the
accusations against such a distinguished person as Simson with fervour
and thus were already being quoted as centres of dissent. Simson's
teaching methods themselves were largely blamed for this sudden out-
pouring of liberalism:

> Students of divinity oppose the Confession of Faith . . . the grace
> of God is openly mocked and ridiculed . . . they [the students] were
> not to regulate themselves by human composures . . . but were to
> reason freely upon things and regulate themselves by scripture and
> reason. The lightness and liberty of speaking allowed by the
> Professor at Glasgow [is] a sad inlet to corruption among the
> youth.[26]

The genie was out of the bottle:

> They [the professors] opened and enlarged the minds of the
> students, which soon gave them a turn for free inquiry, the result of
> which was candour and liberality of sentiment.[27]

It is beyond belief that the young David Home would not have been an enthusiastic participant in these debates and that the extra-mural student life of Edinburgh must have honed his analytical skills. The heat of this debate was fuelled by Simson's partial apostasy, and, if the Scottish Enlightenment can be said to have a finite beginning, it can be argued that Simson's behaviour was the flint that struck the spark that fired the metaphorical tinder.

This tinder had already been put in place with the appointment of Francis Hutcheson as Simson's replacement in the chair of Moral Philosophy in Glasgow. He was a liberal Whig who lectured in English and had been placed in his chair thanks to the patronage of Archibald Campbell, Lord Islay, who was nicknamed the Viceroy of Scotland. Islay ensured that only Whigs held positions of power and he made over fifty university appointments, almost inadvertently completing the modernisation of the universities, not only those changes started by Carstares in Edinburgh, but also in Glasgow. Hutcheson, himself a pupil of Simson, was hugely popular with his students, often lending them money and admitting the poorer ones to his classes without fees. He shone a new light on theology, believing that there was an innate sense of moral good in man; a belief which would later bring him into conflict with Home, as well with his own pupil Adam Smith. He said: 'we are laid under a real internal obligation of a most sacred kind, from the very constitution of our nature, to promote the good of mankind'. But Hutcheson's pupils 'panted to be what they beheld' and he 'spread such a spirit of enquiry . . . that the conversations of students . . . turned upon subjects of learning and taste'.[28] The Scottish Enlightenment was now inextinguishable.

It was at this time that David Home developed the habit of constant debate. Many people use university to try on various personalities, and in this ferment of debate Home clearly found that the role of scholar and philosopher fitted him comfortably. The diversions of literature and philosophy were much more attractive than the study of law which his brother was assiduously following. In *My Own Life* Home says:

> I passed through the ordinary course of education with success; and
> was seized very early with a passion for literature which has been
> the ruling passion of my life, and the great source of my
> enjoyments.[29]

Tantalisingly, only a glimpse of this can be seen in a few pages of an extant essay of Home's now in the care of the National Library of Scotland. The fragment, *An Historical Essay on Chivalry and modern Honour*,[30] is only a few pages long and is written in what appears to be a teenager's fair copy, with no alterations and a meticulously sharp pen. Home's handwriting was, thankfully, extremely clear and varied little throughout his life, but this document has no sign of hesitation or of the urgency sometimes shown in his later correspondence. The essay is a description of the destruction of the true classical virtues by invading Gothic barbarians and the replacement of these virtues by the ludicrous precepts of romantic chivalry. Home sets out his argument calmly inside the logical framework of carefully chosen history. Already it is entertaining and elegant, throwing doubt on it as the work of a young boy. However, Professor E.C. Mossner said of it:

> We are dealing with the mind of genius, in this case a mind that
> indisputably produced the *Treatise of Human Nature* by the age of
> twenty six. That that same mind produced the '*Historical Essay*' at
> the age of fourteen or fifteen does not seem at all incredible.[31]

Although written in the first decades of the eighteenth century, it demonstrates what would become a typical stance of the Age of the Enlightenment. Home starts by pointing out that the seeds of the destruction of classicism lay in the late Roman Empire and its destruction by the Goths:

> Had their invasion and conquest happened while the Grecian
> philosophy was yet in any tolerable condition, they would probably
> have engrafted on this stock; but as that was disgraced and even
> purposely rendered odious by the Christian religion, which then
> prevailed and which they embraced, they were reduced to work
> upon some other, that lay in more common life. Thence they would
> embellish after a method of their own, shoddy excellencies and
> beauties beyond the original from which they drew their first
> notion.

Hume paused in his transcription here – there is a sharpened pen for the remainder. But this passage is a first sign that Hume already was preferring the Greek and Roman virtues to the Christian, which he regarded as the religion of the barbarians. His audience, when he delivered this paper, was largely composed of academics giving up a Saturday morning to hear it, and they would either have muttered agreement or excused this as undergraduate zeal, as yet undimmed by wisdom. But Home went on to say that this hybrid belief produces 'Whimsies and Chimeras' and a new set of 'Passions, Affections and Desires'. Philosophy would supersede nature in raising human behaviour above the savagery of nature while the barbarian Goths, out of a misunderstanding of the classical virtues, erected their own fantastic systems. Gothic art lacks the purity of classical art and architecture. But worse is to come; for now he finds that the most admired virtue in Gothic civilisation is warlike bravery. This is the first difference between classical and modern. When bravery was not controlled by reason it produced 'pirates and robbers' and when it was controlled it took on only an 'affectation of civility':

> One cannot but prefer the plain roughness of the one to the chimerical and affected politeness of the other.

This 'civility' is acquired by mixing love with courage:

> To which almost everyone has a great propensity, and which 'tis impossible to see a beautiful woman without feeling some touches of.

A mistress is as necessary to a Cavalier or knight-errant 'as a god or saint is to a devotee'. Hume is hinting heavily that he finds established religion just as absurd as 'extravagant gallantry', producing 'tilts and tournaments [as] the reigning entertainments'. 'Entertainments' is shown as the first word of the next page but this is, in fact, the end of the fragment.

While the absurdity of formal single combat is obvious, it does not necessarily seem to follow directly from adoration of the female sex, but Hume was a teenager and, while there is no doubting the precocious brilliance of his mind, he could do nothing to halt the rush of hormones in his body. How much more there was we cannot know, but he seemed to be warming to his subject and the fragment probably represents under half of the original. At any rate Home felt proud enough of this essay to preserve the fragment and he had been infected with a persistent and virulent infection. He had discovered that he could use his pen to persuade. He had had contact with liberal thought and debate and had started to examine the received wisdom of the day.

Apart from this fragment David Home appears to have passed through Edinburgh University without making any mark on it. Neither he nor his brother graduated formally, a not uncommon event in this period. The eighteenth century did not pay the slavish lip-service to labels that exists today, and with the obvious exceptions of medicine and science, entry into a profession would merely require some form of apprenticeship or a term of clerkship. Influence and family ties were more important than paper qualifications and the majority of students, having flirted with new ideas, became conventional members of the respectable middle classes. 'All the judicious soon returned to the lower sphere of long established truths.'[32]

However, the education of the Home brothers came to an abrupt halt in 1725 when the house in the Lawnmarket burnt down, as they commonly did, and the Home family had to return to Ninewells to review their future.

TWO

The Disease of the Learned

The family would never again live together in Edinburgh and John Home's university days were over. Together with his fifteen-year-old sister Katherine and his forty-two-year-old mother he started to settle into Ninewells as the farmer he would be for the rest of his life. These three had no option but to put duty before any other feelings they may have had and they focused entirely on the management of the estate. This they did out of necessity, but they willingly allowed David the freedom to continue with his studies for whatever career he chose. John was hardly at the cutting edge of new developments in agriculture, but gradually he improved the estate and left it better and more prosperous than he found it. His tenants and neighbours thought him a good manager and he treated everyone with a due respect which was, in turn, shown to him. Had it not been for his brother we would never have heard of him.

David, however, was an extra mouth to feed with no inclination towards farming. He had, for all practical purposes, finished his formal university education and must now launch himself on a career. The choices for a youth of his birth and education in the early part of the eighteenth century were limited and soon examined. A life in the army or navy would have meant buying a commission and hoping for advancement through prowess in battle but the Ninewells resources could not run to a commission in a sufficiently prestigious regiment. He was already too old to join the navy as a midshipman and in either career he would have been unlikely to make any financial return to his family for a very long time. Also, for the moment at least, Europe was at peace, with the bulk of the British army on half-pay, so a military career was totally impractical. The church cannot have been considered for long. David could not have concealed his growing scepticism, and the position of his minister uncle would have been an example of the backwater to which he might have been condemned. The prospect of scholar/clergyman would have been attractive but would have required an act of intellectual hypocrisy on David's part. David Home possessed not an ounce of hypocrisy. He knew nothing of

medicine, and distrusted the scientists' dogged reliance on what they took
to be irrefutable facts. Since he had attended university he had attained the
demonstrable education to obtain what would inevitably be a lowly post as
a private tutor.

But this would have been no more than a temporary solution with no
possibility of advancement and Home's mind wanted to move forward.
Tying himself to the restrictive world of the academic would have seemed
anathema to his spirit. It was a world then, as now, riven with faction and
extremely hostile to incomers, especially provocative incomers. The Enlightenment was, as yet, too fragile to court open controversy. And biting
his tongue to gain preferment in a university was impossible for David
Home. Politics required money and powerful friends, neither of which the
Homes possessed. Commerce would be just possible since there was little
snobbery in the family and there were already rumours that fortunes could
be made in India, either as a servant of the all-powerful East India
Company, or as an independent trader. It was a highly sought-after
repository for younger sons in search of a fortune. Also young Scotsmen
were well regarded by 'John Company' and recommendations to the
London Directors could have been sought, but David was loath to leave
his family at this stage in his life. His family did, however, have several
powerful connections in the legal profession, as his baptismal witnesses
had demonstrated, and it was therefore overtly to follow the study of the
law that, in 1725, he returned to Edinburgh.

It is curious that, of the paths rejected at this time, he was eventually to
tread most of them. While not exactly a soldier, he would become
secretary to a general and take part in a farcical invasion of France; he
would be engaged as tutor to an aristocrat, albeit a seriously deranged one;
he would be engaged (unsuccessfully) in commerce when employed by
Bristol merchants; and he would be a diplomat and civil servant. He was
true to avoiding medicine and academe (although he applied for professorships) and he never practised as a lawyer. It was usually the need for
immediate funds that drove him into all of these unlikely posts.

We can be sure that it was, above all, to please his family that David
returned to Edinburgh to assume the duties of an apprentice Edinburgh
lawyer. He rejected them almost immediately with revulsion:

> My studious disposition, my sobriety, and my industry gave my
> family a notion that the law was a profession for me: but I found

an insurmountable aversion to every thing but the pursuits of
philosophy and general learning.[1]

Neither brother John nor mother Katherine would have brought any
pressure to bear on David but he was already growing apart from their lives
on the farm. What Home actually wanted at this time, when he was
fourteen years old, was the life of a dilettante scholar, but, he said:

My family . . . was not rich; and being myself a younger brother,
my patrimony, according to the custom of my country, was of
course very slender.[2]

This 'patrimony' was probably less than fifty pounds annually. This would
not allow him the leisure to exist as an independent gentleman, living on
his estate and living the quiet life of a scholar. Forty years later he would
look back and tell us that it would only have taken a hundred pounds a year
to achieve that dream, but that was twice his income and far beyond his
powers.

Thus he returned to Edinburgh, almost by default, to sit at the feet of an
advocate and to attend classes in the law. There is no evidence for his
having been officially articled but he did form what was to be a lifelong
friendship with Henry Home of Kaimes. In a letter of June 1745, Home
calls him 'the best friend that I ever possessed'. He also called him the most
arrogant man in the world. Henry Home, a neighbour but, astonishingly,
no relation, was twice David's age and had been practising as an advocate
for three years. In his portrait he scowls and smiles simultaneously under a
hooked nose and this may reflect his wide variety of interests: metaphysics,
theatre, music, law, and poetry. He once said, 'Anatomy is the only science
I've never studied'. His daily round started at five when he prepared for
court, after which, in late morning, he walked with friends – surely
including Home – before dinner and study. He would then go out to the
taverns where he would sit late and drink hard. Boswell said of him that he
had a large circle of young people whom he would instruct and dictate to,
but when they came to have a mind of their own, he would quarrel with
them. In later life Home's friendship with him did cool considerably. He
introduced his young friends to the delights of Edinburgh's taverns – it
seems that the law was administered in eighteenth-century Edinburgh
through a haze of alcohol and throbbing hangovers. More importantly,
however, Henry Home could extend his borrowing privileges at the

Advocates' Library to his young acolytes. Library time at the university was limited and borrowing was expensive. The key to the 11,000 volumes in the locked cupboards was kept firmly in librarian Robert Henderson's pocket.[4]

Home did borrow books and read extensively but fifty years later in *My Own Life* he admits to a small deceit:

> and while they fancied I was poring over Voet and Vinnius, Cicero and Virgil were the authors I was secretly devouring.[5]

He visited Ninewells often during this time, and though it is unlikely that the family came to Edinburgh, from this remark it is obvious that there was contact between them as to how his studies were proceeding. They had seen him deep in books and presumed that he was following in his father's footsteps.

They would certainly hope so, since the sooner he could produce another income, the sooner their standard of living would return to what they had enjoyed while Joseph had been alive. But David was not reading Johannes Voet's *Compendium* or Arnoldus Vinnius's *Tractatus quinque*, both of whose works on law were, and indeed still are, held in the University Library. However, somehow he did learn enough law to enable him in the future to carry out routine legal tasks.

It was at this time that Home made the acquaintance of Michael Ramsay of Mungale, who was to become one of his firmest friends and a frequent guest of the family at Ninewells. After the death of both Home and Ramsay, Ramsay's son wrote of their correspondence and friendship which:

> proceeded from the purest friendship and the strongest attachment. Nor do I believe there were ever two companions upon earth more respectable for their constancy and mutual esteem for each other.[6]

Ramsay had a dual reputation, being, for some, Michael 'the Archdevil' and for others a 'harmless creature'. He was described as a very debauched and licentious creature, carrying the youth of his acquaintance to lewd women and drunken companions. He was certainly a habitué of Edinburgh's brothels and dram shops, but he could not have held the lifetime friendship of David Home without considerable intellectual acumen, so he may have been both hell-raiser and scholar. Edinburgh has always specialised in such dual personalities.

There is no evidence whatsoever that Ramsay corrupted Home. In later life Home was fond of good food and drink, but sexual delights seemed not to interest him in the least. It would have been unexceptional for a man of his position to use the facilities of brothels, but Home passed his life free of the venereal disease that was the almost inevitable consequence. Ramsay was harshly judged by people who still believed that a man was either pleasure-loving or intellectual. The eighteenth century saw a revival of the belief that it was possible to be both.

Eventually Home, probably on the advice of Henry Home, had to confess his deceit to his family, give up his pretence of studying law and return to Ninewells without a profession or degree. He was aware of costing his family money in Edinburgh rents and achieving nothing. In abandoning formal studies he became Edinburgh University's most celebrated drop-out.

This was, in fact, the end of Home's formal education. His Latin would now be polished, he would have gained a knowledge of Greek and French, and he would be well versed in the Classics. He would have read philosophy from Plato to Locke and he would have honed his skills in logic and metaphysics. He had debated theology and history and, most importantly, had been taught how to use his mind. For most people it was sufficient education for a gentleman and most gentlemen would now let their minds lie fallow. David Home's mind was fertile ground with unexpected blooms germinating. His return home was welcomed without question, and while mother and brother ran the estate, with sister Katherine as housekeeper, David had time to reflect.

His earliest surviving letter – to Michael Ramsay – gives us a hint of the deep introspection to come:

Just now I am entirely confined to myself and library for
diversion . . . I take no more of them than I please, for I hate task
reading . . . sometimes a philosopher, sometimes a poet, which
change is not unpleasant . . . this Saturnian happiness I have in a
great measure come at, just now; I live like a King pretty much by
myself . . . This greatness and elevation of souls is to be found only
in study and contemplation, this alone can teach us to look down
upon humane accidents.[7]

He goes on to tell Ramsay that his brother John, now eighteen, has bought a horse for six guineas and that, lifting himself from 'so low affairs as horses', Home himself is 'mightily delighted' with reading Longinus' treatise on the Sublime. The idea of the Sublime he was reading in Dionysius Longinus was that there was a form of beauty which was daunting to the intellect and 'aweful'. For Home it would have formed part of his investigations into what we could *know* – a thunderstorm in mountain country – and what we could *understand* – why is the thunderstorm beautiful and frightening at the same time? Modern authorities doubt whether Longinus actually wrote the treatise, but its arguments figure strongly in the Romantic Revival of the nineteenth century.

There are also clues to Home's regard for polished style, even when writing chatty letters to friends. Ramsay had obviously reproved Home for earlier lapses:

You say that I would not send in my papers because they are not polished or brought to any form; which you say is nicety. But was it not reasonable? Would you have me send in my loose uncorrect thoughts? Were such worth the transcribing?[8]

All of this gives us substantial clues to Home's activities at Ninewells. In the letter referred to above he thanks Michael Ramsay for sending him books, and it is not unlikely that this service continued during all the time Home was at Ninewells. His education had not stopped and he was, in fact, setting about a course of intellectual regeneration that would drive him to the brink of madness.

Already he was making notes for what would be the *Treatise of Human Nature*, and from the books he was reading we can follow the direction of his thought. None of these notes exists now, although Home kept them for over twenty years. In 1751 he wrote to Elliot of Minto:

And tis not long ago that I burn'd an old Manuscript book wrote before I was twenty, which contained page after page, the gradual process of my thoughts on that subject [religious scepticism]. It begun with an anxious search after arguments, to confirm the common opinion; doubts stole in, dissipated, returned, again dissipated, returned again, and it was a perpetual struggle of a restless imagination against inclination, perhaps against reason.[9]

The knowledge that such notes once existed is hugely frustrating, but there do exist a few pages of what we would now call a commonplace book which gives us a guide to what Home was reading. From this we know that one of these books was the *Réflexions critiques sur la poésie et sur la peinture* by the Abbé DuBos. This highly popular two-volume treatise on aesthetics had first appeared in 1719 and had run through several editions. Since the English translation did not appear until 1748, Home must have read the work in the original French. He referred to the Abbé as 'One of the French mystics'. In the *Réflexions* we find the following passage:

'Tis in vain nevertheless to attempt to persuade young people pressed by emulation, excited by the fire and activity of youth, and spurred on by the impatience of their genius to the pursuit of fame, to defer making their appearance in public, till they have discovered their kind of talent, and sufficiently improved it. It would be to no purpose to tell them that it would be gaining a great point to surprise the public, that they would be much more respected were they never to appear as apprentices in their profession. *Prudentia non cadit in hanc aetatem* [Cicero: Prudence does not fall to young people's share].[10]

Home tells Michael Ramsay:

All the progress that I made is but drawing the outlines in loose bits of paper; here a hint of passion, there a phenomenon in the mind accounted for, in another the alteration of these accounts; sometimes a remark upon an author I have been reading, and none of them worth to anybody and I believe scarce to myself.[11]

So already he was putting some of his thoughts down on paper and had been showing them to Michael Ramsay, who, it would seem, had encouraged the sixteen-year-old to think of publication. But, heeding the advice of DuBos, it would be ten years before Home published his first work and at this time he had no confidence in his powers as a philosopher. Nor could he yet define *how* he thought. Analysing these processes led him inevitably but painfully to deconstruct the processes of intuitive thought. He would scrub his mind clean of all derivative influences with the intellectual equivalent of caustic soda.

He was now solitary and either reading, making notes, writing letters, or walking alone over the hills around Ninewells. Just below the house at Ninewells there is a small cave locally called the 'Philosopher's Cave' and visitors are told that this was where David retired to think. To be fair, the local people do seem ashamed when they tell one this, and given Home's later fondness for fleshly comforts, the idea of such an activity is ludicrous. It is a very small cave and although Home was, at this time, slim built, I doubt if he ever sat in it himself since his games of hide-and-seek as a child.

This idleness was tolerated by his brother, John, who would have watched David's lonely activity in puzzlement while he, necessarily, busied himself with running the farm. David's idleness and withdrawal were a worry and a total wonder to his mother, Katherine. She is reputed to have said, 'Our Davie's a fine good-natured crater [creature], but uncommon wake-minded'.[12] Whether she ever said it or not it is the remark of a mother who has seen her son leave for a country of the mind she cannot understand, let alone inhabit, carried there by his piercing wide-awake observation of everything around him. The sympathy and understanding of brother and mother, to say nothing of his sister Katherine, were a necessary boon to David.

The talk at mealtimes must have been strained almost to breaking point with David showing forced interest in the affairs of the estate while his family made puzzled responses to his comments on what he was reading. He was surrounded by a family who cared for their, now almost estranged, brother but had no idea what he was doing or why he was doing it. They were bound by the seasons and the imperatives of sowing, harvesting, lambing, and selling at market. Maintenance and expansion are progress enough for farmers who live a predictably cyclical life. But David was, bafflingly, moving in straight lines and tangents which were leading him in all sorts of different directions. He must have felt colossal guilt for living among his beloved family like a scholastic parasite.

But Home may well also have reassured himself with the thought that he had a God-given gift, for the Abbé DuBos states:

Now a person must be born with a genius, to know how to invent; but to be able to invent well, requires a long and unwearied application . . . Genius is an aptitude which man has received from nature to perform well and easily, that which others can do but indifferently and with a great deal of pains. We learn to execute things for which we have a genius, with as much facility as we speak our mother tongue . . . Whatever is proposed to him as the object of his application can never fix him unless it be that which nature has allotted him. He never lets himself be diverted from thence for any length of time, and is always sure to return to it, in spite of all opposition, and sometimes in spite of himself. Of all impulses that of nature, from whom he has received this inclination is much the strongest.[13]

Home was preparing himself to 'invent well' and finding the application wearisome, even though it was an 'impulse of nature'. He had had experience of speculative debate at Edinburgh University and had felt the growing atmosphere of intellectual reform. Now he was preparing himself to be part of that movement. And the 'French mystic' reinforced the feeling that the time was ripe:

'Tis easy to judge by the present state of the natural sciences how much our age is more enlightened than those of Plato . . . [Our predecessors] may have surpassed us, if this expression be allowed me, in practical reason, but we excel them in speculative. One may judge of our superiority of wit and reason over men of past ages, by the state in which the natural sciences are at present, and that in which they were in former times.[14]

So, it was during this period that the young David Home was freeing his mind of the conventional beliefs into which he had been educated since his birth and was now establishing his own methods of thought. To this end he was reading the current commentators and examining whether, by logic and reason alone, he could accept their thinking.

Home's reading allows us an insight into his mental struggles in those years and we have already referred to a subsequently burnt manuscript book, in which he had recorded the 'progress of my thoughts' on the existence of God. Throughout his life he would be dogged with the unfair accusation of atheism. The struggle came, simply, to a choice between imagination, or faith, and reason. The arguments would be crucial to his development, since, for example, a simple lack of faith was not a sufficient argument for Hume's rejection of God. That would be simply to allow the imagination to dominate reason without any logical proof. Perhaps he remembered Simson's motto of *Ratio est principum et fundamentum theologiae* and extended it to propose that reason was the fundamental principle, not only of theology, but of all thought. By defining the processes of reason in contrast to imagination Hume would start to try to understand how the human mind worked. This is an awesome task even today with our contemporary knowledge of psychiatry and physiology. After Bertrand Russell completed his *Principia Mathematica* in 1913, in which he undertook a similar task, his friends said he was never the same man again. Hume was to learn that philosophy can seriously damage your health, especially if undertaken in solitude.

The pages headed 'Philosophy' in his few surviving notes are dominated by references to one book in particular. This was 'Bayle' whose *Dictionnaire historique et critique* was published in Paris in 1697. Pierre Bayle was hugely influential: 'in Bayle's writings are to be found all the leading themes of the advanced thinkers of the next century',[15] especially in France, which he had to flee on account of his Calvinism. He was crucial in founding the school of scepticism which led to Voltaire and the Encyclopaedists. He was a sceptical moralist believing that man was capable of making moral judgements independently of a God-given conscience, relying on experience. Governments, likewise, should be judged, not by dogma, but by results. The *Dictionnaire* was an attempt to bring all of these thoughts under one roof and is a vast and well-nigh impenetrable seven-volume work of over 800 folio pages per volume. The footnotes are hugely discursive and are frequently longer than the principal text, and they themselves carry marginal references to other entries in other volumes. The work also lacks any plan of organisation, or logical progression. Even in a modern reprint of an English translation it can turn the calmest researcher into a gibbering wreck. Home presumably read the entire work in the original French since he would have had no translation, and for this alone he is deserving of unstinted praise. Bayle does examine the position of philosophers, and Home would have found some passages of great interest in his conflict between faith and reason. For example, and typically bafflingly, under 'Takiddin, a mahometan author', Bayle tells us that the believers' objections to philosophers are not confined to the Christians alone:

> It is . . . difficult to persuade the world that the followers [of
> Descartes and Gassendi] are good Catholics and that if they were
> allowed to preach publicly their principles they would not quickly
> undermine all the foundations of the Romish religion. The
> Protestants have not a better opinion of Descartes' doctrine . . .
> Their philosophy is very dangerous to Christianity . . . there is but
> little religion among great philosophers . . . devotion is chiefly to be

found among the vulgar, and those who have most carefully examined the marks of divine authority of the holy scripture are commonly less pious and devout than others.[16]

Bayle was a Christian Sceptic and follower of Calvin, but his writing hovered on the brink of accepting a philosopher's totally rational view of the world:

It is an axiom among the schoolmen that a philosopher ought not to have recourse to God to explain the effects of nature. Philosophy will destroy both errors and truths if she be allowed to have her full scope.[17]

Bayle consistently maintained that philosophy achieves not comprehension and contentment, but paradox and puzzlement. From this he advocated questioning all accepted thought, and accepting nothing which could not bear rational examination. However, he did draw the line at total atheism:

I never advance, as my own opinion, any doctrine which is repugnant to the articles of the confession of faith of the reformed church in which I was born and of which I make profession.[18]

Home realised, even at this time, that a system of thought which actively denied the existence of God was practically unachievable, as was a logical proof of his existence. But he examined the subject with meticulous care, keen to note some proofs of the existence of God, and there is a single page of random notes on this subject. Collected over a period of time, they are personal jottings but they give an indication of what was of interest to him gathered together as a summary:

PHILOSOPHY

Though the ancients speak often of God in the singular number, that proves not that they believed in his unity, since Christians speak in the same number of the Devil.
Men love pleasure more than they hate pain.
Men are vicious but hate a religion that authorises vice.
Atheists plainly make distinction betwixt good reasoning and bad.
Why not betwixt vice and virtue?
Three kinds of atheists according to some.

1. Who deny the existence of God, Such as Diagoras, Theodorus.

2. Who deny a providence, such as the Epicureans and the Ionic sect.

3. Who deny the freewill of the deity, such as Aristotle, the Stoics. The argument *a priori*. That no necessary existent being can be limited is only conclusive that there is an intelligent being who intendently [sic] forms the idea of infinite perfection and resolves to work up to his model. Which implies a contradiction.

Those who solve the difficulty concerning the origin of ill by the apology of general laws suppose another master beside goodness in the creation of the world.

The soul; a *carte blanche* indifferent to all perception. What necessity therefore for harmful motions or disagreeable perceptions? Many plans upon which the universe might be formed. Strange that none should be better than the present.

God could have prevented all the abuses of liberty without taking away liberty. Therefore liberty no solution of difficulty.

God does not will sin as sin, but in some other vein. According to Calvin.[19]

Here we can plainly see that the traditional philosophical debates were bound to take account of God although there can be no doubt that at this time Home had abandoned the traditional Christian faith, while studying the best current arguments for such a faith. If he could then refute these arguments by reason, then atheism would be justified. This is typical of a man who was trying to drive his thoughts by logic alone. Simply to say 'I have no faith' was not enough and he would have had to find excuses to give his family on Sundays when they climbed the hill to his uncle's church. Home would continue this debate throughout his life, reaching a summation only posthumously in his *Dialogues concerning Natural religion*. More and more he was becoming an enigmatic cuckoo in the nest at Ninewells.

Home also read François de Salignac de la Mothe Fénelon, Bishop of Cambray's works on the existence of God, and made notes on what he found:

Some pretend there can be no necessity according to the system of atheism. Because matter cannot be determined without something superior to determine it. Being and truth and goodness the same.

Three proofs of the existence of God. 1. Something necessarily existent and what is so is infinitely perfect. 2. The idea of infinite must come from an infinite being. 3. The idea of infinite perfection implies that of actual existence.

Home would have rejected this false logic out of hand but his thinking would have been nearer to Fénelon in *The Difference between a Philosopher and a Christian,* which echoed his own conflicts:

A philosopher is a man that examines everything profoundly by the light of his reason, who will needs know the cause and the reason of everything that is proposed to him . . . this is what has made so many heathen philosophers practise virtue, and combat vice to far greater perfection than many others that call themselves Christians.

Men's reasonings do agree with the teachings of Christ 'to a certain point'.

Humility, which makes us contemptible in our own eyes puts us in the place that belongs to us, annihilates us, as Jesus Christ annihilated himself; as, on the contrary, knowledge puffeth up.

He that desires and aspires after this divine love, shall attain thereto and find by his experience, that this passion surpasses reason, sets the man to rights, and banishes all that disorder with which sin has poisoned him.[20]

Home had no intention of 'annihilating' himself, rather he wanted to liberate his mind without being 'puffed up'. He would also, at this time, be deeply suspicious that passion should surpass reason, although his subsequent investigations would lead him to put the relationship between passion and reason as one of the principal subjects of the *Treatise.* He could not accept Fénelon's assertion that faith 'banishes all disorder'. That sounds very like the oft-quoted definition of the Church as 'the last refuge of the distressed intellectual'. Home was undoubtedly distressed at this conflict, and the battle for a definite course of thought brought about what we now would call a nervous breakdown.

Home was undertaking all of this work with no outside help except by correspondence and in surroundings which were physically comfortable enough but intellectually stultifying. He must have made occasional excursions to Edinburgh – for books – and would have met like-minded souls in the city, but basically he was locked in the solitary confinement of his own intellect.

Home may have been visited by Michael Ramsay, to whom he wrote in 1732 declaring his good health and thanking Ramsay for returning Home's copy of Bayle. He hoped Ramsay would find 'Diversion and Improvement' in it. He reminded him of a promise he had made to visit Home at Ninewells. Ramsay had obviously been dilatory in coming and we have no knowledge of whether Michael Ramsay came or not, but it would have cheered David and lightened the load on his family.

Discarding more and more of conventional thinking left David Home with a mental vacuum and he grew to acknowledge its physical effect on him:

My health was a little broken by my ardent application.[21]

Home was becoming worried about physical symptoms such as 'scurvy spots' which broke out on his fingers. Since this caused him to abandon his studies, he consulted a physician, possibly Dr Cranston, an eminent physician living in nearby Jedburgh, who, confirming Home's self-diagnosis, prescribed anti-scorbutic juices. This was forty years before James Lind wrote his *Treatise on the Scurvy* for the Royal Navy. The anti-scorbutic juices were probably mainly lemon juice and are easily obtainable today, but in 1809, seventy years after Home's illness, the Reverend Sydney Smith described his parsonage in Yorkshire as being 'so remote that it was twelve miles from the nearest lemon'. Ninewells was probably even further, so the cure would be more awkward to achieve. Home was also given a warning against the 'Vapors' and blithely proceeded to ignore it. The result was that in April 1730 another consultation took place about a less troublesome but more persistent symptom, that of 'ptyalism or a wateryness in the mouth'. Ptyalism is excessive salivation and is commonly a symptom of mercurial poisoning, although in Home's case it is more likely to have been linked to the scurvy. Home's physician laughed at all this and welcomed him to the brotherhood, 'for that I had fairly got the Disease of the Learned'. The cure was to be a course of bitters, and anti-hysteric pills. The bitters were Peruvian bark – now called chinchona, a source of quinine – in syrup of lemon, red wine or camomile tea, and anti-hysteric pills were a mixture of musk, opium and castor sugar, sometimes administered as suppositories. William Buchan's *Domestic Medicine* of 1769 also recommended 'agreeable company, variety of amusements and

change of place, especially travelling into foreign countries'.[22] Home
carried out this advice wholeheartedly for the remainder of his life.

The immediate treatment was combined with drinking an English pint
of claret daily and riding eight to ten Scotch Miles. (A Scotch mile was
two hundred yards longer than its English equivalent.) This Home did
methodically for seven months with great improvement at first:

> In this way I lived with satisfaction enough; and on my return to
> town next winter [1730] found my spirits very much recruited, so
> that, though they sunk under me in the higher flights of genius, yet
> I was able to make progress in my former designs.[23]

This tells us that he was working again on his planned project, certainly
the *Treatise of Human Nature*. Since it was not published until 1739,
Home had now only the framework. In 1727 he had hinted to Michael
Ramsay that he had sketches of a work – it can only have been the *Treatise*
– and he then spent three stressful years examining what was current
thought and rejecting most of it. Home had now reached the emptiness of
mind necessary to work from first principles and start to answer two
fundamental questions: 'How do our thoughts occur and how do they
control our actions?' But it had very nearly robbed him of his most
precious attribute – his reason.

Then in the spring of 1731, having wintered in Edinburgh:

> there grew upon [me] a very ravenous appetite and as quick a
> digestion, which I at first took for a good symptom and was very
> much surprised to find it bring back a palpitation of the heart,
> which I had felt very little of before.
>
> This appetite however, had an effect very unusual, which was to
> nourish me extremely; so that in six weeks time I passed from the
> one extreme to the other, and being before tall, lean and raw-boned
> became on a sudden, the most sturdy, robust, healthful-like fellow
> you have ever seen.[24]

Home's life at this time was not, however, an endless treadmill of
intellectual agony and physical ill-health. During his trips to Edinburgh
he had started to display an enthusiasm for whist and for female company.
Not for him the rumbustious wenching of Michael Ramsay, but rather the
polite conversation of the tea table. He may even have considered marriage
at this time but we have only a passing reference to it. In 1770, six years

before his death, Home wrote jokingly to his friend, Baron Mure of Caldwell:

> the taking of a wife is the first [great operation of human life] which I hope will come in time.

This comment is reprinted in the collected Caldwell papers with a gossipy footnote:

> Home had not always been so determined a bachelor as he was in his latter days. Early in his life he paid his addresses to a young lady of good family and great personal attractions in Edinburgh. His suit was unfavourably received; but several years later when he had achieved celebrity, it was hinted to him by a common friend that the lady had changed her mind. 'So have I', replied the philosopher.[25]

It would seem, therefore that the proposal was made – if it was made at all – after Home's recovery in 1731 and before the start of his fame in the 1740s when he was in his twenties, so his rejection – as a youthful second son with no prospects, except for an as yet unpublished book of philosophy – is not surprising. Annoyingly, though, there are no other references to it.

Home was greatly heartened by his recovery and noticed that his family thought him a better companion than before. His riding exercise, which his horse must have found increasingly wearisome as its rider grew more and more sturdy and robust, took him to and from 'a mineral well of some reputation'. This was Duns Spa, six and a half miles distant from his Ninewells home.

He wrote about the period of illness in 1734, while in London, in an enigmatic, unaddressed and anonymous letter telling his mysterious correspondent that he decided to proceed with his philosophy, rejecting the 'moral philosophy transmitted to us by the ancients' as being like their science, 'entirely hypothetical, depending more on invention than experience'. He claims in the letter that he hopes for advice from 'a skilful physician, a man of letters, of wit, of good sense, and of great humanity', but the letter is a total oddity, having no addressee or signature. It begins:

> Sir,
> Not being acquainted with this hand-writing, you will probably look to the bottom to find the subscription, and not finding any will certainly wonder at this strange method of addressing to you.[26]

He also determines in the letter to keep his name a secret, thus making a reply impossible. He goes on:

> Everyone who is acquainted either with the philosophers or the critics knows that there is nothing yet established in either of these two sciences and that they contain little more than endless disputes even in the most fundamental articles. Upon examination of these, I found a certain boldness of temper growing in me which was not inclined to submit to any authority in these subjects, but led me to seek out some new medium by which truth might be established. After much study and reflection on this, at last, when I was about 18 years of age, there seemed to be opened up to me a new scene of thought which transported me beyond measure and made me, with an ardour natural to young men, throw up every other pleasure or business to apply entirely to it.
>
> The law, which was the business I was designed to follow, appeared nauseous to me and I could think of no other way of pushing my fortune in the world, but that of a scholar and philosopher. I was infinitely happy in this course of life for some months, till at last, about the beginning of September 1729 [Hume was then 18] all my ardour seemed in a moment to be extinguished, and I could no longer raise my mind to that pitch, which formerly gave me such excessive pleasure. I felt no uneasiness or want of spirits when I laid aside my book; and therefore never imagined there was any bodily distemper in the case, but that my coldness proceeded from a laziness of temper, which must be overcome by redoubling my application. In this condition I remained for nine months, very uneasy to myself, as you may well imagine, but without growing any worse, which was a miracle.[27]

Home may simply have been recording his past illness and confusion of mind in the form of a letter to a physician and it is probable that the letter was never sent. He may have had a Dr Arbuthnot in mind as recipient, and Professor Mossner certainly makes a strong case for him.[28] Arbuthnot was a Scot as well as a scholar and wit, and he was then practising in London. Alternatively, Home may have had one Dr George Cheyne in mind as the possible recipient. Cheyne had been in correspondence with Dr Cranston, whom Home had probably already consulted. At any rate, the previous year Cheyne had published a book which sounds as if it suited Home's situation perfectly, *The English Malady; or a Treatise of Nervous Diseases of all kinds, as Spleen, Vapours, Lowness of Spirits, Hypochondriacal Distempers, etc.* Cheyne observed:

> It is a common observation, (and I think has great probability on its side), that fools, weak or stupid persons, heavy and dull souls, are seldom much troubled with vapours and lowness of spirits[29]

Cheyne's own regime for his physical health was completely disastrous and the doctor grew to a monstrous weight of thirty-two stones.

Scholars will argue over the respective candidates for receipt of Home's letter, but a third possibility, which seems the most credible, is that the letter was never intended to be sent to anyone. Home was writing to himself with an account of the crisis he had surmounted alone. He had come to the edge of an abyss, looked over and drawn back from it in time. In later life, when confronted with adversity, all he had to do was re-read the letter and think, 'If I could conquer that, then I can conquer anything'.

Philosophically, Home had clearly by now embraced Locke's argument that our knowledge of the world is based, not solely on reason, but on reason moulded by experience. Home found that the moral structures erected by the ancients were without regard for human nature, and it is human nature which he now vows to pursue as his principal study. With the 'boldness of temper' and the confidence of youth (he was twenty-three) he says:

> little more is required to make a man succeed in this study than to throw off all prejudices either for his own opinions or of this for others . . . I have scribbled many a quire of paper in which there is nothing contained but my own inventions.

He is now breathing clear air and this justifies our belief that he had scoured his intellect clean. He had read the major contemporary works in Latin, French, and English and was teaching himself Italian. His depression and illness had prevented him from editing the papers containing the codification of his early thought, and he had found 'two things very bad for this distemper, study and idleness, so there are two things very good, business and diversion'. The mysterious unaddressed letter continues:

> I had no hopes of delivering my opinions with such elegance and neatness, as to draw me to the attention of the world and I would

rather live and die in obscurity than produce [here is the only
correction in the manuscript – 'produce' replaces 'deliver'] them
maimed and imperfect.[30]

So not only was his ambition to redefine human nature by reason but to
achieve worldly fame in the doing of it. Writing after his recovery, he is
full of renewed confidence and feels that he has joined a select club. He
notes that the French Mystics, Abbé DuBos in particular, and 'our fanatics
here' have suffered similar symptoms. The Abbé, rather cumbersomely,
entitles Chapter One of Volume One of his *Réflexions Critiques*:

Of the necessity of occupation in order to avoid heaviness; and of
the attractives which the motions of the passions have with regard
to man.

DuBos goes on:

Let those that instruct the public philosophical tracts, expound the
wonders of divine providence . . . The soul hath its wants no less
than the body, and one of the greatest wants of man is to have his
mind incessantly occupied. The heaviness which quickly attends the
inactivity of the mind, is a situation so disagreeable to man, that he
frequently chooses to expose himself to the most painful exercises,
rather than be troubled with it.

Two methods of occupying the mind are recommended:

The first is when the soul is affected by external objects, which is
what we call a sensible impression: the other is, when she amuses
herself with the speculation of useful or curious objects, which is
properly to reflect and meditate.

Home would deal at length with 'impressions' in the *Treatise*. But DuBos
continues:

The imagination . . . hurried away by a tumultuary succession of
innumerable unconnected ideas, or the mind fatigued with so close
an application seeks to unbend itself and a dull heavy
pensiveness . . . is the fruit of the effort made for its amusement.
Every man must have experienced the weariness of that state;
wherein he finds himself incapable of thinking . . . In fact, the
hurry and agitation, in which our passions keep us, even in solitude,

is of so brisk a nature, that any other situation is languid and heavy, when compared to this motion.

Thus we are led by instinct, in pursuit of objects capable of exciting our passions, notwithstanding those objects make impressions on us, which are frequently attended with nights of pain and calamity; but man in general would be exposed to greater misery, were he exempt from passions, than the very passions themselves can make him suffer.[31]

This made so great an impact on Home that he debated in detail the conflict between imagination and the passions in Book II of the *Treatise*. But activity alone was not enough for him since he was already a perfectionist. Even Fénelon had dealt with depression in his *Instructions et Avis sur divers points de la Morale et de la perfection Chrétienne*:

As to what regards a certain lowness of spirits, that contracts the heart and damps it; these two rules seem to me of importance . . . not to overload ourselves with toilsome affairs that we may not succumb under an unequal burden. To husband not only the strength of the body; but even that of the mind, to reserve always hours for contemplation; for reading; for encouraging ourselves by good conversations; even being gay; in order to unbend all at once the mind along with the body according to the occasion . . . have some discreet person to whom we may unbosom ourselves. The second rule is to bear peacefully all the involuntary impressions of dejection we suffer . . . A step made in this state is always a gigantic one, it is worth more than a thousand made in a disposition more sweet and consoling . . .

The imagination, as St Thèrèse says, is the fool of the house. She never ceases making noise. It must not be imagined that we can enter into this state [of calm] by efforts of our own. Such a struggling would render you constrained, scrupulous, uneasy in the affairs and conversations where you have occasion for being free. You would always be in fear lest the presence of God escaped you. [Therefore turn to God.] But, we reason too much, and hurt ourselves with reasoning. There is a temptation to reasoning we must be afraid of, as of other temptations.[32]

Much of this would have struck a chord with Home. He had no 'discreet person' to whom he could unbosom himself, except possibly on occasional visits from Michael Ramsay, so his chances of 'good conversations' in Fénelon's sense were slim, as were his opportunities for gaiety, and consequently he was 'hurt with reasoning'. Having thus come to a climax and survived, he resolved to 'toss about the world, from one pole to another, till I have this distemper behind me'. He accepted that 'a symptom of this distemper is to delight in complaining and talking of itself'. He later told a correspondent after the publication of the *Treatise* that 'so vast an undertaking, planned before I was one and twenty and composed before twenty five must necessarily be defective'. In other words he was ready to start but was taking a break to correct the necessary defects before plunging in.

David Home had come through the self-imposed ordeal of intellectual regeneration, an eighteenth-century equivalent of an unsupervised doctoral thesis, and had recovered his health. He had laid the foundations for his *Treatise of Human Nature* without as yet writing a word of it. And he had achieved all this, not in the intellectual atmosphere of a university, but in a Berwickshire farmhouse, punctuated by occasional trips to Edinburgh. This had been tolerated by his brother, John, who would have watched David's physical decline with worry while he ran the farm. Likewise, David's seeming idleness and withdrawal had been a total puzzlement to his mother. The sympathy and understanding of brother and mother, to say nothing of his sister Katherine, had been a necessary boon to David.

Home had, quite literally, gathered his thoughts, but had yet to put them in a cogent form, and for this he needed a complete change of scene. He was determined to take a rest from what Paul Strathern called 'thinking himself to bits'.[33] Being the man he was, his choice of a suitable new ambience for this was totally astonishing.

THREE

A More Active Scene of Life

Having thus collected his thoughts and put his mental house in order, Home should have had no reason to delay writing the work that he felt would propel him to international fame, respect, and wealth. His family would probably have continued to support him but there is a limit to how much charity one can tolerate and Home had reached that limit. His next task was to find somewhere in which he could write in comparative peace. Even with his limited funds Edinburgh was a possibility and he would have the necessary access to libraries, although the access would be thanks to the good offices of Henry Home of Kaimes. Henry Home's enthusiastic hospitality in taverns and the conviviality of Michael Ramsay could mean that Edinburgh would be too full of distractions and Home would anyway carry the reputation there of simply being a younger son who had failed to become a lawyer and had now turned to dilettantism.

So if not to Edinburgh, it had to be a move south, to London, armed, no doubt, with letters of recommendation to men of influence provided by Henry Home, and a promise of accommodation from unknown fellow Scots. But Home had, in fact, already made detailed arrangements for his immediate future and he left Ninewells at the end of February 1734, by boat from Berwick. The sea journey was preferable since the journey to London by coach took over two weeks and, in any case, there was only one coach monthly. David Home was putting his family home behind him, at least for the present. His period of solitary study had bred in him a habit of keeping his intentions private and the results of his move south were a complete surprise.

Had he stayed in his family home there was one event that might well have caused him some embarrassment. It became public in Chirnside a week later on 5th March. Three weeks earlier, before Home had left, a pregnant girl had made her way up to the manse of David's uncle, the Reverend George Home. She was Agnes Galbraith and she had named David Home as the father of her child. George did not believe a word of her story and did not even worry David with the accusation, but the minister had no choice except to let the ponderous juggernaut of clerical justice roll forward and to call a meeting of the Kirk Session to hear her case. Agnes did not appear at first when called by the Session, but came of her own volition to a later meeting. The Session was equally suspicious about the allegation. Why had she waited until David had left Scotland before openly accusing him?

> . . . she did not compear [present herself] when cited, about three weeks ago, when he was in the country, and had come this day without being cited when he was gone.[1]

Also this was Agnes's third confession of fornication, and her accusations seemed to be habitual. However, the Session had to take her charge seriously and duly passed the case to be heard by the Presbytery in nearby Duns on 25th June.

It was not uncommon for pregnant girls to bring such accusations to those in authority, or with a position to defend, in the hope of being bought off quickly or of obtaining the eighteenth-century equivalent of a maintenance order. Agnes had chosen the laird's brother and the minister's nephew, who had conveniently left for England and could not defend himself. But in this case, the Presbytery took no action against Home in England, since he was 'out of this Kingdom' (the Union of the Crowns, over a hundred years earlier, clearly had had no effect in the Presbytery of Duns), and Agnes was remitted back to the Session of Chirnside for treatment. As an admitted adulteress she would have stood outside the Church door on a Sunday morning clad in sackcloth, her neck fastened to the wall by an iron collar or 'joug', and then inside the church she would have sat on the 'cutty stool', or stool of repentance, before the congregation while her sins were declared for the third time. Her child was baptised on 5th May with a John Galbraith, almost certainly a relative, as the putative father. She seems not to have restrained her amorous nature since she bore another illegitimate child in 1739 and reappeared in the 'joug'. In this period many parish churches must have looked very odd on Sunday mornings with immoral women shackled to their doors.

David Home could not have been the father of her child. He had been in extremely low spirits for some time and would have been known around the parish as a moody, studious sort of lad. A quick dalliance with a local girl on the rebound from his rejection in Edinburgh is possible but the dates do not make any sense, and to run from his obligations was completely out of character for Home. But Agnes might have thought that waiting until the laird's brother had left for London and then making an accusation he could not defend might shake John Home's purse strings loose. It was certainly worth a try, even though it failed, and David would only have heard about the case many years later, if at all.

Now in London, he took the opportunity to review his past crisis to the point of detailing it all in the 'letter' to a physician. Then, after about a fortnight, in mid-March 1734, without having sent the letter, he left for Bristol a hundred-odd miles to the west. It had been his intended destination from the start. Without realising it and certainly without admitting it to himself, Home was on the second lap of a run for cover. He was unaware that he was running away, or from what, but he was leaving his youth behind, and had re-invented himself, although the new creation would not be complete until he had codified his thoughts some three years later. He was also leaving behind the guilt of being a parasite to his family, no matter how much they would have denied it. And he was running from the memory of the 'Disease of the Learned', which he had confronted in his anonymous letter. But there were three more laps to cover before he could stop running and find a refuge.

He had prepared himself for this particular lap since in *My Own Life* he tells us that he 'had recommendations to some eminent merchants', though how he could have received such recommendations is hard to say. The Edinburgh merchants he or his brother might have known nearly all dealt directly south with London or with the Baltic ports and Edinburgh's growing demand for sugar from the West Indies was largely satisfied by Glasgow importers. Edinburgh was, however, a major importer of wine from Bordeaux, as was Bristol, and this may have established one link.

Of course, this was not the choice of a 'career' in the modern sense but rather the choice of a place where all previous influences would be too remote to be of any importance, and no one in Bristol would have had foreknowledge that Home's baggage included notes on a major philosophical work. He was cut off from the libraries of Edinburgh and from what debating friends he had, so further progress on the *Treatise* would have been all but impossible. But if Home was trying to gain experience of commercial life he could not have chosen a better place.

According to Daniel Defoe in his *Tour through the whole Island of Great Britain* published some ten years earlier, Bristol was:

the greatest the richest and the best Port of Trade in Great Britain, London only excepted [and traded] with more independency upon London than any other town in Britain.[2]

In Bristol, Home was received as a clerk by Michael Miller of 15 Queen Square. Miller did not deal in wine but was a prosperous merchant in the city dealing mainly with the West Indies for sugar, and, probably, slaves, a trade which Home would abominate in later life. It was the most improbable situation Home could have chosen.

Miller's establishment in the city – where he, and probably Home, lived – was on a newly fashionable peninsula lined with dockyards. The River Avon wound round the southern and eastern sides of the peninsula and St Augustine's Reach was on the west. Thirty years previously the area had been simply a marsh with a bowling-green when the first house was built in 1701. Gentrification continued as it was renamed Queen Square in honour of Queen Anne in 1702. Then a rope-walk and tar house were removed in 1712 and by 1716 trees were planted and the square was complete. It was the height of modernity and fashion but since it was within an easy walk to all the wharves it admirably suited the Bristolian spirit of combining elegance with profitable trade.

At this time Home had no concept whatsoever of elegance and even less of trade. He was a tall, now robust, country-born Scot with a thick Scots accent and he made only one concession to his new-found English colleagues. Rather patronisingly and to ease their ignorance of Scottish pronunciations he changed the spelling of his name to Hume. It remained Hume for the rest of his life – as it will remain in this book.

As to Hume's friendships in Bristol, a John Peach is mentioned and there did exist a Samuel Peach who seems to have been born 1713, being thus a near contemporary of Hume's. He was probably a local boy starting out in commerce. A bank, Peach, Fowler & Co, was founded in 1774, forty years after Hume had left Bristol. Hume was probably a friend of the younger members of the family. There are two letters to a James 'Jemmy' Birch who was younger than Hume but equally impecunious and who proposed joining Hume after he left Bristol. The two never, in fact, met again, but they were clearly close friends. Hume would have looked for company with young men of his own age, although he would have found

no fellow spirits. The local clerks' interests would lie more with commercial success and sexual conquests than with philosophy. After Hume's
crisis with the 'disease of the learned' and during this first period of living
alone and out of his native surroundings the atmosphere of alienation
would have been deeply hurtful. It was also a situation from which there
was no easy escape. Hume had changed the spelling of his name since the
English confused its pronunciation – they still do – and he must have
proved a humiliating figure of fun to his fellow clerks. His accent and
manners marked him out as foreign, and it still comes as a shock to all
Scots living in England for the first time to find the differences in
behaviour so clearly marked. Hume's natural sociability turned to caution
as he was asked to repeat nearly every phrase, and his vivacity of mind
faded in the company of merchants' clerks talking about nothing except
commerce, drink and girls.

An independent account of his sojourn in Bristol is given by John
Latimer and is worth repeating:

> His future employer was Mr Michael Miller, a merchant, residing
> at 15 Queen Square who had made a fortune by his enterprise but
> whose education, in the opinion of his new clerk, left much to be
> desired. It is said, and it is practically confirmed in a letter from
> Dean Tucker [Tucker was rector of St Stephen's Church and Miller
> was a parishioner] to Lord Hailes, that Mr Miller, exasperated at
> the criticisms passed on his business letters, told Hume that he had
> made £20,000 with his English, and would not have it improved.
> The offended Scot, who hated all Englishmen, many years later
> took the opportunity of displaying his scornful opinions of
> Bristolians, describing in his *History* the progress of Naylor the
> Quaker fanatic. Hume says, 'He entered Bristol riding on a horse, I
> suppose from the difficulty in that place of finding an ass'. There is
> a tradition, nevertheless, that he kept up a friendship with Mr John
> Peach of Maryleport Street, to whom he sent the manuscript of the
> first volumes of his history, desiring him to remove any dialectical
> barbarisms. The story, if true, does not redound to Mr Peach's
> credit for the first edition abounded with barbarisms.[3]

The contretemps with Miller is also reported in C.H. Cave's *History of
Banking in Bristol*:

I'll tell you what, Mr Hume, I have made £20,000 by my English
and I won't have it mended.[4]

It is not difficult to recreate the scene when Hume's employer, Miller, for
whom one must have some sympathy, confronted his arrogant, alien,
incomprehensible clerk. Criticism of his English from a raw-boned
Scottish clerk was too much to bear and the two parted company. It
was the end of Hume's career in commerce, and this time his desire to 'toss
him about the world' led him for the first time, but certainly not the last,
across the Channel to France. From feeling an alien in the newly created
Britain, he would now be a true alien in a foreign country, whose language
he could read and write with fluency but had probably never used in
conversation.

Retracing his steps to London, after a day's journey by coach to Dover
Hume then took ship for Calais. After what could be a lengthy wait for a
favourable wind he spent between three hours, if he was lucky, or up to
twenty hours if he was not, crossing the Channel for about 10 shillings,
depending on the number of passengers. Nearly all travellers of the time
comment on nausea and fear as the two predominant experiences of the
crossing, and arrival at Calais must have come as a welcome relief. The
standard of accommodation in France varied widely, but at all establishments it was thought wise to lock one's door, sleep with one's valuables
under one's pillow and keep weapons within reach.

Food and wine at the better class of inns were often of a higher standard
than expected as were the tableware and furnishings. Hume's severely
limited budget would exclude him from many of these joys, normal to
those undertaking the Grand Tour. It would also prohibit him from the
hiring of a private chaise, the preferred transport, being the eighteenth-
century equivalent of a chauffeur-driven limousine. Instead of that luxury,
David Hume took the bus!

This was the universally detested 'diligence'. The lowliest English stage
was thought to be a vehicle of some elegance in comparison to it. It carried
about twenty passengers, inside and out, but was usually overcrowded with
up to thirty people aboard. Although French main roads were generally of
a high standard, the diligence's primitive attempts at springing made the
voyage hideously uncomfortable. The diligence could cover up to seventy
miles in a day, thanks to dawn starts, although the food supplied at the
stopping places was usually foul and expensive, as was the accommodation

provided *en route*. At least when the diligence stopped, Hume would be spared Lady Mary Wortley Montagu's experience in 1718:

> While the post horses are changed, the whole town comes out to
> beg, with such miserable starved faces and thin tattered clothes,
> they need no other eloquence to persuade [one of] the wretchedness
> of their condition.[5]

Diligence passengers were known to be too poor to be worth approaching.

In the crowded coach, Hume would be conspicuous as a foreigner with his tentative, nervous attempts at French. Having read Bayle and Fénelon provided no equipment for small talk among his fellow travellers across the Pas de Calais and the Isle de France. And the fellow travellers, often only suffering the diligence for short distances, were not prone to discuss the latest theories of philosophy:

> Chance, indeed, may now and then throw a pleasant man in your
> way, but these are but thinly sown amongst those sour and silent
> gentlemen who are your general associates.[6]

We may be sure that Hume did attempt conversation, even with a broad Scots accent overlaying his French – even thirty years later as a diplomat with the British Embassy in Paris his French accent was thought to be 'atrocious'. And he would have been at laborious pains to point out that he was not 'un Anglais' but 'un Ecossais'.

This Ecossais arrived in Paris in the late spring or early summer of 1734. The shock of seeing Paris must have been even more enormous than his attempt at a life in commerce or his brief stays in London. With a population of 600,000, Paris was the most splendid city he had so far visited. Bridges linked the ancient centre of the Isle de la Cité with both banks of the Seine. On the Left Bank the Latin Quarter had extended itself from the Sorbonne in both directions. The Rue St Honoré on the Right Bank was the principal street of the city, running past the northern side of the Louvre, itself described by one awestruck visitor in 1665:

> I saw also that vast stupendous building the Louvre . . . I think the
> Grand Seigneurs seraglio shall bear no proportion to it.[7]

On the other side of the Rue St Honoré was the Palais Royal where, during Louis XV's minority, the regent Duc d'Orléans had held a scandalous court with his 'roués'. His influence had now passed to the more sober Cardinal Fleury as Chancellor. The Tuileries Gardens were at the furthest end of the city, and to the west beyond them lay open countryside with the gardens of the Champs Elysées and the great houses of the Faubourg de St Honoré. Pedestrians in the city had to take care to avoid the carriages of the nobility, but Hume would have taken part in the promenades in the newly built Place Louis-le-Grand, now renamed the Place Vendôme. His first sight of Parisian women parading in the height of fashion would have been alarming. Even the redoubtable Lady Mary Wortley Montagu commented:

> The French ladies . . . so fantastically absurd in their dress! So monstrously unnatural in their paint! Their hair cut short and curled round their faces, loaded with powder that makes it look like white wool, and on their cheeks to their chins, unmercifully laid on, a shining red japan that glistens in a most flaming manner, that they seem to have no resemblance to human faces, and I am apt to believe took the first hint of their dress from a sheep new raddled . . . Grotesque daubers!![8]

Hume would have seen plenty of sheep marked with red ochre, or reddle, at Ninewells, but even in the drawing rooms and taverns of Edinburgh he would have seen nothing like this human masquerade.

He was visiting France at one of the pivotal points in its history. Alfred Cobban in his *History of Modern France* says of the period:

> The government of France had been left by Louis XIV half-way between the mediaeval personal and the modern administrative regimes.[9]

This political uncertainty made Paris a magnet for the dispossessed and Hume would have met many fellow countrymen since there were certainly more Scotsmen in Paris than there had been in Bristol. Many refugees from the Jacobite rising of 1715 had settled there. Chief of those was the Earl of Mar who had held office under Queen Anne, been dismissed after her death, and then had led the Old Pretender's armies with a spectacular lack of success at Sheriffmuir in November 1725. Now he was a sad exile under the nickname of 'Bobbing John'. Paris and, indeed, all France still had bitter cause to remember the Edinburgh-born John Law, now in uneasy exile in London. Fourteen years earlier Law had risen to be Controller-General of Finances for France, introducing the concept of credit banking based on paper money. He also founded a company trading to Louisiana, known simply as Le Mississippi. When both the wildly over-financed company and the hugely extended bank collapsed, thousands were ruined and the French economy stalled. Law fled.

But central to Hume's stay in Paris was the Chevalier Ramsay. He had been born Andrew Michael Ramsay in Ayr on 9th June 1686 to a reasonably prosperous baker who had suffered exile for his Covenanting activities. Ramsay attended Edinburgh University and while in the capital managed to get the Lord Lyon King-of-Arms to grant him patents of nobility. He was also a companion of Hume's friend Michael Ramsay whom he claimed as a cousin, and it is probable that Hume carried letters of recommendation from Michael. Hume, then, had a failsafe plan for France if his career in Bristol failed. In other words, when he left Ninewells for a 'more active scene of life' he had several options already prepared.

Andrew Ramsay had gone to study at Leyden, as many of his countrymen did, and had managed to meet Fénelon who lived at nearby Cambrai. Thanks to this friendship Ramsay converted to Catholicism and Fénelon then arranged for his appointment as preceptor to the Duc de Chateau-Thierry. He left this post with a knighthood in the order of St Lazarus, and from then on styled himself the Chevalier Ramsay. He climbed his next rung on the ladder of fame in Rome as tutor to the four-year-old Prince Charles Edward Stuart. Now collecting pensions from the Duc de Chateau-Thierry, the Comte d'Evreux, and a colonelcy from the exiled James III, he returned to Paris to pursue 'literary endeavours'. He wrote a life of Fénelon and the quasi-historical *Voyages of Cyrus*, gaining an LLD from Oxford University, becoming a Fellow of the Royal Society and hoping even to become one of the forty 'immortels' of the Académie française. They, sensibly, drew a line at the Chevalier's ambition and he was rejected. Hume lived with the Chevalier at his lodgings with the Duc de Sully – he had a knack for lodging with the richer nobility – near the Place des Vosges. Robert Chambers said the Chevalier:

> was a young man full of literary enthusiasms and haunted with day-dreams of immortality.[10]

He received Hume with 'all imaginable kindness' although one cannot imagine a more disparate pair. Eight years later, after Hume had published the *Treatise,* the Chevalier wrote to Dr John Stevenson in Edinburgh about the character of Hume:

> That bright ingenious young spark does not seem to me to have acquired a sufficient stock of solid learning, nor to be born with a fund of noble sentiments, nor to have a genius capable of all that geometrical attention, penetration and justness necessary to make a true metaphysician. [He is] too dissipated with material objects and spiritual self-idolatry to pierce the sacred recesses of divine truth . . . he seems to me to be one of those philosophers who spin out systems out of their own brain without any regard to religion, antiquity or tradition sacred or profane; but Descartes is a melancholy example that such cobwebs are no use, and yet that philosopher was one of the greatest genis [sic] of his age and far superior to your thin, superficial, meagre, lean skeleton Locke.[11]

Paris did not entirely hold similar opinions to the Chevalier for Voltaire's *Lettres Philosphiques* were published in 1734 endorsing both Locke and Newton. Later Hume said:

> I thought the opinions of the ingenious writer very curious, but I pretend not to warrant the justice of them . . . Chevalier Ramsay, a writer, who had so laudable an inclination to be orthodox that his reason never found any difficulty, even in the doctrines which the free thinkers scruple the most, the trinity, incarnation and satisfaction: his humanity alone, of which he seems to have a great stock, rebelled against the doctrines of reprobation and predestination.[12]

The Chevalier and Hume would have been locked in controversy over an event of seven years previously, which was still very much in people's minds. In 1727 a Jansenist deacon, François de Pâris, died and was buried in the cemetery of Saint-Médard in the Faubourg Saint-Marcel, near the present Gare d'Austerlitz. The Jansenists were originally followers of Cornelius Otto Jansen, a Flemish theologian who denied the freedom of the will and accused the existing church, especially the Jesuits, of moral laxity. He advocated a return to the teachings of St Augustine. The movement had become politicised into attacks on the centralism of royal government and had been condemned by Pope Clement IX in 1713 by the Bull *Unigenitus.* However, at the deacon's tomb, miracles very inconveniently started to occur. Crowds gathered to watch the antics of the *convulsionaries,* or cripples, who lay on the tomb and were cured, leaping extravagantly in relief. This focus for Jansenism could not be tolerated and, on the orders of the Chancellor, Cardinal Fleury (needless to say, he was a close personal friend of the Chevalier), the police closed the cemetery. Hume was astonished at the credulity demonstrated:

> many of the miracles were immediately proved on the spot, before judges of unquestioned integrity, attested by witnesses of credit and distinction, in a learned age and on the most eminent theatre that is the world. Nor is this all, a relation of them was published everywhere . . . and what have we to oppose to such a cloud of witnesses, but the absolute impossibility or miraculous nature of the events, which they relate? And this, surely, in the eyes of all reasonable people will alone be regarded as refutation.[13]

The Chevalier, as a devout Catholic, would have had no difficulty in believing in the miracles, but his friendship with the Cardinal, and the fact that the miracles occurred at the tomb of a Jansenist, would have given him much food for thought. Hume, on the other hand, would have treated the entire affair with utter scepticism, and eventually encapsulated his thoughts in his essay *Of Miracles.*

The Chevalier would have felt it incumbent on himself to introduce his young friend to the intellectual circles of Paris, and Hume would have revelled in their company. But he was getting no nearer to finding the peace he required to write his philosophy. Michael Ramsay's temptations in the taverns of Edinburgh were nothing compared to the cafés and salons of Paris, and Hume was facing another problem. This problem has faced most visitors to Paris, even today. He was running out of money and had to find somewhere cheaper to live.

Hume chose Reims on the recommendation of the Chevalier, and the city could be relied on to have a reasonable library and at least some citizens of education. To modern visitors the two main attractions are, firstly, the magnificent twelfth-century Cathedral of Nôtre Dame, coronation site for the kings of France and, secondly, the local wine. The cathedral would have interested Hume not at all and he does not mention the wine, but what was of interest to him was that two families in Reims were friends of the Chevalier, so armed with the inevitable letters of introduction he left Paris for the north-east.

Almost upon arrival, on 12 September 1734, he wrote to 'Jemmy' Birch in Bristol who clearly had had ideas of following Hume to France with 'a view to studying there':

> Reims is a very famous and ancient town and university situated about 34 leagues from Paris which makes an easy day's journey by post. It is a large town containing they say about 40,000 people; but its buildings are not very beautiful; which proceeds from this that the people of fashion choose to build their house off the streets and by that means they are concealed. There are about 30 families here that keep coaches though they tell me there is not one of £500 a year in the whole town. They are a polite sociable people and what is of considerable advantage to a stranger, are easily made acquaintance with. For having got letters of recommendation to two of the best families in town, I am every day in some of their houses, they make parties of diversion to show me more company, and if I could but speak their language perfectly I would immediately be acquainted with the whole town. But that is a difficulty which will soon be got over; so that when you come I shall have the satisfaction of showing you the best company in town. These letters I got thanks to the Chevalier Ramsay, who received me in Paris with all imaginable kindness. I have another letter from him, which I have not delivered since the gentleman is not at present in town, though he will return in a few days. He is a man of considerable note . . . and one of the most learned in France. I promise myself abundance of pleasure from his conversation. I must likewise add, that he has a fine library, so we shall have all advantages for study . . . I shall write you an exact account of the method of travelling to Paris and shall meet you there . . . I forgot to mention that I think we cannot live under £80 a year and that may do.[14]

He then sends his compliments to 'Mr Peach, and all friends', and the letter goes, via Paris and London, to Mr James Birch, at the Old Market Bristol. The mention of £80 annually for him and Jemmy to live on leads one to think that he was only just managing to exist alone on his allowance of £50.

On the same day he wrote to Michael Ramsay in Edinburgh, giving his address as *Monsieur David Hume, Gentilhomme Ecossois, chez Monsieur*

Mesier, au perroquet verd proche la porte au feron,* proudly maintaining his social standing as a gentleman. Hume repeats most of his description of Reims, including his vexation at not speaking French well enough to 'support a conversation', and then uses 'the freedom to entertain you with any idle thoughts that come into my head'. The Chevalier had given him advice to imitate as much as possible the manners of the French:

> For, says he, though the English perhaps have more of the real politeness of the heart, yet the French certainly have a better way of expressing it . . . in my humble opinion it is just the contrary, viz., that the French have more real politeness and the English the better method of expressing it. By real politeness I mean softness of temper and a very sincere inclination to oblige and be serviceable; which is very conspicuous in this nation . . . so that I have not yet seen one quarrel in France, though they are everywhere to be met with in England. By expressions of politeness, I mean these outward deferences and ceremonies which custom has invented, to supply the defect of real politeness or kindness . . . Thus when the Quakers say 'your friend' they are as easily understood as another that says 'your humble servant.' The French err in the contrary extreme, that of making their civilities too remote from the truth, which is a fault, though they are not designed to be believed, just as it is a transgression of rules in a dramatic poet to mix any improbabilities with his fable.
>
> Another fault I find with French manners, is that like their clothes and furniture, they are too glaring. An English fine gentleman distinguishes himself from the rest of the world by the whole tenor of his conversation, more than by any particular part of it; so that you are sensible he excels, you are at a loss to tell in what . . . The English politeness is always greatest when it appears least. After all it must be confessed, that the little niceties of the French behaviour . . . serve to polish the ordinary kind of people and prevent rudeness and brutality . . . Devotees feel their devotion increase by the observance of trivial superstitions as sprinkling, kneeling, crossing, etc . . . the mind pleases itself by the progress it makes in such trifles . . . and I verily believe that 'tis for this

---

* The Green Parrot was an auberge dating from 1668 at the *porte des ferrons*, or ironworks. Nothing now exists of this.

reason you scarce ever meet with a clown, or an ill bred man in France.

> You may perhaps wonder that I who have stayed so short [a] time in France and who have confessed that I am not master of their language should decide so positively of their manners . . . when I compare our English phrase of 'humble servant' . . . with the French one of 'the honour of being your most humble servant' . . . [it] lets me clearly see the different humours of the nations. The phrase of 'honour of doing or saying such a thing' goes so far, that my washing woman today told me that she hoped she should have the honour of serving me while I stayed at Reims; and what is still more absurd it is used by people to those who are very much their inferiors.[15]

He ends, jokingly, by instructing Ramsay to take more care over writing his letters and hopes that he will have the honour and satisfaction of hearing from him. This is Hume the first-time traveller, making massive and sweeping generalisations. By 'English' he includes the Anglicised Scots, of which he would be one. He takes casual swipes at religious ceremonies and at dramatists including 'improbabilities'. This is absolutely in keeping with the eighteenth-century Whig view that embraced the Church of England and considered Shakespeare as a barbarian. Also, like many people visiting France for the first time, he had become a committed Francophile. He would remain one for the rest of his life.

A few days later, on the 29th September, the gentleman 'of considerable note' had returned to Reims. According to P.H. Meyer[16] the likeliest candidate was Louis-Jean Levesque de Pouilly. He was a distinguished citizen of Reims, author of *Théorie des Sentiments Agréables*, with a keen interest in the philosophic theories coming from England. He was also a friend and correspondent of Claude Helvétius, one of the contributors to the *Encyclopédie* and a profound believer in experience as a basis for intellect. Hume and he would find an easy rapport.

The other, less likely, candidate was the Abbé Noel-Antoine Pluche. He was the distinguished author of *Beautés du spectacle de la nature* in which he proved the existence of God as the creator of the balance of nature – whoever created the fishes, also created the seas for them to live in – as well as some devotional works. He was also professor of rhetoric at the University of Reims. But Pluche was a devout Catholic, indeed a Jansenist, who had undergone exile at nearby Laon as a result of the Papal Bull *Unigenitus*. He had, however, recently returned to Reims. All logic points to Levesque as the sympathetic host and mentor Hume was seeking, as opposed to the stern Christian and Jansenist Pluche. However, on the 29th Hume wrote again to Michael Ramsay:

> I am resolved before the post go away to tell you of the library to which I am admitted here in Reims. I was recommended to the Abbé Noel-Antoine Pluche, which most learned man has opened his fine library to me. It has all the advantages of study and holds an abundance of writings of both the French and English along with as complete a set of the Classics as I have seen in one place. It is my pleasure to read over today Locke's *Essays* and *The Principles of human Knowledge* by Dr Berkeley which are printed in their original state and in French copy. I was told by a student of the University who attends to the books that his master received new works of learning and philosophy from London and Paris each month, so I shall feel no want of the latest books.[18]

There is, therefore, no doubt as to Hume's host in Reims, probably as a result of a recommendation from Chevalier Ramsay, who was well connected in Jansenist circles. Hume lived with Pluche at the corner of the Rue de Marc and the Place du Forum. The house has been demolished and is now a children's playground with a plaque noting the residence of Abbé Pluche but not his more famous guest. Conversation between the two may have raised other difficulties as Hume says he was still learning to speak French. Now, if the Abbé Pluche spoke no English – and it is very likely that he spoke it only as well as Hume spoke French – he and the Abbé would have had to converse in whatever each of them could understand of the other's language. However, Pluche had earlier published a pamphlet in Latin, and both men spoke Latin with ease although their respective accents might have been a problem. In 1666 Christopher Wren tried speaking Latin to his French hosts. He found their attempts at the language totally Frenchified and they found his Latin tainted with an impenetrable English accent.

Of supreme importance to Hume would have been the facility to consult the library of the Jesuit College a kilometre distant. The College had been established by Henri IV in 1606, no doubt to strengthen his credentials as a good Catholic, and was completed in 1678. The College was endowed with a magnificent library. 'The wealth of the decoration perhaps will tire the eyes, but the whole is full of harmony.'[19] Deserted at the suppression of the Jesuit order in 1762, it became a laundry store when the College was converted to a hospital, but is now under restoration. The books have been removed to the Bibliothèque Patrimoine and their catalogue displays a vast breadth of mind. Bayle is present – with four copies of the complete works – as well Locke (in French), and commentaries on Newton and Malebranche. Duns Scotus and Albert Magnus rub shoulders with reflections on Descartes and histories of Calvinism.[20]

Now Hume had all the books he needed, a mentor with whom he could discuss, however haltingly and confrontationally, his philosophy, and his notes from Edinburgh and Ninewells. He had been preparing to write for some years now and the *Treatise of Human Nature* is described in the 'Advertisement' to the posthumous edition of Hume's *Essays* in 1777 as having been 'projected before he left college'. He had lodgings in a comfortable but not overly diverting city and could spend his time as he wished. So why did he not start to write?

The twenty-three-year-old David Hume behaved like someone who has laboriously climbed to the ten-metre diving board in an Olympic-sized swimming pool and looked over the edge. He was fully prepared but the actual height was daunting. 'I'll dive after three – one – two – two and a half – two and three quarters' – and so on. Ordering his thoughts had given him the 'Disease of the Learned', he had run to Bristol where he had, unsurprisingly, failed to accommodate himself with a life of commerce, been plunged into the maelstrom of the Parisian literati, and had now come to a pause in Reims.

In *My Own Life* he says that:

> I went over to France with a view of prosecuting my studies in a country retreat; and I there laid that plan of life which I have steadily and successfully pursued: I resolved to make a very rigid frugality supply my deficiency of fortune, to maintain unimpaired my independency, and to regard every object as contemptible except the improvement of my talents in literature.[21]

Reims was not a country retreat, it was an historic provincial city, where Hume was learning to speak French, taking part in the social life, and probably spending too much money. It took him nearly two more years to dive from the high board, but in 1735 he moved on again for what was to be the last lap of his journey.

His choice this time drove him further into the heart of '*La France Profonde*', to the village of La Flèche in Anjou, far to the south-west of Reims. The population was only a tenth of Reims and La Flèche possessed no venerated cathedral. This was the country retreat Hume had been seeking, in a shaded valley surrounded by vineyards, on the river Loir, flowing westwards into the Sarthe before it, in turn, turned south to join the Loire itself at Angers. Hume gives us a few clues as to why he chose this rustic retreat in a letter to 'Jemmy' Birch of 18 May 1735:

> 'Tis a neat, well-built but small town, very pleasantly situated in the banks of a river and in one of the finest provinces in France. The people are extremely civil and sociable; and besides the good company in the town there is a college of a hundred Jesuits, which is esteemed the most magnificent both for buildings and gardens of any belonging to that order in France or even in Europe. This beside the cheapness of it, has formerly made it so much frequented by our countrymen, that there was once thirty Englishmen boarded in this small town.[22]

Henri IV had also founded a Jesuit college there in 1604 and it had an equally magnificent library which exists to this day. Its most distinguished former pupil was René Descartes who had attended the school since its inception until 1612 when he left convinced he had learned nothing. But the Reims librarians would have told Hume of their sister establishment in rural La Flèche, and the cheapness of the accommodation there would have clinched it. Once again bearing letters of recommendation, he set about on his last lap.

In 1700 Sir Andrew Balfour's *Letters writ to a friend, containing Directions and Advices fro travelling through France and Italy*, were published and in the book he advises:

> 'You may hire horses to La Flèche where the only thing considerable is the Jesuit's College. It is a most noble structure and by far the best that they have in France. Take particular notice of their Church where the heart of Henry IV who gave them the house is kept: the Biblioteck; the bake-house where one man and his dog makes bread for all the college every day . . . The best lodging was *Au Quatre Vents*.[23]

In the terms of the *Guide Michelin* the village was 'worth a detour'. Today it is merely 'interesting'. The inn has long since vanished, and the relics of Henri IV and his Queen Marie de Medici were burnt in the square during the Revolution although the chapel still holds the ashes of their hearts. The college, which in Hume's day was a flourishing Jesuit seminary, is now a prestigious military academy, and smartly clad cadets march briskly where Hume once walked in debate with the learned fathers.

In 1735 the college had an enforced exile within its walls. This was one Père Jean-Baptiste-Louis Gresset, confined to La Flèche after his teaching of the humanities at Tours had become too liberal. Gresset had also published a hilarious verse satire, purporting to be written by 'Vert-Vert, the green parrot of Nevers', who was loved by the sisters of the local convent. Green parrots seemed to loom large in Hume's life at this time. At La Flèche Gresset asked to be released from his vows and the Jesuit order was only too glad to oblige. Gresset left immediately to pursue a successful career as a dramatist in Paris. Later in his life Hume bought Gresset's complete works for the Advocates' Library in Edinburgh on whose shelves they still stand, but in 1735 the twenty-four-year-old Scots scholar and the twenty-six-year-old Jesuit apostate must have been diverting company for each other in the Au Quatre Vents. Gresset wrote of La Flèche:

> La Flèche would be fine
> If it was a beautiful prison;
> A pleasant climate
> Sweet enough little drinks
> A drinkable enough little wine
> Little recitals fine enough
> And passable social life
> La Flèche would be fine
> If it was a beautiful prison.

Likewise at the Au Quatre Vents the hospitality of the lay population of La Flèche would have been open to Hume. 'Their table, their heart and their purse [would have been open] for the *Quatre Vents* was an expensive inn for a young man with more breeding than disposable income.'

Hume did not, in fact, stay at the inn but two kilometres north of the town at the manor house of Yvandeau in the small suburb of Saint-Germain-du-Val. This charming house then belonged to the Jesuits and was at the disposal of their guests. It exists to this day as a delightful residence, with carefully tended gardens facing south with unimpaired views of the spires of the Jesuit chapel in the village below. In this country idyll he was provided with a spacious bed-sitting room on the first floor, amply furnished with bed, writing-table, bookcases and fireplace. The servants of the house also served Hume, delivering his mail from home. 'I perceive a great extent of fields and buildings beyond my chamber'[25] – and he had but a short walk to the Jesuits' library in town. Having survived the 'Disease of the Learned' alone, Hume had no fears in writing his book without the tutelage of learned professors. Earlier in the above mentioned letter he tells Jemmy Birch:

> . . . as you know there is nothing to be learnt from a Professor, which is not to be met with in books, and there is nothing to be required in order to reap all possible advantages from them, but an order and choice in reading them . . . I see no reason why we should either go to an university, more than to any other place, or ever trouble ourselves about the learning or capacity of the professor.[26]

Hume would, however, have had the opportunity of debate, however halting, with the fathers in the seminary and we can construct a portion of such a debate:

> I was . . . engaged in conversation with a Jesuit of some parts and learning, who was relating to me, and urging some nonsensical miracle performed in their convent when I was tempted to dispute against him; and as my head was full of the topics of my *Treatise of Human Nature*, which I was at that time composing, this argument immediately occurred to me, and I thought it very much gravelled my companion; but at last he observed to me that it was impossible for the argument to have any solidity because it operated equally against the Gospel and the Catholic miracles; which observation I thought proper to admit as a sufficient answer . . . the freedom at least of this reasoning makes it somewhat extraordinary to have been the produce of a convent of Jesuits, though perhaps you may think the sophistry of it savours plainly of the place of its birth.[27]

At least there is grudging admiration for the debating skills of the Jesuits. Hume's argument, later codified in *Of Miracles*, was that there could be no proof of a miracle:

. . . No testimony is sufficient to establish a miracle, unless the testimony be of a kind that its falsehood would be more miraculous than the fact which it endeavours to establish; and even in that case there is a mutual destruction of arguments and the superior only gives us an assurance suitable to that degree of force which remains after deducting the inferior.[28]

His Jesuit companion would have believed that proof was unnecessary, if one had sufficient faith. Also, that one of the principal characteristics of a miracle was not necessarily its veracity, but its ability to increase faith. Hume's faith was in reasoned argument. But the incident does show that he was welcome in the seminary and that the brothers of 'some parts and learning' would try their wits with him and he with them. All writers understand that an occasional break from the rigours of the desk is essential, and the intellectual atmosphere of La Flèche was ideal. Isolated in his *manoir* with easy access to a large library when he chose, intellectual conversations in the seminary, and Loire trout available at Au Quatre Vents with the excellent white wine of the region, he found this an ideal retreat. The library of nearly 5,000 volumes contained 157 works of philosophy, by Descartes, Puffendorf, Malebranche, Grotius and Bacon. There were eight works labelled *Vetiti* (the forbidden ones), and there he would have found Bayle, Jansen and Voltaire. 'The presence of controversial works shows that the Jesuits of La Flèche were not disinterested in the huge problems which concerned Christianity.'[29] However, by 1776, when the library had survived the extirpation of the order, it still contained no works by Hume – not even under *Historia Profana*.

Ninewells was a long way away and Hume was under no pressure to achieve anything. His allowance was adequate for his needs and there were no distracting friends expecting a spectacular dive from the high board. Hume could lower himself into the shallow end of the pool and go into as deep water as he wished in perfect privacy. He had brought a plan of his book from Ninewells to France and had fleshed out the framework in Reims. Here in La Flèche there was a specialised library for him to consult. 'Was his thinking entirely new? How did it compare with religious precepts of free will or predestination?' Again and again he would write and then go to check his conclusions on the upper floor of the college which held the library. Then he would walk back with his thoughts to the sunlit room at Yvandeau. For the next two years the time passed 'very agreeably' and in August 1737 he left La Flèche with the first two books of the *Treatise* completed.

He wrote to his old friend Michael Ramsay in Edinburgh while passing through Tours and Orléans *en route* for Paris, hoping to meet Ramsay in London in three to four weeks' time when he intended to let him read what he had written. Dauntingly Hume suggested that Ramsay do a little homework to prepare himself:

> . . . read over once *le Recherche de la Verité* of Père Malebranche, the *Principles of Human Knowledge* by Dr Berkeley, some of the more metaphysical articles of Bailes [sic] *Dictionary*, such as those [of] Zeno and Spinoza. Descartes' *Meditations* would also be useful but don't know if you will find it easily among your acquaintances. These books will make you easily comprehend the metaphysical parts of my reasoning and as to the rest, they have so little dependence on all former systems of philosophy that your natural good sense will afford you light enough to judge of their force and solidity.[30]

In other words, he recommended two rationalists and two sceptics. It is interesting that Hume thought eighteenth-century Edinburgh would easily supply Malebranche and Bayle, hardly known today outside philosophical studies, whereas Descartes might be harder to find. His view of his own contribution is confident if extravagant. His self-confidence is even more assertive when, in the same letter, he talks of his old Paris host, the Chevalier Ramsay:

> I shall be obliged to put all my papers into the Chevalier Ramsay's hands when I come to Paris; which I am really sorry for. For though he be free thinker enough not to be shocked with my liberty, yet he is so wielded [sic] to whimsical systems and is so little of a philosopher that I expect nothing but cavilling from him.[31]

Michael Ramsay had in previous, now missing, correspondence found David cold and distant but David assured him that this was not so:

> . . . you seem to doubt of my present friendship [for] you or of its continuance . . . You know my temper well enough not to expect any romantic fondness from me. But constancy, fidelity and a hearty good you may look for and shall ne[ver] be disappointed.[32]

Hume did pass through Paris although the Chevalier was unavailable. Four years later the Chevalier did receive a copy, and when a mutual friend, a Dr Stevenson of Edinburgh, suggested Hume to the Chevalier as a translator, his reply of 24th August 1742 tells us of his views, both of David Hume and the *Treatise:*

> Dear Sir and best of friends,
> . . . he would no doubt acquit himself very well of such commission, but I am afraid he would not undertake it. If I am not mistaken . . . he is too full of himself to humble his pregnant, active protuberant genius to drudge at a translation . . . if he will out of friendship to you undergo such slavery . . . The gentleman we speak of sent me his essay on human nature about fifteen months ago by one Sir John Ramsay, a friendly enough countryman of ours now in Angers. I have neither had the time nor health to peruse such an obscure, dark, intricate performance. I shall however read it when I go to Boulogne.[33]

Whether the Chevalier did read it or not we do not know, but by September 1737 David Hume was back in London seeking a publisher. This work had nearly cost him his sanity, had been over ten years in the preparation and writing, and was to establish Hume for ever in the world of philosophy. But what did it contain?

FOUR

A Treatise of Human Nature

G eneral readers, that is to say, readers who are not studying philosophy, have often felt baffled and confused by *A Treatise of Human Nature*, a work which does not seem to address any of the issues that they feel it should. It says nothing on ethics, morals, or rules of behaviour. It talks of 'ideas' and 'impressions', of 'causes' and 'effects' and seems not to attempt in any way to clarify the human condition.

But in Hume's time 'philosophy' encompassed every class of intellectual endeavour, dividing itself into natural philosophy, which we would today call science in all its forms, and moral philosophy, which included metaphysics, ethics, logic and indeed moral philosophy itself. Hume would eventually write on all these subjects as well as politics and even the then unheard-of discipline of economics. In the *Treatise* he simply set about defining how we think; therefore, of what we are capable of thinking and how this controls our actions. The work is carefully titled *A Treatise of Human Nature, being an attempt to introduce the experimental Method of Reasoning into Moral Subjects,* and was first published in two parts, looking at *Understanding* in Part I and at *Passions* in Part II. Hume was to alter and amend much of his thinking throughout the course of his life, but the *Treatise* is the beginning of that voyage, and to have a clear picture of the man we must understand his thinking. But first we have to survey the environment out of which the book emerged.

Until the Reformation the Church dominated all thought. By the middle of the fifth century the Greek tradition of empiricism was totally suppressed and Augustine of Hippo continued to codify thought. He believed that reason was the gift of God and should, therefore, be used only to glorify God. Thomas Aquinas and the Schoolmen adapted the teachings of Aristotle and Plato to the Christian tradition, but:

> Even Thomas Aquinas, one of Europe's most outstanding
> champions of rational thought, had to suspend reason when it
> conflicted with orthodoxy.[1]

The philosophical debate was spectacularly restarted by René Descartes who set about using pure reason to examine the validity of what had gone before. In 1637 he published the *Discourse on the Method of Rightly Conducting Reason*, followed in 1641 by the *Meditations on First Philosophy*. With startling boldness Descartes asserted that all precepts were based on faulty reasoning except the very existence of thought itself. All existence, physical and spiritual, could be merely the result of human fantasies and we can have, therefore, no certainty of anything. But since he was aware of thinking, he must, by logic, exist and that is the only fact of which we can have any certainty. This led Descartes to coin the most famous phrase in all philosophy, 'I think, therefore I am' '(*Je pense, ansi je suis*'). Descartes wrote in French, but the phrase is often quoted in Latin. This fundamental, if severely reductive, principle, is the foundation stone of all subsequent philosophy. Henceforth philosophers would have to start by examining the manner in which thought itself operated. This has been declared to be the birth of epistemology, itself defined as the theory of the basis of knowledge.

Confusion of this metaphysical system with the previous moral philosophy has led to the frustration referred to above and has caused many readers needlessly to abandon reading Hume.

But before Hume enters the stage himself we must look at his immediate predecessors, the philosophers John Locke and Bishop Berkeley.

It is said of Locke:

> His philosophy was to lay the foundations of empiricism with its belief that our knowledge of the world is based on experience. It also introduced the idea of liberal democracy.[2]

Locke was a don at Christ Church, Oxford, and was attracted to science. A follower of Newton, he relied on experience rather than tradition and used experiment rather than conviction. He admired Descartes as an iconoclast who had ended the teaching of the mediaeval Schoolmen, who argued over angels and pinheads, and himself used Descartes' logical method. Locke felt that scientific induction was the only way forward. He was a follower of the empiricist Pierre Gassendi who believed that all knowledge was based on sensory perception, and that this could be used to move forward from Descartes' theories. Locke agreed with the belief of Hobbes that, at least in times of war, the life of man was solitary, poor, nasty, brutish and short but he felt that there must be a form of government that would better this. Locke was also a part-time doctor with no training but astonishing success. An asthmatic, he rose to be adviser to Lord Chancellor Shaftesbury and, always a lady's man, died in 1704 in the arms of another man's wife.

However, in 1689, for 'the satisfaction of a few friends' he had produced *An Essay Concerning Human Understanding.* Empiricism was born. (We don't learn from reason, we learn from experience.)

Though he believed in God, Locke didn't believe we have innate God-given ideas about right and wrong. 'There is nothing in the mind except what was first in the senses.' We start with no knowledge and through experience and reflection we discover what we think. We then use reason to draw conclusions from these experiences. Empirical knowledge may infer probability from experience, but only intuition can determine how probable they are. This is the start of taking common sense as a basis for all thinking. Locke goes on to propose that there are two types of idea defining matter. There are simple and indivisible ideas like heat, cold, and smell, and there are complex ideas which are combinations of these. Primary qualities are dimensions and measurable aspects, such as speed or heat. Secondary qualities would be taste or colour, for instance. As a committed Whig, Locke published the *Essay* in 1689 as well as *Two Treatises on Government,* the first justifying parliamentary government and denying the divine right of kings. The second *Treatise* defines basic human rights of freedom and their necessary limitations in a social contract. He also justifies the rights of the people to remove the unjust magistrate. This was an argument of John Knox's and the case for such rights had already been made by Knox's colleague Christopher Goodman in 1558 in his tract *How Superior Powers Ought to be Obeyed.*

Early on in the *Essay,* Locke deals with the acquisition of knowledge through experience:

> Let us suppose that the mind be, as we say, white paper, void of all
> characters, without any ideas. How comes it to be furnished?
> Whence comes it by that vast store which the boundless fancy of
> man has painted on it with an almost endless variety? Whence has
> it all the materials of reason and knowledge? To this I answer in
> one word, Experience; in that all our knowledge is founded, and
> from it ultimately derives itself.[3]

Locke's combination of empiricism – the universe is composed of definable matter and we only know of it what we can experience – and liberal optimism for the human race make him one of the most accessible of the eighteenth-century philosophers as well as a bold pioneer in moving completely away from the past traditions of thought:

> It is ambition enough to be employed as an under-labourer in clearing the ground a little, and removing some of the rubbish that lies in the way to knowledge.[4]

We have seen the cost to David Hume of such 'weed clearance'.

Hume's second predecessor was the Reverend George Berkeley who was to take the theory of experience being all we can know to ridiculous limits. G.J. Warnock in *The Oxford Companion to Philosophy* says of him, 'Berkeley is a most striking and even unique phenomenon in the history of philosophy'.[5] Berkeley was horrified that Locke's common sense arguments might move towards removing the mystery of God, and that Locke's definitions of matter were perilously close to assuming the universe to be a machine as opposed to the divine creation of God. Early in his life Berkeley wrote, 'I wonder not at my sagacity in discovering the obvious though amazing truth, I rather wonder at my stupid inadvertency in not finding it out before'. His 'amazing' discovery was that matter did not exist at all. Clearly, if Locke said that all we knew was what we experienced, then anything external to our direct experience could not be held to exist within our knowledge. Berkeley held that if he turned his back on the land and looked out to sea, then he could not be certain that the land still existed. Famously, Dr Johnson was asked if he could refute this theory and he said, 'I refute it thus', and, closing his eyes, kicked a large stone.[6] Voltaire dismissed him even more thoroughly as not even worth refutation: 'le paradoxe de Berkeley ne vaut pas la peine d'être réfuté'.[7]

Since the deeply Christian Berkeley rose to be bishop of Cloyne, it is not surprising that in his time he also attempted to stem the advances of what he felt to be atheistical science and, as we have heard, he did attempt to found a missionary college in Bermuda, but the project was a failure. Sadly he is now remembered as a comic footnote to eighteenth-century philosophy, although he did make it necessary for Locke's theories to be taken forward and examined in more detail.

This is where David Hume enters, and in spite of Hill Burton's cautionary statements:

It has been generally and justly remarked that the *Treatise* is among the least systematic of philosophical works – that it has neither a definite and comprehensive plan, nor a logical arrangement . . . There can be no more repulsive matter for reading than condensed metaphysics.[8]

we will examine it.

Like all good theorists Hume starts with a definition of terms in Part I – *Of ideas*, thus refuting Hill Burton at the outset:

All the perceptions of the human mind resolve themselves into two distinct kinds, which I shall call impressions and ideas. The difference betwixt these consists in the degrees of force and liveliness, with which they strike the mind, and make their way into our thought or consciousness. Those perceptions which enter with the most force and violence, we may name Impressions; and under this name I comprehend all our sensations, passions and emotions, as they make their first appearance in the soul. By ideas I mean the faint images of these in thinking and reasoning; . . . every one of himself will readily perceive the difference betwixt feeling and thinking.[9]

Already Hume differentiates between feeling and thinking and in this part of the *Treatise* he deals entirely with thinking:

All our simple ideas in their first appearance are derived from simple impressions, which are correspondent to them and which they exactly represent . . . impressions may be divided into two kinds, those of sensation and those of reflexion. An impression first strikes upon the senses and makes us perceive heat or cold, thirst or hunger, pleasure or pain of some kind or other. Of this impression there is a copy taken in the mind, which remains after the impression ceases; and this we call an idea. We find by experience that when any impression has been present with the mind, it again makes its appearance there as an idea, and this it may do in two different ways . . . The faculty by which we repeat our impressions in the first manner is called the memory, and the other the imagination.

Here Hume allows experience to control how we define ideas. He also is predicating that an idea must have an impression as an origin. In other words we grow our ideas on a basis of impressions which we receive through experience. So far, so Locke.

Modern science might disagree with this line of thinking since it is essential to atomic physics that a particle called the 'Higgs boson' should exist. All current atomic theory depends on its existence. But even after £6 billion has been spent on research, science is no nearer finding it except in theory. In Hume's terms it is an idea without an impression and may exist only in theory. However, he allowed for such paradoxes:

> Whatever has the air of a paradox, and is contrary to the first and most unprejudiced notions of mankind is often greedily embraced by philosophers, as showing the superiority of their science, which could discover opinions so remote from vulgar conception.

Accepting this as a piece of intellectual snobbery, while not approving of it, is typical of a man who has himself stifled the arrogance of the auto-didact. But here Hume uses 'philosophers' to include natural philosophers or, in modern terms, physicists, and in Part II – *Of the ideas of space and time* he moves into their territory. But he does make a statement that would trouble modern physicists who can send time rolling through curved space:

> It is universally allowed that the capacity of the mind is limited and can never attain a full and adequate conception of infinity.

Hume does, however, deal with the definitions of time, somewhat to his own puzzlement:

> It is certain, then, that time, as it exists, must be composed of indivisible moments. [Here Hume's thinking predates Max Planck's quantum theory by two hundred years.] For if, in time we could never arrive at the end of a division, and if each moment as it succeeds each other were not perfectly singular and indivisible, there would be an infinite number of co-existent moments, or parts of time; which I believe will be allowed to be an arrant contradiction.

Modern science has accepted the 'arrant contradiction' as fact.

Hume now, with an all too human humility, decides to let well alone:

> My intention never was to penetrate into the nature of bodies or to explain their secret operations. For besides that this belongs not to

my present purpose, I am afraid that such an enterprise is beyond
the reach of human understanding and that we can never know [a]
body other than by those external properties which discover
themselves to the senses. But at present I content myself with
knowing perfectly the manner in which objects affect my senses and
their connections with each other as far as experience informs me of
them. This suffices for the conduct of life; and this suffices also for
my philosophy, which pretends only to explain the nature and
causes of our perceptions and ideas.

Understanding the 'secret operations' of bodies led us not only to nuclear
power but also to Hiroshima and the hydrogen bomb.

In Part III of the first book, 'Of Knowledge and Probability', Hume
starts to look at the relationships between objects and ideas:

There are seven different kinds of philosophical relation, viz.,
resemblance, identity, relations of time and place, proportion in
quantity and number, degrees in any quantity, contrariety, and
causation. These relations may be divided into two classes; into
such as depend entirely on the ideas which we compare
together, and such as may be changed without any change in
the ideas.

Resemblance, contrariety, degrees in quantity, and proportions in
quantity and number, depend solely upon ideas and may be the
objects of knowledge and certainty.

There is no single phenomenon, even the most simple, which can
be accounted for from the qualities of the objects as they appear to
us, or which we could foresee without the help of our memory and
experience with regard to identity, relations of time and place, and
causation.

This is the first mention of 'causation', the phenomenon of cause and
effect, which was to be central to the *Treatise*. Professor A.J. Ayer
commented:

No element of Hume's philosophy has had a greater and more
lasting influence than his theory of causality. It has been frequently
attacked and frequently misunderstood.[10]

Hume goes on to explain:

Resemblance, contrariety and degrees of quality are discoverable at first sight and fall more properly under the province of intuition than demonstration. Proportions in quantity and number are, likewise, precise.

We ought not to receive as reasoning any of the observations we may make concerning identity and the relations of time and place, since in none of them the mind can go beyond what is immediately present to the senses, either to discover the real existence or the relations of objects. It is only causation which produces a connection as to give us assurance from the existence or action of one object, that was followed or preceded by any other existence or action.

In other words causation explains the relationships between actions or objects – and by this Hume includes ideas – and therefore defines their very existence. Everything which exists must have had a cause, although there can be other definitions of identity:

Three relations are resemblance, contiguity and cause and effect. Of these three relations the only one which can be traced beyond our senses and informs us of existences and objects which we do not see or feel is causation. [And] Whatever objects are considered as causes and effects are contiguous; [since] nothing can operate in a time or place which is ever so little removed from those of its existence.

Hume then argues that inevitably the cause must come before the effect. The cause has 'priority of time' before the effect:

For if one cause were co-temporary with its effect, and this effect with *its* effect, and so on, it is plain there would be no such thing as succession, and all objects must be co-existent.

Then, feeling that further examples of the idiocy of universal co-existence are unnecessary, he goes on:

If the argument appear satisfactory, tis well. If not, I beg the reader to allow me the same liberty, which I have used in the preceding case, of supposing it such. For he shall find that the affair is of no great importance.

This refreshing candour permeates the *Treatise* as Hume's own personality breaks through with almost conversational urgency. He is talking rather than expounding.

He goes on to say that priority of time is not enough to prove causality, although all effects must have a previous cause. Nor is contiguity enough alone:

> Hume acknowledges that the relations of priority and contiguity are not sufficient for causality.[11]

And Hume admits that:

> having thus discovered or supposed the two relations of contiguity and succession to be essential to causes and effects, I find I am stopped short, and can proceed no further in considering any single instance of cause and effect.

But with all the diligence of the metaphysician, Hume could not leave the argument there and set about examining what seemed to be self-evident:

> For what reason [should] we pronounce it necessary that everything whose existence has a beginning must also have a cause? Why [should] we conclude that such particular causes must necessarily have such particular effects; and what is the nature of the inference we draw from the one and of the belief we repose in it?

Thus, if a brick is hurled forcefully at a fragile windowpane and the windowpane shatters, we conclude that the cause of the glass shattering is the impact of the brick. However often we see the event occur, the result is always the same. Admittedly, if the brick is smaller or the glass thicker, then the event will not occur, but if the circumstances are exactly the same, then exactly the same event will occur. This inevitability we will quickly learn from experience, but, in fact, it cannot be proved by metaphysics. Hume gives a different example:

> We remember to have seen that species of object we call 'flame', and to have felt that species of sensation we call 'heat'. Without any further ceremony we call the one cause and the other effect. [But] there is only one perceived or remembered and the other is supplied in conformity to our past experience. This relation is [called] constant conjunction. The transition of an impression present to the

memory or senses to the idea of an object which we call cause or effect, is founded on past experience, and on our remembrance of their constant conjunction.

The memory of a brick hitting a window is a constant conjunction. The window always breaks. *Experientia docet.*

Hume hammers the point home:

The idea of cause and effect is derived from experience . . . Thus not only our reason fails us in the discovery of the ultimate connexion of causes and effects, but even after experience has informed us of their constant conjunction, it is impossible for us to satisfy ourselves by our reason, why we should extend that experience beyond those particular instances which have fallen under our observation. We suppose, but we are never able to prove, that there must be a resemblance betwixt those objects of which we have had experience, and those which lie beyond the reach of our discovery.

Before finishing with the subject Hume has another observation to make:

Because a particular idea is commonly annexed to such a particular word, nothing is required but the hearing of that word to produce the correspondent idea.

As in 'flame – hot, bird – flight, garlic – smell, wound – pain', etc. But none of this goes to demonstrate how we acquire knowledge except by experience and memory. Causation is a weak link which cannot be proved:

Though causation be a philosophical relation, as implying contiguity, succession and constant conjunction, yet, 'tis only so far as it is a natural relation, and produces an union among our ideas, that we are able to reason upon it, or draw any inference from it.

A few pages later, Hume draws a line under the argument:

Objects have no discoverable connexion together; nor is it from any other principle but custom operating upon our imagination, that we can draw any inference from the appearance of one to the existence of another.

In other words, all attempts to prove cause and effect by reason alone will fail. But what, then, can be the uses of reason? The eighteenth century was the age of reason like no other, and if reason has no purpose, then as a race we are no better than vegetables. However, we do possess belief and Hume moves to define belief as a lively or vivid idea produced by relation to a present impression. He demonstrates this by the example of two people reading the same book, but one treating the work as true history, while the other regards it merely as fiction. The former, Hume says, will form a deeper conception of the incidents, while the latter will derive little entertainment from it. This seems to be a horrifying and priggish view, implying that *Hamlet*, read as Danish history, is more satisfying than when it is read as a poetic portrayal of human tragedy. In fact, it only tells us that Hume was concurring with the eighteenth-century abhorrence of violent emotion and its embracing of reasoned taste. Shakespeare was 'barbarous' and in 1754 Hume would say of him:

> If Shakespeare be considered as a man, born in a rude age, and educated in the lowest manner, without any instruction, either from the world or from books, he may be regarded as a prodigy: if represented as a poet, capable of furnishing a proper entertainment to a refined or intelligent audience, we must abate somewhat of this eulogy. In his compositions we regret that great irregularities, and sometimes even absurdities should so frequently disfigure the animated and passionate scenes intermixed with them; and at the same time we perhaps admire those beauties on account of their being surrounded with such deformities. A striking peculiarity of sentiment, adapted to a singular character, he sometimes hits, as it were by inspiration; but a reasonable propriety of thought he cannot for any time uphold. Nervous and picturesque expressions as well as descriptions abound in him; but 'tis in vain we look either for continued purity of simplicity or diction. His total ignorance of all theatrical art and conduct, however material a defect; yet, as it affects the spectator rather than the reader, we can more readily excuse, than that want of taste which often prevails in his productions, and which gives way, only by intervals, to the irradiation of genius. A great and fertile genius he certainly possessed, and one enriched equally with a tragic and a comic vein, but he ought to be cited as a proof, how dangerous it is to rely on these advantages alone for the attaining an excellence in the finer arts. And there may even remain a suspicion that we over-rate, if

possible his genius in the same manner as bodies often appear more gigantic, on account of their being disproportioned and misshapen. Johnson [sic] possessed all the learning which was wanting to Shakespeare, and wanted all the genius of which the other was possessed.[12]

This seems to us today a monstrous judgement by a man with little or no experience of the theatre. But eighteenth-century criteria of taste placed elegance and refinement far before passion. Also Hume would have read no novels as we know them. Richardson's *Pamela* was published in 1741, two years after the *Treatise*, while the appearances of *Tom Jones* and *Roderick Random* were over five years away. Also, the extraordinary vividness of Hume's life was, as yet, ahead of him and at this time he had been involved in a purely philosophical view of the world alone in La Flèche.

Hume justifies his analytical search for established reason by a declared faith in scepticism:

No weakness of human nature is more universal and conspicuous than what we commonly call credulity, or too easy a faith in the testimony of others.

However, self-contradictorily, he admits to allowing sentiment to take control when applying reason:

All probable reasoning is nothing but a species of sensation. It is not solely in poetry and music we must follow our taste and sentiment, but also in philosophy. When I am convinced of any principle, it is only an idea which strikes more strongly upon me. When I give preference to one set of arguments above another, I do nothing but decide from my feeling concerning the superiority of their influence.

Hume is beginning to doubt the validity of metaphysics as a logical tool and more than his toe is now in the troubled waters of religious faith:

Belief consists in a lively idea related to a present impression.

Belief, therefore, is nothing but 'a more vivid and intense conception of any idea'. But he is puzzled as to the appeal of the formal religions, based on faith alone, and he describes the Catholic religion as a 'strange superstition', full of 'mummeries', and notes that,

> In matters of religion men take pleasure in being terrified and no preachers are so popular as those who excite the most dismal and gloomy passions.

However, the attraction of regarding experience as our guiding principle is still strong:

> There is nothing in any object, considered in itself, which can afford us a reason for drawing a conclusion beyond it . . . Even after the observation of the frequent or constant conjunction of objects, we have no reason to draw any inference concerning any object beyond those of which we have had experience.

Professor Ayer sums up Hume's thoughts on this:

> All that we have to go on is our past experience of regularity in nature; indeed there is nothing more to be discovered. We become habituated to expecting that this regularity will be maintained. And this habit or custom is so firmly ingrained in us that we project the strength of the association to the phenomena themselves, and to succumb to the illusion that 'necessary connexion' is the name of a relation in which they actually stand to each other.[13]

Hume himself states:

> Without considering . . . the effects of custom on the imagination we shall lose ourselves in perpetual contradiction and absurdity.

Unquestioning faith lets us ignore the 'contradiction and absurdity' and Hume obviously felt that this was impossible for a rational man. It is almost as if the idea that his doubts about conventional religion might somehow be resolved cause him continually to test his current thinking against the traditional views of God's existence:

> The ultimate force and efficacy of nature is unknown to us, and it is in vain that we search for it in all the qualities of matter . . . It is the deity (therefore) who is the prime mover of the universe . . . This opinion is certainly very curious and well worth our attention. If every idea be derived from an impression, [then] the idea of a deity derives from the same origin; and if no impression [of the qualities of matter] . . . implies any force or efficacy, it is equally impossible to discover or even imagine any such active principle in the deity.

Stephen Hawking felt that if a 'Universal theory of Everything' were to be discovered, then we might know the mind of God, but since Hume believes that this theory, like the concept of infinity, is beyond the mind of man, it will be forever unproven. However, it is worth remembering that in the language of the Masai nation, the words for 'God' and 'I do not know' are the same. Hume was merely saying that the existence of God was unprovable by the power of reason. Conversely the non-existence was beyond proof. All his writings on religion explore these doubts in great depth, and to call these doubts atheism is a gross simplification.

Hume would be dogged by the indictment of atheism all his life and he struggled greatly either to prove or disprove the existence of God. At some time around the appearance of the *Treatise* Hume wrote out a debate on aspects of the subject, of which only two pages survive. Tantalisingly they are headed 'Section Seven, fourth objection', and nothing more is known to survive. The manuscript was acquired by the National Library of Scotland in 1993 from a dealer acting for a client in Bristol and it may be that it came from the estate of John Peach of Maryleport Street, whom Hume used from time to time as a sounding board:

> The fourth objection is not levelled against the intelligence of the deity, but against his moral attributes which are equally essential to the system of theism . . . Reason and virtue are not the same nor do they appear to have any immediate connexion in the nature of things. A sound understanding and a hard heart are very compatible . . . Whether the author of nature be benevolent or not can only be proved by the effects, or by the predominancy of good or evil, happiness or misery, in the universe . . . What one may safely pronounce on this head, is that if we compare pains and pleasures in their degrees, the former are infinitely superior; there being many pains, and even durable ones, extremely acute and no pleasure that is at the same time very intense and very durable . . . in this view, therefore pains and pleasures are not to be put in the same balance with each other.

However, Hume's optimism leads him to think that there exist many more pleasures than pains in the world. But these are particular to his own experience and cannot be taken as a generality. Also since the effect of pain is more intense and vivid than the effect of pleasure:

I find myself more inclined to think that evil predominates in the
world, and am apt to regard human life as a scene of misery
according to the sentiments of the greatest of sages as well as the
generality of mankind from the very beginning of the world to this
day . . . Victuals, wine, a fiddle, a warm bed, a coffee-house
conversation make a pitiful figure when compared with racks,
gravel, infamy, solitude and dungeons.[14]

But he reaches no logical conclusion, only an anecdotal impression that
there is more evil and pain than virtue and pleasure in the world. While he
does not deny the existence of God, he finds that logic and experience
cannot establish that existence:

We now see that a significant part of Hume's philosophy of religion
was fully worked out by around the time of the *Treatise* and more
directly indebted to his logical and psychological doctrine than was
previously appreciated.[15]

What other arguments were contained in other sections of what must have
been a considerable document remains a puzzle, attendant on the discovery of other manuscripts. But no part of the *Treatise* deals in such detail
with the arguments for or against the existence of God.

Allowing that experience can show that there are causes and effects,
Hume comes to simple definitions of them:

A [natural] cause is an object precedent and contiguous to another,
and where all objects resembling the former are placed in relations
of precedence and contiguity to these objects that resemble the
latter.
A [philosophical] cause is an object precedent and contiguous to
another, and so united to it, that the idea of the one determines the
mind to form the idea of the other, and the impression of the one
to form a more lively idea of the other. Should this definition be
rejected . . . I know no other remedy.

Steering close to Bishop Berkeley, he allows that we can never have reason
to believe that any object exists, if we have no experience of it in some
form, even theoretically. Hume demonstrated that we can have no reason
to cling to our past beliefs, but he did not assert either that this was
sufficient reason to abandon what we believed in or had experienced.

He now moved to examine the sceptical views of philosophy and to disprove the ludicrous assertions of the good bishop in Part IV of the *Treatise – Of the sceptical and other parts of philosophy*. To this end he proposed the hypothesis:

> That all our reasonings concerning causes and effects are derived from nothing but custom; and that belief is more properly the act of the sensitive than of the cognitive part of our nature.

Once again Hume, the great rational sceptic, allows the imaginative part of human nature dominance over the purely intellectual. He then moves rapidly to a common sense denial of Berkeley. Since it is clear, careful and convincing, it is worth quoting at length:

> We may well ask what causes us to believe in the existence of body? But it is in vain to ask whether there be body or not? That is a point which we must take for granted in all our reasonings. The subject, then, of our present enquiry is concerning the causes which induce us to believe in the existence of body; and my reasonings on this heading I shall begin with a distinction, which at first sight may seem superfluous, but which will contribute very much to what follows. Why we attribute a continued existence to objects, even when they are not present to the senses; and why we suppose them to have an existence distinct from the mind and perception . . . Concerning the senses, they give us no notion of continued existence, because they cannot operate beyond the extent in which they really operate. We may, therefore, conclude with certainty that the opinion of a continued and of a distinct existence never arises from the senses . . . Whatever convincing arguments philosophers may fancy they can produce to establish the belief of objects independent of the mind, it is obvious these arguments are known to very few, and it is not by them that children, peasants and the greatest part of mankind are induced to attribute objects to some impressions and deny them to others . . . this sentiment, then, as it is entirely unreasonable must proceed from some other faculty than the understanding . . . [it] must be entirely owing to the imagination . . . That all these objects to which we attribute a continued existence have a peculiar constancy, which distinguishes

them from the impressions whose existence depends on our impressions.

Those mountains, houses, and trees which are at present under my eye have always appeared to me in the same order; and when I lose sight of them by shutting my eyes or turning my head I soon after find them return upon me without the least alteration.

So, common sense prevails and philosophy can lead us into flights of logic which crash when put to the test of reality. Hume cannot be blamed for his attempt to use metaphysics to describe a system of thought. Indeed Professor Isaiah Berlin states:

This craving for a metaphysical system is one of the most obsessive of all the fantasies which have dominated the human mind.[16]

Or, at least, dominated the minds of philosophers.

Here at the end of the first book of the *Treatise*, Hume stands back, with astonishing self awareness, to examine what he has achieved and what, having dismantled the metaphysician's theory of causality, philosophy can hope to achieve in the future:

I am like a man who, having struck on many shoals . . . has the temerity to put out to sea in the same leaky weather-beaten vessel and even carries his ambition so far as to think of compassing the globe under these disadvantageous circumstances . . . When I look abroad, I foresee on every side, dispute, contradiction, anger, calumny and detraction. When I turn my eye inward I find nothing but doubt and ignorance . . . The memory, senses, and understanding are, therefore, all of them founded on the imagination or the vivacity of our ideas . . . Nothing is more dangerous to reason than the flights of the imagination, and nothing has been the occasion of more mistakes among philosophers . . . The understanding when it acts alone, and according to its most general principles, entirely subverts itself, and leaves not the lowest degree of evidence on any proposition either in philosophy or in common life. We save ourselves from . . . total scepticism by means of that singular and seemingly trivial property of the fancy by which we enter with difficulty into remote views of things, and are not able to accompany them with so sensible an impression as we do those that are more easy and natural. Shall we, then, establish it for a general maxim that no refined or elaborate reasoning is ever to be received?

Very refined reflections have little or no influence upon us; and yet we do not, and cannot, establish it for a rule that they ought not to have any influence; which implies a manifest contradiction. [But] I dine, I play a game of backgammon, I converse, and am merry with my friends, and after three or four hours' amusement, I would return to these speculations, they appear so cold and strained and ridiculous, that I cannot find in my heart to enter into them any further. I make bold to recommend philosophy, and shall not scruple to give it preference to superstition of every kind and denomination. Generally speaking, the errors in religion are dangerous; those in philosophy only ridiculous. We might hope to establish a set of opinions which, if not true (for that, perhaps, is too much to be hoped for) might at least be satisfactory to the human mind and might stand the test of the most critical examination . . .

[The study of] Human nature is the only science of man; and yet has been hitherto the most neglected. It will be sufficient for me if I can bring it a little more into fashion.

A few paragraphs later, writing about his time in La Flèche either at Yvandeau or by the banks of the Loir, he said:

At the time therefore, that I am tired with amusement and company, and have indulged in a reverie in my chamber or in a solitary walk by the riverside, I feel my mind all collected within itself and am naturally inclined to carry my view into those subjects about which I have met with so many disputes in the course of my reading and conversation. I cannot forbear having a curiosity to be acquainted with the principles of moral good and evil, the nature and foundation of government, and the cause of those several passions and inclinations which actuate and govern me . . . I feel an ambition to arise in me of contributing to the instruction of mankind and of acquiring a name by my invention and discoveries.

These quotations are almost a credo for the whole life of David Hume. He has a self-mocking view of his intellectual rigour, a rigour which can probably never be sustained. The emotions will probably always win and

Hume has no regrets about this. Whether he had read Alexander Pope's *Essay on Man* of 1733, we will never know, but Hume's views are an echo of:

> The proper study of mankind is man.
> Plac'd on this isthmus in a middle state,
> A being darkling wise, and rudely great:
> With too much knowledge for the sceptic side,
> With too much weakness for the stoic's pride.[17]

Book II is entitled 'Of the Passions', by which Hume means the emotions: pride, humility, love, hatred and the will. Once again Hume starts with a definition of terms:

> All the perceptions of the mind may be divided into impressions and ideas, so the impressions admit of another division into original and secondary . . . of the first kind are all the impressions of the senses, and all bodily pains and pleasures; of the second are the passions, and other emotions resembling them, i.e. impressions of sensation (original) and reflection (secondary).
>
> Impressions of sensation belong to anatomy and natural philosophy [physiology]. Reflective impressions divide into calm and violent. Of the first kind is the sense of beauty and deformity in action, composition and external objects. Of the second are the passions of love and hatred, grief and joy, pride and humility . . . When we take a survey of those passions there occurs a division of them into direct and indirect. Under the indirect passions I comprehend pride, humility, ambition, vanity, love hatred, envy, pity, malice, generosity, with their dependents. And under the direct passions [I comprehend] desire, aversion, grief, joy, hope, fear, despair and security.

First he deals neatly with pride and humility:

> Pride and humility cannot be defined but they can be described. The object is always self. A man may be proud of a beautiful house, the object of the passion is himself, but the cause is the house.

Since the emotions are a human attribute, this is unsurprising, and Hume quickly leaves pride and humility to deal with love and hatred. *En passant*, however, he moralises on the state of philosophy and why it can never satisfactorily describe anything so vibrant as human nature. He is being drawn to the superiority of emotion over reason, but reaching that conclusion by reason:

> Moral philosophy is in the same condition as natural [philosophy] with regard to astronomy before Copernicus. The ancients, though sensible of that maxim that nature does nothing in vain, contrived such intricate systems of the heavens, as seemed inconsistent with true philosophy and gave place at last to something more simple and natural. We only desire by a number of falsehoods, to cover our ignorance of the truth . . . It is impossible for the mind to fix itself steadily upon one idea for a considerable time, nor can it by its utmost efforts arrive at such a constancy. All resembling impressions are connected together, and no sooner one arises than the rest immediately follow. It is difficult for the mind when actuated by any passion to confine itself to that passion alone without any change or variation. Human nature is too inconstant to admit of any such regularity. Changeableness is essential to it. And to what can it so naturally change as to affections or emotions which are suitable to the temper, and agree with that set of passions which then prevail?

This is not written by the cold mind of the abstract metaphysician, but by a man who has admitted the frailties of the human intellect. When dealing with hatred he comes quickly to the conclusion that the effects are the subjective view of the causes:

> Nothing is more evident than that any person acquires our kindness or is exposed to our ill will in proportion to the pleasure or uneasiness we receive from him . . . If the general of our enemies be successful it is with difficulty we allow him the figure and character of a man . . . if the success be on our side, our commander has all the opposite good qualities, and is a pattern of virtue. It is evident the same method of thinking runs through common life.

'Amorous love', not normally dealt with by philosophers, comes next to be examined and Hume, unsurprisingly, has a brisk commonsense view:

> Amorous love is a compound passion derived from the conjunction of three different impressions or passions, viz., the pleasing

sensation arising from beauty; the bodily appetite for generation; and a generous kindness of good-will. Sex is not only the object but also the cause of the appetite. We not only turn our view to it when actuated by that appetite, but the reflecting on it suffices to excite the appetite. But as this cause loses its force by too great frequency, it is necessary [that] it is quickened by some new impulse; and that impulse we find to arise from the beauty of the person; that is from a double relation of impressions and ideas.

The sexuality of David Hume seems completely normal as stated here even if the sexual drive is viewed with the detachment of the scientist.

Finally Hume talks of the will and Direct Passions which he has already defined as desire and aversion, grief and joy, and hope and fear. But insofar as the will is concerned, he looks first at just how much liberty is, in fact, possessed by the will. His conclusions are surprising:

Necessity is regular and certain. Human conduct is irregular and uncertain. The one, therefore, proceeds not from the other . . . Necessity makes an essential part of causation; and consequently, liberty, by removing necessity, removes also causes, and is the very same thing as chance. Few are capable of distinguishing betwixt the liberty of spontaneity as it is called in the schools, and the liberty of indifference.

In other words, there really is no such thing as will controlled purely by reason; the action of the will is controlled entirely by chance and, in any case, the majority of people are too lazy to be ruled by anything other than chance. He condemns anyone taking moral stances over this rather gloomy assertion:

There is no method of reasoning more common, and yet more blameable, than in philosophical debates to endeavour to refute any hypothesis by a pretext of its dangerous consequences to religion and morality.

But he goes on to claim that he can prove that reason cannot control the will:

Every rational creature, it is said, is obliged to regulate his actions by reason . . . I shall attempt to prove first, that reason alone can never be a motive to any action of the will, and, secondly, that it can never oppose passion in the direction of the will.

He argues that experience gives us only information regarding the abstract relations of our ideas and therefore has no place in the world of reality. Thus demonstration and volition are separated from each other:

A merchant is desirous of knowing the sum total of his accounts . . . that he may learn what sum will have the effect of paying off his debt . . . abstract or demonstrative reasoning, therefore, never influences any of our actions, but only as it directs our judgement concerning causes and effects . . . It is obvious that when we have the prospect of pain or pleasure from any object, we . . . are carried to avoid or embrace what will give us this uneasiness or satisfaction . . . the impulse arises not from reason but is directed by it . . . Since reason can never produce any action, or give rise to volition, I infer, that the same faculty is as incapable of preventing volition, or of disputing the preference with any passion or emotion.

But Hume is not cast down by his proofs of the inadequacies of philosophy:

Upon the whole, this struggle of passion and reason, as it is called, diversifies human life, and makes men so different not only from each other, but also from themselves in different times. Philosophy can only account for a few of the greater and more sensible events of this war; but must leave all the smaller revolutions, as dependent on principles too fine for her comprehension.

The human mind cannot comprehend infinity and philosophy cannot comprehend the fine divisions of emotion that control our day-to-day lives.

In the last two chapters of Book II Hume looks at pain, pleasure, good and evil:

Nothing has a greater effect both to increase and diminish our passions, to convert pleasure into pain, and pain into pleasure than custom and repetition. It is easy to observe that the passions both direct and indirect are founded on pain and pleasure, and that in order to produce an affection of any kind, it is only requisite to present some good or evil. Upon the removal of pain and pleasure there immediately follows a removal of love and hatred, pride and humility, desire and aversion, and of most of our reflective or secondary impressions. Desire arises from good considered simply and aversion is derived from evil. The will exerts itself when either the good or the absence of the evil may be attained by any action of the mind or body.

To sum up the *Treatise*, then, human behaviour cannot be explained by metaphysics, there can be no proof of cause and effect, but an acceptance of events can be gained only by observation and experience. God is never mentioned, except as 'the deity', which could as easily mean Allah or Mazda, and man has now become the centre of existence. He recommends philosophy over superstition, i.e. religion, and hopes that a system might be found 'satisfactory to the human mind'. But man was not, and could not be, controlled entirely by reason. This is reinforced in the most famous phrase of the *Treatise*:

Reason is, and ought only to be, the slave of the passions, and can never pretend to any other office than to serve them.

This is the view of the humanist. Far from denying or suppressing the passions as many tried to do in the eighteenth century, Hume gave reason the role of servant to the emotions. Hume, who was steeped in classical studies, would have remembered that the man who stood behind a triumphant Roman, holding a victor's wreath over his head and whispering in his ear, 'remember you are only a man', was a slave. But reason was a slave, part of whose task was maintaining balance between the unreasoning brute and the unfeeling logic of the 'control freak'. Bayle believed that only the Zoroastrians had found a balance between good and evil, and balance was at the forefront of eighteenth-century thought. Belief and disbelief were balanced by experience. Therefore the idiocy of Berkeley was refuted since experience counts for more than logic and Dr Johnson's rebuttal was perfectly legitimate. Descartes' theory of existence, being only valid because of the thought that allowed the question to be asked, had been extended by including passion as well as reasoned thought. 'I think, therefore I am' now could be rewritten as 'I think and feel, therefore I behave thus'. But Hume had examined all the arguments logically, reducing thought to the closely defined limits of 'ideas' and 'impressions' and had found as many shortcomings as truths. He had moved forward from the pure empiricism of Locke. To his own satisfaction Hume had proved the case for empirical scepticism from first principles. Bishop Berkeley would now be sidelined as having reduced thought to an absurdity without ever seeing the joke.

The *Treatise* would put Hume at the leading edge of European philosophy. Now philosophers would have to take the existence of man as a sentient being into account and the *Treatise* drew a line under all that had gone before. All Hume had to do now to claim his place in the sun was to publish the *Treatise* and immediately become rich and famous. After all, the *Treatise* is 'by common consent the greatest work of philosophy to have appeared first in the English language'.[18] But that opinion was written nearly two hundred and fifty years after its publication.

FIVE

Dead-Born from the Press

H aving found creative calm in France and having used the interlude to accomplish his task there, Hume left for London in September 1737. His visit to France had given him a taste for the country and its attitudes. He had, it is true, experienced only the salon life of Paris and the intellectual life of the scholars in Reims and La Flèche and he had no experience of the social conditions in either town or country to compare with Edinburgh or Berwickshire. But he had started a love affair with France that would continue for the rest of his life. Four years later he wrote:

> The most eminent instance of the flourishing of learning in absolute governments, is that of France, which has scarcely enjoyed any established liberty, and yet has carried the arts and sciences as near perfection as any other nation. The English are, perhaps, greater philosophers, the Italians better painters and musicians; the Romans were greater orators; but the French are the only people, except the Greeks, who have been at once philosophers, poets, orators, historians, painters, architects, sculptors, and musicians. With regard to the stage, they have excelled even the Greeks, who far excelled the English. And in common life, they have in a great measure, perfected that art, the most useful and agreeable of any, L'Art de Vivre, the art of society and conversation.[1]

Even allowing for the rather grudging praise for English philosophers, one of whom he would now consider himself – Hume always thought of the Scots as English – this was a eulogy reflecting his wide reading and, most probably, the warmth of his welcome into the polite society of Reims and the more bucolic tables of the Quatre Vents.

But the *Treatise* needed a publisher and the most eminent of those were to be found in London, and so his stay in London was to be one of necessity rather than pleasure. He clearly would have preferred to be in France or Edinburgh.

The London that Hume came to in the autumn of 1737 was a city vivid with extremes. The sophisticated delights of Gainsborough's portraits, Handel's oratorios, Wedgwood's porcelain, Pope's satires, Chippendale furniture, and the architecture of the Adam brothers, contrasted with public executions, exposure in the pillory and watching the lunatics being flogged at Bedlam. The poor, who were plentiful and, when they could afford the very few pence needed, completely drunk, lived in Hogarthian squalor. Street crime was rampant and the local journals abounded with advertisements offering to buy back pocket watches, walking sticks and even handkerchiefs. Only the brave or foolhardy walked in the streets by night, and then only in armed groups.

The rich aristocracy, the Lords Cavendish, Grosvenor, and Burlington, were building their town houses in the West End, often creating elegant squares around them. The rebuilding of the City after the Great Fire was almost complete, as was Westminster Bridge, destined to be the second bridge to cross the Thames since Roman times. Nicholas Hawksmoor was still adding the towers to Westminster Abbey and London was spreading inexorably westward:

> Pease cabbages and turnips once grew where
> Now stands New Bond Street and a newer Square.[2]

George II, in a fit of Hanoverian pique, had exiled his son Frederick, Prince of Wales, from St James's Palace, along with his pregnant wife Augusta, to nearby Leicester House. George's unpopularity with his subjects grew when, in November 1737, his wife, Caroline of Brandenburg-Anspach, endured a long and painful death from a ruptured womb. As she was dying George assured her that he would never marry again but merely find solace in his numerous mistresses, principally Amalia Wallmoden, later Countess of Yarmouth.

The determined and power-hungry Robert Walpole was Prime Minister, his political brilliance hidden by a deceptive inactivity. A gross and self-indulgent man – he was rumoured to open letters from his huntsman and his gamekeeper before those from the King – he lived in flagrant adultery with an accommodating Irish girl, Maria Skerret. But, hypocritically, whatever licence he allowed himself in his personal life, he felt there was too much in the theatre and introduced the Licensing Act giving a royal patent for theatrical performances only to Drury Lane and Covent Garden for drama, with loosely defined opera confined to the Haymarket

Theatre. This often took the form of a play with musical interludes. Hume took a keen interest in all this, later commenting that a performance by Colley Cibber at Drury Lane interested the public more than the Prime Minister's machinations. But the Prime Minister's machinations were establishing the supremacy of parliament over the crown.

Hume had taken lodgings in Lancaster Court. This was a narrow street running north and south at the western end of the Strand with the newly built church of St Martin's in the Fields at its northern end. Not far to the east lay Covent Garden with its many attractions ranging from the theatres of Drury Lane and the Covent Garden market itself to its many taverns and coffee houses. The entertainment available was plentiful and varied. The theatres presented nearly 500 productions each year while at the Shakespeare Head tavern Jack Harris, a waiter, could provide you with *Harris's List of Covent Garden Ladies, or the Man of Pleasure's Kalendar.* Hume would have found a welcome, had he wanted one, either at the St James's Coffee House at 87 St James's Street – it was a celebrated meeting place for the leading Whigs – or at the British and Forrest's Coffee House in Cockspur Street – near his lodgings, the favoured haunt of visiting Scots.

Numerous countrymen of David Hume trod the corridors of power and as a Scot he had access to many of the great and the good in Government. Lord Polwarth and his brother Alexander Hume-Campbell were family neighbours from Berwickshire and both men were Members of Parliament. Hume certainly approached them, albeit half-heartedly, as well as Alexander Broadie, a parliamentary member for far-off Caithness, but the extent of their favours appears to have been only in supplying Hume with ready franked letters so that he had post-free correspondence with Scotland. The most powerful Scot in government was Lord Islay, soon to be Duke of Argyll. As Keeper of the Great Seal he had control of Government patronage in Scotland, but apart from attending one of Islay's levées Hume made no attempt to curry his favour. Indeed he showed no interest in the great men of the day, vivid though they were.

Instead he chose, possibly for reasons of economy or shyness, not to socialise while in London and his choice of address may have been influenced by the presence of the Rainbow Coffee House in Lancaster Court itself. He certainly gave this coffee-house as an address for his correspondence.

There is nowhere in which it is so easy to maintain anonymity as a great city, and here Hume could still keep his head well below the parapet. In a sense while living in London he continued his French exile in the Rainbow Coffee House, which was itself a place for Protestant exiles and, since exile lends a special intensity to belief, the conversations would be equally intense. In the nineteenth century London had many such meeting houses for political and religious refugees. They flourished again in the '30s and '50s of the twentieth century, always filled with the smoke of exotic tobaccos, foreign newspapers and heated political debate taking place over hotly contested games of chess. The Rainbow must have been an earlier version of such a place, and if Hume had chosen to be a philosophical exile, it would have been the ideal refuge.

But one of the habitués of the Rainbow, Pierre Desmaizeaux, was the biographer and literary executor of Pierre Bayle. He was also the London correspondent of many European literary journals. Hume certainly knew Desmaizeaux well enough to ask him his opinion of the *Treatise*. It is highly likely that Hume was recommended to look up Desmaizeaux by friends in Paris, possibly the ever helpful Chevalier Ramsay, or even by the Abbé Pluche in Reims. Hume certainly made friends with Desmaizeaux.

The principal purpose of his visit, however, was to find a publisher, and London was being flooded with philosophical or religious works, most of which have been quietly and deservedly forgotten along with their authors. Hume was determined not to be one of these and did not embrace the idea of publication at any price. He made three non-negotiable demands on any publisher to whom he offered the *Treatise*. Firstly, that no nobleman should be approached as patron, since Hume wanted total control of the contents for himself. Secondly, that the work should be published anonymously, as was common practice, and was still not uncommon in the next century. And finally, that the contract would be for a first edition only, all subsequent rights remaining with Hume. After the *Treatise* was published he would have second thoughts about the lack of patronage. These demands display a degree of arrogance for a first-time author, although he continued to dislike the system of patronage for, in 1766, when he was rich and famous, he wrote:

> Too many men of letters have debased their characters stooping so low as to solicit the assistance of persons of wealth or power, unworthy of affording them protection.[3]

He seems to have gained the possibility of publication several times and then drew back. It is almost as if he had climbed back up to the high diving board and once again been daunted by the distance he had to plunge.

Hume had, however, no doubts as to the importance of his thought. But now he could run no further and had to declare his hand. Why had he not returned to Edinburgh with his manuscript under his arm? He could have divided his time between finding a publisher in Edinburgh – there were plenty – and rejoining his family at Ninewells. Or, while in London, he could have used his access to the influential Scots to ease his path to publication. Instead of any of these courses of action he buried himself among political exiles in London and erected obstacles in his own path to a publisher. There is a substantial clue in a letter he wrote to his old Edinburgh friend Henry Home on 2 December 1737:

. . . my opinions are so new and even some terms I am obliged to make use of that I could not propose by any abridgement to give my system an air of likelihood, or so much as to make it intelligible . . . I have greater desire of communicating to you the plan of the whole, that I believe it will not appear in public before the beginning of next winter . . . I must confess I am not ill-pleased with a little delay, that it may appear with as few imperfections as possible. I have been here near three months always within a week of agreeing with the printers, and you may imagine that I did not forget the work itself during that time, where I began to feel some passages weaker for the style and diction than I could have wished. The nearness and greatness of the event roused up my attention and made me more difficult to please than when I was alone in perfect tranquillity in France. But here I must tell you one of my foibles. I have a great inclination to go down to Scotland this spring to see my friends and have your advice concerning my philosophical discoveries; but cannot overcome a certain shame-facedness I have to appear among you at my years without having yet a settlement or so much as having attempted any. How happens it that we philosophers cannot as heartily despise the world as it despises us? . . . [I] accordingly enclose some reasonings concerning miracles which I thought of publishing with the rest, but which I am afraid will give too much offence even as the world is disposed at the present . . . tell me your thoughts of it. Is the style not too diffuse? . . . let me know at your leisure that you have received it, read it, and burnt it. I would not even have you make another nameless use of it, to which it would not be improper, for fear of accidents . . . I am at present castrating my work, that is, cutting off its noble parts, that is, endeavouring that it shall give as little offence as possible . . . This is a piece of cowardice for which I blame myself; though I believe none of my friends will blame me. But I was resolved not to be an enthusiast in philosophy, while I was blaming other enthusiasms.[4]

This is almost Hume thinking aloud. The passage on miracles he talks of would not be published as a separate essay until 1748, but it does sound as if he is getting editorial advice from publishers. And he is ashamed to show his face in Scotland until he has established himself. His guilt at having lived at Ninewells without having made any concrete contribution to his family's living is foremost in his mind and this guilt never left him. His brother John should have followed his father's footsteps into the law, but father's early death made this impossible, and John, robbed of any financial freedom to train for any other career, had no option but to become a farmer. David was allowed that freedom to study for a profession, but instead of going into some gainful employment and contributing to the family income, he chose to give himself a nervous breakdown, and then fled into French exile, having failed at commerce in Bristol. Now he was twenty-six and returned to Britain with only an unpublished manuscript to show for his efforts. And what if these efforts were worthless? Hume must have suffered more extremely from the doubts and paranoia that normally afflict any writer.

He did try to gain an opinion from Dr Joseph Butler who had been Clerk of the Closet to Queen Caroline and was Dean of St Paul's Cathedral. In the year of Hume's arrival Butler had published *Analogy of Religion, Natural and Revealed, to the Constitution and Course of Nature*, a rebuttal of Deism. Deism was, in the eighteenth century, a belief in God justified by reason as opposed to being justified by simple faith. Deists like Voltaire believed that God was a human construct and Butler pointed out that by their own arguments their beliefs could be invalidated as easily as those of the conventional faiths.

Hume had been given a letter of introduction to Butler by Henry Home but, rather weakly, failed to meet him:

I have called upon the Doctor with a design of delivering him your letter; but find he is at present in the country. I am a little anxious to have the Doctor's opinion. My own I dare not trust to, both because it concerns myself and because it is so variable that I know not how to fix it. Sometimes it elevates me above the clouds: at other times it depresses me with doubts and fears; and so whatever be my success I cannot be entirely disappointed.[5]

Some might say Hume was hedging his bets, others that here is a young philosopher using his own reason to insure himself against future hurt.

However, in September 1738 Hume did finally achieve the conditions for publication he was seeking when, just over a year after his arrival in London, he made an agreement with Joseph Noon, at the White Hart, near Mercer's Chapel in Cheapside, to publish the *Treatise*. Noon was a respected publisher of religious and philosophical works and Hume's *Treatise* would join a distinguished list. For 1738 this comprised twenty-one books including *Paraphrase with notes on The Epistles of St Paul, the Revelation of St John the Divine*, a *Dissertation on the Civil Government of the Hebrews, The Philosophical Grammar, The young student's memorial book*, a *History of the Sevarambians*, and *The Negotiator's Almanack (all of great use to Merchants)*. Hume's is the only anonymous work. Also in the list is George Turnbull's *The Principles of Moral Philosophy, an Enquiry into the Wise and Good Government of the Moral World*,[6] the title of which tells us what was expected of a philosopher. Hume's work did none of this moral exploration and some of his trepidation came from knowing that his work contained much that was pure novelty.

But although Hume's conditions for publication were met, Noon added some of his own. The book would be a first edition of two volumes in octavo. Hume would receive £50 to be paid in six months plus twelve bound copies. Publishers were also booksellers, printers and binders, and usually sold books as loose sheets. Noon kept the sole profit of the first edition, which was not to exceed a thousand copies, and Hume could not sell a second edition until the first thousand copies were sold, although the unsold copies could be bought by Hume at current prices.[7]

The two volumes were *Book I, Of the Understanding* and *Book II, Of the Passions*, priced at ten shillings. There was, in fact, a third book, *Of Morals*, but Hume did not feel this was ready for publication and held it back. This also meant that, since it was to be a separate publication, he could look for another publisher. Once again he hedged his bets.

At about the same time as Hume agreed this contract, Michael Ramsay, his old companion and correspondent from Edinburgh, visited London and provided a relief from endless philosophical discussions at the Rainbow Coffee House. Ramsay was keen to gain some office or sinecure from the Government and Hume did try to help but it is more likely that the two young men spent a large part of their time together enjoying at least some of the delights of eighteenth-century London which Hume had hitherto denied himself.

For theatre at Drury Lane they could have seen Colley Cibber as Foppington in *The Relapse* or as Glendower in *Henry IV Part One*, with James Quinn as Falstaff, then Quinn again as Falstaff but Cibber switching to Pistol in *Henry IV Part Two*. Across the road at Covent Garden they could pick from *Oronooko, Venice Preserv'd*, or *All For Love*. Performances started at six o'clock and there was much socialising before and after among the audience. Eating, drinking and conversation were all available nearby and Hume would have introduced his friend to his new acquaintances at the Rainbow Coffee House. During Ramsay's visit a troupe of French actors had, extraordinarily, been given a licence to perform at the Haymarket Theatre, previously licensed only for music. On 9 October the Londoners' objections to their taking employment from British actors boiled over into a street riot. Hume and Ramsay would have been caught up in the event, taking place not half a mile from Hume's lodgings. Hume must have been ambivalent, given his belief in the superiority of French theatre.

The two young men would also have visited Vauxhall Gardens, only a short journey by boat from Hume's nearest landing place at Hungerford Stairs. Travel by river was then by far the most convenient in London, and for a shilling entrance money the young men would have entered a baroque wonderland. There were twelve acres of formal woodland with triumphal arches, ruined grottoes, even a Chinese pavilion serving cold suppers. The gardens were lit by 3,000 coloured lanterns and Handel's latest music was played by an orchestra in a treetop bandstand. There were secluded alcoves for supper, and while David dined reflectively no doubt Michael availed himself of the ladies of the night who plied their amorous trade among the shaded bowers. Vauxhall was a Disneyland for grown-up gallants.

Ramsay was passing through London *en route* for the south of France and Hume wrote to him at Marseilles in February 1739, allowing that perhaps he had been unwise in refusing to seek out any patronage for his book, also saying that gaining any profitable place for Ramsay would require Ramsay's personal attendance in London:

> I expect every hour to have a call from a ship to go to Scotland . . . As to myself no alteration has happened in my fortune, nor have I taken the least step towards it. I hope things will be riper next winter; and I would not aim at anything till I could judge of my success in my grand undertaking and see upon what footing I shall stand in the world. I am afraid, however, that I shall not have any great success of a sudden. Such performances make their way very heavily at first, when they are not recommended by any great name or authority . . . I have had a conversation with Mr Hume* since I wrote this. He is entirely of my opinion that nothing can be done till you be on the place . . . I saw My Lord Polwarth but he was with some great folks . . . and [he] did not give me an opportunity of speaking to him.[9]

But the memories of cold suppers in Vauxhall had faded as Hume waited for the appearance of the *Treatise*. He had voiced his misgivings about not having sought out a patron – Turnbull's *Principles of Moral Philosophy* was dedicated to the Earl of Stanhope – and Hume felt that he had been hasty in agreeing to Noon's terms out of 'indolence and an aversion to bargaining', but old doubts must have raised themselves again. Near the end of Book I of the *Treatise* is a passage which may have been a late insertion as part of the revisions he undertook in London:

> I am affrighted and confused with that forlorn solitude in which I am placed in my philosophy, and fancy myself some uncouth monster, who not being able to mingle and unite in society, has been expelled all human commerce, and left utterly abandoned and disconsolate. Fain would I run into the crowd for shelter and warmth; but cannot prevail with myself to mix with such deformity. I call upon others to join me, in order to make a company apart, but no one will hearken to me. Every one keeps at a distance, and dreads that storm, which beats upon me from every side. I have exposed myself to the enmity of all metaphysicians, logicians, mathematicians, and even theologians; and can I wonder at the

---

* Alexander Hume-Campbell, son of the 2nd Earl of Marchmont, MP for Berwickshire.

insults I must suffer? I have declared my disapprobation of their
systems; and can I be surprised if they should express a hatred of
mine and of my person? When I look abroad, I foresee on every
side, dispute, contradiction, anger, calumny and detraction. When I
turn my eye inward I find nothing but doubt and ignorance. All the
world conspires to oppose and contradict me; though such is my
weakness, that I feel all of my opinions loosen and fall of
themselves, when unsupported by the approbation of others. Every
step I take is with hesitation and every new reflection makes me
dread an error and absurdity in my reasoning. For with what
confidence can I venture upon such bold enterprises, when beside
those numberless infirmities peculiar to myself, I find so many
which are common to human nature?[10]

There can be no better description of first-night nerves, and it is an
exceptional athlete on the starting blocks who does not wonder at how
much fitter his rivals appear. But it is the exceptional athlete who wins and
the focused actor who overcomes first-night nerves. Hume could console
himself with the thought that his publisher, Joseph Noon, had a distinguished reputation for scholarship and had many learned works in his
list. Noon, having no desire to attract ridicule, would have read the
Treatise with care, but Hume, the man of reason, was beset by irrational
fears which no logic could allay.

Publication would answer all the questions and by the end of January
1739 the *Treatise of Human Nature* was published.

In *My Own Life* he tells us:

Never literary attempt was more unfortunate than my Treatise of
Human Nature. It fell *dead-born from the Press;* [Hume's italics; he
is quoting from Alexander Pope, 'All, all but truth, drops dead-born
from the press, like the last Gazette, or the last Address'.] without
reaching such distinction as even to excite a murmur among the
Zealots.[11]

The lull before the storm is terrifying enough, but when the storm fails to
materialise at all the reaction can be devastating. In fact the book caused
quite a stir in literary circles, but it had a delayed reaction and Hume seems
to have expected instant fame, or notoriety. To his chagrin, neither was
immediately apparent. He goes on:

But being of a cheerful and sanguine temper, I very soon recovered from the blow, and prosecuted with great ardour my studies in the country.[12]

Bear in mind that Hume wrote this in 1776, thirty-seven years after the event and thus distance had enchanted him. He was, in fact, desperate for some kind of reaction and on 13 February 1739 he wrote to Henry Home:

I thought to have wrote this to you from a place nearer you than London, but have been detained here by contrary winds, which have kept all Berwick ships from sailing. 'Tis now a fortnight since my book was published and besides many other considerations I thought it would contribute very much to my tranquillity and might spare me many mortifications to be in the country when the success of my work was doubtful. I am afraid it will remain so very long . . . My principles are also so remote from all the vulgar sentiments on this subject, that were they to take place, they would produce almost a total alteration in philosophy; and you know that revolutions of this kind are not easily brought about. I am young enough to see what will come of the matter; but am apprehensive lest the chief reward I shall have for some time will be the pleasure of studying on such important subjects and the approbation of a few judges. I shall present you with a copy as soon as I come to Scotland and hope your curiosity as well as friendship will make you take the pains of perusing it . . . In looking over your letters I find one of a twelve-month's date wherein you desire me to send down a great many copies to Scotland. You proposed no doubt to take the pains of recommending them and pushing the sale. But, to tell the truth, there is so little to be gained that way in such works as these, that I would not have you take the trouble . . . You'll excuse the natural frailty of an author in writing so long a letter about nothing but his own performances. Authors have this privilege in common with lovers and founded on the same reason, that they are both besotted with a blind fondness of their object. I have been on my guard against this frailty; but perhaps this has turned to my prejudice. The reflection on our caution is apt to give us a more implicit confidence afterwards, when we come to form a judgement.[13]

The silence was indeed deafening for Hume. Having spent so long on the diving board, he had finally summoned up his courage and dived. It seemed to him as though no one had been looking. A whole fortnight had passed and he was still not famous. He had sent copies to the Bishop of Bristol and to Alexander Pope but had had no response from them either. He had also given a copy to Pierre Desmaizeaux, his old friend from the Rainbow Coffee House, and in April he wrote to him:

> Wherever you see my name, you'll readily imagine the subject of my letter. A young author can scarce forbear speaking of his performance to all the world; but when he meets with one that is a good judge and whose instruction and advice he depends on, there ought some indulgence to be given him. You were so good as to promise me, that, if you could find leisure from your other occupations, you would look over my system of philosophy and at the same time ask the opinion of such of your acquaintance as you thought proper judges. Have you found it sufficiently intelligible? Does it appear true to you? Do the style and language seem tolerable? These three questions comprehend everything; and I beg you to answer them with the utmost freedom and sincerity.[14]

Hume had no need to add 'and with the greatest speed', but asked for the reply – which no longer exists – to be addressed to him at Ninewells. He had obviously discussed the *Treatise* with Desmaizeaux in the days of the Rainbow Coffee House and knew that his 'other occupations' would unlock the doors to continental reviews.

The first of these came while Hume was still in London. The *Bibliothèque Raisonnée des ouvrages des savans* [sic] *de L'Europe* was published in Amsterdam and in the spring of 1739 names Hume as the author of the *Treatise* and states:

> those who demand the new will find satisfaction here. The author reasons on his own grounds; he goes to the very bottom of things and traces out new routes. He is very original.[15]

Desmaizeaux knew Hume to be the author, and although the brief notice is a very friendly one, he had blithely destroyed Hume's anonymity. Desmaizeaux had launched his friend in Europe.

In May 1739 there was a second acknowledgement in the *Neue Zeitung von gelehrten Sachen* [The new journal of learned affairs]. It gave the *Treatise* a short review, noting Hume's evil intentions as a free thinker.

This change of tone announced that a storm was about to break, but a passage on a ship for Berwick became available, and possibly by April 1739 David Hume had returned to Ninewells. He had been absent for five years and four months. His 'shame-facedness' and lack of settlement weighed heavily on him. There are no extant letters from Hume to his family for the years of separation and, in any case, there can have been little of interest to pass between them. Farming news from the Scottish borders would have had no relevance to a budding philosopher surrounded by French vineyards, and the society gossip of Paris and Reims was of no interest whatsoever to the Homes of Ninewells. However, the now much more mature – and bulky – David did return to his family with some copies of his *Treatise,* bound according to his contract. It is very doubtful if his brother, mother or sister had a moment's respite from their farming labours even to open a copy, far less debate it with its author. Although John must have wondered if, had it not been for his father's premature death, he, as well as David, might have followed the intellectual life.

Hume's interest now was mainly in the reactions of his friends, and especially in the opinion of Henry Home. Much later, James Boswell recalled what took place:

> When David Hume arrived home from his travels, he had his two volumes of the *Treatise of Human Nature* printed and published. He brought them to Lord Kames,* and begged he would read them. My Lord told him he was quite out of the train of metaphysics, in which he found that he never got more light, and declined reading them. About a month after, David came back and begged he would read them to oblige him. Said my Lord: 'I'll do anything to oblige you. But you must sit by and try to beat your book into my head.' He did so. Yet my Lord had no more than a glimmering of what was his meaning. Some time after this, my Lord, who had a farm in the country and had got up at six in a May morning when there was nothing to do in the fields, took up David's book, and as a proof that thoughts ripen in the mind imperceptibly, he read it, to his astonishment with the clearest understanding. And he sat down and wrote his observations upon it. David who used to come

* Henry Home was raised to the bench in 1752 and became Lord Kames.

frequently to him, came soon after. 'Well, David, I'll tell you news. I understand your book quite well.' He shewed him his objections, and David, who was not very ready to yield, acknowledged he was right in every one of them. He said he never did think as David does in that treatise.[16]

In spite of the differences between them their friendship continued. By June Hume had received no further reviews and was feeling, unjustly, considering the speed of the academic mills, neglected. A correspondent, reminiscing in the *Edinburgh Amusement* in July 1771, recalls:

I was in Edinburgh soon after the original publication and well remember how much and how frequently it was mentioned in every literary conversation.[17]

The *Treatise* had certainly been read by Thomas Reid, later Regent in Philosophy at King's College, Aberdeen. 'At which period [1739] the publication of the Treatise induced him "to call in question the principles commonly received with regard to the human understanding". In his youth he had admitted Hume's scepticism and the consequences of these opinions roused his opinions concerning the truth.'[18]

In spite of this Hume's despondency is apparent in a letter to Henry Home of 1st June 1739:

You see I am better than my word, having sent you two papers instead of one. I have hints for two or three more, which I shall execute at my leisure. I am not much in the humour of such compositions at present, having received news from London of the success of my philosophy, which is but indifferent, if I may judge by the sale of the book, and if I may believe my bookseller. I am now out of humour with myself, but doubt not, in a little time, to be only out of humour with the world, like other unsuccessful authors. After all, I am sensible of my folly, in entertaining any discontent, much more despair, upon this account; since I could not expect any better from such abstract reasoning; nor indeed did I promise myself much better. My fondness for what I imagined new discoveries made me overlook all the rules of prudence; and having enjoyed all the usual satisfaction of projectors, 'tis but just I should meet with their disappointments. However, as 'tis observed with such sort of people, one project generally succeeds another, I doubt not but in a day or two I shall be as easy as ever, in hopes that truth will prevail at last over the indifference and opposition of the world.[19]

In spite of his reluctance to write again, Hume still had hope for the unpublished Part III of the *Treatise*, as well as the excised portion referring to miracles, and had obviously started to write essays. But more continental reviews were appearing and were probably being forwarded to Ninewells.

The *Nouvelle Bibliothèque*, published in The Hague, carried the following notice in October 1739:

the ideas of the author approach closely in some places to those of Dr Hutcheson on the moral sentiment and on the human passions, there are yet many original things in this new treatise, which, however, is only the commencement of a more extended and complete work.[20]

Hutcheson, Professor of Moral Philosophy at Glasgow University would differ widely from Hume and reject his views in place of the idea of an inherent moral good in mankind. But the review was, in general, friendly. The *Bibliothèque Britannique*, also of The Hague, in its winter quarter edition of 1739 simply notes the anonymous *Treatise*:

This is a system of logic, or rather of metaphysics, as original as can be, in which the author claims to rectify the most ingenious philosophers, particularly the famous Mr Locke, and in which he advances the lost unheard-of paradoxes, even to maintaining that operations of the mind are not free.[21]

But this was merely a notice and not a review and Hume was still waiting for a reasoned judgement. Such a judgement was about to come and with devastating effect. It was a review in the November and December editions of the influential *History of the Works of the Learned*. The other works reviewed in these issues of the journal were *Memoirs of the Duke of Ripperda* (Dutch Ambassador to Spain), *The new book of Constitutions of the ancient and honourable Fraternity of Free and Accepted Masons*, by James Anderson D.D., an examination of the last edition of St Jerome, an essay on a particular passage of Virgil, and a biography of Prince Eugene of Savoy. This journal was, then, an eighteenth-century version of the *Times*

Literary Supplement or the *London Review of Books* with the difference that today reviewers use the journals to display their own erudition and seldom mention the book they are reviewing while in Hume's day the reviews were largely lengthy quotations from the work with bland explanatory passages. Hume's review had the lengthy quotations certainly, but they were wrapped around not with blandness but with bitter vituperation:[22]

> I do not recollect any writer in the English language who has
> framed a system of human nature, morally considered, upon the
> principle of this author, which is that of necessity in opposition to
> liberty or freedom . . . our author has sufficiently (he says)
> explained the design of this work in the introduction. Perhaps he
> expects we should understand it by the following passages . . .

There follows three pages of direct quotation from the *Treatise*, summed up dismissively:

> Here the reader has all that I can find in the introduction to this
> work which can in the least give him any idea of the design of it:
> How far he will thereby be instructed in it must be left to his own
> judgement: I go on to set before him the several topics therein
> treated of.

But before doing so the reviewer objects to Hume's use of the personal pronoun in the text, resorting to a footnote for his objection:

> This work abounds in egotisms. This author would scarcely use that
> form of speech more frequently, if he had written his own memoirs.

In the same tone he finds Hume's brisk prose self-satisfied, although the arguments are often beyond him:

> When he has fixed this assertion [the relationship of ideas to
> impressions] beyond contradiction he reflects on what he has done
> with great satisfaction . . . There are many instances of our author's
> inscrutability in this work of his.

Hume's views on space and time, which, as we have seen, predated much of modern physics, are altogether too revolutionary for the reviewer and hover on the verge of bad taste. That is to say, they diminish the work of God:

The infinite divisibility of space is, I think, an impropriety. Space is, in the strictest sense, an *individuum*, yet [our author] seems by his subsequent reasoning (if it may so be called) to intend by *space, matter* or *solid extension* . . . He wades still further therein [the concept of space] through several pages mixing time along with it, and viewing both in a variety of lights. Some of these are too dazzling for my weak sight. I must therefore shun them; only telling the reader, whose eyes are strong enough for such views, where to look for them . . . I will venture to affirm his philosophy will never suffice to acquaint us with either the nature or causes of our perceptions; any farther than any man's consciousness will do without it. We now come to the fourth part of this volume, of which we shall not offer to make any exact analysis, only select a few curious passages, such as we think conducive to the reader's pleasure and edification.

Having thus given up any rational analysis the reviewer quotes at such length that the remainder of the review was held over until the January issue of *The History of the Learned*. The reviewer, perhaps revealing a clerical background, recoils in horror at Hume's discussion of the immateriality of the soul:

This is indeed a lamentable case; for such is the absolute pleasure of our author, and we must submit; neither Locke nor Clarke, nor the most venerable names shall usurp the place of truth in his affections.

This is the tone of a senior don's disgust at a whipper-snapper of an undergraduate daring to question the status quo. But when Hume does honestly admit to personal doubt, the critic cruelly satirises Hume's thoughts in the passage, 'I am like a man, who having struck on many shoals . . .' with:

What heart would not almost bleed? What breast can forbear to sympathise with this brave adventurer? . . . I will take leave of our author while he is in this cheerful mood, in this agreeable situation; for, by looking forward, I perceive him extremely ready to relapse into profound meditations on incomprehensible subjects, and so into scepticism, chagrin and all the gloomy frightful train of ideas from whence he is but this moment engaged . . .

Then, astonishingly, in the final paragraphs of the review there is a complete *volte face*. The review concludes:

> Perhaps I have sufficiently answered the end of this article, which is to make the treatise it refers to more generally known than I think it has been; to bring it, as far as I am able, into the observation of the learned who are the proper judges of its contents, who will give a sanction to its doctrines, where they are true and useful, and who have authority to correct the mistakes where they are of a different nature; and lastly to hint to this ingenious writer, whoever he is, some particulars in his performance, that may require a very serious reconsideration. It bears indeed incontestable marks of a soaring genius, not young, and not yet thoroughly practised . . . we shall probably have reason to consider this [the *Treatise*] compared with his later productions, in the same light as we view the juvenile works of Milton, or the first manner of a Raphael, to other celebrated painters.[23]

This passage, which ends the review, must have been written by a different person to the bulk of the foregoing demolition, and given that whoever did write it must also have read the *Treatise*, it seems safe to presume that it was the editor of *The History of the Learned* himself, probably feeling that the foregoing article was altogether too savage. This was highly possible since in the October 1741 issue the editor appears to answer a complaint about a reviewer:

> all I can say of him is, that by the verisimilitude of the MSS I believe him to be the person who drew up the account of the *Treatise of Human Nature* . . .[24]

The final paragraph of the review is a wonderful example of an editor regretting his choice of reviewer and trying, belatedly, to make amends. There can be no certainty as to the identity of the reviewer but all evidence (endorsed by Professor Mossner) points to William Warburton, later Bishop of Gloucester. He was the deeply conservative author of *The Divine Legation of Moses* and a violent opponent of Voltaire and the Deists. He would snap at Hume's heels again in the future.

Hume was deeply distressed by the review and there is a totally ludicrous legend that he threatened the printer of it at sword point. This is not only out of character, but since Hume was in Scotland and the printer in London it is clearly a fabrication, however much Hume would have liked to skewer his attacker. But he was not going to let his *magnum opus* be condemned out of hand by a man whose prejudices had prevented him from understanding it, and to this end he wrote a summary of its main points and swiftly sent it to Charles Corbet, a publisher at Addison's Head, 'over against St Dunstan's Church in Fleet Street'. Hume had determinedly refused to allow the *History of the Learned* to publish the work. 'There having been an article with regard to my book, somewhat abusive, printed in that work.' It was advertised in the *Daily Advertiser* of 11 March 1740 for sixpence as *An Abstract of a late Philosophical performance, entitled a Treatise of Human Nature, etc., wherein the chief Argument and Design of that Book, which has met with such Opposition, and been represented in so Terrifying a light, is further illustrated and explained.* His 'cheerful and sanguine nature' had, in fact, been stretched to breaking point, but when the *Abstract* was, in fact, published in 1740 the latter part of the title had been considerably amended, probably by the publisher, to *the Chief Argument of that book is further Illustrated and Explained.* But, curiously, Charles Corbet was no more than a front for the actual publisher. The *Abstract* was in fact printed by William Strahan, for none other than James Noon, the publisher of the *Treatise.* He obviously felt that Hume had been unfairly treated and tried to help by distributing Hume's explanation. This we know from Strahan's ledgers, preserved in the British Library.[26] The *Abstract* is comparatively short and is a simple summary of his main points, principally in Book I 'Of the Understanding', since Book II had largely been ignored by *The History of the Learned*. He repeats the principles of cause and effect and reiterates his assertion that the two are only linked by experience. Hume gives the example of one billiard ball striking another. 'Jupiter' Carlyle tells us that there was a billiard table within fifty yards of the University, so Hume would have been well acquainted with the game. Since, like him, we have seen this event many times we know that the stationary ball will move. If we could find someone who had never seen a billiard table, he might not make this presumption. He refers to the passions and his belief that reason comes from them and is their servant. Hume preserves his anonymity in the *Abstract* and it is written in the style of an explanation by a third party.

The *Bibliothèque Raisonnée* noted, 'some people having found that the *Treatise of Human Nature* of Mr Hume was a little too abstract, a brochure has been published to help them understand it'. Most probably this notice was the work of Desmaizeaux who clearly had no regard for Hume's desire for anonymity. Hume would have known of these later French and German reviews and would have either read them personally or, as far as the German reviews were concerned, had the gist of them translated to him. Hume spoke no German.

There were two main prongs to the criticism, both of which would have hurt Hume deeply. The review in the *History of the Learned* attacked his prose style and his manner of writing as though making a personal address. This was simply the established generation recoiling from anything new. Good prose, for them, consisted of long, complex sentences with numerous complementary clauses, all with a sound classical base. Hume wrote in brisk contemporary English. Next, his arguments made no allowance for inherent knowledge but only for knowledge derived from experience. This comes very close to denying the existence of an immortal soul and to giving God no part in creating the human psyche. The result of this was that many reviewers, when they grasped the direction of the argument, either ceased to read any further or simply skimmed the remainder in growing horror. One German reviewer, having summed up the main arguments against logical proof of cause and effect, states, 'Oddly enough we shall not even think of the consequences the author derives there from!' One of the consequences was to cause Immanuel Kant to say that Hume had 'wakened philosophy from its dogmatic slumber'. But in 1740 the 16-year-old Kant had only just entered the University of Königsburg. Derision and satire largely protected these critics from having to consider Hume's thought. Some called his thought 'baffling', and where his anonymity was respected he is 'the English savant'.

One letter to the journal *Common-Sense, or the Englishman's Journal*, talking of the *Treatise* on 5 July 1740 does, however, state:

> Our author has handled his subject with a perspicuity that one does not often find in Treatises of this nature. We can everywhere understand him, if we cannot in all things agree with him; though I think throughout he is a rational as well as a clear writer.

The writer was also the author of *An essay towards demonstrating the Immateriality of the Soul.* However, he goes on to give:

A short account of a long book, the author of which seems, if I understand him, which I confess I am not quite sure of . . . [to give a] tedious performance. I shall take no note of this novel sort of diction, because most metaphysicians, to the great prejudice of their science, affect to think and to express themselves in a manner peculiar to themselves . . . I am convinced no man can comprehend what he means. This will be sufficient for preventing my author's philosophy from having any mischievous effect upon the opinions or morals of mankind. [As to anonymity] I can upon honour declare I never had the least information who he is, so that my criticism cannot proceed from any malice or ill will.[27]

He goes on to object to Hume's classification of the will, pride, humility, love and hate being 'impressions' since this denied their God-given qualities.

An anecdote concerning the young Adam Smith shows the depth of penetration achieved by the *Treatise:*

Something had occurred while Smith was at Oxford to excite the suspicion of his superiors with respect to the nature of his private pursuits, and the heads of his college, having entered his apartment without his being aware, found him engaged in perusing Hume's *Treatise of Human Nature,* then recently published. This the reverend inquisitors seized, while they severely reprimanded the young philosopher.[28]

So, the thought police of Balliol College, Oxford, were well aware of the work in 1740. Smith may have been reading the work on the recommendation of Hutcheson, his late professor at Glasgow University.

Therefore, far from falling 'dead-born from the press', the *Treatise* was severally reviewed although the reviewers largely failed to understand it, out of an inability to grasp innovation in philosophy. The fact that thinking would now have to change from explaining a God-created world to explaining a world in which man stood centre stage using experience and reason to understand his feelings and impressions was horrifying to the established philosophers. The Church would not easily loosen its grip on thought. The debate rumbled on – it still does – and in the *Edinburgh Amusement* of 1771 is an essay on genius by James Beattie, Professor of Moral Philosophy at Marischal College, Aberdeen, and a vehement opponent of Hume. The same issue carries a letter by 'Orthodoxus' which defends Hume without agreeing with him:

Mr Hume is no doubt an avowed sceptic, but you have charged him with being an avowed and dogmatical teacher of atheism, a charge which, in my opinion is unjust . . . Can this man be so formidable an enemy to religion and the good order of society as you represent him? . . . Mr Hume wrote a book upon human nature which was never or by a few people read or understood . . . Mr Hume has never, so far as I have heard, signed our confession of faith, or sworn to the Calvinistic doctrines – he then certainly escapes the charge of perjury. There has been a time for burning Arminians, as well as other heretics. God forbid it should return. It is impossible, as Arian expresses it, to be both a blockhead and a philosopher.[29]

The cudgels on behalf of Hume were taken up again on 25 July, in a letter:

This persuasion is equally sanguine that the *Dissertation on Human Nature* has never been read, or but by a few: that it is now forgotten, and hardly to be met with in any bookseller's shop in Great Britain. How true the last of these facts may be, I pretend not to judge; but the first and second . . . are absolutely false, and so grossly contradictory to universal knowledge and conviction, that he must be charitable indeed who can palliate them with excuse of mistake. I was in Edinburgh soon after the original publication, and well remember how much and how frequently it was mentioned in every literary conversation: and if it is now so irrecoverably involved in oblivion, how should it have happened that Dr Reid, and a number of other venerable names have opposed the full strength of their genius to its malignity? I will, however, do Mr Hume the justice to assert that no performance written with so much taste and genius as his own will ever be forgotten.[30]

Hume's disputes with Thomas Reid will be dealt with later. However, the relative reputations of Hume and Beattie were put into perspective in Hume's obituary in the *Annual Register* for 1777, under Characters, pages 27–32:

This work [the *Treatise*] though not inferior to anything of the moral or metaphysical kind in any language was entirely overlooked, or decried at the time of publication, except by a few liberal minded men, who had courage to throw aside their popular and literary prejudices and follow sound reasoning, without being afraid of any dangerous conclusion, or fatal discovery. Dr Beattie has been so successful as to obtain a pension by his *Essay on the Immutability of Truth;* in which he discovers all the violence of a sectary, and all the illiberality of a pedant, and abuses rather than refutes Mr Hume.[31]

Therefore, so far from being ignored, Hume's work was a topic of lively controversy. It was reviewed in England, France and Germany. It was 'frequently mentioned in every literary conversation' in Edinburgh, but it was not a bestseller and that was what Hume wanted. His aspiration was for the entire philosophical, literary and clerical world to say, 'Oh, I see. I have been grievously mistaken all my life, but I am grateful to Mr Hume for pointing out my errors and showing me the path of truth'. Hume had talked to Michael Ramsay about the work and Henry Home had read it and had disagreed with it. Like all first-time authors Hume was hurt by negative criticism and suspicious of praise. But he desperately wanted to engage in a reasoned debate with a figure of authority who might give him the encouragement he needed to continue with his chosen career of letters. He had produced an unsupervised dissertation of startling originality and he desperately needed a supervisor. Such a one was Adam Smith's professor at Glasgow University, Francis Hutcheson.

SIX

Improvement of Fortune

F rancis Hutcheson has already been mentioned as a charismatic Professor of Moral Philosophy at the University of Glasgow. He was now 46 years old, an Irish-born Whig with a 'just abhorrence of all slavish principles' and a passionate belief in the rights of the people to oppose unjust rule. From the Earl of Shaftesbury's school of thought in Dublin he had absorbed the ideas of 'politeness' and 'refinement' as virtues of a civilised society. Alexander 'Jupiter' Carlyle (he was thought to resemble a Classical God) said that it was due to him that:

> a new school was formed in the western provinces of Scotland, where the clergy till that period were narrow and bigoted, and had never ventured to range in their mind beyond the strict bounds of orthodoxy.[1]

He did, however, believe that God had given humanity a fundamental understanding of the moral virtues, and that mankind was inherently good. The highest goal in life was happiness and this was achieved by ensuring the happiness of others. This follows the German jurist Samuel Puffendorf's belief that our own self-interest will make us strive for the good of the community. Hutcheson built on this, believing that since we are part of that very community, a God-given sense of moral correctness will influence our reasoning toward virtue. Now, when Hume wrote to Henry Home on 13 February 1739:

> If you know anybody that is a judge, you would do me a sensible pleasure in engaging him to a serious perusal of the book. 'Tis so rare to meet one that will take pains on a book, that does not come recommended by some great name or authority, that I must confess, I am as fond of meeting with such a one, as if I were sure of his approbation.[2]

Hutcheson would have seemed the obvious person for Henry Home to contact since it was said of him that:

He loved truth and sought after it with impartiality and constancy . . . his heart was finely turned for friendship . . . students advanced in years and knowledge choosed [sic] to attend his lectures of Moral Philosophy for four, five, or six years together.[3]

Henry Home duly sent the two volumes of the *Treatise* to Francis Hutcheson who replied in April 1739 with typical generosity:

I deferred acknowledging the most obliging present I received of your friend's book upon Human Nature, by my Lord Kilmarnock, till I could find leisure to peruse it: and unluckily I met with more than ordinary interruptions by unavoidable business. I perused the first volume and a great part, indeed, almost all the second. And was everywhere surprised with a great acuteness of thought and reasoning in a mind wholly disengaged from the prejudices of the learned as well as those of the vulgar. I cannot pretend to his tenets as yet, these metaphysical subjects have not been much in my thoughts of late; though a great many of these sentiments and reasonings had employed me about 10 or 12 years ago. The teaching in a college, and a more important work of inspecting into the conduct of several young folk committed to me leaves very little leisure for close attention to a long scheme of philosophy not in my province. This book will furnish me matter for a good deal of thought next vacation, now coming on in less than six weeks. I shall have the greatest pleasure in communicating to the ingenious author whatever occurred probable to me on these subjects . . . I should be very glad to know where the author could be met with if a lazy umbratick,* very averse to motion, ever takes a ramble in a vacation.[4]

Henry Home obviously transmitted this answer to Hume who, having suffered from the 'prejudices of the learned', found it encouraging enough to send Hutcheson the unpublished manuscript of Part III of the *Treatise, On Morals.* We can deduce his views on this since Hume wrote to thank him on September 17:

I am much obliged to you for your reflections on my papers. I have perused them with care and find they will be of use to me. You

---

* shade-seeking, or, metaphorically, reclusive.

have mistaken my meaning in some passages; which upon
examination I have found to proceed from some ambiguity or
deficit in my expression.[5]

This is Hume at his mildest and he clearly feels that, at last, here is a
master at whose feet he would be willing to sit. Not, of course, without
disputing with the master.

Hutcheson had found Hume to have a lack of warmth for the cause of
virtue, and Hume defended this, saying it had not happened by chance but
by the application of reason which has no inherent virtue. Although he
wished to be esteemed a friend of virtue, he must always cling to the
rigours of taste. However, he hoped in the future to make the moralist and
the metaphysician agree a little better. Hume excused the cold vigour of
his analysis, as being like an anatomist who can advise a painter on the
structure of the body. This analogy is carried further in the *Enquiry
concerning Human Understanding*, published in 1748.[6] Hume disagreed
with Hutcheson, as philosophers will, over a word, 'natural'. Hume had
examined the methods by which man discerns the difference between
good and evil actions[7] and Hutcheson had countered that there was a
natural mechanism inherent in man. Hume disputed this:

'Tis founded on final causes, which is a consideration, that appears
pretty uncertain and unphilosophical. For pray, What is the end of
Man? Is he created for happiness or virtue? For this life or for the
next? For himself or his maker? Your definition of natural depends
upon solving these questions, which are endless and quite wide of
the purpose. I have never called justice unnatural, but only
artificial . . . Grotius and Puffendorf, to be consistent, must assert
the same.[8]

However, Hume assured Hutcheson that he would alter the passages
found defective, although he thought Hutcheson was 'a little too delicate'.
Hume tried to justify sugaring the pill for the general reader and hoped he
could consult with Hutcheson when in any difficulty. In fact, he took the
opportunity to do so then and there in a lengthy postscript:

I cannot forbear recommending another thing to your consideration.
Actions are not virtuous nor vicious; but only so far as they are
proofs of certain qualities or durable principles in the mind . . . I
desire you to consider if there be any quality that is virtuous

without having a tendency either to the public good or to the good of the person who possesses it. If there be none without these tendencies we may conclude that their merit is derived from sympathy. I desire you would only consider the tendencies of qualities not their actual operation, which depends on chance . . . 'tis upon the goodness or badness of the motives that the virtue of the action depends. This proves that to every virtuous action there must be a motive or impelling passion distinct from the virtue and that the virtue can never be the sole motive to any action. You do not assent to this, though I think there is no proposition more certain or important. I must own my proofs were not distinct enough and must be altered. You see with what reluctance I part with you; though I believe it is time I should ask your pardon for so much trouble.[9]

Here, at last, Hume is writing to a man whose advice he is willing to take, and with whom he feels comfortable in debate. The gulf between them is, however, wide, with Hutcheson believing that there is an inherent God-implanted good in humanity, allowing for motiveless virtue, and Hume arguing that, since this belief has no validity except faith, it cannot be reasonably maintained. Hume must also have been delighted to find an authority who would treat his efforts with the seriousness he felt they deserved. He knew full well that many of the reviewers of the *Treatise* had read no further than their prejudices would allow. He complains of this in Part III of the *Treatise*, *Of Morals*:

I am hopeful it may be understood by ordinary readers, with as little attention as is usually given to any books of reasoning . . . the greatest part of men seem agreed to convert reading into an amusement, and to reject everything that requires any considerable degree of attention to be comprehended.[10]

What Hume would have thought of the present age where comprehension scarcely extends beyond the soundbite can easily be imagined. He did, however, have a very contemporary curiosity as to the commercial world of publishing, and on 4th March 1740 he wrote again to Hutcheson asking what kind of advance, or 'copy-money', he might expect and also if Hutcheson could recommend a publisher. He still thought his work would be controversial, however:

'Tis with reluctance I ask this last favour, though I know your authority will go a long way to make the matter easy for me. I am sensible that the matter is a little delicate. Perhaps you may not care to recommend even to a bookseller a book that may give offence to religious people. Perhaps you may not think it calculated for public sale. I assure you I shall not take it amiss if you refuse me . . . the book is pretty much altered since you first saw it; and though the clergy be always enemies to innovations in philosophy, yet I do not think they will find any great matter of offence in this volume. On the contrary I shall be disappointed if impartial judges be not much pleased with the soundness of my morals.[11]

Hume had already taken Hutcheson's advice and had sent copies of the *Treatise* and the manuscript of the *Abstract* to Hutcheson's publisher John Smith 'at the Philosopher's Head on the blind Quay' in Dublin. Nothing came of this. But in less than a fortnight Hutcheson came up with a recommendation for his new-found colleague, for on 16th March Hume responded to him:

I must trouble you to write that letter you was [sic] so kind as to offer to Longman the bookseller. I concluded somewhat of a hasty bargain with my bookseller from indolence and an aversion to bargaining.[12]

Thomas Longman, of the Ship at Paternoster Row, beside St Paul's Cathedral, was Hutcheson's own publisher and did, in fact, publish Hume's Part III of the *Treatise*, *Of Morals*, in 1740. No evidence of Hume's contract with Longman exists, but if it resembled his agreement with Noon, it was again £50, at least equal to his annual allowance.

In his reply to Hutcheson Hume went on to doubt the importance of his thought and promised to 'consider more carefully all the particulars you mention to me'; he also asked Hutcheson's opinion of other points, including a quandary as to the influence of Superior Beings:

If morality were determined by reason that is the same for all rational beings: but nothing but experience can assure us that the sentiments are the same. What experience can we have with regard to superior beings? How can we ascribe to them any sentiments at all? They have implanted those sentiments in us for the conduct of life like our bodily sensations, which they possess not themselves. I expect no answer to these difficulties in the compass of a letter. 'Tis enough if you have patience to read so long a letter as this.[13]

Here Hume is touching on a major difference between himself and Hutcheson. While Hutcheson believed that knowledge of God was not a prerequisite for an inherent sense of moral virtue, he did believe that the sense of virtue was God-given. Hume was not so sure but was certainly not willing to alter his work to coincide exactly with Hutcheson's thinking. He was, however, grateful for his advice as to a publisher.

Before publication took place he made an albeit half-hearted effort to find another source of income beyond his publisher's advance and his annual allowance of £50, and on 12 November 1739 he wrote to George Carre of Nisbet, an advocate and neighbour from Berwickshire:

'Tis natural for a man that has not been much accustomed to solicit for favours, to be a little shy in that particular; especially if there is required in the person to whom he applies himself, not only a good will to him, but a good opinion of him in order to the granting of the request. Yet this is my present case. I am informed that your cousins, my Lord Haddington and Mr Baillie [the 19-year-old heir to the earldom and his younger brother] are going abroad and want a governor. I have an intention of offering my service and know no person so proper to apply as myself: and the more so that I hope if you do not think the matter feasible or proper, you will be so free as to tell me so. If you approve of the project, you both know the proper persons to apply to and will be able to give me the proper advice in that respect. There are many inviting circumstances with regard to these young gentlemen which have engaged me to make this step. They have a very good character; I have the honour to be their relation [the earldom was a Home nobility and 'nearly every Home and Hume could call cousins with every other'] (which gives a governor a better air when attending his pupils) and I have at present some leisure to bestow. As I was uncertain whether or not they might be provided and would not willingly be named in the affair, if it do not succeed, I desire it may be conducted with all possible secrecy. I have enclosed this to Harry Home as not knowing your direction. He will confer with you about the matter and to your friendship and discretion, I commit myself.[15]

Since Lord Haddington was currently a student at Oxford, it is unsurprising that they went abroad under the care, not of David Hume, but of the Rev John Williamson, an English cleric.

The letter is interesting in that it is clumsily written, showing signs of haste, and its diffidence is almost as if Hume wished he did not have to write it. It also reveals Hume's shyness, and although he consorted with some of the greatest figures in European culture, his inferiority complex as a Berwickshire farmer's son was always present. There is none of the confidence of style here that we see in his letters to Hutcheson or Henry Home, and he may well have been relieved when he was rejected for this post. There would, however, be other opportunities in the near future, no matter how disastrous.

His first priority was to oversee the publication of *Of Morals* and by June 1740 he was in London. He had met up with William Mure of Caldwell, who was *en route* for Leyden to complete his legal studies, and while in London the two young men became guests at a house at nearby Richmond-upon-Thames. From there Mure wrote to his sister Agnes on 5 June 1740, giving an intimate picture of the young philosopher:

> We have been here now these ten days, and pass our time in a very agreeable way. We have our countryman Mr Hume, the author of the metaphysical books we heard so much of last summer, as a party in our retirement. He is a very sensible young fellow and extremely curious in most parts of learning and how much soever he has shown himself a Sceptic upon subjects of speculation and enquiry, he is as far from it as any man with regard to the qualities of a well natured disposition, and an honest heart which are no doubt of greater consequence to the intrinsic worth of a character than any abstract opinions whatever. As he is very communicative of all his knowledge, we have a great deal from him in the way of dispute and argument, and not a little too in the way of plain information. We reason upon every point with the greatest freedom, even his own books, (which we are working at at present), we canvass with ease, and attack him boldly wherever we can get the least hold of him, and question or contradict his most favourite notions; all this goes on with the greatest good humour, and affords us entertainment both within doors and in the fields at our walks in this delightful country, which is the finest that we can possibly

imagine, and has the preference by people that has travelled through most of Europe, to any that they ever saw. We make use of our philosopher too in another way less becoming to the dignity of his character, as we keep family within ourselves, he manages all the necessities of household economy and manages all the affairs of house keeping. For these few hints you may imagine we spend our time here in a pleasant enough manner, and much more to all our satisfaction than in the noise and hurry of the town.[16]

It is not difficult to imagine that the person 'who has travelled through most of Europe' was David Hume displaying his nascent diplomatic skills, but the picture of the celebrated philosopher as expert housekeeper comes as a surprise although those too were to prove hidden skills. The picture is of a healthy relaxed young gentleman enjoying the company of friends, and especially enjoying friendly debate by way of conversation, a situation Hume revelled in whenever it was available to him. There is no suspicion of priggishness or pomposity. Such society repaid him for his early solitude of thought.

Volume III of the *Treatise, Of Morals,* was duly published on 5 November 1740 to a silence even more deafening than that which had greeted the first two volumes. The *Bibliothèque Raisonnée* found it baffling and gave it a 'mixed notice', and it is indeed a mixed work, having almost entirely departed from the metaphysical rigour of the first two parts. There is an immediate assertion that morals do not derive from reason since reason 'is, or ought to, be the slave of the passions':

Morals excite passions, and produce or prevent actions. Reason of itself is utterly impotent in this particular. The rules of morality, therefore, are not conclusions of our reason.

He deals quickly with effects of introducing God into the equation and replacing reason with faith, leading in turn to dogma:

In every system of morality which I have hitherto met with I have always remarked that the author proceeds for some time in the ordinary ways of reasoning and establishes the being of a God, or makes representations concerning human affairs; when of a sudden I am surprised to find that instead of the usual copulations of propositions, 'is' and 'is not', I meet with no proposition that is not connected with an 'ought' or an 'ought not'.

Hume does allow that there is a sense of virtue and that the basic ability to know right from wrong does exist. The question of whether this sense was inherent or learned proved too complex and Hume simply agreed that it was too difficult:

> Should it . . . be demanded whether the sense of virtue be natural or artificial, I am of the opinion that 'tis impossible for me at present to give any precise answer to this question.

This question is still unanswered and the battle of psychologists favouring either 'nature' or 'nurture' rages to the present day.

In Part II of the book, *Of Justice and Injustice,* Hume starts to examine the practical applications of the sense of virtue. He proposes that it is the wish of most people to live in peace and tranquillity and that to achieve this end a sense of justice in its broadest form has emerged. Justice is one of the virtues:

> that produce pleasure and approbation by means of an artifice or contrivance, which arises from circumstances and necessities of mankind . . . No action can be virtuous or morally good unless there be in human nature some motive to produce it, distinct from the sense of its morality.

In other words, our desire for well-ordered peace has produced a system which we applaud, since we both needed and invented it. This forerunner of Utilitarianism grows out of the thinking of Samuel Puffendorf, the German jurist. However, as to the desire for self-gratification at the expense of society:

> Self love is the source of all injustice and violence.

The maintenance of the wellbeing of society is paramount and our instinctive feelings for self-gratification must be curbed if society is to operate efficiently. Hume argues that from the earliest times man had to co-operate in order to hunt, and this need for co-operation brought about a structured society. Thus his thinking coincides with John Donne's *Meditation*, 'No man is an island, entire of itself':

> There is no human, and indeed no sensible creature, whose happiness or misery does not in some measure affect us when brought near to us.

And he still retains a refreshing optimism about the human condition:

> I am of the opinion that though it be rare to meet with one who
> loves any single person better than himself; yet 'tis as rare to meet
> with one in whom all the kind affections taken together do not
> over balance the selfish.

The idea that there was a primitive paradise inhabited by inherently virtuous savages is always lurking in the recesses of eighteenth-century thought:

> In the state of nature which preceded society there be neither
> justice nor injustice, yet I assert not that it was allowable to violate
> the property of others. I only maintain that there was no such thing
> as property, and consequently could be no such thing as justice or
> injustice.

Now, it is true that in the language of some primitive societies there are no possessive or personal pronouns, since the concept of private ownership does not exist. But these people frequently wage savage tribal wars. Their need to protect their society, or at least its often limited gene pool, results in their regarding incest, which is surrounded by complex and intricate laws, as the greatest crime, punishable by death. Although Hume was unaware of this, the sanctions applied here to protect the stability of society still fall within his definition of an artificial contrivance arising from the necessities of mankind. The arrival of the concept of possession of property has given rise to much of current commerce and he goes on to define the practice of trade and finance:

> The invention of the law of nature concerning the stability of
> possession has already rendered men tolerable to each other; that of
> the transference of property and possession by consent has begun to
> render them mutually advantageous . . . A promise would not be
> intelligible before human conventions had established it, and that
> even if it were intelligible it would not be attended by any moral
> obligation . . . A promise is the sanction of the [self] interested
> commerce of mankind . . . Afterwards a sentiment of morals
> concurs with interest and becomes a new obligation upon mankind.
> This sentiment of morality in the performance of promises, arises
> from the same principle as that in the abstinence from the [taking
> of] property of others.

Thus Hume defines the laws of nature while, in fact, defining commerce and starting a train of thought that would be continued by his great friend Adam Smith as a foundation stone in the new science of economics:

> [There are] three fundamental laws of nature, that of stability of possession, of its transference by consent, and of the performance of promises.

He is in danger of straying far from his point to define moral laws and swiftly returns to look at the foundations on which justice is built:

> We are to consider this distinction between justice and injustice as having two different foundations, viz. that of self-interest, when men observe that 'tis impossible to live in society without restraining themselves by certain rules, and that of morality when this interest is observed to be common to all mankind, and men receive a pleasure from the view of such actions that tend towards the peace of society . . . Nothing is more certain than that men are, in a great measure, governed by interest, and that even when they extend their concern beyond themselves 'tis not to any great distance . . . In the execution and decision of justice, men acquire a security against each other's weakness and passion, as well as against their own, and under the shelter of their governors, begin to taste at ease the sweets of society and mutual assistance . . . There is evidently no other principle than interest and if interest first produces obedience to government, the obligation to obedience must cease when the interest ceases in any great degree.

Now, astonishingly, he confirms himself as a true Whig, totally endorsing the events of the Hanoverian succession:

> Here an English reader will be apt to enquire concerning that famous revolution which has had such a happy influence on our constitution . . . When the public good is so great and so evident as to justify the action [removal of an unjust sovereign] the commendable use of this licence causes us naturally to attribute to parliament the use of further licences.

This endorses the right of the people to remove an unjust sovereign through Parliament acting for the people, although in foreign policy he finds it less reprehensible to allow the deceits of diplomacy:

The natural obligation to justice among different states is not so strong as among individuals, the moral obligation which arises from it must partake of its weakness; and we must necessarily give greater indulgence to a prince or minister who deceives another than to a private gentleman who breaks his word of honour.

Having endorsed diplomatic deceit as a necessary evil, he now turns to chastity and modesty on which he has equally astonishing views. Since men do not get pregnant they, logically, do not cause so much damage to society, therefore they can be given greater licence:

'Tis contrary to the interest of civil society that men should have an entire liberty of indulging their appetites in venereal enjoyment; but as this interest is weaker than in the case of the weaker sex, the moral obligation arising from it must be proportionably weaker.

After this quite outrageous statement it is as if he pulls himself together and remembers what his original purpose was as he starts Part III, rather weakly entitled, *Of the other Virtues and Vices*. He starts with a bold definition:

Meekness, beneficence, charity, generosity, clemency, moderation and equity are the social virtues, marking their tendency to the good of society. The good arising from them is the object of natural passion, justice is only the concurrence of mankind . . . Every quality of the mind is denominated virtuous which gives pleasure by the mere survey; as every quality which produces pain is called vicious . . . These sentiments produce love or hatred; and love or hatred by the original constitution of human passion is attended by benevolence or anger; that is, with a desire of making happy the person we love and miserable the person we hate.

Readers may recall that a page of rough notes simply entitled 'Philosophy' and made some fifteen years previously was quoted earlier in this book. They were largely unattributed though Bayle had clearly been a powerful influence. These notes included the following entries: 'Men love pleasure more than they hate pain. Men are vicious but hate a religion that authorises vice. Atheists plainly make distinction betwixt good reasoning and bad. Why not betwixt vice and virtue?' Here, in *Of Morals* Hume is putting flesh on these thoughts and brings himself back to his main theme by setting out to define 'greatness of mind'. There are two principles at work here which Hume quotes as 'sympathy' and 'comparison':

> The direct survey of another's pleasure naturally gives us pleasure; and therefore produces pain when compared with our own. His pain, considered in itself, is painful; but augments the idea of our own happiness and gives us pleasure . . . If the idea be too faint, it has no influence by comparison; on the other hand, if it be too strong, it operates entirely on us by sympathy, which is contrary to comparison. Sympathy being the conversion of an idea into an impression, demands a greater force and vivacity in the idea than is requisite to comparison.

Although sympathy arises from some comparisons, in some cases it can lead to animosity:

> The gay naturally associate themselves with the gay and the amorous with the amorous; but the proud never can endure the proud . . . a fool must always find some person that is more foolish in order to keep himself in good humour with his own parts and understanding.

However, self-esteem is no bar to greatness of mind and is often essential to a rational view of one's demerits and merits. Hume goes on to describe the beneficial effects of:

> That merit which is commonly ascribed to generosity, humanity, compassion, gratitude, friendship, fidelity, zeal, disinterestedness, liberality and all those other qualities which form the character of the good and the benevolent.

But have we any choice in embracing these virtues? Hume thinks not:

> First many of these qualities which all moralists . . . comprehend under the title of moral virtues are equally involuntary and necessary with the qualities of the judgement and the imagination. Secondly I would have anyone give me a reason why virtue and vice may not be involuntary as well as beauty and deformity. These moral distinctions arise from the natural distinctions of pain and pleasure. Thirdly, as to free will, it has no place with regard to the actions, no more than the qualities of men . . . Our actions are more

voluntary than our judgements, but we have not more liberty in one than in the other.

So both vice and virtue are inherent and we are governed by self-interest. Their balance, so beloved of the eighteenth century, will produce harmony of action.

As Hume draws to the end of the *Treatise* he makes generalisations about the importance and weight of the men possessed of these virtues:

> The histories of kingdoms are more interesting than domestic stories; the histories of great empires more than those of small cities and principalities; and the history of war and revolution than those of peace and order. We sympathise with the persons that suffer, in all the sentiments which belong to their fortunes . . . The mind is occupied by the multitude of the objects and by the strong passions that display themselves. And this occupation or agitation of the mind is commonly agreeable and amusing. The same theory accounts for the esteem and regard we pay to men of extraordinary parts and abilities. The good and ill of multitudes are connected with their actions. Whatever they undertake is important and challenges our attention . . . And where any person can excite these sentiments, he soon acquires our esteem; unless other circumstances of his character render him odious and disagreeable.

Before the conclusion of the *Treatise* Hume deals with 'further reflections concerning natural virtues' and immediately looks at the advantages and disadvantages of the body. His first example is astonishing:

> 'Tis a general remark, that those whom we call good women's men, who have either signalised themselves by their amorous exploits, or whose make of body promises any extraordinary vigour of that kind, are well received by the fair sex, and naturally engage the attentions even of those whose virtue prevents any design of ever giving employment to these talents. Here 'tis evident that the ability of such a person to give enjoyment is the real source of the love and esteem he meets with among the females; at the same time that the women who love and esteem him have no prospect of receiving that enjoyment themselves and can only be affected by means of their sympathy with one that has a commerce of love with him. This instance is singular and merits our attention.

The example does indeed merit our attention, especially when coupled with the passage on male venereal pleasure. Men should be less harshly criticised for sexual immorality than women, and women are more easily attracted by the macho Don Juan. These two passages stand out as though they were additions to the text inserted at a much later date than the main body. They read as if Hume had received some hurt from a woman which turned him temporarily against the female sex. Now, while preparing the text for final publication we have heard that Hume was in the company of Mure of Caldwell, who, as we have heard, much later as Baron Mure, recounted the story of Hume being jilted in Edinburgh. It is possible that Hume's rejection was still painful and that Mure was told of it while the friends were at Richmond. The passages certainly read like the reaction of a young man whose past rejection had rendered him bitter.

However, Hume goes almost directly to the conclusion to this final section of the *Treatise* and the style is now brisk and logical:

> Virtue is considered as a means to an end. Means to an end are
> only valued so far as the end is valued. But the happiness of
> strangers affects by sympathy alone. To that principle, therefore, we
> are to ascribe the sentiment of approbation, which arises from the
> survey of all those virtues that are useful to society, or to the person
> possessed of them. These form the most considerable part of
> morality . . . The most abstract speculations concerning human
> nature, however cold and unentertaining, become subservient to
> practical morality, and may render this latter science more correct in
> its precepts, and more persuasive in its exhortations.

Hume also felt that some of the criticisms of the first two books had been brought about by his own lack of clarity, and to amend this he added an *Appendix* 'to guard against all mistakes in the readers'. It is largely a re-statement of the arguments of the first two books with some clarifying notes to be inserted. With this he completes his three-volume *Treatise*.

He has proved, at least to his own satisfaction, that no matter of fact can be believed without experiencing its cause or effect and that there can be no metaphysical link between the cause and the effect. Only experience can show cause and effect to be present and only experience can lead us to presume their results. From this he asserts that the feelings, sentiments, or passions, actually exert greater control than the reason. This leads to his famous phrase, 'reason is, or should be the slave of the passions'. His views on morals have been taken by some to be depressing in that, while accepting that there is an inherent sense of virtue in man, it arises from man's need for peaceful co-operation, which in itself arises from man's self-interest. Nowhere is God mentioned as part of the human psyche, but, equally importantly, nowhere does Hume deny His existence. Hume's reputation as an atheist is thus unfounded. He would re-examine all of these ideas for the rest of his life in essays and further enquiries, but today his principal reputation as a philosopher rests on the *Treatise*, practically unread in his own time.

It was, however, time for Hume to move on, and the discursiveness we find in the later parts of Volume III of the *Treatise* shows us that, far from abandoning philosophy altogether, as some commentators have suggested, he was finding it convenient to deal with discrete aspects of the subject in a shorter form. There was also no doubt that Hume needed money and felt that he could earn more by essay writing as well as, he hoped, reaching a wider audience.

The essay was a literary form dating back to Francis Bacon in the late sixteenth century. Joseph Addison and Richard Steele had polished the essay to a high degree in the *Tatler* and the *Spectator* in the early part of the eighteenth century, and Charles Lamb would carry the form on into the nineteenth with *Essays of Elia*. Hume had already sent 'papers' to Henry Home and these must have been early sketches of essays. Also, he had *Of Miracles* yet to be published:

> Hume's *Essays* do not mark an abandonment of philosophy, as some
> have maintained, but rather an attempt to improve it by having it
> address the concerns of common life.[17]

His first idea seems to have been to start a weekly paper in which his essays would be published individually, but by 1741 he had abandoned this idea, and a collection of fifteen essays was printed by R. Fleming and A. Alison for the publisher Alexander Kincaid who sold the work at 'his shop above the cross', in other words in Edinburgh's High Street, for two shillings and sixpence. After what he considered to be the failure of the *Treatise* Hume wrote a modest *Advertisement*:

> Most of these essays were wrote [sic] with a view to being
> published as weekly papers and were intended to comprehend the
> designs of the spectators and craftsmen. But having dropped that

undertaking, partly from laziness, partly from want of leisure, and being willing to make trial of my talents for writing before I venture upon any more serious compositions, I was induced to commit these trifles to the judgement of the public. Like most new authors, I must confess I feel some anxiety concerning the success of my work: but one thing makes me more secure, that the reader may condemn my abilities, but, I hope, will approve of my moderation and impartiality in my method of handling political subjects: as long as my moral character is in safety, I can with less concern, abandon my learning and capacity to the most severe censure and examination. Public spirit methinks, should engage us to love the public, and to bear an equal affection to all our countrymen, not to hate one half of them, under colour of loving the whole. This 'party rage' I have endeavoured to repress as far as possible; and I hope this design will be acceptable to the moderate of both parties; at the same time that, perhaps, it may displease the bigots of both. The reader must not look for any connexion among these essays, but must consider each of them as a work apart. This is an indulgence given to essay writers; and perhaps, such a desultory method of writing, is an equal ease both to the author and reader, by freeing them from any tiresome stretch of attention and application.

Hume was keen that his writing should reach the general public and had to balance the brevity needed to reach the short attention span of his public with the complexity of his thought. This, however much of a compromise for Hume, has led to an urgency of prose style which is extremely attractive for the contemporary reader. Even allowing for their considerable shortcomings, it is sad that his *Essays* are now rarely read even by philosophers and students of politics, and are largely disregarded as literature.

The variety of subjects dealt with in the first edition gives us an idea of how he was surrounding his philosophy with other subjects. The fifteen essays were, *Of Delicacy of Taste and Passion, Of the Liberty of the Press, Of Impudence and Modesty, That Politics may be reduced to a Science, Of the First Principles of Government, Of Love and Marriage, Of the Study of History, Of the Independency of Parliament, Whether the British Government tends more to absolute Monarchy than to a Republic, Of Parties in General, Of Parties of*

Great Britain, Of Superstition and Enthusiasm, Of Avarice, Of the Dignity of Human Nature, Of Liberty and Despotism. A very mixed bag indeed. Hume was sugaring his pill and it was so effective that a second, longer two-volume edition appeared, still from his Edinburgh publishers, with the original *Advertisement*.

The first volume of this second edition is simply a reprint of the first edition but in the second volume Hume added twelve more essays, *Of Essay Writing, Of Eloquence, Of Moral Prejudice, Of the Middle Station of Life, Of the Rise and Progress of the Arts and Sciences, Of the Epicurean, Of the Stoic, Of the Platonist, Of the Sceptic, Of Polygamy and Divorces, Of Simplicity and Refinement,* and *A Character of Sir Robert Walpole.* These twenty-seven essays were to contain the core of Hume's essay writing although with additions and subtractions as subsequent editions followed.

Three of these essays appeared only in the second edition, *Of Essay Writing, Of Moral Prejudices,* and *Of the Middle Station in Life.* In *Of Essay Writing* Hume divides the world into the learned or intellectual and the conversible. The latter he finds unentertaining and unprofitable; they are what today would be dismissed as the 'chattering classes'. For himself, however:

> I cannot but consider myself as a kind of ambassador from the dominions of learning to those of conversation . . . Women of sense and education (for to such alone I address myself) are much better judges of all polite writing than men of the same degree of understanding . . . I hope they will never be guilty of so wrong a choice as to sacrifice the substance for the shadow.

Hume was clearly aiming at the wit shown by Addison and Steele, but he lacked their experience of life, and although his prose is entertaining and elegant, his writing lacks authority. His attempts in these three essays to be jocular become patronising and uncharacteristic. This is not the incisive mind of the *Treatise*, rather it is hack work designed to bulk out a book. Hume must have been relieved when subsequent editions gave him the opportunity to consign these essays to the dustbin.

The remaining essays divide themselves into social, philosophical, and political subjects, and even they are of variable quality. Hume is on much stronger ground when considering political and philosophical subjects: *Of the Liberty of the Press*:

Nothing is more apt to surprise a foreigner than the extreme liberty which we enjoy in this country of communicating whatever we please to the public . . . As long, therefore, as the republican part of our government can maintain itself against the monarchical it will be naturally careful to keep the press open as of importance to its own preservation.

But there are reservations:

It must, however, be allowed that the unbounded liberty of the press, though it be difficult, perhaps impossible, to propose a suitable remedy for it, is one of the evils attending mixed forms of government.

Government is too important to be left to the 'casual humours and characters of particular men' and therefore stability of government can only be provided by a system of just laws. 'Effects will always correspond to causes, and wise regulations are the most valuable legacy that can be left to future ages.' He is sharply critical of the self-importance displayed by the political press:

I would not be understood to mean that public affairs deserve no care or attention . . . but such questions are of little importance to the public, and lay those who employ their pens upon them under a just suspicion of either malevolence or flattery.

He had already noted that the theatrical news of Colley Cibber was of more interest than parliamentary debates.

The nine essays, *Of the Liberty of the Press, That Politics may be reduced to a Science, Of the First Principles of Government, Of the Independency of Parliament, Whether the British Government tends more to absolute monarchy than to a Republic, Of Parties in General, Of Parties in Great Britain, Of the Dignity of Human Nature,* and *Of Liberty and Despotism,* all first appearing in both the first and second edition, encapsulate Hume's political thought during the 1740s. He justifies the rule of law and the governance of Parliament by philosophical methods, written in elegant prose, and it easy to imagine that these were the 'papers' that passed between himself and Henry Home.

The balance between freedom, with its inherent danger of anarchy, and control, with its equally dangerous curtailment of liberty, colours most of the other essays even when religious topics appear. In *Of Superstition and Enthusiasm,* for example:

> Weakness, fear, melancholy, together with ignorance, are . . . the true sources of superstition. Hope, pride, presumption, a warm imagination, together with ignorance, are . . . the true sources of enthusiasm. Superstition is favourable to priestly power, and enthusiasm not less, or rather more, contrary to it, than sound reason and philosophy. Religions, which partake of enthusiasm are, on their first rise, more furious and violent than those which partake of superstition, but in a little time become more gentle and moderate. Superstition is an enemy to civil liberty and enthusiasm a friend to it.

Avarice is dismissed as an irredeemable vice and true eloquence is seen to have died with the ancients. Man may fall short of perfect wisdom but is redeemed by his love of virtue. All the arts and sciences flourished under free nations, although he finds France a notable exception to this rule. He regards the past culture of an England under the absolute rule of the Stuarts as a desert. 'We have no dictionary of our language and scarcely a tolerable grammar.' Hume was wrong. There had been a short dictionary in 1558 and in 1604 Robert Cawdrey published a *Table Alphabetical* of some 3,000 words, expanding to 38,000 words by 1706, and by the time of Johnson's Dictionary in 1755 several others had been published. 'The first polite prose we have was writ by Dr Swift, a man still alive.' So much for Francis Bacon and Thomas Browne! All this can be mended by the moderation of the Whigs. 'The balance of power is a secret in politics, fully known only to the present age.'

There are four essays on strictly philosophical subjects with a preface:

> The intention of this and the following essays is not so much to explain accurately the sentiments of the Ancient sects of philosophy, as to deliver the sentiment of the sects as they naturally form themselves in the world, and entertain different ideas of human life and happiness. I have given each of them the name of the philosophical sect to which it bears the greatest affinity.

Hume also attempted, with wildly varying success, to write in the supposed style of each sect:

'Tis proper to inform the reader, that, in those essays entitled The Epicurean, the Stoic, etc., a certain character is personated, and, therefore no offence ought to be taken at any sentiments contained in them.

He would polish this technique when he wrote the *Dialogues Concerning Natural Religion*.

The first essay on *The Epicurean, or the Man of Elegance and Pleasure* is a mock pastoral hymn to pleasure. Wildly overdone and full of hyperbole, it fails on all counts:

Fear not my friends, that the barbarous dissonance of Bacchus and of his revellers should break in upon this entertainment, and confound us with their turbulent and clamorous pleasures. The sprightly muses wait around, and with their charming symphony, sufficient to soften the wolves and tigers of the savage desert, inspire a soft joy into every bosom.

He is on surer ground with *The Stoic, or the Man of Action and Virtue*:

Brute creatures have many of their necessities supplied by nature . . . but man exposed naked and indigent to the rude elements, rises slowly from that helpless state by the care and vigilance of his parents. Nature – a sublime celestial spirit – has given man intelligence . . . The great end of all human industry is the attainment of happiness . . . When we have fixed all the rules of conduct we are philosophers. When we have reduced these rules to practice we are sages. The man of virtue looks down with contempt on all the allurements of pleasure, and all the menaces of danger. Death itself loses its terrors, when he considers that its dominion extends only over a part of him, and that, in spite of death and time, the rage of the elements, and the endless vicissitudes of human affairs he is assured of immortal fame among the sons of men. There is surely a being that presides over the universe, and, with infinite wisdom and power has reduced the jarring elements into just order and proportion. He [the Man of Virtue] thinks not virtue an empty name, but justly esteeming it to be its own reward, he gratefully acknowledges the bounty of his creator, who by calling him forth into existence, has thereby afforded him an opportunity of once acquiring so invaluable a possession.

This has gone beyond doubt and Deism and it is all too easy to replace 'bountiful creator' with 'God' although here Hume stops short of acknowledging the immortality of the soul. But not so in the next essay, *The Platonist or the Man of Contemplation and Philosophical Devotion*:

> O philosopher! Thy wisdom is in vain, and thy virtue unprofitable. Where is the adoration due to infinite perfection . . . where is the gratitude, owing to thy Creator, who called thee forth from nothing? Where is the beauty to be found equal to that of the universe? Or virtue which can be compared to the benevolence and justice of the Deity? But it is our comfort that, if we employ worthily the faculties here assigned us, they will be enlarged in another state of existence, so as to render us more suitable worshippers; and that the task, which can never be finished in time, will be the business of an eternity.

Here is total acknowledgement of established religion. Hume's tongue must have been firmly in his cheek. Removing it, he demolishes all philosophy with a dismissive sting in the tail of *The Sceptic*:

> Human life is more governed by fortune than by reason: it is to be regarded more as a dull pastime than a serious occupation; and is more influenced by particular humour than by general principles. Shall we engage ourselves in it with passion and anxiety? It is not worthy of so much concern. Shall we be indifferent about what happens? We lose all the pleasure of the game by our phlegm and carelessness. While we are reasoning concerning life, life is gone; and death, though perhaps they receive him differently, awaits alike the fool and the philosopher. To reduce life to exact rule and method is commonly a painful, oft a fruitless, occupation: and is it not also a proof that we overvalue the prize for which we contend? Even to reason so carefully concerning it, and to fix with accuracy its just idea, would be overvaluing it, were it not that, to some tempers, this occupation is one of the most amusing in which life could possibly be employed.

After these intellectual exercises the edition ends with *A Character of Sir Robert Walpole*, a short essay which was subsequently demoted to being a footnote to *That Politics may be reduced to a Science* and was finally dropped altogether after 1770. Hume provides an introduction:

The Character of Sir Robert Walpole was drawn some months ago, when that great man was in the zenith of his power. I must confess that, at present, when he seems to be upon the decline, I am inclined to think more favourably of him and to suspect that the antipathy, which every true born Briton naturally bears to ministers of state, inspired me with some prejudice against him. The impartial reader, if any such there be; or posterity, if such a trifle can reach them, will best be able to correct my mistakes in this particular.

In the *Character* Hume obviously had ambivalent feelings towards the Prime Minister. As a devoted Whig he had established the supremacy of Parliament over the crown. Walpole had consistently opposed all forms of strife, since they were costly and interrupted business, including the ridiculous War of Jenkins' Ear which had broken out in October 1739. In 1731 a Captain Jenkins had been attacked by Spanish coastguards in what claimed to be Spanish territorial waters on the grounds, probably justifiable, that he was interfering with their trade in the West Indies. In the fight he had had an ear cut off which he kept bottled in preservative until displaying it in righteous indignation before the House of Commons in 1738. The Commons, in line with the fervent anti-Spanish feeling in the country, declared war. Walpole objected to this, as he had to causing any disruption, and he finally resigned in 1742. The war, as such, was of no interest whatsoever to Hume. But Walpole's character was:

I wish for the honour of our country, that any one character of him had been drawn with such judgement and impartiality, as to have some credit with posterity, and to show that our liberty has, once at least, been employed to good purpose . . . a man of ability, not a genius, good natured, not virtuous, constant, not magnanimous, moderate, not equitable (Moderate in the exercise of power, not equitable in engrossing it) . . . During his time trade has flourished, liberty declined, and learning gone to ruin. As I am a man, I love him, as I am a scholar, I hate him, as I am a Briton, I calmly wish his fall. And were I a member of either house, I would give my vote for removing him from St James's, but should be glad to see him retire to Houghton Hall to pass the remainder of his days in ease and pleasure.

Hume obviously approved Walpole's Whig politics, but decried his studied philistinism. Walpole had said, 'I always talk bawdy at the table, because in that all could join'.[18] This was certainly not David Hume's idea of table talk.

There is no doubt that the *Essays* would have benefited from a firmer editorial view, rather than relying on Hume's own judgement over the years. His attempts to sugar the pill of politics with diversions into *Impudence and Modesty* or *Essay writing* were embarrassingly unsuccessful and Hume later withdrew many of them. His attempts at satire and pastiche were heavy-handed and dull. But when writing what he wanted to and not what he thought he ought to, his style is elegant and remarkably polished. The philosophical essays contained much, in more palatable form, from the *Treatise* and Hume must have hoped that, at last, his philosophy would interest the general public. Instead he had established for himself a reputation as a political essayist. He was not altogether unhappy with this state of affairs although his most popular essay was his *Character of Sir Robert Walpole*, which was reprinted widely. The *Newcastle Journal* of 13 February 1742 listed ten questions to be answered by the author, and the *Scots Magazine*, which had published the *Character* in full, gave Hume the chance to reply. This was the eighteenth-century version of a television interview even although it was still presumed to be anonymous:

Q. In what sense may a person be allowed a man of ability in that business which at the same time it is asserted he has no genius for?
A. A genius, in English, signifies a man of extraordinary capacity, such as Richelieu, Cromwell, the Duke of Marlborough, the Duke of Orleans. Walpole and Fleuri, though great men are both inferior to the former.
Q. Upon what principle can it be supplied that a man of no magnanimity is able to support the character of constancy against a long and mighty opposition?
A. A Man of constancy perseveres in safe and constant measures: A magnanimous man perseveres in great and bold enterprises. It is not asserted that the minister is pusillanimous, but only that his character does not rise up to that height as to deserve the epithet of magnanimous.
Q. May the qualities of moderation and iniquity be placed in contrast without impropriety?

A. The author explained this by a note Viz., 'Moderate in the exercise of power not equitable in engrossing it.'

Q. With how much consistency may a man be termed not virtuous, who at the same time is characterised for virtues in several instances, free from the allay of vice; and, in others, his virtues more than his vices?

A. Virtue is, properly, good nature made steady and extensive by good principles. A man may have many virtues without deserving so noble a character.

Q. By what rule or method can it be discovered that a person whose abilities only appear fit for the second place in government would, nevertheless, have been esteemed worthy of the first, if he had never possessed it?

A. If his conduct in the first part of his life, prognosticates more genius than what appears in the latter. A man is well qualified for the second place in a government who excels in the detail of public business, by his affability, good sense, method, and application. Other qualities are requisite for the first place.

Q. Will the author of the character attribute the flourishing of trade to the measures of the Prime minister?

A. Yes: so far as the administration has been pacific, and private property has been preserved inviolate, by keeping parties from the courts of judicature. I speak with regard to England.

Q. What instances have we of the declension of liberty?

A. There are many instances, though, I hope, none fatal. Such as the increase of the civil list, votes of credit, and too large a standing army, etc.

Q. Is learning really gone to ruin?

A. To a great degree. What successors have Addison, Congreve, Prior, Newton, etc., left in Britain? Who are to succeed Pope, Swift and Bolingbroke?

Q. Are a man, a scholar, and a Briton so distinct things and opposite in their natures as that what is the object of love in one is the object of hate in another?

A. The same person may without any inconsistency be considered in several different reviews.

Q. Would not a plain and honest answer to the above enquiries greatly illustrate and confirm the justice of the character?

A. The character seemed as clear as was consistent with brevity.[19]

Hume's last answer is typical of an interviewee who is getting slightly cross with the interviewer and it, as well as the answer to question three, make it quite clear that Hume had not written the questions as well as the answers.

Henry Home had been asking his London friends to do what they could for the sales of the *Essays* and had been in touch with James Oswald of Dunnikier, the 27-year-old MP for Kirkcaldy who provided Home with gossip and new works hot off the press including Pope's *Dunciad*. He had been to school in Kirkcaldy where a school-fellow was Adam Smith. In later life it was said of him:

> His accurate discernment, consummate knowledge of business, indefatigable application, unquestionable integrity and disinterested friendship were relied on by all who were connected to him.[20]

In January 1742 Oswald wrote:

> Nothing can be more agreeable to me than either to recommend our friend Hume or his book . . . I am convinced Mr Hume's things will make their way and nothing shall be left on my part to let them be known as far as I can.[21]

A year later Hume was recommending to William Mure, now MP for Renfrewshire, that he strike up a friendship with Oswald:

> You cannot possibly find a man of more worth, of a gentler disposition, or better understanding.[22]

So Henry Home's introductions were proving worthwhile.

At the moment, however, Hume's spirits were high. He had visited the west of Scotland where he clearly had continued his friendship with Hutcheson as he wrote to Mure in September:

> I say not a word of Mr Hutcheson for fear you should think I intend to run the whole circle of my West Coast acquaintance.[23]

In November he wrote again to Mure asking him to vote against a Bill of Pains and Penalties against Walpole, now Earl of Orford, on 14 November 1742:

> having published to all Britain my sentiments on that affair, it will be thought by all Britain that I have no influence on you if your sentiments be not conformable to mine . . . I entreat you to get the

Bill about witches [it repealed the existing legislation making witchcraft a capital offence. Hume is being ironic] repealed and to move for some new Bill to secure the Christian Religion by burning Deists, Socinians, Moralists and Hutchinsonians . . . Make my humble compliments to the ladies and tell them I should endeavour to satisfy them if they would name the subject of the essay they desire . . . I see you are tired of my long letter and begin to yawn. What! Can nothing satisfy you and must you grumble at everything. I hope this is a good prognostic of your being a patriot.[24]

However varied we may find the *Essays* in quality, the publication was a success. David Hume had written a bestseller. Although a London correspondent of Henry Home's wrote to him that the public only appreciated 'flashy lively things' and 'trash', - a comment that would still find support today – the *Essays* were sold by three booksellers including 'A. Millar, over against St Clement's church in the Strand', who would become Hume's principal publisher:

In 1742 I printed at Edinburgh the first part of my Essays: The work was favourably received, and soon made me entirely forget my previous disappointment. I continued with my mother and my brother in the country; and in that time recovered the knowledge of the Greek language, which I had too much neglected in my early youth.[25]

Now the shame of unproductiveness was leaving him and by June 1742 he was, at last and at the age of 31, a successful author. He wrote a long letter to Henry Home on the 13th in great high spirits, discussing Cicero's *Orations*, gossiping about 'my flame' Betty Dalrymple [she married well elsewhere] and finishing with:

The Essays are all sold in London, as I am informed by English gentlemen of my acquaintance. There is a demand for them; and, as one of them tells me, Innys, a great bookseller in Paul's churchyard, wonders there is not a new edition for that he cannot find copies for his customers . . . They may prove like dung with marl and bring forward the rest of my philosophy, which is of a more durable, though of a harder and more stubborn nature. You see I can talk to you in your own style.[26]

Marl was a clay soil often used as a fertiliser, but when mixed with dung and straw, it set like concrete and was commonly used as a replacement for mortar in plastering. Hume here is talking to Home, a known enthusiast for modern farming methods, as a fellow country dweller.

Hume was now dividing his time between Edinburgh and the family farm at Ninewells where, with his brother and sister, John and Katherine, as well as his mother, the estate was starting to flourish. David with his temporarily meagre earnings, combined with his allowance, could maintain this style of life with comparative ease although it was not the life of total independence he hoped his pen might bring him. He was able to socialise with his aristocratic neighbours, however, and on 30 June 1739 had been 'very late' at Redbraes Castle, home of the Marchmont family at nearby Polwarth. George Hume, Master of Polwarth, had been Hume's godfather, and the young Lady Jane would have been part of the company. No matter what the circumstances Hume enjoyed female company, even if protected by the formal gallantry of his age, and he was always welcome in their drawing rooms.

However, more importantly, from now on he had no difficulty in attracting editors as well as admirers. Also, if we presume, and there is no proof, that he received a similar advance for Vol III of the *Treatise* as for Vols I and II, i.e.£50, then the same amount for the *Essays*, first edition, and the same amount again for the added essays in the second edition, Hume would have received earnings of £200 in the years 1740 to 1742. Add to this his allowance of £150 for these three years and he was on his way at least to comfort if not prosperity.

SEVEN

A Critical Season

David Hume may have been on his way to comfortable, if modest, prosperity, but his situation in Edinburgh was still precarious. The ruling establishment in Edinburgh was still deeply conservative and Hume was a liberal with dangerous Whig tendencies. The city could easily dismiss any fame brought about by the *Essays* as merely London-based, and, therefore, of no importance, and continued to regard Hume simply as a dangerously sceptical philosopher. In an age when patronage and sinecures were the order of the day Hume had no official position in the city. When he criticised the Whigs for rampant corruption they presumed he had turned Tory. The church still maintained a powerful grip on most aspects of the city and Hume was already labelled as a dangerous atheist. He would find no place in the establishment and would need to be carefully watched. The opportunity for him to become a part of the establishment came about because Frederick the Great of Prussia did not trust the Empress Maria Theresa.

The Holy Roman Emperor Charles VI had died in 1740 and his daughter Maria Theresa had inherited the throne of Austria. Immediately, as always with a female inheritrix, the vultures gathered. They quickly formed alliances with Bavaria, France, Spain and Prussia, led by Frederick the Great, on one side, with Britain, Holland, and Hanover coming to the aid of Austria on the other. James III & VIII, the Old Pretender, opportunistically allied himself with France and Prussia, hoping for a British defeat. Fortunes swung backwards and forwards, but with the withdrawal of Frederick from the Franco-Spanish alliance the Anglo-Dutch forces smelt victory after their successful battle at Dettingen in 1743. This can hardly have been achieved solely because George II led his forces in person, but he was the last British sovereign to do so. Frederick then re-entered the conflict, giving the French enough spirit to defeat the British army at Fontenoy and Lauffield. Walpole had foreseen that the struggle might resolve itself into a war between Britain and France, which, if Britain lost, could see a Stuart back on the throne.

As always, he opposed the war, but was replaced as Prime Minister, with the real power being held by Lord Carteret at the Foreign Office, and there was now a British army pinned down in the Netherlands.

The Physician-General to these forces was one Dr John Pringle who also held the chair of Ethics and Pneumatical Philosophy at the University of Edinburgh. 'Jupiter' Carlyle, who was a pupil of Pringle's, recollects:

> Dr Pringle . . . was an agreeable lecturer, though no great master of the science he taught. His lectures were chiefly a compilation from Lord Bacon's works. And had it not been for Puffendorf's small book, which he made his text, we should not have been instructed in the rudiments of the science. Once a week, however, he gave a lecture in Latin, in which language he excelled.[1]

In a footnote Carlyle comments, 'he held the chair of Moral Philosophy, which he clearly considered a secondary subject'. Such pluralism was quite typical of the time, and during his increasingly frequent absences his chair was occupied by a William Cleghorn. Pringle had offered his resignation in June 1744, but added that he would only deliver it formally if specifically required by the City Council, who held the ultimate authority to appoint university staff. The Provost, John Coutts, father of the brothers who founded the famous bank, was a friend of Hume's and immediately suggested that Hume should apply for the post. In a letter to Mure on 4 August 1744 Hume takes up the story:

> I accordingly did so, and being allowed to make use of the Provost's name, I found presently that I should have the whole Council on my side, and that indeed I should have no antagonist. But when the Provost introduced the Doctor's letter [of his willingness to resign if asked], he discovered that he had in secret wrote differently to some of his friends who still insisted that the town should give him [an] allowance to be absent another year. The whole Council, however, except two or three exclaimed against this proposal and it appeared evidently that if the matter had been put to a vote there would have been a majority of ten to one against the doctor. But Mr Couts [sic], though his authority be quite absolute in the town, yet makes it a rule to govern them with the utmost gentleness and moderation and this good maxim he sometimes pushes even to an extreme. For the sake of unanimity, therefore, he agrees to an expedient started

by one of the doctor's friends, which he thought would be a
compliment to the doctor, and yet would serve the same purpose as
the immediate declaration of a vacancy in the office. This expedient
was to require either the doctor's resignation, or a declaration upon
honour that, whether it were peace or war in any event, he would
against November 1745 return to his office and resign his
commission as physician to the army, or any other emolument
incompatible with his attending in this place . . . we shall receive
his answer in a fortnight, upon which my success seems entirely to
depend.[2]

It is easy to see Hume's frustration both with Pringle's prevarication,
unsurprising on Pringle's part since he was being paid a guinea a day as
physician to the army, and with Coutts's even-handedness. All of this
meant further delays, and Hume had to turn down the offer of a tutorship
to the son of Murray of Broughton in Dumfriesshire in order to stay in
contention for the professorship.

Pringle replied promptly that were he free to return he would, but he
was a soldier and therefore not free. But since the city was happy to cope
with his absence for another year, he assured them that by April he would
tell them whether or not he would return by the winter of 1745. This was
totally unacceptable and Coutts demanded Pringle's immediate resignation. Pringle refused and promised to return by November 1745. There
was a change of Provost in November 1744 and in March 1745 the chair
was declared vacant and the way for Hume was clear. But the lapse of time
had allowed the opposition to Hume to muster its strength:

The accusation of heresy, deism, scepticism atheism, etc., was
started against me, but never took being bore down by the contrary
authority of all the good company in town. But what surprised me
extremely was to find that this accusation was supported by the
pretended authority of Mr Hutcheson and Mr Leechman
[Hutcheson's successor], who, 'tis said, agreed that I was a very
unfit person for such an office.[3]

It is not surprising that Hutcheson and Leechman felt Hume to be
unsuitable since one of the professorial duties was to lecture each Monday
on the truth of the Christian religion. It is inconceivable that Hume
thought he could carry out such duties with tongue in cheek, but it is likely

that he thought an atmosphere of healthy debate could be created. In the academic climate of the time healthy debate was still encouraged only when it led to the confirmation of existing dogma. Debating the *Treatise* with Hume was pleasant enough intellectually for Hutcheson but orthodoxy was orthodoxy. Hume was quite simply moving too fast.

The Council met again on 3rd April and elected Francis Hutcheson to the post, calling for the Edinburgh clergy to ratify the appointment by giving an *avisamentum*, or note of advice. This they presumably did in Hutcheson's favour and the call for his appointment went ahead. For Hume, now living in England near St Albans, the matter seemed to be closed.

In fact the affair was only just starting to heat up since on 10th April Hutcheson refused the appointment on the grounds of his age – he was 51 and would, in any case, die in a year's time. Hume and the substitute professor William Cleghorn were now the only two other reasonable candidates, and a vote at this time would probably have gone in Hume's favour. But again the Council delayed asking the clergy for another note of advice. The delay also allowed political interests to take a part since the Council's troubles were widely known, even reaching the ever open ears of the Marquess of Tweeddale, Secretary of State for Scotland, and Prime Minister Carteret's son-in-law. He had followed his father in belonging to a now almost defunct breakaway Whig faction opposed to the Act of Union known as the 'Squadrone Volante' and was bitterly opposed to Coutts's traditional Whig views. He could also use the power of patronage to ensure that Hume's supporters changed their minds. William Wishart, the Principal of the University, was drawn into the fray and wisely, if dishonestly, reported on Hume's unsuitability by distorting Hume's conclusions 'in the grossest way in the world'. Hume did find a significant supporter in Robert Wallace who was an influential minister, an ex-Moderator of the General Assembly, who had written a sermon entitled *Ignorance and Superstition, a Source of Violence and Cruelty.* He was, however, loath to come forward. The writer of a letter correcting the report of the affair in Hume's obituary in the *London Chronicle* had some inside information:

> In an account of the life and writings of the late David Hume esq., inserted in your and several other newspapers, I observe one particular related in the following words, 'In 1746 he stood

candidate for the chair of Moral Philosophy at the University of
Edinburgh then vacated by the then present Sir John Pringle,
appointed physician to the army. Every one was convinced of Mr
Hume's abilities and his interest was warmly supported by the
nobility and the gentry; but the presbytery of Edinburgh, having a
right to object to one out of three candidates named by the council
put their negative upon honest David whose sentiments were too
liberal for their narrow minds.'[4]

This is full of inaccuracies. The Lord Provost, magistrates, and Council of
Edinburgh possessed an exclusive right of choosing most of the professors
of the University, but every election had to be made with the advice of all
the ministers of that city, not just the presbytery. The vacancy was in 1745,
not 1746. Hume's interest was not supported by the nobility and gentry,
but 'depended chiefly on the influence of his friend Mr Coutts, the late
provost, a spirited man'. The clergy grounded their objection on the
Treatise, but Dr Wallace did not 'think himself entitled to give an opinion,
on pretext too of a juvenile as well as anonymous performance which had
been little read and which was less understood'.

The last two phrases have a familiar ring to them, even today, when
books, plays and films are usually objected to by someone who has never
read or seen them but has 'been informed about them'. First-hand
knowledge can be bad for bigotry. In August 1744 Hume, now fairly
certain that his candidature was in the hands of factionalism, came North
to spend a week in Kirkcaldy with James Oswald. Along with Henry
Home they visited Cupar where the threesome, in best eighteenth-century
fashion, got uproariously drunk while David regaled them with his views
on corruption far into the night.

Back in Edinburgh, the ministers, unsurprisingly, voted against Hume,
and although the Council had the power to ignore their *avisamentum*,
with the Marquess of Tweeddale's influence hanging above them, they
chose not to use that power. 'Provost Coutts was pleased to say in the
meeting this week that he believed that most of the clergy who gave their
avisamentum against Mr Hume had never read the pamphlets whence
people had taken a bad impression of him.'

All this was reported to Hume in St Albans and he wrote a defence of
the *Treatise* to Henry Home who rushed it into print on 21st May, under
needless anonymity, as *A Letter from a Gentleman to his Friend*.

In it Hume restates much of the *Treatise* as 'arguments that would stand at Salamanca' – a Spanish university known since the Middle Ages for the rigour of its logic – including his arguments on cause and effect as well as denying that he had ever attacked natural religion. All the time he knew that his arguments would fall on deaf ears:

> 'Tis impossible ever to satisfy a captious adversary, but it would be easy for me to convince the severest judge that all the solid arguments for natural religion retain their full force upon the author's principles concerning causes and effects and that there is no necessity even for altering the common methods of expressing or conceiving these arguments.[5]

At the Council meeting on 5th June Cleghorn was sworn in as Professor of Pneumatics and Moral Philosophy. He continued uneventfully in the post until his death without ever publishing a word:

> The matter was brought to an issue and by the cabals of the Principal, the bigotry of the clergy, and the credulity of the mob, we lost it.[6]

This was Hume's last official contact with the University from which he had failed to graduate. He is remembered by a truly awful building in his name – the David Hume Tower – built when the University vandalised one of Edinburgh's most beautiful Georgian squares.

The *Treatise*, however, was far from dead and its misinterpretation would haunt Hume for the rest of his life. He put a brave face on his rejection, saying that he was never 'very fond of this office', and he does not mention it in *My Own Life* but he was understandably hurt by it. He had rejected the offer of a tutorship during the campaign since he realised that he must find employment apart from his pen, but when a second offer of a tutorship came along he accepted it with alacrity:

> In 1745 I received a letter from the Marquess of Annandale inviting me to come and live with him in England: I found also that the friends and family of that young noblemen were desirous of putting him under my care and direction, for the state of his mind and health required it. I lived with him a twelvemonth: my appointments during that time made a considerable accession to my small fortune.[7]

The Marquess was said to have been 'charmed with some things in your essays', and the first accession to Hume's fortune was an advance paid by 'Ronald Crawford Writer to the Signet by direction of the Marquess of Annandale, one hundred pounds sterling'.[8] The Marquess was indeed in need of a companion. He already had had several and his story is briefly told:

> George van den Bempe, 4th Marquess of Annandale. Born 29th May 1720. He became deranged by the death of his brother John in 1742. On 5th March 1747 an inquest found that the Marquess was a lunatic, incapable of governing himself and managing his own affairs; and that he had been in this state of mind from 12th December 1744. He survived until the 18th April 1792 when he died at Turnham Green after having completed the seventy second year of his age.[9]

Hume was about to learn a hard lesson in the deviousness of men, a trait he had as yet encountered only marginally in the appointment to the professorship. But, at first, all went well:

> Every thing is much better than I expected from the accounts I heard after I came to London . . . my Lord was never in so good a way before. He has a regular family, honest servants, and everything is managed genteely and with economy. He has entrusted all his English affairs to a mighty honest friendly man Captain Vincent, who is cousin germain* to the Marchioness. And as my Lord has now taken a turn to solitude and repose as he formerly had to company and agitation 'tis to be hoped that his good parts and excellent dispositions may at last, being accompanied with more health and tranquillity, render him a comfort to his friends and his country.[10]

So Hume had been warned already that the situation might be complicated and Henry Home had not been wholehearted in recommending Hume for the post since he felt that his friend would be better occupied in pursuing his literary career in Edinburgh. Henry Home, as a neighbour of Hume's family, suggested that Hume should make sure that his brother and sister had more social life and that his brother, John, should marry

* second cousin

soon. This was becoming a necessity since mother Katharine was now seriously ill. But all seemed well enough and in April Hume moved in with the Marquess in his house at Weldehall, four miles south of St Albans, although he did ask Sir James Johnstone, the Marchioness's brother-in-law and business manager in Scotland, for a written contract. This came via that 'mighty honest and friendly man' Captain Philip Vincent of the Royal Navy. Hume was to be paid £300 a year and, if he chose to leave, he would be paid in full for the quarter in which he left. If the Marquess chose to dismiss Hume on a whim, as he had done with previous companions, he would be paid for the full year. Life with the Marquess was not of the easiest and he had to write to Sir James explaining a small but necessary deception:

> You would certainly be surprised and vexed to receive a copy of the
> novel which was in your hands when you left London . . . the
> vanity of the author returned with redoubled force . . . in short we
> were obliged to print off thirty copies, to make him believe that we
> had printed a thousand, and that they were to be dispersed all over
> the kingdom. My Lady Marchioness will also receive a copy.[11]

The warning was needed since the Marquess's 'novel' was an account of an affair he had unsuccessfully attempted, and the deceit was clearly successful since his behaviour caused Hume 'ennui sometimes' but no more. The Marquess even composed some French verses in praise of Hume.

The situation was working to Hume's advantage since his daily attendance was not needed. In fact Hume was planning to divide his time between Weldehall and London and use what leisure he had for essay writing and spending time with James Oswald. Vincent had proposed to Sir James that 'my friend Mr Hume, a very worthy and knowing man', should be given an annuity of £100 for life. Sir James felt, correctly, that the Solicitor General for England, in whose gift such payments were, would refuse.

The Marquess was now becoming more and more withdrawn, demanding total solitude, and suffering from self-imposed bulimia. Also Vincent had written to Sir James giving an account of the state of affairs at Weldehall which caused Hume to write on his own behalf asking for a meeting. Since this letter would have arrived in Dumfries at about the same time as Charles Edward Stewart, the Young Pretender, defeated the English army of Sir John Cope at Prestonpans and began his march south into England, Hume realised that journeying across the country might be difficult on account of the 'present unhappy troubles'. Hume was feeling friendless, and misrepresented by Vincent, and later would say that he felt all his letters were opened. Relations between the 'mighty honest and friendly man' and the 'very worthy and knowing man' were now reduced to hostility. By October he was desperate and told Sir James:

> God forgive you, Dear Sir, God forgive you, for neither coming to us nor writing to us. The unaccountable, and, I may say, the inhuman treatment we meet with here, throws your friend into rage and fury, and me into the greatest melancholy.[12]

And then a week later:

> I must begin by complaining of you for having yoked me to a man of the Captain's character, without giving me the least hint concerning it, if it was known to you, as it is no secret to the whole world.[13]

Hume had suggested moving the Marquess and his establishment to a smaller house, while Vincent was blackening his name to the Marchioness:

> Mr Hume is a scholar, and I believe an honest man; but one of his best friends at Edinburgh first wrote me, he had conversed more with books than the world, or any of the elegant part of it, chiefly owing to the narrowness of his fortune. He does not in this case seem to know his own interest, though I have long perceived it is what he mostly has a peculiar eye to. Hereafter I shall consider him no more than if I had never known him. Our friend in reality does not desire that he should stay with him.[14]

Hume must have got wind of these slanders, for he wrote to Vincent:

> My Lord, far from having a quarrel with me, said this evening that he wished one could form a plan by which we might go together to some foreign country, change our names, and remain absolutely concealed and unknown. You see then, that his proposals proceed only from his excess of solitude.[15]

He also made his views on Vincent known to Sir James:

I shall not, however, conclude without telling you that, when I became absolutely certain of this man's character, I was anxious to know the character he bore in the world, and for that purpose wrote to Mr Oswald (with whom I live in great intimacy), to desire him to inform himself of the matter, which he was easily enabled to do by his connexions in the navy. He answered me that he was universally regarded as a low, dirty despicable fellow; and particularly infamous for pimping his wife to another peer.[16]

But provided no harm came to her son, the Marchioness was unconcerned about the conflict occurring at Weldehall, and Sir James was content to vacillate to the end of time. The referees had no interest in anything but a quiet life. Hume continued to apply himself as a companion, but was finding his master's moods more and more wearisome:

Paniotty [the Marqess's valet] desired him to rise and take a little exercise, and, in my sight, he tried him with one of the rudest exercises in the art of fencing (which I remembered had almost dislocated my whole body when I tried it) and yet he never complained. He had today several short fits of high spirits mixed with his low ones. This is not a history of the weather, but of something as uncertain.[17]

Vincent now openly demanded Hume's departure, and Hume voiced his discontent to Lord Elibank who wrote to Sir James:

I own it is my opinion that Vincent's only view in turning off Hume is that he finds him an obstacle to selfish views of his own, to which even lady Annandale may in time become a sacrifice. This I say from my personal knowledge of the man.[18]

Henry Home entered the fray, but as he had been uneasy at Hume's appointment, the possibility of his being dismissed was not unattractive in itself, but 'I thought instantly of writing him a letter not to stay under any terms after such an affront'. He advised James Johnstone to 'interpose that no more attempts of this kind be made'.[19] But on 16th April Hume and the Marquess parted for the last time.

He wrote to Sir James:

My only crime has been too little dissimulation, and too strong an indignation at meeting with treachery and perfidiousness when I did not expect it . . . I shall always have a grateful regard and memory of your friendship. I have found in this whole affair that some men are honest and sincere and others not so. A very slender discovery you'll say; but which, however, may be useful to me by teaching me not to trust too much to professions and appearances. I am, dear sir, your most humble and obedient servant, David Hume.[20]

And that should have been the end of the sorry affair. But while Vincent paid Hume his £300 for the year 1745, he refused to pay him the £75 due for the first quarter of 1746. This was a meaningless act of petty revenge in which he was clearly in the wrong, but Vincent died in 1746, and Hume, on advice from Henry Home, went to the Court of Session and by 1761 the matter was finally settled out of court. He had conquered his 'indolence and aversion to bargaining'. He had also had a lesson in the perfidy of his common man and was becoming more streetwise, even if the experience had been a painful one.

His other painful experience in the early part of 1745 was to hear of his mother's death while he was at Weldehall. The date of her death is unrecorded but on 15th June he wrote to Henry Home:

I receive very melancholy letters from my brother, which afflict me very much. My mother's death, which makes an immense void in our family, along with my absence, and his disappointment in love, sink him I find very much.[21]

In *My Own Life* he had described his mother as being 'of singular merit' and she had, in fact, been both mother and father to David. He would have known the economic struggles she had during his youth and education and her bafflement at the course of life he had chosen. She had been in poor health since 1743, when he had refused to leave home, but now she had died while he was absent from Ninewells. She was probably 62 years old and her cause of death is unknown. Eight years later, Mrs Carlyle, wife of 'Jupiter' Carlyle, was debating Hume's supposed atheism with Patrick Boyle, minister of Irvine in Ayrshire:

Mrs Carlyle asked Mr Boyle if he thought David Hume was as great an unbeliever as the world took him to be? He answered that the world judged from his books, as they had a right to do; but he thought otherwise, who had known him all his life, and mentioned the following incident: when David and he were both in London, at the period when David's mother died, Mr Boyle, hearing of it went into his apartment – for they lodged in the same house – when he found him in the deepest affliction and in a flood of tears. After the usual topics of condolence, Mr Boyle said to him. 'My friend, you owe this uncommon grief to your having thrown off the principles of religion; for, if you had not, you would have been consoled by the firm belief that the good lady, who was not only the best of mothers, but the most pious of Christians, was now completely happy in the realms of the just.' To which David replied, 'Though I threw out my speculations to entertain and employ the learned and metaphysical world, yet in other things I do not think so differently from the rest of mankind as you may imagine.' To this my wife was a witness.[22]

Hume's reaction could also be interpreted as 'atheists also cry', but he was undoubtedly deeply distressed at the news of his mother's death. Nothing is known of John's unsuccessful suit, but he was obviously following Henry Home's advice and looking for a wife. Ninewells needed a chatelaine and sister Katharine might marry and leave. At the moment, however, David Hume was becoming more and more remote from his family.

He did also manage to remain aloof from the other great event of 1745, the Jacobite Rebellion of Charles Edward Stewart – 'Bonnie Prince Charlie' – to install his father in London as James VIII and III. 'Jupiter' Carlyle called it a 'trifling insurrection'. Hume, a devoted Whig, viewed the possibility of a Stewart restoration with horror but some of continental Europe looked on it with more than a modicum of enthusiasm. On 25 July 1745 Prince Charles Edward landed, almost alone, in Scotland and called on the Highland clans to form an army. By September, due to luck and the ineptitude of General Sir John Cope, he was threatening Edinburgh itself where the population trembled at the approach of what was regarded as a horde of uncivilised barbarians set on rape and pillage. In fact the Jacobite army numbered only about 5,000 but rumour put the number at three times that amount. Hume expressed the views of an educated but prejudiced Lowlander:

The Highlanders are altogether as ignorant of Discipline as the Low-Country Ploughmen and know as little the Nature of Encampments, Marches, Ranks, Evolutions, Firing, and all other parts of Military exercise which preserves order in an Army, and renders it so formidable. They advance to battle in a confused heap, which some people have been pleased to call a column: they can use no weapon but a broadsword which gives not one wound in ten that is mortal, and obliges each combatant to occupy double the ground that would suffice did he employ the pushing sword or the bayonet. They become weaker by their victories; while they disperse to their homes, in order to secure the plunder they have acquired . . . The barbarous Highlander, living chiefly by pasturage, has leisure to cultivate the idea of military honour; and hearing of nought else but the noble exploits of his Tribe or Clan he soon fancies that he himself is born a hero as well as a gentleman.[23]

Hume had an equally bleak view of the forces deployed to defend the capital after the regular dragoons had fled to nearby Prestonpans:

There were of the Town Guards ninety six men, augmented at that time to 126. These are rather elderly men, but pretty well disciplined; and, indeed, the only real force the Provost was master of. The rest were, in a word, undisciplined Britons, which implies just as formidable an idea as undisciplined Romans, or undisciplined Indians. They were nominally divided into the Trained-Bands, the Edinburgh Regiment and the Volunteers. But this division was really what the schoolmen call a distinction without a difference. For with regard to military prowess they were much the same. As to the Trained-Bands (commonly about 1200 men) In what condition that formidable body may be at present, or might have been in at the time of the rebellion, I cannot tell; But I remember, when I was a boy, I had a very contemptible idea of their courage . . . for as they were usually drawn out on birthdays, and marched up through the main street, it was very common for any of them that was bolder than usual, and would give himself airs before his wife or mistress, to fire his piece in the street, without any authority or command from his officers. But I always observed that they shut their eyes before they ventured on this military exploit; and I, who had at that time been accustomed to fire at rooks and magpies, was very much diverted by their timorousness. (But their arms were so bad that a very moderate charge of powder would have made them burst about their ears.)[24]

The Jacobite army passed through the city to rout the Government forces at Prestonpans (sometimes called Gladsmuir). Prince Charles took up residence in Holyrood Palace and prepared for an ill-fated march on London. Many of the leading Whigs simply kept their heads down and waited for the storm to pass. 'Jupiter' Carlyle was ordered to stop on the highway by four armed Highlanders, but he gave them a shilling and they went away happy. One of their officers told him that they would desert as soon as they had either a full purse or a full belly. Henry Home, 'to divert him from brooding over the fate of his country', retired to Berwickshire and wrote *Essays upon several Subjects concerning British Antiquities*, a Whig justification of the Union of the Parliaments. He argued that Scotland's first law came with Malcolm Canmore and was inspired by Norman feudalism. The Scottish parliament was unicameral and, thus, too close to the power of the crown, while the British parliament's bicameral system allowed for resistance to royal power:

> The late King James was set aside by the sovereign authority of the nation . . . the peace of society is an object of greater importance than the right of any particular man can be, supposing him to be descended from a thousand kings.[25]

During the main part of the Rebellion Hume was at Weldehall with, when the Marquess was calm enough, occasional excursions to London for research and relaxation. As the Highland army, such as it was, neared the capital, anti-Scottish feeling rose and London became a dangerous place for a Scotsman. On the 4th December the Jacobites reached Derby where Prince Charles realised that his army was fading away and England was not rising in support. It was to be their furthest point of advance and they began the long march north which would end outside Inverness, on Culloden Moor. There the exhausted, ill-armed, untrained and ill-disciplined remnant were brutally annihilated by well-trained Lowland and English regiments. Prince Charles Edward had led the Highlanders into a campaign which would bring about the collapse of their traditional culture. Such sentimental romanticism had no place in the mind of a rational sceptic such as Hume who believed, not in feudal loyalty to a clan chief, but in individual freedom. When the news of Culloden arrived in London, the Scots Carlyle and Smollett walked with drawn swords:

lest the mob should discover my country and become insolent, 'For John Bull,' says he, 'is as haughty and valiant tonight as he was abject and cowardly on the Black Wednesday when the Highlanders were at Derby'.[26]

One aftermath of the Rebellion was that Archibald Stewart, Hume's old supporter for the professorship, was now a prisoner in the Tower of London. He had been Provost of Edinburgh and had been imprisoned by the Jacobites for opposing them when they occupied the city, and then, to double his misfortune, when the city was liberated by Government forces, he was sent to the Tower for having surrendered the city. He was taken back to Edinburgh and tried before the High Court of Justiciary on 24 March 1747 for 'neglect of duty and misbehaviour in his office', and after numerous adjournments by the now embarrassed court he was acquitted eight months later.

Hume had written to John Coutts to know the facts of the Jacobite occupation of Edinburgh and on 8 November 1745 Coutts wrote to Mure:

I wrote to Mr Oswald last post and sent him a state of facts relating to the rebel army into Edinburgh as I could make them out from memory. Mr Hume wrote anxiously to know the state of that affair. I wrote him enclosed in my letter to Mr Oswald and I desired Mr Oswald to furnish him with a copy of the facts. In case my letter to Mr Oswald has miscarried you'll please forward to Mr Hume the enclosed letter with a copy of the enclosed narration which you may put, if you please, in some better order or dress.[27]

Hume had leapt to his old friend's defence in a pamphlet entitled *A True Account of the Behaviour and conduct of Archibald Stewart Esq*. It was dated 20 October 1747 with a postscript on 4th November. In fact Stewart's acquittal took place on the 2nd, so the pamphlet was too late to influence the trial, but Hume went ahead with publication, anonymously of course, the following year, declaring in it that 'I had just obligations to Mr Stewart as well as great personal regard for him'. All Edinburgh could identify the author. There had been some doubts as to whether Stewart would be acquitted, not because of his guilt, but because:

Several of the jury had been volunteers during the Rebellion and all of them were particularly distinguished by their warm zeal for the government.[28]

These jurors were largely Tory and Stewart's Whig friends dreaded 'Party Zeal'. 'Hypocrisy, violence, calumny, selfishness are, generally speaking the true and legitimate offspring of this kind of zeal.' Even among Whigs Hume found the 'religious Whigs' an altogether loathsome division and far removed from the 'political Whigs' with their love of 'laws and liberty' and 'whose chief regard is to the public good'. The pamphlet is a first example of Hume as an historian who delivers not merely a list of events but shrewd personal political judgements as well. The injustice he saw being meted out to Archibald Stewart from purely political malice must have reminded Hume of the factionalism he had suffered under during his bid for the professorship.

Stewart rewarded Hume for his albeit tardy support with a 'batch of uncommonly good burgundy'. Hume said, 'The gift ruined me. I was obliged to give so many dinners in honour of the wine'.[29] At the time burgundy was practically unknown in the capital, and to this day Edinburgh thinks of itself as a 'claret' city with all other wines being viewed by the city's élite as mildly eccentric.

Hume's departure from Weldehall meant that he was once again without employment. He had earned over £400. His first act was to visit London, coincidentally on the date of the battle at Culloden. He was welcomed no doubt into the circle of James Oswald, but there was no possibility of Hume staying in London and he prepared himself to return to Ninewells. By the morning of Sunday the 18th May Hume had embarked his heavy baggage and was ready to sail for Berwick, when:

> I received a sudden invitation from General St Clair . . . a few
> hours before I was due to go to Edinburgh.[30]

This last-minute reprieve came from the Honourable James St Clair, who had been a Colonel in the 1st Regiment of Foot, the Royal Scots, had already served in Flanders and would eventually rise to be a General in 1761. 'He does not seem to have been a brilliant soldier but possibly never had much luck.' He was a Scottish Member of Parliament and probably a friend of Oswald in whose company he would have met Hume. A friendship was formed between the two men and, when St Clair was given his orders he had to assemble a personal staff with the utmost speed. A secretary was essential, and one with some knowledge of the law was an advantage. Hume was a fellow Scot, likeable, with some legal training and immediately available. He accepted with enthusiasm and told his erstwhile employer, Sir James Johnstone:

I doubt not but you will be glad to hear, that I have not changed
my situation for the worse. The office is genteel: I have 10 shillings
a day besides perquisites, which may be considerable; and can be
put to little expense, because I live with the General. The invitation
I received was as unexpected as that which your friend [the
Marquess] gave me.[32]

Hume now had not only a healthy retainer as secretary to the General, but
the opportunity to charge a supplementary fee for every task he carried
out. The General was being paid £10 per day.

The orders St Clair had received were complex. Britain had established
a foothold on Cape Breton Island off the coast of French-occupied
Canada after Sir William Pepperell had taken the fortress of Louisburg
on the east of the island from the French in 1745. Patriotically, Pepperell
had spent £20,000 of his own money to equip the expedition. The island
guarded the southern entrance to the St Lawrence River and provided a
land approach through Nova Scotia to mainland Canada. Its position
meant that a two-pronged attack on French Canada was possible if
undertaken speedily enough. Speed, however, was not the watchword of
the government of the day. The landward attack would comprise forces
raised in America which could march from Albany to Montreal. Forces
landed from Britain at Louisburg could move up the St Lawrence and
seize Quebec. It was these forces that St. Clair was to command, and on
21st May the General left for Portsmouth. His orders were to proceed to
Louisburg and then move on to capture Quebec, preparing it as base for
the total conquest of Canada. If Louisburg had already been recaptured
by the French, St Clair was to retake it, and if he could not he was
instructed to withdraw to Boston for the winter and there reflect on
future action.

On 18th May David Hume had been an unemployed ex-tutor; now,
three days later, he was about to invade Canada. He managed to catch his
breath at Portsmouth and write to Henry Home:

A letter you have good reason to expect from me before my
departure for America; but a long one you cannot look for, if you
consider that I knew not a word of this matter till Sunday last at
night, that we shall begin to embark from hence in two or three
days, and that I had very ingeniously stripped myself of everything
by sending down my whole baggage for Scotland on Sunday

morning. Such a romantic adventure and in such a hurry, I have
not heard of before.[33]

But from a romantic adventure the expedition turned quickly to farce. By
25th May all the troops, except an infantry regiment, the Royals, were
embarked on transports at Portsmouth and on 30th May Commodore
Coates, the Naval officer in charge of the escorts, was given the order to
sail, only to have it rescinded on the same day. On 12th June the fleet of
transports was finally loaded with St Clair's troops, about 4,500 men.
They were escorted by three frigates and sloops, their provisions were
loaded for a six-month period and General St Clair boarded the *Superbe*
on the 14th. On the 15th they set sail, but due to contrary winds only
reached St Helens, a few miles away on the Isle of Wight, where they
anchored. After much tacking and fighting unfavourable winds they were
still at St Helens ten days later. Hume's spirits were still high although he
fretted at the delays. On 24th June he wrote to Henry Home:

> We are still dependent on winds and ministers of state and
> consequently in a very uncertain condition . . . The General is ill;
> though we hope that his distemper will prove only a fit of the gout
> and be no way dangerous . . . The season in which we can safely
> sail is limited to 10 days or a fortnight and the admiral's ship is still
> in the harbour and 'tis a great chance if she can get out to the road
> in that time. This joined to the declared aversion of the greatest
> part of the ministry to this project, renders our condition very
> uncertain . . . I shall mention the chief circumstance that
> prognosticates success, that the General is undoubtedly the only
> officer of his rank in Britain fit for this undertaking . . . As to
> myself, my way of life is agreeable, though it may not be as
> profitable as I am told, yet so large an army, as will be under the
> General's command in America, must certainly render my
> perquisites very considerable. I have been asked whether I would
> incline to enter the Service? My answer was, that at my years
> [Hume was 35] I would not decently accept of a lower commission
> than a company [i.e. become a Major]. The only prospect of
> working this point would be to procure at first a company in an
> American regiment, by the choice of the Colonies. But this I build
> not on, nor indeed am I very fond of it.[34]

Hume was becoming accepted by his military companions and this had clearly prompted his thoughts on accepting a commission. Thankfully he thought no more of it, although as events will show, he could scarcely have been a worse soldier than the professionals. He was already making his own account of the expedition: 'Having had opportunity of knowing [the] secret springs and causes of the whole I shall endeavour, for my own amusement to collect [the events]'.[35]

On the 25th, after a French squadron was heard to have sailed west for an unknown destination, St Clair was ordered back to Portsmouth and on the same day the Secretary at War, Henry Fox, ordered all the troops, except three regiments, to disembark.

Although Henry Fox may have been the Secretary at War, the orders were coming from Thomas Pelham-Holles, Duke of Newcastle, Secretary of State for the Southern Department:

> Personally the Duke was a petty creature, as much afraid of a damp bed as of the barest demonstration by a mob, insanely jealous of power, ridiculous in his tearful embraces and gabbling ejaculations.[36]

He was described by colleagues as a man who lost half an hour every morning and spent the rest of the day searching for it.

In late July he reinforced the expedition with Admiral Lestock in command over Coates, and gave orders to re-provision the fleet and prepare to sail. The troops were re-embarked for a second spell of misery on the transports. Hume was trying to ensure a modicum of rations were provided, and, as secretary, his signature appears on victualling orders as well as supplying stationery and office equipment. He even ordered fishing tackle to be issued to all ships with a view to some level of self-sufficiency. His housekeeping skills were coming in useful:

> The captains of the transports were croaking about the difficulties of a voyage across the Atlantic so late in the year and set the crews croaking likewise. Furthermore the soldiers and their officers were weary to death of the expedition to Quebec and would be thankful to hear it had been countermanded. Lastly, scurvy was raging in one regiment which had been on board ship for sixteen weeks, and this was not calculated to encourage the rest.[37]

The scurvy stricken regiment was the East Lancashires. By 1st August they sailed but by 8th August had to anchor in Sandown Roads on the east coast of the Isle of Wight having travelled about twelve miles on this occasion.

However, on the 3rd August St Clair, who now, reasonably, thought that they would never cross the Atlantic, decided to ensure that Hume would, at least, profit from the débâcle. He appointed his Judge Advocate, one Captain Grant, to be his aide-de-camp and gave the vacated position to Hume. This would mean that his current pay of ten shillings a day would, at the end of the engagement, which seemed imminent, continue as a lifelong pension of five shillings a day. Interestingly, Hume, as secretary, was to write and sign his own commission. He also continued to act as secretary to St Clair, thus for the moment collecting both fees.

It was now too late in the year for the assault on Canada, and simply transferring the troops to Louisburg would be an unnecessary expense. There was a safe harbour in Boston, but the prospect of paying an army for winter quartering was distinctly unappealing. This left Newcastle with the problem of making a decision and unfortunately St Clair had previously mentioned the idea of using the assembled force for a landing on France. He later said it was:

> at random and as the first thing that came into my head . . . why may we not frighten the French and alarm them as they have done us, by sending this squadron with the troops now ordered to some part of the coast of France, and as all their regular troops are on the Flanders and German frontiers it's not impossible but that such an alarm may make them recall some of them.[38]

Since there were large Huguenot populations on France's west coast, there was even a chance they might rise to ally themselves with the Protestant British. Hume pooh-poohed this idea: 'It is as if we were living in the time of the League [of Augsburg?] or during the confusion of Francis II's minority'.[39] But Newcastle seized on the idea since it would at least show some sign of activity. This was sorely needed since after the withdrawal of British troops from Flanders to stiffen resistance to the Jacobite rising of 1745 the French Marshal Saxe had won victory after victory. Therefore, on 26th August St Clair was ordered to go to Plymouth to await orders to procure a diversion, 'which is one great end of this expedition'. His orders, given on 22nd August, were somewhat lacking in precision: 'I doubt not but that you be able to suggest something of great service.'[40]

> Make a descent on some part of the Western coast of France . . .
> which might greatly annoy the French . . . give assistance to any of
> the French Protestant in Bretany [sic] who have risen and may be
> disposed to rise and cause an immediate diversion in Flanders. Take
> on pilots in such a manner that the secret may not transpire.[41]

How one hires pilots in secret was not made clear. The King was known to
be very keen that Bordeaux should be attacked, but Newcastle issued
orders to attack L'Orient or Rocehfort or La Rochelle. With consideration
of the need for secrecy St Clair could not ask his friends for maps of
Brittany, and begged Newcastle for intelligence of the coast of France,
although Hume felt that he might as well have asked for news of the coasts
'of Japan or California'. St Clair now faced the prospect of sailing without
'intelligence, good pilots, and beer for the squadron and transports'.
Newcastle sent maps of Normandy and Gascony, telling St Clair that
if the weather was bad he could always invade Normandy. He also
despatched a Major Macdonald, an expert on the Normandy coast,
and Captain Ephraim Cook, a pilot for the harbours of northern France.
Macdonald had a plan for taking Rouen, or Dieppe, or Abbeville, or Caen
by a force of 300 cavalry and 'accoutrements for three or four hundred
horsemen'. A few questions revealed both men to be rank impostors
although Newcastle excused this by saying on 11th September that Major
Macdonald might well be an impostor but he was the only expert who
could be found. Both Admiral Lestock and St Clair complained repeatedly
that they had no siege equipment, indeed no draught horses, little in the
way of artillery, and money only in the form of Mexican dollars. They did
have trappers and experts in the Indian languages of southern Canada. But
they had no maps of France. This latter problem was finally solved by
Captain Grant, St Clair's ADC, going into a bookshop in Plymouth and
buying a book which contained a map of France.

   L'Orient was the final choice for an attack since it was the headquarters
for the French East India Company with their rich warehouses. They had
also heard an unsubstantiated rumour that L'Orient was weakly defended
on the landward side. Hume commented that they were:

> to sail with the first fair wind, to approach an unknown coast,
> march through unknown country and attack the unknown cities of
> the most potent nation of the universe.[42]

Hume made several accounts of the campaign, some for 'my own amusement', some as official despatches, as well as sending a long letter to his brother.[43] A pocket book now in the British Library, was written as events unfolded[44] and the National Library of Scotland holds two other versions; one is a much corrected manuscript[45] and the other is the final version to be sent to London.[46] There are no major discrepancies between these accounts and Hume's trenchant comments appear in all of them.

This time they had favourable winds and in three days they lay off the coast of France. Hume describes the situation of L'Orient:

> L'Orient, formerly a small village, now a considerable town on the coast of Brittany, lies in the extremity of a fine bay, the mouth of which is very narrow, and guarded by the strong citadel of Port Louis . . . The town itself is far from being strong. Two sides of it, which are not protected with water, are defended only with a plain wall near thirty foot high, of no great thickness, and without any fosse or parapet. But the water which covers the other two sides rendered it impossible to be invested, and gave an opportunity for multitudes of people to throw themselves into it from every corner of this populous country . . . The East India Company had numbers of cannon in their magazines and had there erected a School of Gunners for the service of their ships and settlements. The vessels in the harbour supply them with more cannon and with seamen accustomed to their management and use, and whatever was wanting either in artillery or warlike stores could easily be brought by water from Port Louis with which the town of L'Orient kept always an open communication.[47]

The wind was offshore and landing had to be delayed, losing what little surprise they had had. They were awaited by 200,000 of the Gardes des Côtes who were ill-armed and ill-disciplined, 'formidable alone by their numbers, and in Brittany by the ferocity of the inhabitants esteemed of old and at present, the most warlike and least civilised of all the French peasants'.[48] But by a diversion St Clair landed 600 troops south of L'Orient and interrogated prisoners as to the best way to the town. The prisoners only spoke Breton and there were no translators. However, 'they were informed by a lame curate, the only person remaining in the village, that about a league* from hence there were two roads leading to

* A league was approximately four terrestrial miles.

L'Orient'.[49] The Militia fled and at first the campaign went in favour of St
Clair with his advance guard soon at the gates of L'Orient. The Governor
of L'Orient, the Marquis de L'Hôpital, was offered terms of surrender,
signed by 'David', who was still acting as secretary as well as Judge-
Advocate. The negotiations broke down and St Clair had to set about
laying a siege for which he had no equipment. He now had about a
thousand men ashore, from the Royals, the Gloucesters, the Black Watch,
the East Yorkshires and the East Lancashires, but under musketry fire
from the town the vanguard panicked and fled. In their flight they met
newly arriving soldiers who presumed they were the attacking French and
about twenty of St Clair's men were shot by their own side. These men
had been cooped up in appalling conditions in the transports, suffering
from sea-sickness as the unwieldy craft lumbered about at sea, and were
poorly fed and stricken with dysentery and scurvy. They also had probably
no idea where, or why, they were in France:

> Meanwhile every accident concurred to render the enterprise of the
> English abortive and some deserters got into the town who
> informed the garrison there of the true force of the English, which,
> conjecturing from the greatness and number of the ships they had
> much magnified.[50]

St Clair now had his somewhat depleted force of 3,000 men ashore and
was assured by his engineers that the walls of L'Orient could be breached
in twenty-four hours. Hume, with hindsight, commented:

> It has long been the misfortune of English Armies to be ill-served
> in engineers, and surely there never was on any occasion such an
> assemblage of ignorant blockheads as those which at this time
> attended us.[51]

Lestock agreed to unship four twelve-pound guns, which, with a mortar
firing red-hot shot, would breach the walls and quickly reduce the East
India depot to ashes. This plan took no account of the fact that, lacking
any horses, the guns had to be manhandled by the sailors some ten miles.
The now incessant rain turned the countryside into a quagmire. However,
St Clair still supported his engineer and his Director of Artillery:

> Though the general offered to place and support the battery
> wherever the engineer thought proper, he chose to set it above six

hundred paces from the wall where such small cannon find no manner of execution. He planted it at such an oblique angle to the wall that the ball thrown from the largest cannon must have recoiled without making any impression.[52]

The gunners did not have sufficient ammunition for the continuous bombardment needed and had forgotten to bring the furnace to heat the shot. A council of war was held on board the *Princessa* at which St Clair reported:

It appears by the Admiral's message to me by Brigadier Graham that he disapproves of the project and that the generals are unanimously against it, I give it up.[53]

St Clair decided to blow up what ammunition they did have, spike the guns and retire to the ships. However, the Marquis de L'Hôpital, hearing the explosions of what he took to be the start of a second onslaught, decided to surrender. He had seen that the British artillery was totally ineffectual, he had had sight and intelligence of St Clair's forces and so knew that he had a five-to-one superiority of numbers against a sick and ill-fed enemy. He also probably knew that a relieving force of battle-hardened troops were marching from Flanders to his aid. In spite of all this he marched out in full military glory with drummer, trumpeter and white flag. Unfortunately he found the field deserted with no one to receive his sword and he had to turn round and march back into L'Orient, having failed to surrender.

He had, at least, the satisfaction of watching the invading fleet depart and move south heading for Quiberon Bay. The inevitable storm blew up from the south, dispersing the fleet and five transports that found themselves separated and, without any orders to the contrary, turned for home.

The broad farce of the expedition was not without its tragedies and, in a letter of October Hume wrote to his brother of the tragic death of a friend, Major Alexander Forbes of the Black Watch:

a man of the greatest sense, honour, modesty, mildness, and equality of temper in the world. His learning was very great for a man of any profession, but a prodigy for a soldier. His bravery had been tried and was unquestioned . . . I found him with small remains of life, wallowing in his own blood, with the arteries of his arm cut asunder. I immediately sent for a surgeon, got a bandage tied to his arm and recovered him entirely to his senses and understanding . . . I die, says he, from a jealousy of honour, perhaps too delicate; and do you think, if it were possible for me to live, I would now consent to it, to be a gazing-stock to the foolish world . . . he became delirious a few hours before he died.[54]

Landing parties raided the two small and totally insignificant islands of Houat and Hoedic, gaining perhaps the only plunder of the expedition. The Governor of one of the islands was parted from his purse. 'It contained the important sum of ten sous, which is less than sixpence of our money.' Hume defended St Clair hotly:

A certain foreign writer, more anxious to tell his story in an entertaining manner than to assure himself of their reality, has endeavoured to put the expedition in a ridiculous light, but as there is not one circumstance of his narration which has truth in it, or even the least appearance of truth, it would be needless to lose time in refuting it. With regard to the prejudices of the public a few questions may suffice. Was the attempt altogether impracticable from the beginning? The general neither proposed nor planned it, nor approved it, nor answered for its success. Did the disappointment proceed from the want of expedition? He had no pilots, guides nor intelligence afforded him and could not possibly provide himself in any of these advantages, so necessary to all military operations. Were the engineers blameable? This has always been considered a branch of military knowledge distinct from that of a commander, and which is altogether entrusted to those to whose profession it properly belongs.[55]

St Clair also complained bitterly over the inefficiency he found:

The engineers . . . seem totally ignorant of what belongs in their profession; and I must particularly mention Mr Armstrong, the Director, as one who appears to me absolutely incapable to execute that employment, or to be entrusted with the command of the detachment of the train of artillery sent on the expedition.[56]

St Clair received a letter clearing him of all blame from the Duke of Cumberland, youngest son of George II. However, a pencil-written note in Hume's pocket book reveals the confusion that raged in the General's mind:

1. To sail immediately with the Guards alone.
2. To wait for the transports of 'Huske's regiment'
3. To put the Guards on board the men of war.
4. To replace them in the transports.
5. To disembark.
6. To re-embark.
7. To sail to the Downs.
8. To sail to Plymouth.
9. To disembark at Dover.
10. To disembark at Gravesend.
11. I omitted an order to wait till further orders.[57]

Finally they did none of these things. Hume and St Clair landed in Cork on the south coast of Ireland on 29th October having achieved nothing but at least with little loss of life. Marshall Saxe, having successfully completed his conquest of most of the Netherlands, put his troops into winter quarters. St Clair, to whom no blame had been attached, was now bound for Flanders and asked Hume to accompany him, although with no specific post in mind. Hume duly reported the offer to Henry Home:

> I have an invitation to go over to Flanders with the General, and an offer of table, tent, horses, etc. I must own I have a great curiosity to see a real campaign; but I am deterred by the view of the expense and am afraid that, living in a camp without any character and without any thing to do, would appear ridiculous. Had I any fortune which could give me a prospect of leisure, and opportunity to prosecute my historical projects, nothing could be more useful to me . . . But what can all this serve? I am a philosopher and so, I suppose, must continue.[58]

Hume was turning his thoughts to writing history and was now feeling himself to be a reluctant philosopher. He had enjoyed his time in the General's mess – 'a gay pleasurable life' with 'much enjoyment' – but recognised the essential shallowness of such an existence. To continue it without employment and, more importantly, without pay was pure folly. The matter of pay was much in Hume's mind since 'I am very uncertain of getting half-pay, from several strange and unexpected accidents'. He does not elaborate on these 'accidents' – they were 'too tedious to mention' – but he did not receive his due until sixteen years later. His bonhomie had assured him of entrée to the world of St Clair. It had also, thanks to the excellence of the General's table, provided Hume with the establishment of the waistline for which he would be famous. The days of the 'disease of the learned' were far behind him now.

His intentions were to return to London with the rather vague hope of finding something new, and, if not, to return to 'books, leisure and solitude in the country, an elegant table has not spoilt my relish for sobriety; nor gaiety for study'. In London he made the first steps to recovering his pension in motion and by August was back at Ninewells writing to his old whist opponent Colonel Abercromby of the Royal Scots for news of his erstwhile brother officers as well as asking for advice on how best to approach the Secretary for War in pursuit of his pension.

He was not totally indulging in leisure at Ninewells for he used the time available to look again at the *Treatise*. This revision would emerge in 1748 as *An Enquiry concerning Human Understanding*, but while at leisure he thought of publishing the work at once and confided to Oswald that he had mentioned his intentions to Henry Home who thought it 'indiscreet':

> I am at a critical season in life; and if I retire into solitude at
> present I am in danger of being left there, and of continuing a poor
> philosopher for ever . . . if I wait till I shall be able to make my
> name more generally known, something may offer of itself and even
> seek me in my solitude, as everything that has yet presented itself
> has done.[59]

This was not in any way true since it had been his own actions that had resulted in the publication of the *Treatise*. The result of that publication was his subsequent friendship with Hutcheson, which, in turn, had eased the path to his publishing the *Essays*, and thus his name came to the ears of the Marquess of Annandale. Acquaintance with Oswald had brought him to the notice of St Clair. But all of this stemmed from the *Treatise*. What Hume was suffering from was an exaggerated attack of self-pity, since he was not yet world-famous. He was increasingly prosperous and had a justified expectation that his subsequent work would be published, but he had had first-hand experience of the rich and powerful 'warts and all'. So why could he not have their wealth and influence? He was socially quite acceptable in their company and he knew he was intellectually their master, but he was taken up by them and dropped when his usefulness expired. Hume was merely experiencing what had been normal treatment for Mozart or Michelangelo and he was resentful. But then, so were they.

Hume's 'leisure' was, in fact, well occupied since, as well as revising the *Treatise,* he was preparing an edition of three more essays, *Of National Characters, Of the Original Contract* and *Of Passive Obedience,* to be published by Millar and Kincaid in 1748 as *Three Essays, Moral and Political,* before being incorporated into a third edition of the *Essays, Moral and Political* in the same year. Hume had originally intended to publish an essay *On the Protestant Succession* and had sent the manuscript to Oswald who gave it 'his approbation'. However, Hume was using Charles Erskine, Lord Tinwald as his agent in London for these essays and it was Erskine who, using the freedom Hume had given him, decided against *On the Protestant Succession* and to replace it with *Of National Characters.* Hume himself said of them: 'one is against the Original Contract, the system of the Whigs, another against passive obedience, the system of the Tories . . . I have established it as a maxim never to pay court to my superiors by any of my writings; but it is needless to offend them.'[60] In these essays Hume is writing with more assurance and style than previously but, naturally, still showing some of the entrenched attitudes of his century.

In *Of National Characters* he accepts that there are defining national characteristics which derive from either moral, or political, or physical causes such as air and climate. Moral causes such as proximity of profession appear in Hume's examples of soldiers and priests. He had just had experience of life among soldiers and his spectacles were strongly rose-coloured:

> The uncertainty of their life makes soldiers lavish and generous, as well as brave. Their idleness, together with the large societies which they form in camps and garrisons, inclines them to pleasure and gallantry . . . as they use the more the labour of the body than that of the mind, they are commonly thoughtless and ignorant.[61]

Priests, on the other hand:

> must not, like the rest of the world, give scope to their natural movements and sentiments. This dissimulation often destroys the candour and ingenuity of their temper, and makes an irreparable breach of their character.[62]

In the edition of 1753 he inserted a surprising footnote:

> Revenge is a natural passion to mankind; but seems to reign with
> the greatest force in priests and women. Because being deprived of
> the immediate exertion of anger in violence and combat, they are
> apt to fancy themselves despised on that account; and their pride
> supports their vindictive disposition.[63]

Later in the same essay comes another note which has hung around
Hume's neck like a millstone:

> I am apt to suspect the Negroes to be naturally inferior to the
> whites. There scarcely ever was a civilised nation of that
> complexion, nor even any individual eminent either in action or
> speculation . . . Negro slaves are dispersed all over Europe, of
> whom none ever discovered any symptoms of ingenuity . . . In
> Jamaica, indeed, they talk of one Negro as a man of parts and
> learning, but it is likely he is admired for slender accomplishments,
> like a parrot who speaks a few words plainly.[64]

However loathsome this opinion sounds to twenty-first century ears
Hume was, with very limited experience, merely reflecting the views of
his time. In 1758 he published *Of the Populousness of Ancient Nations* which
contained a lengthy condemnation of slavery, so there is some mitigation
of his patronising comments.

He makes wide generalisations over national characteristics:

> The French, Greeks, Egyptians, and Persians are remarkable for
> their gaiety. The Spaniards, Turks, and Chinese are noted for their
> gravity and serious deportment.[65]

He concludes that climate has little effect on national character and ends
by coming dangerously close to recommending selective breeding:

> The race of animals never degenerate when carefully tended; and
> horses, in particular, always show their blood in their shape, spirit,
> and swiftness. But a coxcomb may beget a philosopher; as a man of
> virtue may leave a worthless progeny.[66]

He draws no conclusions except to say that national characteristics do
exist, although there is no proof as to why they occur. It is a light-hearted
essay with a wittier style than some previous works, but still reads much

more like a first draft than a finished piece. Given that these three essays were published in what Hume knew to be a gap in his life, it seems that, in the tradition of the L'Orient expedition – 'go somewhere and do something' – these essays were rushed into print. Aware of this tendency in himself, Hume revised nearly all of his work throughout his life. The other two essays deal more directly with contemporary matters.

In *Of the Original Contract* and the extremely short *Of Passive Obedience* Hume deals with the philosophy behind the creation of political parties and again examines the vexed question of loyalty from the people to the sovereign and vice versa. Much of the ground had been covered in the *Treatise* and by Locke in his *Second Treatise* but Hume reassembles the arguments in what he hopes is a purely philosophical manner. He also attempts to put the arguments for government by a divinely appointed sovereign – the Tory view – and government by the will of the people – the Whig view – in an even-handed way. His conclusion is that the current compromise government of Britain is the best, or, possibly, the least bad form of government:

> The doctrine which founds all lawful government on an original
> contract, or consent of the people, is plainly of this kind; nor has
> the most noted of its partisans, in prosecution of it, scrupled to
> affirm that absolute monarchy is inconsistent with civil society and
> so can be no form of civil government at all; and that the supreme
> power in a state cannot take from any man, by taxes and
> impositions, any part of his property without his own consent or
> that of his representatives. What authority any moral reasoning can
> have, which leads into opinions so wide of the general practice of
> mankind, in every place but this single kingdom, it is easy to
> determine.[67]

He then leads into the question of passive obedience by citing Socrates' refusal to escape from prison and certain death because he had promised to obey the law. Hume says that this is a Tory conclusion from a Whig undertaking.

He continues the theme in *Of Passive Obedience*: 'the obligation to justice is founded entirely on the interests of society' and later '*salus populi suprema lex* – the safety of the people is the supreme law', and he goes on to say that Charles I and James II ruled as absolute sovereigns:

These were harmless, if not in their private character, good men: but mistaking the nature of our constitution, and engrossing the whole legislature, it became necessary to oppose them with some vehemence, and even to deprive the latter formerly of that authority, which he used with such impudence and indiscretion.[68]

Thus passive obedience can lead rulers to acts of injustice and thus to their downfall, destabilising the state. This stability can only be maintained by the populace shouldering their responsibilities to keep a rein on their rulers. But this must be a legal rein, since Hume had a horror of the mob. They represented animal emotion, not ordered reason. Hume's obvious desire to put both points of view, to praise and criticise both parties equally, led eventually to his being accused of Toryism by the Whigs and Whiggism by the Tories. This would depress him although he still corresponded cheerfully enough with Henry Home, praising Home's *Essay on British Antiquities* and, jokingly, accused him of 'borrowing some principles from a certain book'.

But then, as in the experience of Wilkins Micawber, 'something turned up'. So, by January 1748, Hume's address was first London, then Harwich, as he left on a military embassy which would take him to Vienna and Turin.

EIGHT

Like a Grocer of the Trained Bands

B y 1748 Europe was tiring of war. Marshal Saxe, having defeated Cumberland at Maastricht, controlled nearly all of the Netherlands, and Maria Theresa, the source of all the trouble, was losing her resolve for war, so Britain despatched an urgent embassy to remind her of her promise to invade Italy. After this not inconsiderable task they were to go to Turin and attach themselves to the King of Sardinia whom nobody trusted. The head of the mission was General St Clair. Such was his fondness and admiration for Hume that he sent for him to be his secretary and cipher clerk once more. Hume was delighted and, leaving the task of overseeing the publishing of the three essays with Erskine along with Oswald, set off for Harwich by coach. He wrote to his brother of the journey:

> Mr Wilson . . . who sat next to me in the coach, complained
> grievously at every jolt we received, of the enormous weight that
> was thrown on his little carcass, and swears that all his body,
> especially his shoulders are as black as his beard . . . But as this is
> only one jest in a thousand to which we fat people are exposed, I
> have borne it with great patience: Though I confess it has
> frequently excited my admiration why fat people should be so much
> the object of mirth, rather than lean, I am at a loss whether to
> ascribe it to the cowardice or benevolence of mankind. Perhaps we
> are not so commonly witty as you and, consequently, men think
> they will have an easy conquest in attacking us. Perhaps we are
> better natured and men think they run no risk of offending us. I
> leave this as a problem for you to discuss[1]

As we have seen, Hume had written, 'for my own amusement', a lengthy account of the *Descent on the Coast of Brittany* and in the spring of 1747, the previous year, had written to Henry Home about seeking 'opportunity to prosecute my historical projects'. Now, between March and June of 1748, he sent his comments on the embassy to his brother John Home: 'I have taken a fancy, for your amusement, to write a sort of journal of our travels'.

Hume was living in a time when political parties as we know them were only starting to emerge, and even in monarchies such as Britain the rights of the Parliament were being asserted and formalised. The rights of royal succession had been in armed dispute and Hume's embassy concerned itself, nominally at least, with France and Spain wishing to influence the succession in Austria. Worldwide trading posts were being turned into colonies and Hume had been part of an, albeit abortive, attempt to seize Canada from France. Many of his essays had a historical basis and Hume's personal involvement in diplomacy and the politics of the day must have stimulated him to examine the history of his own country. He had been reading classical history since his youth and was now experiencing the contemporary version. Before long he would have to fill in the gaps and he realised that this expedition would provide him with a first-class opportunity.

Before departing he had told James Oswald:

> I shall have a opportunity of seeing courts and camps; and if I can afterwards be so happy as to attain leisure and opportunities, this knowledge may even turn to account for me, as a man of letters, which I confess has always been the sole object of my ambition. I have long had an intention, in my riper years, of composing some history; and I question not but some greater experience of the operations of the field, and the intrigues of the Cabinet, will be requisite.[2]

Hume landed in Holland at Helvoetsluys (he named it Helvoet Sluice) after only a day's crossing. However, the disadvantage of a fast crossing was the roughness of the sea. 'I had the misfortune to be excessively sick. But the consolation to see an Admiral as sick as myself.'[3] He found Holland dull, 'for every part of it is like another. 'Tis an unbounded plain, divided by canals and ditches and rivers. The sea higher than the country; the towns higher than the sea; and the ramparts higher than the towns'. He visited the Hague, 'the beauty and elegance of which nothing can exceed', where he was less than impressed with the calibre of the Dutch troops but found the Prince of Orange had 'something of innocence and simplicity in his character which promotes more his popularity than the greatest capacity'. Three days later and by horseback to Breda where after the snow melted, 'we discovered Holland in all its native deformity. Nothing can be more disagreeable than that heap of mud and ditches and reeds, which they here call a country, except the silly collection and clipped evergreens which they call a garden'. In Breda he saw some French prisoners – 'such pitiful fellows as man never set eye on . . . Are these the people that have beat us so often?' At Nijmegen the confluence of the Rhine and Waal rivers had caused him to 'see nothing but the tops of trees standing up against the waters, which recalls the idea of Egypt during the inundations of the Nile'. But it was here that the party were joined by their wheeled transport. This was a chaise for the servants and a Berlin for the General and his immediate staff. This was a four-wheeled covered carriage, and as the now admittedly corpulent David Hume sank into its leather seats he must have had memories of the 'diligence' fourteen years earlier. His route was through Bonn (where he slept under his first duvet – 'too warm and suffocating'), Koblenz, Frankfurt, Würzburg and Ratisbon (Regensburg) to the Danube. He found this journey through the Rhine vineyards delightful, stopping off to visit battlefields and to notice, as one raised on a Scottish Border farm would, 'I never saw such rich soil, nor better cultivated'. He was hugely impressed with the several states and petty princedoms, having 'passed through many a Prince's territories and have had more masters than many of these Princes have subjects. Germany is undoubtedly a very fine country, full of industrious honest people, and were it united it would be the greatest power that ever was in the world. The people here . . . are not very much inferior to the English, notwithstanding all the airs the latter give themselves'. Finally at Ratisbon they took boat for Vienna. 'We were all very glad of this variety, being a little tired of our Berlin.' As no doubt Hume's companions were a little tired of the space he occupied. Their boat was newly built of fir planks and would be dismantled and sold as timber in Vienna while the erstwhile boatmen walked the 200-odd miles back home.

They arrived in Vienna on 7th April after travelling for just over a month, but had a delay of another week since the court could receive no one during Easter Week. They finally met Maria Theresa on the 15th. Count Podewils, the Prussian Ambassador, said:

> Her demeanour is sprightly and happy, and her greeting always warm and pleasant; there is no denying that Maria Theresa is a most charming and delightful woman.[4]

Hume found her not to be a great beauty or well shaped, but a woman 'of sense and spirit'. They were also presented to the Empress Dowager, Elisabetha Christina of Brunswick-Wolfenbüttel, the widow of the Emperor Charles VI, in whose august presence special protocols applied:

> You must know that you neither bow nor kneel to emperors and empresses, but curtsey. So that after we had had a little conversation with her Imperial Majesty, we were to walk backwards through a very long room, curtseying all the way: and there was a very great danger of our falling foul of each other, as well as of tumbling topsy-turvy. She saw the difficulty we were in and immediately called to us, 'Come, come, Messieurs, no ceremony. You are not accustomed to this exercise and the floor is slippery'. We esteemed ourselves very much obliged for this attention, especially my companions who were desperately afraid of my falling on them and crushing them.

Hume found the Austrian ladies delightful, especially Mademoiselle Stahrenberg, whose father was assistant to Prince Kaunitz, Maria Theresa's Chancellor, as well the countess Palfi, wife to the commander of the Hungarian army, who was 'worthy of a toast'. The men, however, with red heels to their shoes and well-dressed wigs, were ugly and awkward:

> A Court of Chastity is lately erected here, who send all loose women to the frontiers of Hungary, where they can only debauch Infidels and Turks; all whore-masters are punished as they deserve, that is, very severely. The promotion of several officers has been stopped by aspersions of this nature. And the Emperor lately could not prevail with the Queen to give a regiment to a young nobleman because it was supposed he wanted his maidenhead . . . There has been great noise made with us on account of the Queen's new palace at Schönbrunn. It is indeed a handsome house, but not very great, nor richly furnished . . . There is no very great amusement in this place. No Italian Opera: No French Comedy: No Dancing. I have however, heard Monticelli, who is the next wonder of the world to Farinelli. [Farinelli was the most famous castrato of his day, so we must presume Monticelli was another whose fame has, sadly, not lasted.]

So even allowing for the, in Hume's eyes, limited amusements, the embassy was enjoyable. But, unfortunately, it had to move on to Turin and the court of the King of Sardinia. The journey, in April 1748, was not, as Hume had hoped, via Venice, but directly over the Alps. Passing through Styria – present-day Steiermark – near Graz, Hume was horrified by the appearance of the population:

> The country is agreeable in its wildness; as much as the inhabitants savage and deformed and monstrous in their appearance. Very many of them have ugly swelled throats; idiots and deaf people swarm in every village, and the general aspect of the people is the most shocking I ever saw. One would think, as this was the great road through which all the barbarous nations made their irruptions into the Roman Empire, they always left here the refuse of their armies before they entered into the enemy's country; and that from thence the present inhabitants are descended.

The description of goitrous throats tells of thyroid disorders on a huge scale, probably from iodine deficiencies of one sort or another in the local diet. But Hume's fantasising about the destruction of Classical Rome is pure eighteenth-century belief. The ugliness continued until they climbed into the Tyrol but the descent into springtime on the Lomardy plain was delightful:

> every hour's travelling showed us a new aspect of spring. So that in one day we passed through all the gradations of that beautiful season, as we descended lower into the valleys, from its first faint dawn till its full bloom and glory.

They passed through Trent where had met an 'assembly of philosophers and divines who established such rational tenets for the belief of mankind'. This was the Counter-Reformation Council of Trent which met from 1545 to 1563 and codified Catholic belief, doctrine and ritual throughout the world. One can only think that here Hume is commenting with heavy irony.

They reached Turin on 8th May, twelve days after leaving Vienna. According to the Earl of Sandwich, 'Turin is the best place you can go to now. They have a polite and friendly court'. It was ruled by Charles Emmanuel III, King of Sardinia, who, confusingly, also controlled Savoy and Piedmont. It was he that St Clair was urging to greater military efforts. Unknown to both of them there was also a British mission meeting the French at Aix-la-Chapelle to negotiate a peace. One mission urging war and the other, simultaneously, negotiating peace provides a vivid example of the left hand not knowing the actions of the right. Unfortunately both hands were on the same man.

By 16th June Hume wrote to his brother that he had no idea when they might return but he hoped to tour France and Italy. This would be Hume's Grand Tour and would let him share the experience of most of his better-off contemporaries. This was not to be. The Treaty at Aix-la-Chapelle, while solving nothing politically, meant that his usefulness to St Clair was now limited but he remained with the General until his departure on 29th November.

During his time in Turin, he made the acquaintance of James Caulfield, Earl of Charlemont. He was an 18-year-old Irish peer, who had acceded to the earldom at the age of eight. His portrait by Hogarth at 13 shows a velvet-clad youth trying to look serious and instead looking vacantly pompous. In Turin he was attending the Royal Academy and it was probably there that he met with Hume, who was now famous if not notorious:

> [I met] The celebrated David Hume, whose character is so high in the literary world, and whose works, both as a philosopher and as an historian, are so wonderfully replete with genius and entertainment, when I was at Turin. He had then lately published those philosophical essays which have done so much mischief to mankind, by contributing to loosen the sacred bonds by which man alone can be restrained from rushing to his own destruction . . . their admired author was already, by public opinion, placed at the head of the dangerous school of sceptic philosophy . . . He had kindly distinguished me from among a number of young men . . . and appeared so attached to me, that it was apparent he not only intended to honour me with his friendship, but to bestow upon me what was, in his opinion, the first of all favours and benefits, by making me his convert and disciple . . .[5]

Grateful as the young peer was for Hume's friendship, his description of the philosopher's appearance is less than kind:

> Nature, I believe, never formed any man more unlike his real character than David Hume. The powers of physiognomy were baffled by his countenance: neither could the most skilful in that

science, pretend to discover the smallest trace of the faculties of his mind, in the unmeaning features of his visage. His face was broad and fat, his mouth wide, and without any other expression than that of imbecility. His eyes were vacant and spiritless and the corpulence of his whole person was better fitted to communicate the idea of a turtle-eating alderman, than of a refined philosopher. His wearing a uniform added greatly to his natural awkwardness, for he wore it like a grocer of the trained bands. His speech in English was rendered ridiculous by the broadest and most vulgar Scottish Accent, and his French was, if possible still more laughable. So that wisdom most certainly, never disguised herself before in so uncouth a garb. Though now near fifty years old [he was, in fact, thirty-seven. But to a teenager . . .], he was healthy and strong; but his health and strength, far from being advantageous to his figure, instead of manly comeliness, had only the appearance of rusticity. It was thought necessary that his secretary should appear to be an officer, and Hume was accordingly disguised in scarlet, while his broad face was rendered still broader by a wig *à la Militaire*.[6]

Many have commented on Hume's apparently vacant expression. The Scots description of it would, unfairly, be 'glaikit', and it is not uncommon among highly intelligent, but painfully shy, people. They simply put their mind into a receptor mode until they have collated enough information for a response. But Charlemont, like many after him, did feel himself admitted to Hume's friendship and he acknowledged Hume's love of mankind and total absence of rancour:

> Of all the philosophers of his sect none, I believe, ever joined more real benevolence to its mischievous principles than my friend Hume. His love to mankind was universal and vehement and there was no service he would not cheerfully have done to fellow creatures, excepting only that of suffering them to save their souls in their own way. He was tender-hearted, friendly, and charitable in the extreme.[7]

Charlemont had a close friend in the beautiful Countess of Duvernan, a 24-year-old lady of 'great sense and spriteliness'. Married to an 'old decrepit man', she was childless and a learned conversationalist:

> far from incurring any of those disgusting defects which study usually produces in a female scholar. Such was the woman to whom

I had the honour of paying my court, and in whose company I
regularly spent my evenings.[8]

Following his praise of her beauty and wit to him Hume was eager to meet
her, and Charlemont introduced Hume to the lady, whereupon David was
not only a regular visitor but appears to have fallen madly in love. She
questioned Charlemont closely about Hume, since 'I must inform you that
I have made a complete conquest of the great philosopher'. She then
invited Charlemont to witness her conquest of Hume:

> At his next visit which will probably be this evening, only take the
> trouble to hide yourself behind the curtain, and you shall be witness
> to a scene, which, if it does not make you angry, as indeed it ought
> not, will at least make you laugh, and when the comedy is over and
> your doubts removed, you must give me leave finally to discharge
> my troublesome admirer. Give me your word that you will on no
> account discover yourself, as that might not be to my advantage.
> The illustrious philosopher lost no time in preliminaries. No sooner
> was he in the room than he plumped down on his knees before her.
> He addressed her in the usual commonplace strain, that he was
> smothered with love. 'Dear, dear lady I am desolate, cast into an
> abyss and totally destroyed.' The lady replied that it was nothing
> more than a natural operation of his philosophy and asked him to
> rise. It was a picture of old ugly, blubbering, fat, ungainly passion.
> Silenus on his knees to one of the Graces or a bear making love to
> an Italian greyhound would be objects ridiculous enough – but
> neither Silenus nor the bear are philosophers.[9]

Hume was dismissed with grace after a few moments and his next visit was
his last. His passions had erased his reason altogether. The Countess had,
unfeelingly, cast herself in *Twelfth Night* as a composite Olivia and Maria
with Charlemont combining Sir Andrew and Sir Toby, while Hume was
an unwitting Malvolio. Charlemont did confess his part in the adventure
to Hume who took it in good part and advised him:

> You are young, you are amiable, you are beloved, all that is
> precisely as it should be. Yet let me make one short observation –
> in French also, althought that is not my talent, 'Cueillez, Milord,
> les fleurs – cueillez les fleurs – mais ne vous faites pas jardinier.'
> [Gather flowers, but do not be a gardener]

Hume and Charlemont remained friends, but his *Memoir* was not published until well after Hume's death. Nor did Hume seem to mind that Charlemont had made the event a matter of public gossip, as Hume became the butt of many jokes among his friends in Turin. Charlemont also treated lightly an apparent relapse into the 'Disease of the Learned':

> He was affected by a most violent fever, attended with its natural symptoms, delirium and ravings. In the paroxysms of his disorder he often talked with much perturbation of the Devil, of Hell, and of damnation, and one night, while his nurse-tender happened to be asleep, he rose from his bed and made towards a deep well, which was in the courtyard, with a design, as was supposed, to drown himself, but finding the back door locked he rushed into a room where the gentlemen of the family were, he well knew, used to deposit their swords, and where he was found by the servants . . . and was forcibly brought back to bed . . . this whimsical adventure was, as may well be supposed, after his recovery, a subject of merriment among his friends, and we all agreed in laughing at the philosopher's fears and desperation.

Hume was aware of this and protested to his seeming friends:

> 'Why, you boobies, what would you have of a madman? Do you suppose philosophy to be proof against madness? The organisation of my brain was impaired, and I was as mad as any man in bedlam.'

The cause of this attack is unknown and physical reasons – malaria, typhus, etc. – are a possible cause. In such cases the arrival of a fever was enough for all hope to be abandoned. In this case, it was severe enough for his Italian hosts to have summoned a priest, and there is a rumour that, while delirious, the great infidel received extreme unction. One George Norvell accused Hume of being a sincere Catholic since he had once received extreme unction. Hume said, 'I was in a high fever then and did not know what I said or what they did with me.' After the accusation Norvell said, 'David and I for years after were tolerable friends but never so cordial as before'.[11]

But a psychological reason is also possible. Hume's reason was unseated by the force of the emotions to which it was the slave.

Hume was undaunted by this experience and always enjoyed the company of ladies: 'I took particular pleasure in the company of modest women, I had no reason to be displeased with the reception I met with from them'.[12] Perhaps the Countess Duvernan was not 'modest'. Later on in Edinburgh he was a sought-after adornment in the drawing rooms as, in Paris, he would grace the salons. So, notwithstanding his corpulence and strange accent, he had enough wit and charm to be attractive. He had been rejected once in Edinburgh although that seems to have been the result of a youthful infatuation. This, however, if Charlemont is to be believed – and there is no reason to doubt him – was a full-blown *amour fou*. The Countess was flattered to win the friendship of a famous philosopher, but had hoped for no more than an intellectual companion, certainly not declarations of love from a fat foreign gentleman 13 years her elder. While handsome, vigorous admirers of her own age lacked the wit and learning of Hume, they understood the rules of flirting and even seduction. Hume did not, and as often happens with one's first experience of love, threw caution to the winds and burst forth in full passion. This might have been acceptable at 15, but was thought ludicrous at 37. He was an embarrassment to the Countess who had to be rid of him. This blow would be received with the same intensity of feeling as he had experienced in his infatuation. Being an apprentice in love meant that he had no means of tolerating the undoubted hurt, and this may have produced his temporary madness. He was already suspicious of female psychology, as we have seen in his essays, and this event must have confirmed his suspicions. Henceforth his defences would remain strong and he would remain safe behind gentle, amusing conversation and mild flirting.

Intending to reach England for Christmas, the embassy set out to return on 29th November and reached Paris in mid-December. Their last stop for a change of horses was at Fontainebleau, and while St Clair and his party were refreshing themselves a soldier, hoping, no doubt, for a tip, motioned them to a back room where a 28-year-old man was being held under close guard. He was wearing the Order of the Garter and was immediately recognisable as Prince Charles Edward Stewart *en route* for exile first in Switzerland and then Rome. He had become a nuisance in Paris, but had refused to leave voluntarily, so on 10th December the Duc de Biron was ordered to arrest him. He was taken as he arrived at the Opera and held in Vincennes prison. His house was searched and a considerable private arsenal was found. In Vincennes he had a suite of well-heated rooms, with the best of food and wines. In high spirits he said, 'Tell my friends that I am well. My head has never left my shoulders'.[13]

However, a contemporary memoir in the *Edinburgh Magazine* tells a different story: 'they put him in that part of the castle called the dungeon, a little dark hole of a place. He said, "it was not quite as good as the bothies in the Highland hills"'.[14] The truth, as always with this slippery character, is elusive. Thus David Hume, democrat and freethinker, met the Catholic embodiment of the Divine Right of Kings. If they ever spoke, there is no record of the conversation, and it seems likely that the Prince was treated to one of David's glassy stares.

By Christmas Hume was back in London and looked back on his career as secretary, first, to a general and then to an ambassador. ' We shall have seen a great variety of Dutch, German, Italian, Spanish and French courts in this jaunt.'[15] At least he hoped so in Turin on 16th June, although he failed to mention Austria, and Spain was to remain merely a hope. In *My Own Life* he summarises the events:

> These two years were almost the only interruptions which my
> studies have received in the course of my life: I passed them
> agreeably and in good company; and my appointments, with my
> frugality, had made me reach a fortune, which I called independent,
> though most of my friends were inclined to smile when I said so: in
> short I was now master of near a thousand pound.[16]

Remembering that he felt he could live the life of a scholar at Ninewells on a hundred a year, he had a considerable cushion even although his wealthier friends patronised his feelings. But then the wealthy friends were not the second sons of Scottish border farmers.

While in Italy Hume had read an edition of *L'Esprit des Lois* by the Baron de Montesquieu. This was an examination of the necessity for a system of law and an examination of the systems of law then prevailing, greatly praising the methods adopted by England where he had spent two years. On returning to London, on 10th April Hume wrote to him, praising the book and making detailed comments. This caused Montesquieu to comment that Hume's letter was full of 'light and good sense'. He intended to make use of Hume's comments in a subsequent edition. Montesquieu replied to Hume that his comments were so judicious and sensible that he could not tell Hume by which point he was most delighted. These letters mark the start of Hume's friendships with the leading French intellectuals.

During his absence his three essays, *Of National Characters, Of the*

Original Contract, and *Of Passive Obedience*, had been published and were reprinted in November of the same year as part of *Essays, Moral and Political, Third edition*. This edition was important for several reasons; it marked the start of his association with Andrew Millar as his London publisher, the now redundant anonymity was dropped, and, most importantly, it carried the additional essay *Of Miracles*. It was to have been part of the *Treatise*, but had been dropped on the advice of Henry Home, who still had reservations about it. Before sailing Hume had written Oswald:

> I have some thoughts of taking advantage of this short interval of liberty that is indulged us and of printing the philosophical essays I left in your hands. Our friend Harry is against this as indiscreet. But in the first place I think I am too deep engaged to think of a retreat. In the second place, I see what bad consequences follow, in the present age, from the character of an infidel, especially if a man's conduct be in other respects irreproachable.[17]

Among the other papers he had left to be published during his absence was a reworking of Part I of the *Treatise*. This was now entitled *Philosophical Essays Concerning Human Understanding* although after 1758 it was re-titled *An Enquiry Concerning Human Understanding*.

Though much of the *Enquiry* was a re-statement of the *Treatise*, he went on to apply what has come to be called by philosophers 'Hume's Fork'. This defined ideas as discoverable by thought alone – pure mathematics, for example – while facts cannot be discovered only by thought but require experience both for their proof and disproof. This led him to look at demonstrative arguments such as deduction and probable or causal reasoning. But as if Hume himself was wearying of this pure philosophy, he ends with this advice:

> When we run over libraries, persuaded of these principles, what havoc must we make? If we take in our hand any volume – of divinity or school metaphysics, for instance – let us ask, does it contain any abstract reasoning concerning quantity or number? No. Does it contain any experimental reasoning concerning matter of fact and existence? No. Commit it then to the flames, for it can contain nothing but sophistry and illusion.[18]

Crucially, however, the *Enquiry* contained the long-awaited essay, *Of Miracles*. Hume defines a miracle as 'a transgression of a law of nature by a particular volition of the Deity, or by the interposition of some invisible agent'.[19] He continues with the assertion that no testimony is sufficient to establish a miracle, unless the testimony be of such a kind that its falsehood would be more miraculous than the fact which it endeavours to establish. He finds no evidence for any such occurrence in history since humanity does not apply such a rigorous proof to its acceptance of miracles. After an examination of miracles from the past and a lengthy account of the miracle of the Abbé Paris he concludes, 'The gazing populace receive greedily, without examination, whatever soothes super-stition and promotes wonder'. He applies the same tests to prophecies, fulfilled or not, and extends the argument against acceptance by faith alone to the whole Christian religion:

> So that, upon the whole, we may conclude, that the Christian
> religion not only was at first attended with miracles, but even at
> this day cannot be believed by any reasonable person without one.
> Mere reason is insufficient to convince us of its veracity: and
> whoever is moved by faith to assent to it, is conscious of a
> continued miracle in his own person, which subverts all the
> principles of his understanding, and gives him a determination to
> believe what is most contrary to custom and experience.[20]

Reading the essay today, it is difficult to understand why Hume, and his mentor Henry Home, were so reluctant to publish it. It is written in a rational style, without vehemence, and simply puts the case that, if you have faith you can believe anything. Many leading churchmen of today find no truth in miracles and regard them rather as the myths which will attend any ancient system of belief. But in 1748 this was new and Hume expected thunderclaps of vituperation for the works published in his absence. However:

> I had always entertained a notion that my want of success in
> publishing the *Treatise of Human Nature* had proceeded more from
> the manner than the matter; and that I had been guilty of a very
> usual indiscretion in going to the press too early, I therefore cast
> the first part of that work anew in the *Enquiry concerning Human
> Understanding* which was published while I was in Turin. [It was
> published in April 1748.] But this piece was at first but little more
> successful than the *Treatise of Human Nature*. On my return from

Italy, I had the mortification to find all England in a ferment on account of Dr Middleton's *Free Inquiry* [Conyers Middleton, librarian to Cambridge University, had, in 1747/8, published an attack on the miraculous powers asserted by the Church], while my performance was entirely overlooked and neglected. A new edition which had been published in London of my *Essays, Moral and Political* met not with a much better reception.[21]

This was the third edition of the *Essays,* published by Millar in November 1748, and, at last, they were not anonymous but bore Hume's name. But once again, although Hume had been provocative and innovative, it seemed no one was listening. He was respected and modestly successful but, still, his prizes did not glitter:

Such is the force of natural temper that these disappointments made little or no impression on me. I went down in 1749 and lived two years with my brother at his country house for my mother was now dead.

The household consisted of John, as laird and farmer, with sister Katharine as housekeeper, taking the place of Hume's mother until such time as John listened to David's advice and took a wife. David was now, as we have heard, comparatively affluent, and his guilt at not contributing to the family expenses must have been assuaged. He had time, in February 1751, to concoct a heavy-handed practical joke on one James Fraser, a physician whom Hume had met on the L'Orient expedition. He tried, through third parties, to convince Fraser that he was about to publish a scurrilous broadsheet accusing Fraser of having treated Dame Public to heavy doses of Jacobitism and Catholicism, and begging that he desist. Reading the broadsheet today, it is lugubriously unfunny[22.] He also wrote, 'at an idle hour', the *Bellman's Petition, or the Petition of the grave and venerable bellmen, or sextons, of the Church of Scotland to the honourable House of Commons.* This was aimed at satirising the claim by ministers and schoolteachers for higher stipends. The controversy was such that Edinburgh printers, totally lacking any sense of humour, refused to print Hume's pamphlet. He writes in the character of 'Zorobabel McGilchrist, Bellman of Buckhaven' and claims that since the bellmen were sextons and gravediggers and therefore employees of the church, they should be included in the claim. The 'half ecclesiastics' are 'not altogether unreasonable nor exorbitant in their demands' since 'the boldest tremble when they think of us'. 'The cardinals who are now princes were once nothing but parish curates of Rome, your petitioners observing the same laudable measures to be prosecuted, despair not of being one day on a level with the gentry and nobility of these realms.' This was accompanied by a 'letter':

> We saw a kind of Pisgah [from which Moses viewed the Promised Land] prospect opened to us of better days, by the application of the Reverend Ministers and Learned Schoolmasters for an augmentation of their stipends and salaries; and we having no less zeal in our inferior station, for the same holy cause, have also agreed upon a napplication [sic] for a like purpose: which I am empowered to transmit to you by the conveyance commonly called by the profane the *Post*. For I do not find there is any gospel name for it . . . Now, worthy and honourable Sir, if you will be the instrument of the Lord in this holy undertaking, I do hereby promise you in my own name, and in that of all of my bretheren, that he amongst us whom the Lord will bless with the comfortable task of doing you the last service in our power, shall do it so carefully, that you shall never find reason to complain of, I am, etc.[23]

Clearly in high spirits and with time to indulge himself, his trips backwards and forwards to Edinburgh were now more easily arranged. He threw himself into writing further essays, sending manuscripts for criticism to Oswald, sketching out a dialogue between himself and one Palamedes, and writing his *Enquiry concerning the Principles of Morals*. This work Hume, 'who ought not to judge on that subject,' regarded as, 'of all my writings, historical philosophical, or literary, incomparably the best'. Typically, 'it came unnoticed and unobserved into the world'.

It was, indeed, the finest to date, being clearly focused with a direct argument proceeding without diversions, possessing wit and humour, and written in an elegant style. From the outset the reader is in no doubt as to Hume's intention and since he is dealing with what a modern reader would consider 'Moral Philosophy' without metaphysics or epistemology it is the most accessible of his philosophical works. Indeed, if the general reader started by reading the *Enquiry concerning the Principles of Morals* instead of the *Treatise*, Hume might not be regarded as such a 'difficult' writer. He had made an effort to write more simply and the effort shows in an Appendix when, having put forward an argument, in exasperation he says, 'If you call this metaphysics, and find anything abstruse here, you need only conclude that your turn of mind is not suited to the moral sciences'.[24]

The *Enquiry* starts by looking at the social virtues of Benevolence and Justice:

> Nothing can bestow more merit on any human creature than the sentiment of Benevolence in an eminent degree . . . that Justice is useful to society . . . it would be a superfluous undertaking to prove . . . the good of mankind is the only object of all these laws and regulations . . . the necessity of Justice to the support of society is the sole foundation of that virtue.

He moves to consider the conflict between political parties and concludes that 'common interest and utility beget infallibly a standard of right and wrong among the parties concerned'. This is the first mention of 'utility', a word which would echo down the corridors of John Stuart Mill's 'utilitarianism'. But Hume asks 'useful to whom' and answers, 'useful to those who are served by the character of the action approved of'. He reviews the various vices and virtues that beset mankind. Avarice and prodigality are condemned as honesty, fidelity and truth are praised, and cowardice can be forgiven after subsequent acts of bravery. Women are particularly at risk since chastity, once lost, cannot be regained and the woman for ever after is 'cheap and vulgar, and exposed to every insult'.

He reviews systems of government and is sharply critical of both parties. While monarchies respect genealogies and military virtue, 'unactive and spiritless minds remain in haughty indolence'; however, in republics 'where riches are the chief idol, corruption, venality, [and] rapine prevail:[while] arts, manufactures, commerce [and] agriculture flourish . . . And we accordingly find that each of these forms of government, by varying the utility of those customs, has commonly a proportionable effect on the sentiments of mankind'.

Next he looks at the qualities immediately agreeable both to ourselves and to others and concludes that self-interest is a driving force in our moral judgements and that self-love drives most of our actions. And then, 'It is requisite that there be an original propensity of some kind, in order to be a basis for self-love, by giving a relish to the objects of its pursuit; and none more fit for this purpose than benevolence or humanity'. Thus self-interest drives us towards the greater good of humanity:

> And in a view to pleasure, what comparison between the unbought satisfaction of conversation, society, study, even health and the common beauties of nature, but, above all, the peaceful reflection on one's own conduct; what comparison, I say, between these and the feverish, empty amusements of luxury and expense? These natural pleasures are, really, without price; both because they are below all price in their attainment, and above it in their enjoyment.

The *Enquiry concerning the Principles of Morals* is a vindication of the theory that the greatest good of humanity can be achieved through the self-interest of the individual. Virtue is its own reward. And the reward is the eighteenth-century ideal of calm satisfaction with no regard for dangerous enthusiasms and passions. He follows this work with four appendices of examples to drive home the point and then gives the reader *A Dialogue*. This is a curious, very short, work, affecting to be a dialogue between Palamedes, 'as great a rambler in his principles as in his person', and Hume. Palamedes is cast in the role of Devil's advocate, describing the mythical country of Fourli where vice is applauded and virtue condemned. Swift's *Gulliver's Travels* was published in 1724 and Voltaire would publish *Candide* in 1758, four years after the *Enquiry,* so the fashion for creating fantastic lands as a basis for philosophic or political speculation was well established in the eighteenth century. Hume realises at once that Palamedes is criticising the Classical Greeks and rushes to their defence, claiming that they should not be judged by contemporary standards. Hume has to allow that the virtues of the Classical world would not stand close examination by today's moralists. Palamedes responds, 'I only meant to represent the uncertainty of all these judgements concerning characters; and to convince you that fashion, vogue, custom and law were the chief foundations of all moral determinations'. Hume goes on to assert that moral excellence consists only in being advantageous and agreeable to a man himself, or to others, no matter how many disagreements there may be as to the usefulness of his actions. He then finds himself in what appears to be a side issue. In Ancient Greece, women were largely excluded from society, and, excepting Helen and Clytemnestra, no events occurred as a result of female intrigue. However, in a thinly disguised reference to contemporary France, he claims that, 'no man can expect success, who takes care not to obtain their good graces'. He sees the acceptance of female infidelity increasing and quotes La Fontaine on infidelity: 'if one knows it, it is but a small matter, if one knows it not, it is nothing'. Hume's admiration for the cynicism of La Fontaine would cause him personal conflict in the near future, but he goes on to condemn the gallantry of the past races of Spaniards and Italians. This is an echo of his student essay *Of Chivalry* but Hume now uses this as a basis for a skilful shift of emphasis. This 'gallantry' is artificial and, in past times, men showed a similarly artificial respect for religion when they confined their religious beliefs to the temple, leaving philosophy alone to regulate men's affairs. However, 'At present, when philosophy has lost the allurement of novelty, it has no such extensive influence'. His disillusion with the reception of the *Treatise* is still apparent:

> Its place is now supplied by the modern religion, which inspects our whole conduct, and prescribes an universal rule to our actions, to our words, to our very thoughts and inclinations . . . when men depart from the maxims of common reason and affect these artificial lives, no one can answer for what will please or displease them.

This somewhat odd essay raises two questions. Was Hume calling down a curse on both the houses of philosophy and religion? Were women to be sidelined as dangerous intriguers? To answer the first question: Hume is saying that the obligations of unthinking ritual allow a hypocritical freedom which Protestantism deplores. But the cost of this is the Puritanical removal of individual liberty. The old philosophies, that is, the systems before Descartes, have been abandoned and the newer ones, especially his, are being ignored. The result will be an anarchy of the mind devoid of reason. Therefore the way forward for mankind is to pursue reason. His views on women are, in fact, unnecessary to the essay, as in essays of the past, but Hume does allow them to appear. He was troubled by the place of women in society. Socially, he enjoyed their company and they sought his – his size and clumsiness allowed his female acquaintances to 'mother' him, but they had no place in ideas of politics or philosophy. The word 'bluestocking' was not attached to women until later in the century. Hume had been, in real terms, fatherless, and would be looked after by his sister, so women held atypical positions of power in his background. He was clubbable with male friends and easy company with a few friends but he felt himself an outsider in society at large.

In his papers there is an unexplained scrap, perhaps a relic of one of those paper and pencil games, where you had to evaluate yourself and the others had to guess the identity from the description:

Character of ——————— written by himself.
1. A very good man the constant purpose of whose life is to do mischief.
2. Fancies he is disinterested, because he substitutes vanity in place of all other passions.
3. Very industrious, without serving either himself or others.
4. Licentious in his pen, cautious in his words, still more so in his actions.
5. Would have had no enemies had he not courted them; seems desirous of being hated by the public, but has only attained the being railed at.
6. Has never been hurt by his enemies, because he never hated any one of them
7. Exempt from vulgar prejudices – full of his own.
8. Very bashful, somewhat modest, no way humble.
9. A fool, capable of performances few wise men can execute.
10. A wise man, guilty of indiscretions which the greatest simpletons can perceive.
11. Sociable though he lives in solitude.
12. [Indecipherable and heavily scored through]
13. An enthusiast, without religion; a philosopher who despairs to attain truth.
14. A moralist who prefers instinct to reason.
15. A gallant, who gives no offence to husbands and mothers.
16. A scholar without the ostentation of learning.[25]

There is ample food here for teams of psychoanalysts, but the paper displays a great deal of self-knowledge:

Meanwhile, my bookseller, A.Millar, informed me that my former publications, (all but the unfortunate *Treatise*) were beginning to be the subject of conversation, that the sale of them was gradually increasing, and that new editions of them were demanded. Answers, by Reverends and Right Reverends came out two and three in a year: and I found by Dr Warburton's [the hostile reviewer of the *Treatise*] railing that the books were beginning to be esteemed in good company. However, I had fixed a resolution, which I inflexibly maintained, never to reply to anybody; and not being very irascible in my temper, I have easily kept myself clear of all literary squabbles. These symptoms of a rising reputation gave me encouragement as I was ever more disposed to see the favourable than unfavourable side of things; a turn of mind which it is more happy to possess than to be born to an estate of ten thousand a year.[26]

It is interesting that, in 1759, the young James Boswell left Scotland for London to be among 'the great, gay and the ingenious', and while David Hume still hankered after fame, it was fame in London that he sought. Both men considered Edinburgh a backwater.

But in March of 1751, events at Ninewells took control and David left home permanently. John Home found a suitable chatelaine for Ninewells and married Agnes Carre from Cavers in the neighbouring county of Roxburghshire. A cautious man, 43-year-old John had hesitated long and calculated hard before taking the leap:

Our friend, at last, plucked up a resolution and has ventured on that dangerous encounter, he went off on Monday morning; and this is the first action of his life wherein he has engaged himself without being able to compute exactly the consequences.[27]

The immediate consequence was that sister Katherine was no longer to be chatelaine of Ninewells, and David clearly felt that he could not ask his new sister-in-law to look after him. The logical step would be for David and Katherine to leave the family home:

Since my brother's departure, Katty and I have been computing in our turn, and the result of our deliberation is that we are to take up house in Berwick, where, if our arithmetic and frugality don't deceive us (and they are pretty certain arts) we shall be able, after providing for hunger, warmth, and cleanliness, to keep a stock in reserve which we may afterwards turn to hoarding, luxury or charity. But I have declared beforehand against the first. I can easily guess which of the other two you and Mr Dysart [his correspondent was Mrs Dysart, wife of the minister of Eccles, fifteen miles to the south-west of Ninewells] will be most favourable to. But we reject your judgement. For nothing binds one so much as inveterate habits.[28]

Hume had decided on luxury, but with a proper regard for finance. He continues the letter with his regards to Alexander Home, the Solicitor General for Scotland, who was a guest of the Dysarts, and:

> Unfortunately, I have not a horse at present to carry my fat carcase to pay its respects to his superior obesity. But if he finds travelling requisite either for his health or the Captain's [another guest ?] we shall be glad to entertain him here, as long as we can do it at another's expense: in hopes that we shall soon be able to do it at our own.[29]

Alexander Home was obviously as large as David and Hume reminds him that in ancient Gaul there was a law fixing a size for bellies and, if any exceeded the legal size, the owners were fined 'proportionable to its rotundity'. He praises Julius Caesar for preferring fat men to lean. Hume was in happy, gossipy and witty mood, but eight years later he wrote:

> I lived several happy years with my brother at Ninewells, and had not his marriage changed the state of the family, I believe I should have lived and died there . . . No man was ever endowed with so great a portion of the *vis inertiae*.[80]

For a man who led an internationally peripatetic life it is odd that he complains of being stricken with inertia. Hume was emotionally attached to the family home and to the countryside of the Scottish Borders. His reputation has given us a picture of a metropolitan man, only at home among libraries and coffee houses, but, although his reason may have been straightforward, his emotions were as complex as everyone else's.

Berwick, once a major centre, was now neither country nor city and it was to Edinburgh that he would go. In June he set out his arrangements in a long, reassuring letter to his oldest friend, Michael Ramsay:

> The concern you take of others is so warm, even after so long absence and such frequent interruptions as our commerce has unhappily met with of late years, that the most recent familiarity of others can scarcely equal it. I might perhaps pretend, as well as others, to complain of fortune; but I do not and should complain of myself as unreasonable, if I did. While interest remains as at present, I have £50 a year,* £100 worth of books, great store of

* The Bank of England rate was 5%, so Hume had invested £1,000.

linens and fine clothes and nearly £100 in my pocket, along with
order, frugality, a strong spirit of independency, good health, a
contented humour, and an unabating love of study. In these
circumstance, I must esteem myself one of the happy and fortunate:
and so far from being willing to draw my ticket over again in the
lottery of life, there are very few prizes with which I would make
an exchange.

After some deliberation, I am resolved to settle in Edinburgh . . .
besides other reasons which determine me to this resolution, I would
not go too far from my sister, who thinks she will soon follow me;
and in that case we shall probably take up house either in Edinburgh
or the neighbourhood. Our sister-in-law behaves very well and seems
very desirous we should both stay . . . and as she [Katharine] can join
£30 to my stock and brings an equal love of order and frugality, we
doubt not to make our revenues answer. Dr Clephane, who has taken
up house [a colleague from the L'Orient expedition, now living in
Golden Square, London], is so kind as to offer me a room in it, and
two friends in Edinburgh have made me the same offer: but having
nothing to ask or solicit at London, I would not remove to so
expensive a place, and am resolved to keep clear of all obligations and
dependencies even on those I love the most.

Part of my baggage is already packed up, and I remove in a few
weeks; but as I cannot give you any other direction at present, I
must beg of you to direct here as usual. I believe I shall live at Mrs
Fairbairn's till Kitty come to a resolution this autumn.[31]

Hume was making the jump and would now be an independent literary
gentleman. In *My Own Life* he says that he 'removed from the country to
the town; the true scene for a man of letters'. As a man of letters he had
another work awaiting publication, a further group of twelve essays, to
appear in 1752 as *Political Discourses*, 'the only work of mine that was
successful on its first publication: it was well received at home and abroad'.
It was, in fact, so successful as to have a second edition within the year and
a third in 1754. In the same year a translation of the *Discourses* into French
by the Abbé Le Blanc, author of *Letters concerning government, politics and
customs of the French and English*, was, 'thanks to the excellence of the
original, selling like a novel'. Hume was famous at last.

The essays in the *Discourses* were, *Of Commerce, Of Luxury* (later changed to *Of Refinement in the Arts*), *Of Money, Of Interest, Of the Balance of Trade, Of the Balance of Power, Of Taxes, Of Public Credit, Of Some Remarkable Customs, Of the Populousness of Ancient Nations, Of the Protestant Succession,* and the *Idea of a Perfect Commonwealth.*

In *Of Commerce* Hume starts with a general statement and a warning:

> General principles, if just and sound, must always prevail in the general course of things, though they may fail in particular cases: and it is the chief business of philosophers to regard the general course of things. I may add, that it is also the chief business of politicians.[32]

He greatly praises the industriousness of the nation, but with qualification:

> Their own steel and iron [that of the manufacturers], in such laborious hands, become equal to the gold and rubies of the Indies . . . Where the riches are engrossed by a few, these must contribute very largely to the supplying of the public necessities.

After this early advocacy of socialism Hume passes to *Luxury* or *Of Refinement in the Arts,* and while allowing that luxury can be seen as a vice, it is only vicious when enjoyed at the expense of a virtue. Needless to say, he finds that the refinement of the arts as seen in the Classical Age is a mark of civilised virtue.

Money, however, '. . . is one of the wheels of trade. It is the oil which renders the motion of the wheels more smooth and easy'. But a plentiful money supply will increase prices disadvantageously.

He then differentiates between wealth and money, but acknowledges that forward investment needs an abundant supply of money, as does the need for a war chest available at any time. It must be remembered that when Hume was born the War of the Spanish Succession was raging, he had just taken part in the final acts of diplomacy in the War of the Austrian Succession, while colonial struggles flared into intermittent conflict throughout the century. So war was a constant likelihood. However, men and commodities are the real strength of any community. And 'Nothing is esteemed a more certain sign of the flourishing condition of any nation than the lowness of interest'. Hume argues that low interest arises from the success of industry and commerce, reducing the need to borrow.

In *Of the Balance of Trade* Hume wants to see the lively manufacturing industry producing a healthy export trade, since 'The more that is exported of any commodity the more will be raised at home, of which they themselves [the manufacturing nation] will always have the first offer'. Hume favours free trade without trade barriers and argues that government restriction of the circulation of money can be destructive: 'A government has great reason to preserve with care its people and its manufactures. Its money, it may safely trust to the course of human affairs, without fear or jealousy'.

Instead of continuing here with a discussion of fiscal and economic policy, he has his first diversion to discuss *The Balance of Power,* and shows that the need for such a political balance between nations is age-old: 'The maxim of preserving the balance of power is founded so much on common sense and obvious reasoning that it is impossible it could altogether have escaped antiquity'. But in modern times he blames Britain's militaristic stance: 'Above half our wars with France and all our public debts are owing more to our own imprudent vehemence than to the impatience of our neighbours.' But the existence of large states is a contributing factor: 'Enormous monarchies are probably destructive to human nature; in their progress, in their continuance, and even in their downfall, which can never be very distant from their Establishment'. Throughout the *Discourses* Hume returns again and again to favour the small democratic city-state in a federation. This is fed by his admiration for Classical Greek society, but the examples of his contemporary society lend validity to many of his arguments. For example, 'The Bourbons trusting to the support of their brave, faithful and affectionate nobility, would push their advantage without limitation'. The limitation would start in just 24 years with the fall of the Bastille.

Returning to economics, he deals briefly with taxes and, unsurprisingly, finds that 'The best taxes are such as are levied upon consumptions, especially those of luxury, because such taxes are least felt by the people . . . the most pernicious are the arbitrary . . . In general all poll-taxes, even when not arbitrary, which they generally are, may be esteemed dangerous'. Equally dangerous, he feels, is the maintenance of Public Credit: 'Why should the case be so different between the public and an individual as to make us establish different maxims of conduct for each? It would scarcely be more prudent to give the prodigal son a credit in every banker's shop in London, than to empower a statesman to draw bills in this manner upon posterity'. And if a person can earn five per cent (as Hume himself was doing) by investing in the funds, then he is less likely to look for a similar profit by being industrious. This will lessen commerce with disastrous results: 'Either the nation must destroy public credit or public credit will destroy the nation'. He allows that such credit might be used to finance a war, but unless it is limited to extreme emergencies it must collapse under its own weight.

He then has two diversions from the general thrust, firstly, in *Of Some Remarkable Customs,* where he asserts that authority must come from law and not from violence. He excepts the practice of forcibly recruiting seamen, 'pressing', since the practice is itself legally authorised. This is wobbly logic and shows the lack of an editorial hand. *Of the Populousness of Ancient Nations* sprang from a contemporary dispute that the ancient world was more populous than in Hume's time and there was, therefore, a theory that mankind was declining. Hume disagreed and gives pages of more or less spurious calculations to support his claim. It is one of the few examples of Hume's writing that is of interest to his own time only, since most of his arguments have a much more universal application. As if to prove the point he compares various aspects of liberty in the Classical world with his own: 'Nature in general, really enjoys more liberty at present, in the most arbitrary government of Europe, than ever it did during the most flourishing period of ancient times'. Almost arguing against his own belief in 'small is beautiful', he proposes a long chain of command from the monarch: 'The more the master is removed from us in place and rank, the greater liberty we enjoy'. This is almost like saying, 'if we're small and quiet, he'll never notice and we can get away with whatever we please'. This an advocacy of anarchy and atypical of Hume.

But Hume then examines the practice of slavery in Rome and Greece and finds it totally repellent. However, while the ancients limited family size by exposing unwanted children, modern society uses convents or the priesthood: 'To kill one's own child is shocking in nature, and must therefore be somewhat unusual; but to turn over the care of him to others is very tempting to the natural indolence of mankind'.

In spite of his proposing a long chain of command, small states are preferable to large monarchies. 'All small states naturally produce equality of fortune, because they afford no opportunities of great increase; but small commonwealths much more, by that division of power and authority which is essential to them.'

Then, as if he could hear his wayward and digressing thoughts being criticised, he excuses himself: 'What can we do but amuse ourselves by talking pro and con on an interesting subject and thereby correcting all hasty and violent determinations?'

His conclusion is decidedly in favour of his own time: 'The equality of property among the ancients, liberty, and the small divisions of their states were indeed circumstances favourable to the propagation of mankind: but their wars were more bloody and destructive, their governments more factious and unsettled, commerce and manufacture more feeble and languishing, and the general police more loose and irregular. These latter disadvantages seem to form a sufficient counterbalance to the former advantages: and rather favour the opposite opinion to that which commonly prevails with regard to the subject'.

In *Of the Protestant Succession* he starts by discussing the condition of monarchy itself: 'An anatomist finds no more in the greatest monarch than in the lowest peasant or day labourer, and a moralist may, perhaps, frequently find less'. Perhaps the ideal method would be to choose a monarch as a 'creature of the public' with conditions. Since the Hanoverian succession had been brought about by Parliament, this was moving toward an endorsement of that. But Hume did not embrace full-blown republicanism since 'The people cherish monarchy, because protected by it: the monarch favours liberty because created by it'. Then, as if remembering his subject, he examines the respective advantages and disadvantages of Stuart and Hanover. For religion alone, Hanover is preferred, in spite of their hated loyalty to their estates in Hanover. Also, being foreign, Hanover has, to date, let us govern ourselves, and so the status quo is preferable.

Lastly Hume gives us his *Idea of a perfect Commonwealth*. He proposes a senate of 100 elected annually by 100 county representatives, and they then, in conclave, elect a protector and various officers of state who must be re-elected every year. Thus every county – there would be 100 of them – would be a republic within itself. It bears a resemblance to the Dutch model with a militia based on the Swiss. He would retain the House of Lords, but without the bishops or the Scotch peers. All would be life peers and they would re-elect their own membership. However, even such a limited monarchy does not remove the difference between court and country parties, there is no sanction against the king's personality, and the king is still the commander-in-chief of the army. He rejected the conventional thinking that no large state could ever be modelled into a commonwealth, but that the contrary was probable. 'In a large government . . . there is compass and room enough to redefine the democracy . . . at the same time, the parts are so distant and remote, that it is very difficult, either by intrigue, prejudice or passion, to hurry them into any measures against the public interest.' When James Madison was planning the new American Constitution in 1787 he included these thoughts in his *Notes on the Confederacy*. 'Such a state ought to establish a fundamental law against conquests: yet republics have ambitions as well as individuals, and present interest makes men forgetful of their posterity. It is a sufficient incitement to human endeavour that such a government would flourish for many ages, without pretending to bestow, on any work of man, that immortality which the Almighty seems to have refused to his own productions.'

These *Political Discourses* can be regarded as Hume's political testament although in today's world of party dogmas they may seem contradictory. Hume is enthusiastically in favour of a free market without government control. But he lived in a time when the intervention of the state, by way of subsidies and tax rebates, was unheard of. Control of the general standard of living was not yet in government hands. Education, health care, and policing were largely the concern of private organisations. Foreign trade was largely untrammelled by government intervention and the rivalry between Parliament and the East India Company was still below the horizon. Hume's *Idea of a perfect Commonwealth* was pure theory and was never meant as a cry to man the barricades. Taken together the *Essays* reflect the pragmatic views of a democratically positioned liberal and they sealed his reputation as a writer of merit and influence. He had moved from pure Whig dogma to allowing some power to the sovereign. In time he would move even further to the right. The London-based *Monthly Review* of January 1752 said of the *Discourses*:

> Few writers are better qualified, either to instruct or entertain their reader than Mr Hume. On whatever subject he employs his pen, he presents us with something new; nor is this his only merit, his writings (as we observed in the preceding article) [an earlier review of the *Enquiry*] receive a further recommendation from that elegance and spirit which appears in them, and that clearness of reasoning which distinguishes him from most others. The discourses now before us, are upon curious and interesting subjects; abound

with solid reflections; and show the author's great knowledge of
ancient and modern history, and his comprehensive views of things.
To such indeed, as have not accustomed themselves to general
reasonings on political subjects, several principles laid down in
them, will, doubtless, appear too refined and subtle: but, as our
author observes, when we reason upon general subjects, it may be
justly affirmed, that our speculations can scarce ever be too fine,
provided they be just.[33]

The review continued for some pages to précis and quote from Hume's
work with few other comments. The reviewer, one William Rose, said of
Money, that it was 'a subject on which he has made many curious and
uncommon observations'. The review was continued in the February 1752
issue when he called *Of Populousness of Ancient Nations* 'the longest and
most curious' without quoting from, or referring to, the crucial passage
condemning slavery.

As we have said above, the January issue also carried a review of the
Enquiry Concerning the Principles of Morals:

The reputation this ingenious author has acquired as a fine and
elegant writer, renders it unnecessary for us to say anything in his
praise. We shall only observe in general, that clearness and precision
of ides on abstracted and metaphysical subjects, and at the same
time propriety, elegance and spirit are seldom found united in any
writings in a more eminent degree than in those of Mr Hume. The
work now before us will, as far as we are able to judge, considerably
raise his reputation; and, being free from that sceptical turn which
appears in his other pieces, will be more agreeable to the generality
of readers. His subject is important and interesting and the manner
of treating it is easy and natural: his design is to fix the just origin
of morals, in the execution of which he has shown a great deal of
judgement as well as ingenuity, as every candid reader must allow,
whatever sentence he may pass upon his scheme in general, or how
much so ever he may differ from him in regard to what he has
advanced on the subject of justice.[34]

As was normal, the remainder of the review of this 'ingenious' and 'very
entertaining' work consisted of description and quotation.

Hume had been criticised for *Of Miracles* but even that criticism had been polite. However, the critique itself was reviewed as, *'A Review of an Essay on Hume's Essay on Miracles*, by William Adams, minister of St Chad's, Salop and chaplain to the bishop of Llandaff, who said:

> Among the many useful and valuable productions that have lately been published, this is not the least considerable. The subject is very important, and handled with judgement and accuracy: the full evidence, possibility, and propriety of miracles are distinctly shown; and the objections of Mr Hume, although urged with great acuteness, are inconclusive. Nor is it the least praise of this performance that it is written with candour, and in such a manner as shows the author to have enlarged and generous notions of Christianity, and a temper free from sourness and bigotry.[35]

This was a great change from the vituperation of *The History of the Learned*. Hume now had an income and a reputation, growing across Europe. The *Essays* continued to be reissued in various editions with growing success. Throughout their existence he added some, dropped others, and altered the texts of some as his views matured. With his various versions of the *Treatise* we can see that he never regarded any of these works as finished. He admitted to impetuousness and acknowledged the fault of going into print too early. As has already been said, in *Réflexions critiques sur la poésie at sur la Peinture* by the Abbé DuBos, which Hume had read, there is a very relevant passage which is worth requoting:

> 'Tis vain nevertheless to attempt to persuade young people . . . spurred on by the impatience of their genius to the pursuit of fame, to defer making their appearance in public till they have discovered their kind of talent and sufficiently improved it.[36]

Hume was hardly a 'young man' – he was 42, but his standards were such that 'sufficient improvements' were infinite. He could sum up his preferences of the *Essays* and the *Enquiry*, writing to the Abbé Le Blanc, probably advising him on translations in 1754:

> The only good edition of my *Essays, Moral and Political* is the fourth; It begins with the sentence, 'some people are subject to a certain delicacy of Passion, etc.' The best edition of the *Enquiry concerning the Principles of Morals* is the second. The booksellers in

London are now reprinting the philosophical essays, but the second edition differs very little from this new one. I doubt these essays are both too bold and too metaphysical for your climate.[37]

Hume had now served his lengthy apprenticeship, and had been diverted from his main intentions by St Clair at L'Orient, in Vienna and Turin, but now he could leave home and start a career: the career he had always wanted. On 24th September he had written to Adam Smith:

I confess, I was once of the same opinion with you and thought that the best period to begin an English history was about Henry the 7th. But you will please to observe that the change which then happened in public affairs was very insensible and did not display its influence until many years afterwards. 'Twas under James that the House of Commons began first to raise their head, and then the quarrel betwixt privilege and prerogative commenced . . . I confess that the subject appears to me very fine and I enter upon it with great ardour and perseverance. You need not doubt of my perseverance.[38]

Hume the historian had started work in earnest.

NINE

A Post in the English Parnassus

H ume was now established in Edinburgh, albeit as yet in lodgings, when, with the perversity of fortune, the opportunity arose to move to Glasgow. Thomas Craigie, the Professor of Logic, had died and Adam Smith, who had been Professor of Moral Philosophy, took his place. Although at this time Smith had no personal knowledge of Hume, he strongly recommended him for the now vacant philosophy chair. But Smith also felt, correctly as it turned out, that public opinion would disbar Hume. Hume's principal supporter was William Cullen, Professor of Medicine at Glasgow, but Hume, with his customary realism, did not expect to succeed. The old complaints of atheism were raised, almost ritually, but the killer blow came from the Duke of Argyll, who as the 'King of Scotland', had the patronage of this post. He simply felt that Hume 'cannot be recommended . . . for many reasons that must easily occur'. Hume was rejected but unsurprised, and his main regret seems to have been that he was 'deprived of great opportunities of friendship' with Cullen. In fact, Cullen eventually came to Edinburgh University and became Hume's personal physician.

By February 1752 Hume was in high spirits as he gained another post, 'a petty office of forty or fifty guineas a year'. Since that was what he had been paid for the publication of the *Treatise*, he had raised his financial sights considerably. He wrote to Clephane on 4th February:

> You have probably heard that my friends in Glasgow, contrary to my opinion and advice, undertook to get me elected into that College; and they had succeeded, in spite of the violent and solemn remonstrances of the clergy, if the Duke of Argyle had had the courage to give me the least countenance. Immediately upon the back of this failure, which should have blasted for some time all my pretensions, the office of library-keeper to the Faculty of Advocates came vacant, a genteel office, though of small revenue; and as this happened suddenly, my name was immediately set up by my friends without my knowledge.[1]

The *Minute book of the Faculty of Advocates* has the following entry:

28 January 1752

In the next place the Faculty proceeded to the choice of a Keeper of their Library in place of the said Mr Thomas Ruddiman, and some members proposing that a dignified member of their own body, viz., Mr Kenneth Mackenzie, Advocate, Professor of the Civil Law in the University of Edinburgh should be named to that office and others inclining that Mr David Home be elected. It was agreed that the matter should be put to a vote: and the Rolls being called and votes distinctly marked and taken down & numbered it was found that the majority had declared for the latter; upon which the Dean and Faculty declared the said Mr David Home duly elected Keeper of their Library, and appointed that the usual salary of forty pounds sterling be paid to him yearly on that account, and in regard that he was to have their minutes, acts and records under his custody, they appointed him also Clerk to the Faculty . . . with power to the said Mr Home to officiate therein by a depute.[2]

The faculty clearly chose to ignore Hume's change of name and, given that none of the Faculty minutes are in Hume's hand, he did use a deputy. The salary was of secondary interest to Hume since what was hugely important was the access now allowed him to one of the major libraries in the country. Founded in 1689 with 3,140 volumes, it came to be situated in the Laigh, or Lower, Hall of the Parliament building. The Copyright Act of 1709 made it into a library of legal deposit whereby it received, via Stationers Hall, a copy of every book published in the United Kingdom. The Library, according to Hume, held 30,000 volumes.

His letter to Clephane continues in great high spirits, and, since he was not present at the meeting of the Advocates, shows a good intelligence service in action:

The bigots joined them [the opposition to Hume's appointment] and both together set up a gentleman of character, and an advocate, and who had great favour on both these accounts. The violent cry of Deism, atheism and scepticism was raised against me; and 'twas represented that my election would be giving the sanction of the greatest and most learned body of men in this country to my profane and irreligious principles . . . 'twas vulgarly given out the contest was betwixt Deists and Christians, and when the news of my success came to the playhouse, the whisper ran that the Christians had been defeated . . . the whole body of cadies brought flambeaux and made illuminations to mark their pleasure at my success, and next morning I had the drums and town music at my door, to express their joy, as they said, of my being made a great man.[3]

He was formally appointed on 6th February:

Mr David Home was received as Keeper of the Advocates Library and Clerk to the Faculty and had thereupon the oath *de fideli* administered to him.[4]

Hume inherited Walter Goodall as Under-Keeper, a post he held from 1735 until 1763. He had been Clerk to the faculty at the sederunt, or meeting, which appointed Hume, and now spent most of his time as creator of the *index materiarum* until his departure from the library. He died, in poverty, in 1766 and his daughter Mary was given a grant of £10 for funeral expenses. An avid admirer of Mary, Queen of Scots, he was the author of a book proving the Casket letters to be forgeries. He was also prone to extended naps at his desk after alcoholic over-indulgence and, on one occasion, when Hume was looking for a book:

He was sitting in his elbow-chair so fast asleep, that neither David nor a friend who accompanied him could wake him by any of the usual means. At last David said, 'I think have a method of waking him,' and bawled into his ear, 'Queen Mary was a strumpet and a murderer!' 'It's a damned lie', said Goodall, starting from his sleep, and David obtained the book he sought.[5]

Hume now had a position, albeit almost honorary, in Edinburgh society he was respected, published and, probably in May 1752, he became a householder in Edinburgh:

About seven months ago [this letter is dated January 1753] I got a house of my own and completed a regular family: consisting of a head, viz., myself, and two inferior members, a maid and a cat. My sister has since joined me and keeps me company. With frugality I can reach, I find, cleanliness, warmth, light, plenty, and contentment. What would you have more? Independence? I have it

in a supreme degree. Honour? That is not altogether wanting.
Grace? That will come in time. A wife? That is none of the
indispensable perquisites of life. Books? That *is* one of them; and I
have more than I can use. In short, I cannot find any blessing of
consequence which I am not possessed of, in a greater and a lesser
degree; and, without any great effort of philosophy, I may be easy
and satisfied.[6]

Hume's house was in Riddel's Land on the south side of the Lawnmarket,
opposite the now rebuilt house in which he had been born. By way of
France, Austria, Italy and London he had travelled less than a hundred
yards, and Edinburgh, with excursions to London and Paris, would be his
home for the rest of his days. The house still stands at the top of the High
Street, and reached through Riddel's Close, an entry too narrow even for a
sedan chair. It is a typical six-storey house of which Hume's establishment
would have occupied a floor, or 'land', much as had his father's. Today
many visitors feel it looks dark and slum-like, but appearances are indeed
deceptive, and the even darker court behind it held the house in which a
town councillor had entertained James VI and his new Danish queen. On
the arch leading to this court is carved the motto *vivendo discimus* (by
living we learn) and a better motto for one who believed that knowledge
was based purely on experience is hard to imagine. But apart from the
inspirational qualities of the carvings, it was prime real estate.

These houses with their dark, stone staircases housed several families,
causing many people to refer to them as 'vertical streets', and it is true that
all social levels could be found on one stair. But this provides no evidence
that these classes mixed socially. Edinburgh, with a population of 57,000
crowded onto its spine of rock, was more democratic than many eighteenth-century cities, but while a viscount might talk easily to a fish-
monger, the route of the conversation was along a one-way street.
Familiarity upwards was amusing and tolerated but it was not encouraged.
The building of a spacious New Town in the later part of the century saw
the affluent flee the congestion of the mediaeval city. David Hume would
join that exodus.

Sir Gilbert Elliott of Minto, a friend and fellow club member of
Hume's, who sought Hume's company despite having 'a marked disapprobation for the Sceptical Philosophy', wrote a report on the city
within two months of Hume's taking up residence:

Proposals for carrying on certain public works in the city of Edinburgh,
The healthfulness of its situation and its neighbourhood to the
[River] Forth must no doubt be admitted as very favourable
circumstances. But how greatly are they overbalanced by other
disadvantages almost without number? Placed upon the ridge of a
hill, it admits but of one good street, running from east to west;
and even this is tolerably accessible only from one quarter. The
narrow lanes leading to the north and south, by reason of their
steepness, narrowness, and dirtiness, can only be considered as so
many unavoidable nuisances. Confined by the small compass of the
[city] walls, and the narrow limits of the royalty, which scarcely
extends beyond the walls, the houses stand more crowded than in
any other town in Europe, and are built to a height that is almost
incredible. Hence necessarily follows a great want of free air, light,
cleanliness, and every other comfortable accommodation. Hence also
families, sometimes no less than ten or a dozen, are obliged to live
overhead of each other in the same building; where, to all other
inconveniences, is added that of a common stair, which is no other
in effect than an upright street, constantly dark and dirty. It is
owing to the same narrowness of the situation that the principal
street is incumbered [sic] with the herb-market, the fruit-market,
and several others; that the shambles [slaughterhouse] are placed on
the side of the North Loch, rendering what was originally an
ornament to the town an insufferable nuisance.[7]

He complains that there is

no merchants exchange, no repository for state records, no meeting
place for magistrates or town council, no persons of rank reside
within the city, it is rarely visited by strangers, and . . . local
prejudice and narrow notions are obstinately retained. For such
reasons alone it must be imputed that Edinburgh, which ought to
have set the first example of industry and improvement, is the last
of our trading cities that has shook off the unaccountable
supineness which has so long and so fatally depressed the spirit of
our nation.

Elliot proposed building a merchants' exchange on the north side of the
High Street, on the ruins of Parliament Close, along with courts of justice

to be built with town offices and new premises for the Advocates' Library. He wanted to turn the North Loch into a canal with walks and terraces on each side. However, he felt, hopefully, 'As it is not the seat of government it can never become the centre of luxury and vice'.

It was a city shaking off the Middle Ages in some respects and embracing the modern world in others. Most journeys inside the city were easily made on foot and Hume would have walked the four hundred yards between his lodgings and the Advocates' Library, close to the cathedral of St Giles and the Tolbooth, Edinburgh's prison. At the north front of the cathedral were the Luckenbooths, literally 'Lockable booths' where, among other trades, Allan Ramsay had his bookshop. To ensure that he sold no corrupting texts, his shop was raided, but, since he had received ample warning, only uplifting works were on the shelves.

To the east of St Giles was the Mercat Cross where miscreants could be seen with their ears nailed to the pillory – they were left there until they had the courage to tear themselves free. Children always gathered to watch this. However, Mr Amyat, chemist to the King, stated that he could stand by the Mercat Cross, which was also a sort of informal meeting place for merchants, and in the course of a few minutes shake fifty men of genius and learning by the hand. Also by the Mercat Cross he would have found Edinburgh's 'cadies' looking for employment. These men looked disreputable, often slept in the street, but were indispensable jacks-of-all-trades. They would act as porters or guides and knew the movements of all citizens in and out of town. They would guard vacated property against burglary and run all sorts of errands – Boswell sent one to fetch him a whore – and, thanks to a collective code of conduct, could be trusted with anything. On one occasion a cadie who was delivering several hundreds of pounds lost the money, but the owner was reimbursed in full by their collective. Shouted imprecations in incomprehensible Gaelic to clear a path would be heard from the sedan chair carriers who were exclusively Highland, and one particular, apparently empty, chair could be seen on rainy evenings as the courts closed their business. Lord Monboddo always walked to his home, but, if it rained, he sent his wig home in a chair. Wigs were expensive – Edinburgh had 65 wig-makers – and his scarlet and silver silk robes could take their chances in the rain. Most of the legal and clerical fraternities would dress in their robes and gowns at home and walk to their places of business in splendour through the street. Ladies of style would promenade on high-heeled pattens to raise them above the filth.

They were frequently masked, with the left-hand string of the mask coiled around an ear and the loose end held in their mouth. Thus they could drop their mask without taking their hands out of their muff.

Off the High Street were the vertiginous 'wynds' (alleyways) leading south to the Cowgate, a parallel street of unsavoury reputation, or north to the Nor' Loch. 'The steepness of the wynds leading to the Cowgate requires great attention to the feet. But so well accustomed are the Scotch to that position of the body required in descending these declivities, that I have seen a Scotch girl run down them in pattens.'[8]

The High Street swept on downhill to the east, passing John Knox's last house, until it reached the City gate at the Netherbow. The actual gates were pulled down in 1764. This was the easternmost limit of the city itself, and beyond this was the Canongate, a separate burgh with its own Tolbooth jail, and two major inns with stabling for over a hundred horses. 'Since 1769 the Canongate included amongst its inhabitants 2 dukes, 16 earls, 2 dowager countesses, 7 lords, 7 lords of session [law lords], 13 baronets, 4 commanders of forces, 4 men of eminence.'[9] It also had a proliferation of brothels catering to all tastes. They were so famous that a person with venereal disease was said to be wearing 'Canongate Breeches'.

The city was lavishly equipped with taverns, both elegant and sordid. Edmund Burt dined in one of the latter in the 1720s:

I was invited to sup at a tavern. The cook was too filthy an object to be described, only another English gentleman whispered to me and said, he believed that if the fellow was to be thrown against the wall he would stick to it . . . We supped very plentifully and drank good French claret, and were very merry until the clock struck ten, the hour at which everybody is at liberty, by the beat of the city drum, to throw their filth out at the windows. Then the company began to light pieces of paper, and throw them on the table to smoke the room, and, as I thought, to mix one bad smell with another. Being in my retreat to pass through a long narrow wynd, or alley, to go to my new lodgings, a guide was assigned me, who went before me to prevent my disgrace, crying out all the way, 'Haud your hand'. The throwing up of a sash or otherwise opening of a window made me tremble, while behind and before me, at some little distance fell the terrible shower. Well, I escaped all the danger and arrived, not only safe and sound, but sweet and clean at my new quarters; but when I was in bed I was forced to hide my head between the sheets, for the smell of the filth, thrown out by the neighbours on the back side of the house, came pouring into the room to such a degree I was almost poisoned with the stench.[10]

This disgusting effluent lay in the streets until morning when, with the exception of the Sabbath, it was swept away. These were the 'Flowers of Edinburgh'.

In some drinking establishments the entertainments went on long into the night. 'At an early hour of the morning you hear a little party at the taverns amusing themselves by breaking the bottles and glasses, but this is all in good humour.'[11]

Edward Topham, extraordinarily for a Captain in the Guards, was amazed at the Edinburgers' capacity for drink:

The gentlemen, pay rather too much respect to the divinity of Bacchus, and offer too copious libations at the shrine of that jovial deity. The wines, indeed, of all kinds are excellent, and their climate not the most comfortable; so that some allowance ought to be made in that respect.[12]

For most people the day would have begun at five or six, although the High School delayed its opening until nine in winter – to spare 'those of tender years' the rigours of winter frosts. Then, Topham noted, breakfast was taken at about 8 a.m, washed down with brandy or ale at breakfast. 'Jupiter' Carlyle gives a picture of Hume's day a few years later:

When he lived at the Canongate during the time he wrote his history, he was an early riser and being very laborious in his studies . . . his custom was to rise early in the morning and to walk round Salisbury Crags and return to breakfast and his studies. He was much abroad at dinner, which in those days was at 2 o'clock – and what was singular at the time he gave no veils [gratuities] to servants tho' he was invited to dinner 4 or 5 times a week, and what was more singular still tho' he was a great eater, he drank but very moderately, he returned to his studies in the evening with clearness and assiduity. With respect to his not giving veils, the truth is that in those days he could not afford it, for he had not £50 per annum tho' he wore fine clothes. The servants too finding that he was facetious and good company and made their masters and mistresses very happy, were always glad to see him as if he had paid them for every dinner.[13]

As we shall see, the practice of giving veils was abolished in 1760. The circuit of Salisbury Crags made by this radical thinker was about four miles over hilly ground.

The bells of St Giles rang at 11.30 – the 'gill-bells' – when the citizenry had their second drink of the day. In the taverns the wine was served by the pint (a Scotch pint was equivalent to two English quarts – a more common quantity was a mutchkin, being three-quarters of an English pint) in metal jugs with a single glass to each jug irrespective of the number of drinkers. A second glass was served with the second pint of wine, though Henry Home found this 'excessively luxurious'.

Not so luxurious was the life of the poor, even in their oyster and porter bars. 'No people in the world undergo greater hardships or live in a worse degree of wretchedness and poverty than the lower classes here.'[14] They slept where they could find any kind of shelter, the women being forced into prostitution for the short period while looks and health held up, the men into begging. Repeated begging would result in a public flogging and exile from the city, although by the years immediately after Hume's death there were twelve charities for the poor inside the city. 'Edinburgh sought to house its settled poor while purging itself of vagrants and only sending those tainted by criminality to the house of correction. Scotland's capital aimed simply to control rather than to repress and exploit the poor.'[15] However, William Creech estimated that between 1763 and 1783 the number of brothels had risen twenty fold and the number of prostitutes had increased 100 times. This is a wild exaggeration, but it strengthens the point of increasing poverty in a city that was largely concerned with linen and leather manufacture as well as trade. The professions, law, university, medicine came second in number with the crafts last. Between 1690 and 1760 the status of elders at the Tolbooth Church was 'merchants 59, professionals 30 and craftsmen 10'.[16] Since the aristocracy formed a transient population, Edinburgh was a largely middle-class city with middle-class values.

'An execution was a rare event . . . for the fifteen year before 1782 only three persons were hanged in Edinburgh every two years.'[17] Although hanging was reserved for the most severe crimes, and often then only after a previous offence, justice was severe and, often, random. One 'panel', or prisoner, made an intelligent plea in his own defence to the judge, Lord Braxfield, who regarded intelligence as highly suspect, and declared, 'you are a clever cheil [man] but you'll be none the worse for a good hanging'.

This was the loathsome underside of Hume's world of reason and gentility:

> In the mid-eighteenth century the search for status was played out in the coffee-shops, promenades, social assemblies and salons for prizes in the marriage market or for something as intangible as the esteem of one's peers.[18]

Hume's search for status was now, temporarily, in abeyance. He had a comfortable, if not lavish, lifestyle with his political writings going through numerous editions and being translated and praised in France and receiving praise, at last, in Germany. He had ready access to his literary friends in Edinburgh and, most importantly, access to a major library. His position:

> gave me the Command of a large Library. I then formed the plan of writing the History of England; but being frightened with the notion of continuing a narrative through a period of 1700 years, I commenced with the accession of the house of Stuart; an epoch when, I thought, the misrepresentations of faction began chiefly to take place.[19]

Hume did not regard his position as a sinecure and took an active part in acquiring books for the Library. Unfortunately, not always with the approbation of the curators, for, in 1754 Hume had bought a batch of 74 books from Thomas Osborne, a London bookseller, including three French works: *Contes* by Jean de La Fontaine, *L'Écumoire* by Claude Prosper Jolyot de Crébillon, and *Les Histoires amoureuses des Galles* by Roger, Comte de Bussy-Rabutin.*

The curators of the library were distinguished Edinburgh lawyers, some of whose descendants still grace Edinburgh committees, but David Hume had the reputation of a dangerous radical, a reputation that had already cost him two university chairs, and, by association with him, these seemed to be dangerous books. Also, they were from France, Britain's enemy through the eighteenth century, and if not downright filthy, then they

---

* For details of these books, see Appendix 2.

were almost certainly seditious. It is more than probable that none of the curators had actually read them, but on 27th June 1754 they were removed from the shelves as indecent and unworthy of a place in a learned library. The catalogue shows an addendum in Hume's hand excising the entries for these books. By the Copyright Act of 1710 the Advocates' Library was a library of legal deposit and, had these books been published in London, the advocates would have had a legal obligation to accept them – this obligation still applies today and the National Library of Scotland has a highly restricted section of erotica. But lawyers often feel that the law is one of their personal playthings, and thereafter no purchases could be made without the curators' permission. This was a hugely time-consuming instruction and soon was allowed to wither on the vine. All the banned books are now in the Library's collection.

Hume, however, was deeply hurt by the affair and, having been in conversation with Robert Dundas, the Lord Advocate, wrote to him on 20th November 1754:

> The expelling these books I would conceive in no other light than as an insult upon me which nothing can repair but re-instating them . . . there is a particular kind of insolence which is more provoking as it is meaner than any other, 'tis the *Insolence of Office* which our great poet mentions as sufficient to make those who are so unhappy as to suffer from it seek even a voluntary death rather than submit to it. I presume it is chance, not design, which has exposed some of the Curators to the reproach of this vice . . . As to the three books themselves . . . I will venture to justify before any literary society in Europe, that if every book not superior in merit to La Fontaine be expelled from the library, I shall guarantee to carry away all that remains in my pocket. I know not indeed if any will remain except our fifty pound Bible, which is too bulky for me to carry away . . . By the bye, Bussi Rabutin [sic] contains no bawdy at all, though if it did, I see not that it would be a whit the worse. For I know not a more agreeable subject for both books and conversation, if executed with decency and ingenuity.[20]

Hume did seriously consider resigning the post, but his own advantage lay with continuing and he eventually came up with a face-saving alternative, worthy of the subtlest diplomat, which he communicated to his friend Adam Smith:

1. David Hume (1711-76) painted when he was 55 years old by Allan Ramsay. He is pictured in the quasi-military dress of an Embassy secretary. Hume perhaps showed an over-fondness for fine clothes. *(Scottish National Portrait Gallery)*

2. The Lawnmarket, Edinburgh. Hume was born somewhere in the triple-gabled building to the right and his penultimate house at James's Court was entered by the passageway at the extreme left. *(Author's Collection)*

3. Ninewells Farm, Chirnside. Hume spent his childhood here and suffered 'the Disease of the Learned' in this typical Border farmhouse. *(National Library of Scotland)*

4. Henry Home, Lord Kames. A judge of deep learning and even deeper drinking. Although both Whigs, Hume and he often disagreed, especially over the existence of God, but Home called him 'the best friend I ever possessed'. *(Scottish National Portrait Gallery)*

5. The library of the Jesuit College in Reims. Hume studied here in 1734. Some have thought that the beauty of the room would disturb the true scholar, but, sadly, it now no longer functions as a working library. *(Bibliothèque de L'Ancien Collège des Jésuites de Reims, Photo: Ville de Reims/Robert Meuille)*

6. The library of the Prytanée National Militaire in La Flèche, Anjou. It was once a Jesuit College, and is now a Military College. Hume worked here while writing the *Treatise of Human Nature.* Today it does not contain a single one of his works. *(Author's Collection)*

7. Yvandeau, above La Flèche in Anjou. The Jesuits gave accommodation here to Hume in 1735 and he wrote the *Treatise* in the left-hand room on the first floor. *(Author's Collection)*

8. The view from Hume's room, Yvandeau. 'I perceive a great extent of fields and buildings beyond my chamber.' The towers of the Jesuit College Chapel can be seen in the centre of the town. *(Author's Collection)*

A

TREATISE

O F

Human Nature :

BEING

An ATTEMPT to introduce the experimental Method of Reafoning

INTO

MORAL SUBJECTS.

*Rara temporum felicitas, ubi fentire, quæ velis; & quæ
fentias, dicere licet.*   TACIT.

VOL. I.

OF THE
UNDERSTANDING.

LONDON:
Printed for JOHN NOON, at the *White-Hart*, near
Mercer's-Chapel, in *Cheapfide.*

M DCC XXXIX.

9. The title page of the 1739 edition of *A Treatise of Human Nature.* Instead of
making Hume instantly famous, it 'fell dead-born from the press'. Never reprinted
during his lifetime, it is now readily available and translated into most languages.
(National Library of Scotland)

10. A page from the 1759 purchase ledger of the Advocates' Library showing the cancellation of three books which had been bought by Hume. The entry, in Hume's hand, reads, 'expunged by order of the curators, after mature deliberation'. *(The Faculty of Advocates)*

11. 'Thé à 'l'Anglais' chez le Prince de Conti. In the 'English Style', tea was served by the ladies themselves, without any servants present. The Comtesse de Boufflers stands in the centre in white, wearing an apron. The Prince is in the left-hand corner with his back to us and also to the small boy playing the harpsichord. He is Mozart. *(Agence Photographique RMN)*

12. A Gala given by the Prince de Conti for the Duke of Brunswick. Boufflers is mounted, uneasily, with a feather in her hat. The Prince, in livery and with a hunting horn, is on foot. This is the world in which *Le Bon David* moved in Paris. *(Agence Photographique RMN)*

13. The Oise today with L'Isle Adam under the willow trees on the right. It was here that the Comtesse de Boufflers found the folio size of Hume's *Essays* too large to be carried for easy reading in the open air. The foreground lamp-post and the diving nymph are recent additions. *(Author's Collection)*

14. Jean-Jacques Rousseau painted by Allan Ramsay in 1766. Hume arranged for his portrait to be made as a gift for Rousseau and received nothing but abuse for his pains. Not for the first time Rousseau bit the hand that fed him. *(National Gallery of Scotland)*

15. Alexander Carlyle painted by Henry Raeburn in 1796. He was nicknamed 'Jupiter' since he was thought to resemble a Roman god. He was an affectionate friend of Hume and one of Edinburgh's greatest gossips. *(Scottish National Portrait Gallery)*

L'historien hume!

16. David Hume painted by Louis Carrogis. The title of the painting would have pleased Hume as he is referred to as 'the historian Hume'. *(Scottish National Portrait Gallery)*

17. Hume's tomb in the Old Calton Burial Ground, Edinburgh. Designed (with some care) by Robert Adam, it is a sadly neglected memorial to one of Edinburgh's greatest citizens. *(Author's Collection)*

. . . being equally unwilling to lose the use of the books and to bear an indignity, I retain the office but have given Blacklock, our blind poet, a bond of annuity for the salary. I have now put it out of those malicious fellows' power to offer me any indignity, while my motives for remaining in this office are so apparent. I should be glad that you approve of my conduct; I own I am satisfied with myself.[21]

Another version of this event is given by 'Jupiter' Carlyle:

he was visited by his friend Blacklock, the poet, who is much better known by his poverty and blindness than by his genius. This poor man began a long descant of misery, bewailing his want of sight, his large family of children, and his utter inability to provide for them, or even to procure them the necessities of life. Hume, unable to bear his complaints, and destitute of money to assist him, ran instantly to his desk, took out the grant, and presented it to his miserable friend, who received it with exultation, and whose name was soon after, by Hume's interest, inserted instead of his own. After such a relation it is needless that I should say any more of his genuine philanthropy.[22]

Hume continued to take an interest in Blacklock's care and in October 1754 was recommending John Wilkes to join in subscribing to a volume of his poetry.

He carried on in his now nominal post until January 1757 when he told Alexander Wedderburn, a curator, that, while conscious of the honour the Library had done him, he wished to resign. The faculty then asked him to submit a formal resignation which he did on 8th January. Meanwhile the faculty set about finding a replacement. The fact that his resignation was accepted and Adam Ferguson was appointed in his place at the same meeting seems to imply that the resignation was not unexpected. Hume was found to owe the Library £7.10. 9 pence, a debt both parties chose to ignore.

Hume was now one of the established figures of Edinburgh and in 1754 Allan Ramsay painted his portrait. It shows a man relaxed with still a hint of the unresponsive expression Charlemont had commented on in Turin. 'Jupiter' Carlyle's remark about Hume's fondness for fine clothes is evident, and when George III saw the portrait he rebuked Ramsay, saying

210 THE GREAT INFIDEL

that he thought the coat too fine. Ramsay riposted that he had painted it so luxuriously in order that future generations would know that during His Majesty's reign at least one philosopher had a decent coat for his back.

Hume would now seek out like-minded companions in Edinburgh. He and Henry Home (elevated to the bench in 1752, and now Lord Kames, as he will now be called) formed a 'triumvirate of taste' with Lord Elibank. Elibank was Patrick Murray, a man of fashion, a patron of letters and a *bon viveur*. He and Hume were firm friends and part of a circle to be found in the various clubs of the city. There were many to choose from.

Under 'Convivialia' in his *Traditions of Edinburgh* Robert Chambers quotes forty-odd clubs of all sorts. Some were self-consciously depraved such as the *Hell-fire* and downright pornographic such as the *Beggar's Benison*; the *Sweating Club* whose members drank solidly until midnight, then roamed the streets beating and robbing whoever they met; and the *Wig Club* who made obeisance to a centuries-old wig, and whose new members had to drink a quart of claret at a single draught, but then, 'the Wigs usually drank twopenny ale on which it was possible to get satisfactorily drunk for a groat' (fourpence).[23] A little less disreputable were the *Facer Club* where, if a member had failed to drain his glass at each draught he was required to throw the dregs in his own face, and the *Soaping Club*, the origin of whose name is obscure, but members were required to compose comic verse, usually obscene. James Boswell was, needless to say, an enthusiastic member.

However, with more intellectual aims, there was the *Philosophical Society*. A Medical Society had been formed in 1731, with Alexander Monro *primus* (the grandfather of the three Professors of Anatomy of the same name at Edinburgh University) as secretary. It was then enlarged in 1737 to encompass Philosophy and Literature when it changed its name to *The Society for Improving Arts and Sciences*, or, more generally, the *Philosophical Society of Edinburgh*. It ceased to meet and broke up during the '45 but restarted in 1752 with Hume and Alexander Monro as joint secretaries. The first volume of the *Transactions of the Philosophical Society of Edinburgh* was accordingly published in 1754 under the title of *Essays and Observations, Physical and Literary*, with a preface almost certainly written by Hume:

The object of this society is the same with that of other academies which have been established in other parts of Europe, the promoting of natural philosophy and of literature, by communicating to the public such dissertations as shall be transmitted to them, either by their own members or by others. 'Tis allowed that these two branches of learning, especially the former, are more promoted by the observation of facts than by the most ingenious reasonings and disputations . . . The sciences of theology, morals, and politics the society are resolved entirely to exclude from their plan. However difficult the inferences in these sciences, the facts on which they are founded are extremely obvious; and we could not hope by our collections to be in this respect of any service to the public. The great delicacy of the subject, the imperfections of human understanding, the various attachments and inclinations of mankind, will forever propagate disputes with regard to these parts of erudition. And 'tis the peculiar happiness of geometry and physics that as they interest less the passions of men, they admit of more calm disquisition and enquiry . . . They assume not such authority as to stamp their approbation on any performance, even those which they communicate, much less those which have been barely read before them.[24]

He might as well have said that the Society was interested in just about everything else, for the collection of essays ranges from lightning rods (Benjamin Franklin) and shallow-ploughing (Kames) through the anthelmintic [of medicinal use against worms] virtue of Bulgewater bark (Peter Duguid, a surgeon in Jamaica), chemistry (Black), thermodynamics (Cullen), mathematics (Colin Maclaurin), and the metaphysics of motion (Kames again) . . . 'a rough and ready frontier spirit enlivened their meetings'.[25] All papers for inclusion were to be sent, either to Monro or Hume, and about the end of 1782 the club was incorporated as the Royal Society of Edinburgh.

Hume was also involved in the foundation of the *Select Society*. According to Dugald Stewart, who is, largely, quoting Carlyle:

The Select Society owed its rise to the ingenious Allan Ramsay, son of the poet of that name, and was intended for philosophical inquiry, and the improvement of the members in the art of speaking. They met for the first time in May 1754, and consisted only of fifteen who had been nominated and called together by Mr Ramsay and two or three of his friends. At that meeting they formed themselves into a society, into which the members were ever after elected by ballot, and who met regularly every Wednesday evening at St Giles Masonic Hall, during the sitting of the Court of Session, both in summer and winter.[26]

The Society gave gold medals for the finer arts and cash awards for the more useful arts:

. . . what chiefly renders us considerable is a project of engrafting on to the Society a scheme for encouraging the arts and sciences and manufactures in Scotland, by premiums, partly honorary, partly lucrative. A box is open for donations and about one hundred guineas has been given in. We hear of considerable sums intended by Lords Hopetoun, Morton, Marchmont, etc., who desire to be members. Nine managers have been chosen; and to keep the business distinct from reasoning, the first Monday of every month is set apart for these transactions, and they are never mentioned in our Wednesday meetings. Advertisements have been published to inform the public of our intentions. A premium, I remember, is promised to the best discourse on Taste, and on the Principles of Vegetation. These regard the *belles lettres* and the sciences, but we have not neglected porter, strong ale, and wrought ruffles, even down to linen rags.[27]

It did, indeed, form a new, parallel, society, the Edinburgh Society for Encouraging Arts, Sciences, Manufactures, and Agriculture in Scotland. In 1755 Hume said of it:

It has grown to be a national concern. Young and old, noble and ignoble, witty and dull, laity and clergy – all the world are ambitious of a place amongst us and on each occasion we are as much solicited by candidates as if we were to choose a member of Parliament.[28]

According to Dugald Stewart and 'Jupiter' Carlyle, Hume and Adam Smith 'never opened their lips', but this is almost certainly untrue. Smith did have an embarrassing stutter, and Hume would have been reluctant to speak in public, but 'never' is unlikely. Stewart quotes the minute for 4th December 1754:

Mr David Hume Preses [Presiding]
The Society entered upon the debate for the question appointed for
this night, viz., Whether ought we to prefer ancient or modern
manners with regard to the condition and treatment of women?
And after some reasoning and speeches on that subject, the question
named by the President, and allowed by the Society, for the subject
of the ensuing night's debate was, 'Whether the difference of
national characters be chiefly owing to the nature of different
climates, or to moral and political causes.'
The President then left the chair.[29]

In accordance with normal debating procedure the President would leave
the chair because he wished to take part in the debate – especially when the
subject was one which Hume had already written about. It is true that he
disliked public speaking and orating, preferring the conversation of a few
around a dinner table to an open debate, but the picture of two of the
greatest intellects in Scotland sitting mute for meeting after meeting is
ludicrous.

The subjects debated varied widely. The Select debated the cessation of
obligatory veils (gratuities to house servants) and they disappeared, in spite
of a vociferous protest by Edinburgh's footmen, in 1760. Other topics
included: Was paper credit advantageous? Should poor relief be given in
their own houses or in work-houses? Did Brutus do well in killing Caesar?
Should the stool of repentance be abolished? The Society did not allow a
proposed debate on whether licensed stews were advantageous to a nation.

All in all, a picture emerges of educated, and where they could afford it,
philanthropic gentlemen engaging in formalised discussion of the sort one
hopes might circulate in clubs, and even pubs, today. The flame of the
Enlightenment was starting to burn more brightly.

They even ventured forth on a subject which still finds column inches in
today's Scottish press – the vexed question of a Scottish accent. Scottish
MPs were found to be unintelligible in Parliament, and the accent was
derided as barbaric once it had progressed south of Berwick. However, the
converse could also be said of the Scots understanding of the southern
English. In Edinburgh a gentleman's daughter had been to see *Love for
Love* and *The old Bachelor*, two mildly racy plays by Congreve. She was told
they were smutty plays not suitable for young women and she answered,
'Indeed they did nothing wrong that I saw, as for what they said, it was

high English, and I did not understand it'. The debate continues vociferously today but in 1761 the Society made *Regulations of the Select Society for Promoting the Reading and Speaking of the English Language in Scotland* and set up another sub-society to promote it.

This fissiparous tendency meant the Select Society was no longer select and its activities were becoming altogether too diverse. The Select Society lasted until 1764, and by 1765 the Edinburgh Society for Encouraging Arts, Sciences, Manufactures, and Agriculture in Scotland, as well as the Select itself, died.

The third club of which Hume was an active member was the Poker Club. This was founded in 1762 to agitate for a militia in Scotland which had not existed since the '45. 'About the third or fourth meeting the members thought of giving it a name sufficiently significant to the initiated but of uncertain meaning to the general public, and not so directly or obviously offensive as that of *Militia* Club which would have been to the adversaries of any such object.'[30] It met between two and six o'clock on Fridays in Nicolson's tavern with an average attendance of ten or twelve members. Dinner was priced at 2/- plus sherry and claret, although its meetings were exceptional for their sobriety. Hume was appointed assessor and admired the 'plain roughness of the Poker', where he was often held up to satire. The need for a Scottish Militia was seldom mentioned. After a row with their host Nicolson in 1769 they moved to the more fashionable Fortune's tavern but this proved more expensive and many members left.

The Enlightenment might have been under way, but Hume was still not beyond criticism. Early in 1753 an anonymous pamphlet appeared in Edinburgh entitled, ponderously, *A Delineation of the Nature and Obligation of Morality with Reflexions on Mr Hume's book entitled an Enquiry concerning the Principles of Morals.* The author was, in fact, James Balfour, the Professor of Moral Philosophy at Edinburgh University. Hume answered this immediately on 15th March and left the response with Balfour's publisher. In a good mood, he begs the friendship of his unknown critic, but points out that the views of Palamedes, the cynic in the *Dialogue,* are not those of Hume. He finds Balfour too fervent an advocate of chastity, gracefully criticises his prose style, and repeats his hopes for face-to-face debate. The offer was never taken up, but Hume was wrong to say that the work 'came unnoticed and unobserved into the world'. Other reviews of his writings were now appearing but Hume stuck firmly to his precept to be unaffected by adverse comments.

Hume had, with Katherine and his maid Peggy Irvine, moved again, on Whitsunday 1753, to Jack's Land in the Canongate. The house no longer exists but it would have stood between a newsagents at 208 and a public house at 232 Canongate.

It was at this house in July 1758 that James Boswell met Hume:

> Mr Hume is, I think, a very proper person for a young man [Boswell was 18] to cultivate an acquaintance with; though he has not, perhaps, the most delicate of taste, yet he has applied himself with great attention to the study of the ancients, and is likewise a great historian, so that you are not only entertained in his company, but may reap a great deal of useful information.[31]

In 1801, for reasons unknown, the reverend Ebeneezer Marshal of Cockpen wrote to Alexander Carlyle asking for anecdotes of David Hume. Carlyle replied, somewhat reluctantly, since he was writing his autobiography at the time, and wished to use these anecdotes himself:

> Apropos of good humour, at a time when he was called Hume the Atheist, and when good people were really afraid to meet with him, a worthy lady of Edinburgh [Mrs Adam, mother of architect Robert] who gave good dinners, said to her son that she had always made his companions very welcome, there was one person she begged she might never see and that was David Hume the Atheist – the son said that he would pay respect to her injunction, but not long after invited David to dine and contrived to conceal from his mother who he was. In the evening when the company broke up, she told her son that the company he had assembled was very agreeable, but above all the fat man who sat next to her, for she had never seen so pleasant a man in all her life. When she was told who he was she explained that she wondered how slanders rose, for that honest man was no more an atheist than she was, and hoped that whenever a dinner was given to the literati he might always be one. Mr Hume was obliged to live very frugally for tho' he had £40 from the Advocates' Library, he had sought that merely for the use of the books, he gave the whole salary away to charity. He had a very small home in Jack's Land in the Canongate and kept only one

maidservant, whom he never parted with all her life, and such was the sweetness of his sister that even when he became opulent and this manner of living rose in proportion to his circumstances, he never put a housekeeper over her for fear of affronting her.

When he lived in the Canongate he gave little suppers to select friends, but when he enlarged his manner of living he entertained much and well, and nobody since his death has taken the pains he did to bring together a convivial society.[32]

Hume was somewhat in awe of his maid, the faithful but redoubtable Peggy Irvine, who despaired of his lifestyle but tolerated it provided it did not interfere too much with her own. Carlyle recalls an evening when the party was settling in for some late-night drinking and debate:

David Hume, who having dined abroad, came rather late to us, and directly pulled a large key from his pocket and laid it on the table. This he said was given to him by his maid Peggy (much more like a man than a woman) that she might not sit up for him. As [his] circumstances improved he enlarged his mode of living, and instead of the roasted hen and minced collops and a bottle of punch, he gave both elegant dinners and suppers, and the best claret, and, which was best of all, he furnished the entertainment with the most instructive and pleasing conversation, for he assembled whosoever was the most knowing or agreeable among the laity or clergy . . . For innocent mirth and agreeable raillery I never knew his match.[33]

The clouds of David Hume's early life had cleared and he was now writing the work by which he most wanted to be remembered. He was writing the *History of England.*

In fact he had thought about this project for some time, and some of his earliest pages of jottings show a profound love of the history of all ages. In a notebook his early classicism is evident with studies of the tax laws of Imperial Rome, and pages of the economic statistics of Rome, Greece, and Persia. He had also read, and noted, the Comte de Boulain-Villiers' accounts of the great French families. Boulain-Villiers was described by Voltaire as 'the most learned historian in France'. He was greatly interested in international trade and the benefits and disadvantages it might bring about. Hume's notes contain many comments on current affairs:

The Pension Bill [for royal pensions] failed passing along with the Triennial [of 1694, to prevent Parliament sitting for more than three years] in a Whig Courtier Parliament only by some idle disputes about the Expression of the King and his heirs and successors . . . The reason why the Court has a greater superiority among the Lords than the Commons, beside the bishops, is that the Court gives places to the Lords chiefly for their interest among the Commons . . . Within the last 2000 years almost all the despotic Governments of the world have been improving and the free ones degenerating so that now they are nearly on a par.[34]

Hume here is showing signs of disillusion with the corruption-ridden Whig hierarchy.

There exists in the National Library of Scotland, a box containing MSS 732-734, three fascicles entitled *Memoranda for my History of England written in July 1745 or 46.* They are subscribed *James Court 1750* to *1759* and carry the signature *David Hume.* A fourth such manuscript exists in the Huntington Library in California. They carry detailed notes on English history from the Roman invasion of 55 BC to AD 1701 and the reign of William III and, for a researcher into the workings of Hume's mind provide an invaluable insight. Unfortunately, they are clearly not in Hume's bold hand and Hume did not move to James's Court until 1762. In September 1977 these fascicles were shown to be forgeries. They are probably the work of Alexander Howland Smith, a forger of historical documents, who, obligingly, provided a counterfeit keyhole into Hume's mind. The box carries a warning from Dr Alan Bell, Asisstant Keeper of Manuscripts in the 1970s, who also published an article on the forgeries in the December 1979 issue of *Notes and Queries*.[35] The fact that these documents are totally unreliable has not been noted by Mossner or by Victor Wexler in his *David Hume and the History of England,* published by the American Philosophical Society in 1979. *Caveat lector.*

However, Hume had been putting down some sketches for the work while with the Marquis of Annandale, and using his contacts with great men to consult their libraries. In the eighteenth century there were no libraries with open access to the public. Richard Meade, physician and antiquary, had allowed Hume access to his collection in London in 1750, and others would have obliged willingly, but Hume needed an entire library to consult on demand. The Advocates' Library answered the bill completely, and he had now, as he had indicated to Adam Smith in September 1752, started to write his *magnum opus,* the *History of England.*

Hume had deliberately called his work the *History of England* since he would have been aware that William Robertson had been writing the *History of Scotland* since 1753. It was published in 1759 and Hume and Robertson had corresponded amicably over the proofs. Robertson appears to have accepted Hume's, altogether quite minor, criticisms. Hume also set out his plan to Clephane back in January 1753, with confusion over the title:

> I have begun a work which will employ me several years, and which yields me much satisfaction. 'Tis a History of Britain, from the Union of the Crowns to the present time. I have already finished the reign of King James [1603 – 1625]. My friends flatter me, (by this I mean they don't flatter me) that I have succeeded. You know there is no post of honour in the English Parnassus more vacant than that of History. Style, judgement, impartiality, care – everything is wanting to our historians, and even Rapin, during this latter period is extremely deficient. I make my work very concise, after the manner of the Ancients. It divides into three very modest volumes; one to the death of Charles the First; the second at the Revolution; the third at the Accession [of the House of Hanover in 1714], for I dare come no nearer the present times.[36]

The reference to 'Rapin' is interesting. Paul de Rapin-Thoyras was a Huguenot refugee who published a six-volume *History of England* between 1723 and 1725. Hume was greatly influenced by Rapin while writing his historical essays. In the letter to Clephane, his disillusion has started and by 1757, 'To tell the truth, I was carried away with the usual esteem paid to that historian, till I came to examine him more particularly when I found him altogether despicable, and I was not ashamed to acknowledge my mistake'.[37] Admission of mistakes is a rare attribute.

To understand this change of view it must be understood that Hume had been born into a Whig family and had swallowed their politics along with his childhood porridge. But this was Whig thought oversimplified into a choice between the Stewarts and absolute rule, and a monarchy controlled by Parliament, and, as so often happens, the principles of popular freedom so often expressed in opposition disappeared when political power was achieved. The Whigs, in power, proved to be as greedy for corrupt sinecures and pocket-lining, in the name of the people, as had been the Tories in the name of the King.

Hume also showed in undertaking this mammoth task that he had an enormous appetite for work. He used to say that he did not find it an irksome task to go through a great many dull books when writing his history. 'I then read,' said he, 'not for pleasure, but in order to find out facts.' He compared it to being a sportsman seeking hares, who does not mind what sort of ground he goes over provided he finds hares in it.[38] He found it impossible to believe that any man of learning was not also thoroughly well read. Boswell contributes another anecdote told to him by Sir David Dalrymple:

> When Mr David Hume first began to be known in the world as a philosopher, Mr Thomas White, a decent rich merchant of London, said to him, 'I am surprised, Mr Hume, that a man of your good sense should think of being a philosopher. Why, I now took it into my head to be a philosopher for some time, but tired of it most confoundedly and gave it up.' 'Pray, sir,' said Mr Hume, 'in what branch of philosophy did you employ your researches? What books did you read?' 'Books?' said Mr White; 'nay, sir, I read no books, but used to sit you whole forenoons a-yawning and poking the fire.'[39]

David Hume was doing no fire-poking or yawning. By 26th May 1753 he told Adam Smith he had reached the Long Parliament, which sat from November 1640. In other words, he had nearly completed his first volume, in spite of his 'scrupulous method of composing'. By 28th October he told Clephane:

> I have now brought my history down to the death of Charles the first; and here I intend to pause for some time: to read and think and correct: to look forward and backward: and to adopt the most moderate and reasonable sentiments on all subjects. I am sensible that the history of the first two Stuarts will be most agreeable to the Tories: that of the two last, to the Whigs. But we must endeavour to be above any regard either to Whigs or Tories.[40]

Having no political bias would, of course, mean that he would be attacked by both sides. Hume's next task would be to arrange for a publisher, but while he was making up his mind to contact Andrew Millar he received an offer from a totally unexpected quarter:

From Bailie Gavin Hamilton to William Strahan, 29 January 1754.

In any important step I make, in business, I should reckon myself very much out of my duty to you as one of my dearest friends if I did not unbosom myself, let this serve as preamble to what I am going to say. I have within these ten days concluded a bargain that is reckoned very bold by everyone that hears of it, and some think it rash, because I have never heard of the like pass here; though at the same time I remain very well content with my bargain.

John Balfour and I have agreed to pay £1200 sterling of copy money, for a single impression of a book, 'tis the great history of Britain [sic] by David Hume our scots author . . . the book will sell at 15/- bound or ten shillings to booksellers in sheets . . . all I can say to you in the bounds of a short letter is that we have been at due pains to inform ourselves of the merit of the work and are well satisfied on that head, that it is the prettiest thing that was ever attempted on the English History, the three volls [sic] contains three grand periods, the first from the union of the crowns to the death of the king, the 2nd voll from the death of the king to the Revolution, and the last till the treaty of Utrecht, the facts are well vouched for and thrown together in a light as to give the true character of the times it is neither whig nor tory but truly impartial.[41]

The treaty of Utrecht in 1714 marked the end of Louis XIV's power, and the year itself saw the accession of George I.

Hamilton's offer is truly amazing. He was a bailie, that is, a member of the city council with the powers of a magistrate and an established Edinburgh bookseller. Hume had, as keeper of the Advocates' Library, bought many books from him, but he had no great experience of publishing. Yet his business sense told him that an investment of £1,200 (£107,200 in present-day values) would return him a profit with a print run of 2,000. It demonstrates the strength of Hume's reputation, as well, perhaps, as Hamilton's naïveté. There is, perhaps, another aspect to the size of the advance. Hamilton, as senior partner in Hamilton and Balfour, was Edinburgh's second leading publisher and, therefore, bookseller. The leader was Alexander Kincaid, who had published Hume's *Essays* in 1741.

But while Hume was Keeper of the Advocates' Library he had bought heavily from Hamilton, spending £448 4s 0d, as opposed to £261 12s 9d spent with Kincaid. The *Essays* had been a moderate success, but when Hume is said to have offered another book to Kincaid, he rejected it, possibly on account of Hume's alleged atheism. We may guess at a falling-out between the two men, but can presume no more.

Hume, however, did not accept the initial offer. As usual he would not contract for more than one volume at a time, and then only for one edition. For this he agreed £400, with £600 for a second edition.

Having completed the work in 470 quarto pages, Hume summed it up:

> . . . my narration is rapid, and I have more proposed as my model the concise manner of the ancient historians, than the prolix, tedious style of some modern compilers. I have inserted no original papers, and entered into no detail of minute uninterested facts. The philosophical spirit, which I have so much indulged in all my writings, finds here ample materials to work upon . . . A few notes, to clear up passages obscure to foreigners may also be requisite.[42]

A cautionary note even for today's authors.

The intrepid and optimistic Hamilton went to London and set up shop at the 'Golden Head, next Pinchbeck's Toyshop, facing the Haymarket'. He advertised in the *Daily Advertiser,* and arranged with other booksellers to offer the book for sale. Hume was pleased with the sales in Edinburgh and awaited the comments of reviewers. He wrote to the Earl of Balcarres:

> The misfortune of a book, says Boileau, is not the being ill spoke of, but the not being spoke of at all. The sale has been very considerable here, about four hundred and fifty in five weeks. How it has succeeded in London I cannot tell. Only, I observe that some of the weekly papers have been busy with me. I am as great an atheist as Bolingbroke, as great a Jacobite as Carte; [author of *the Irish Massacre set in a Clear Light*]; I cannot write English, etc.[43]

He goes on to note the book is more popular with the Tories than the Whigs, but that the Tories, being in opposition, had much less to lose. He sums up his own reaction in *My Own Life*:

> I was, I own, sanguine in my expectations of the success of this work . . . but miserable was my disappointment . . . Mr Millar told

me that in a twelvemonth he sold only forty five copies of it. I scarcely indeed heard of one man in the three kingdoms, considerable for rank or letters, that could endure the book . . . I was, however, I confess, discouraged; and had not the war been at that time breaking out between France and England, I had certainly retired to some provincial town of the former kingdom, have changed my name, and never more returned to my native country. But as this scheme was not now practicable, and the subsequent volume was considerably advanced I resolved to pick up courage and persevere.[44]

The war referred to was the Seven Years War, when France and England finally settled the limits of their respective empires. This letter gives his first reference to a wish to live outside Scotland. He would reiterate this several times at moments of irritation with his fellow countrymen. However, the letter is at variance with that to Balcarres, and could hardly take account of the fact that the *History* would become the internationally bestselling book of its type until Gibbon's *Decline and Fall of the Roman Empire*.

In his own time Hume's *History* was his most famous work, and after its publication he always insisted on being named as a historian, not as a philosopher.

TEN

The Prettiest Thing That Was Ever Attempted

The first surprise on reading the *History*, is that the title page of the 1754 edition calls it *The History of Great Britain* although it is written entirely from the standpoint of an Englishman and only deals with Scottish history when it touches on that of England. Hume would leave the detail of Scotland to William Robertson. For example, he refers to James VI & I as James I throughout, and he regards England as the home country, telling us that James was born and educated amid a foreign and hostile people. He judges that James was guided through his whole reign by 'temper and inclination rather than by the rules of political prudence'. But it is not long before he brings a swarm of angry hornets about his head by reviewing the two religions current in England:

> The first reformers, who made such furious and successful attacks on the Romish SUPERSTITION [Hume's capitals], and shook it to its lowest foundations, may safely be pronounced to have been universally inflamed with the highest ENTHUSIASM. These two species of religion, the superstitious and the fanatical, stand in diametrical opposition to each other; and a large portion of the latter must necessarily fall to his share who is so courageous as to control authority, and so assuming as to obtrude his own innovations upon the world.[1]

The principal hornet was Daniel MacQueen, who wrote the *Letters on Mr Hume's History of Great Britain*, a turgid book of 328 pages containing 9 'letters'. In the first he reports a fictitious debate between a supporter of Hume and an antagonist. The supporter thought 'A minute detail of particular incidents was of little significancy [sic] in history . . . as it perplexed the mind. Mr Hume's history was elegant, the diction generally clear and correct, and the narrative succinct and animated'. The antagonist argued a lack of research and distinguished between history and memoir writing. He regretted the 'author's indecent excursions on the subject of religion, the genius of the Protestant faith, and the characters of the first reformers'.[2] The character supporting Hume said that he addressed himself to 'a distant posterity' and had merely said that Superstition was the characteristic of Catholicism and fanaticism or enthusiasm of the Protestant faith. He cannot see that mere opposition to Rome is fanaticism. MacQueen restates the Reformation view of the Catholic Church and defends the early reformers from the charge of fanaticism, saying that they were simply 'severe' or 'lively'. Luther was no more than a calm intellectual. MacQueen finds the subject of importance, and Hume's 'misinterpretations' are dismissed as 'gross'. Finally he sums up: 'I have done, sir. And shall not take any further notice of the loose and irreligious sneers which Mr Hume has not been afraid to throw out on a subject of the highest dignity and of infinite importance. We have had enough of his confused ideas and speculations about superstition and enthusiasm'.

People felt that Hume, with his dangerous philosophy of scepticism, was unfit to comment on established religion. But to Hume history and philosophy were inseparable, and today's divisions of Political History, Social History, Economic History, etc., were meaningless:

> Through many decades the critics have insisted on a rigid
> dichotomy between Hume the philosopher and Hume the historian.
> The two Humes cannot, however, properly be separated. Descartes,
> with his admiration of certainty, distrusts history, Hume with his
> distrust of certainty admires history.[3]

Hume is still accused today of having written a Tory history while Thomas Carlyle said he was the 'father of all succeeding Whigs'. He himself said:

> My views of things are more conformable to Whig principles, my
> representations of persons to Tory prejudices. Nothing can so much
> prove that men commonly regard more persons than things as to
> find that I am commonly numbered among the Tories.[4]

Hume felt a certain satisfaction that he had now been attacked by both sides, and 'the reader, putting the whole together, concludes that I am of no sect, which to him will appear the same thing as being of no religion'. But he was wise enough to cut the passage from the second edition while justifying the position of a historian in what was meant to be a preface, but appeared as a footnote. He defines the proper office of religion and asserts that when religions of whatever persuasion carry it out wholeheartedly, these religions are then of no interest to the historian, who concentrates on the excesses which give rise to conflict. He reasserts that reformers of both sides have behaved from time immemorial with excessive zeal, even in the 'most happy medium' of the Church of England, 'although during the age of which these volumes treat there was a tincture of enthusiasm in their antagonists'. As to politics, perhaps a totally objective view will only be held by 'a distant posterity'.

This retraction was seized upon in 1757 by the Reverend John Brown in his *An Estimate of the Manners and Principles of the Times,* a two-volume work filled with vinegary gloom. From the start his view is clear: 'We are rolling to the brink of a precipice that must destroy us'. But he warms to his task as a bigot, without naming Hume:

> A certain historian of our times, bent upon popularity and gain, published a large volume and omitted no opportunity offered to disgrace religion. A large impression was published and a small part sold. The author being asked why he had so larded his work with irreligion, his answer implied, 'that he had done it that his book might sell.' It was whispered him that he had totally mistaken the spirit of the times: that no allurements could engage the fashionable infidel world to travel through a large quarto: and that as the few readers of quartos that remain lie mostly among the serious part of mankind, he had offended his best customers and ruined the sale of his book. This information had a notable effect: for a second volume, as large and instructive as the first hath appeared, not a smack of irreligion is to be found in it, and an apology for the first concludes it.[5]

Then having put unsubstantiated words into Hume's mouth, he continues in the second volume:

> . . . he would not offend the Godly. Now this very man, in defiance of all decency, hath for several years carried on a trade of essay-writing, in the course of which he hath not only misrepresented, abused, and insulted the most essential principles of Christianity, but to the utmost of his power, shaken the foundations of all religion. In these sorry essays he had no fear of offending the godly, because he knew the godly were not to be his buyers, but when he finds that his history must sell among the godly, or not sell at all, then comes the panic upon him; then, forsooth he will not offend

the godly. Here, therefore, a character is clearly developed. With St Paul godliness was gain, but with this man, gain produceth godliness.[6]

This contorted logic in pursuit of an epigram attributes completely unwarranted motives to Hume, who could be content with knowing that he was only being given as an example of the general decay described in this narrow, unpleasant work. Brown's conclusion is inevitable: 'The honest pride of virtue is no more, or, where it happens to exist, is overwhelmed by inferior vanities'.[7] Hume was justly furious with this attack and with Brown's implied claim to be privy to Hume's instructions to his publisher, and on 20 May 1757 he wrote to Andrew Millar, who had taken over the publishing of the *History* from Gavin Hamilton:

> All I can recollect of the matter is this that above two years ago when Bailie Hamilton was in London, he wrote me that the stop in the sale of my history proceeded from some strokes of irreligion which had raised the cry of the clergy against me . . . I doubt not but that I could easily refute Dr Brown, but as I had taken a resolution never to have the least altercation with these fellows, I shall not readily be brought to pay any attention to him . . . Since you are acquainted with Dr Brown, I must beg of you to read this letter to him; for it is probably or indeed certainly all the answer I shall ever deign to give him.[8]

The attack, coming from a reactionary clergyman, does show that religion was still not a subject to be debated. Millar took over the publishing of the *History* when the London booksellers closed ranks against Hamilton, a newcomer to the trade, and gravely inhibited the sale of the book.

Hume starts by describing James's accession:

> The crown of England was never transmitted from father and son with greater tranquillity than it passed from the family of Tudor to that of Stuart.[9]

Hume goes on to accuse James I of:

> timidity, his prejudices, his indolence, prevented him from making any progress in the knowledge or practice of foreign politics, and in a little time diminished that regard, which all the neighbouring nations had paid to England, during the reign of his predecessor.

Then, as a result of describing the Gunpowder Plot, he looks at the Reformation:

> Like the ancient pagan idolatry, the popular religion consisted more of exterior practices and observances, than any of the principles which either took possession of the heart or influenced the conduct. [The Church of Rome] extended her jealousy against learning and philosophy, whom in her supine security she had previously overlooked . . . the dreadful tribunal of the inquisition, that utmost instance of human depravity, is a durable monument to instruct us what a pitch iniquity and cruelty may rise to when covered by the sacred mantle of religion.

Of James's character he said:

> Many virtues, it must be owned, he was possessed of; but not one of them pure or free from the contagion of the neighbouring vices. His generosity bordered on profusion, his learning on pedantry, his pacific disposition on pusillanimity, his wisdom on cunning, his friendship on light fancy and boyish fondness.

And he sums up the reign:

> Upon the whole we must conceive that monarchy on the accession of the House of Stuart, was possessed of a very extensive authority . . . by the changes which have been introduced, the liberty and independence of individuals has been rendered much more full, entire and secure; that of the public more uncertain and precarious.

Charles I deserves:

> the epithet of a good rather than a great man, and was more fitted to rule in a regular established government, than either to give way to the encroachments of a popular assembly, or finally to subdue their pretensions . . . The tragical death of Charles begot a question whether the people, in any case, were entitled to judge and punish their sovereign . . . government is instituted in order to restrain the fury and injustice of the people; and being founded on opinion not on force, it is dangerous, by these speculations, to weaken the reverence which the multitude owe to authority.

This is moving away from the absolute right of the people to replace the sovereign. It would have delighted the Tories, and Hume was presumed to have joined their ranks, some critics going as far as to call him a Jacobite. Hume would have none of it. 'I have the impudence to pretend that I am of no party and have no bias. Lord Elibank says that I am a moderate Whig and Mr Wallace that I am a candid Tory.'[10]

On 12th April 1754 he told Millar, 'I have always said to all my acquaintance that if the first volume bore a little of a Tory aspect, the second would probably be as grateful to the other party. The first two princes of the House of Stewart were certainly more excusable than the two second . . . I need not mention the oppressions in Scotland nor the absurd conduct of K James the 2nd.'[11]

A year later, he is complaining vociferously to William Strahan:

> Surely, there was never a man so torn in pieces by calumny. I thought I had been presenting to the public a history full of candour and disinterestedness, where I conquered some of the prejudices of my education, neglected my attachments and views of preferment and all for the sake of truth. When behold! I am dubbed a Jacobite, passive obedience man, papist and what not. But all this we must bear with patience. The public is the most capricious mistress we can court; and we authors who write for fame, must not be repulsed by some rigours, which are always temporary, where they are unjust.[12]

Then:

> In 1756 two years after the fall of the first volume was published the second volume of my history, containing the period from the death of Charles I till the Revolution. This performance happened to give less displeasure to the Whigs and was better received. It not only rose itself, but helped to buoy up its unfortunate brother. But though I had been taught by experience that the Whig party were in control of bestowing all the places, both in the states and in literature, I was so little inclined to yield to their senseless clamour, that in above a hundred alterations, which further study, reading or reflection engaged me to make in the reigns of the first two Stuarts, I have made all of them invariably to the Tory side. It is ridiculous to consider the English Constitution before that period as a regular plan of liberty.[13]

He dealt severely with the 'sectaries' of Cromwell's time:

> Though the English nation be naturally candid and sincere,
> hypocrisy prevailed beyond any example in ancient or modern
> times . . . the Old Testament, preferably to the New, was the
> favourite of all the sectaries. The eastern poetical style of that
> composition, made it more easily susceptible of a turn, which was
> agreeable to them.

And Cromwell's rule without Parliament is treated with loathing:

> All reasonable men now concluded that the very masque of liberty
> was thrown aside, and that the nation was subjected to military and
> despotic government, exercised, not in the legal manner of
> European nations, but according to the maxims of eastern tyranny.

He is casually dismissive of Milton who is 'admirable, though liable to
some objections, his prose writings disagreeable, though not altogether
defective in genius'. In general, he bemoaned the decline of culture and the
arts under the Commonwealth, and possibly with this in mind, welcomed
the Stuart Restoration.

Charles II he thought good in private but dangerously incompetent in
public and he quoted the old saying that Charles 'Never said a foolish
thing nor ever did a wise one'. Nor did civil liberty find in him a very
zealous patron.

James II had 'many of the qualities which form a good citizen', and was
'more unfortunate than criminal'. But he was 'swallowed up in bigotry'.

The convention for the settlement of the crown on the house of Orange
is reported in careful detail and 'the powers of the royal prerogative were
more narrowly circumscribed and more exactly defined than in any former
period of the English government'; Hume reprints the Declaration of
Rights as an appendix.

The four reigns exemplified the 'continued struggle between Privilege
and Prerogative ever at variance' that he mentioned to Adam Smith, and
the result is that 'we in this island have ever since enjoyed, if not the best
system of government, at least the most entire system of liberty, that ever
was known amongst mankind . . . The Whig party, for a course of near
seventy years, have, almost without interruption, enjoyed the whole
authority of government, and no honors [sic] or offices could be obtained
but by their countenance and protection . . . They have thus had un-

opposed control of press and publication to the detriment of historical truth'.

Here lies the basis for Hume's wish to distance himself from the ruling Whigs. The stink of the jobbery and corruption which disgraced eighteenth-century politics nauseated him. He had not become more Tory, but he had never been a party Whig. Such minds, which do not conform to party labels, are anathema to politicians who rely on unquestioning devotion. Lord David Cecil referred to them as 'parcel people'. If you know just one thing about a person, say, that he rides to hounds, then you can guess the rest of the parcel. He will be a homophobic, xenophobic, anti-intellectual country dweller. And his voting intentions will be easily deduced. Therefore if Hume criticised Whigs, he must be a Tory. But it was his critics whose ideas were closely wrapped in small parcels. Samuel Johnson came closer to the mark when he described Hume as 'a Tory by chance'. 'Hume did not change his principles or party allegiance in the second volume; it was history that changed and as a result he changed sides.'[14] In the slippery science of politics, party loyalists are as bigoted as religious fanatics and, as has already been stated, to the bigot, criticism, or even doubt, is denial.

Similarly he tried to protect himself from unjust criticism on religious grounds. 'It is no proof of irreligion in a historian that he remarks some fault or imperfection in each sect of religion, which he has occasion to mention.'[15]

Turning to the condition of Scotland in 1688, however, his view would, even today, cause a wholly justifiable uproar:

> The Scotch nation, though they had never been subject to the arbitrary power of their prince, had but very imperfect notions of law and liberty, and scarce in any age had they ever enjoyed an administration which had restrained itself within the proper boundaries. By their final union with England, their once hated antagonist, they have happily attained the experience of a government perfectly regular and exempt from all violence and injustice.

Hume is foreseeing the union of 1707 with gleeful anticipation.

In his *David Hume and the History of England*, Victor Wexler says of the book:

Hume set himself many goals in becoming a historian. One of them was to provide the British audience with a readable narrative history, the type of work it simply did not have in the eighteenth century . . . Hume's *History* is both economical and eloquent. He deliberately placed any lengthy digressions into footnotes and his own gift for carefully balanced sentences and subtle ironies that graced the finest neo-classical prose makes his *History* infinitely more attractive than the heavy sentences of Tindal's translation of a foreign work.[16]

Nicholas Tindal had been the translator of Rapin.

But Hume managed to have a second bite of the cherry with his essay, *Of the coalition of Parties*, published in 1758:

Liberty is a blessing so inestimable, that, whenever there appears any probability of recovering it, a nation may willingly run many hazards, and ought not even to repine at the greatest effusion of blood or dissipation of treasure.[17]

He argues for control of the despotism, not only of the sovereign, but also of the people:

The true rule of government is the present established practice of the age . . . If the origin of all power be derived, as is pretended, from the people, here is their consent in the fullest and most ample terms that can de desired or imagined.[18]

He concludes the essay with strong recommendations for compromise and tolerance:

There are many invincible arguments which should induce the malcontent party to acquiesce entirely in the present settlement of the constitution. They now find that the spirit of civil liberty, though at first connected to religious fanaticism, could purge itself from that pollution, and appear under a more genuine and engaging aspect; a friend to toleration, and an encourager of all the enlarged and generous sentiments that do honour to human nature.[19]

Hume's capacity for work at this time was extraordinary. In June 1755 Millar had had the intention of setting up a weekly paper and had asked Hume to take part in its founding, but David had excused himself on the grounds of needing to finish writing Volume Two of the *History*. But in the same letter:

> There are four short dissertations which I have kept some years by me in order to polish them as much as possible. One of them is that which Alan Ramsay mentioned to you. [It became *The Natural History of Religion*.] Another *Of the Passions*, a third *Of Tragedy*, a fourth, *Some Considerations previous to Geometry and Natural Philosophy*. The whole I think will make a volume a fourth less than my *Enquiry*, as nearly as I can calculate, but it would be proper to print it in a larger type, in order to bring it to the same size and price. I would have it published about the new year: I offer you the property for about fifty guineas.[20]

The contents of what would be published as *Four Dissertations* varied greatly before its entry into the world. *Geometry and Natural Philosophy* was dropped at Hume's request, since he was persuaded by Lord Stanhope that there was 'some defect in the argument or in its perspicuity'. Millar insisted that the three remaining essays were not enough for a volume on their own and so Hume suggested that the gap should be filled with *Of Suicide* and *Of the Immortality of the Soul*, both subjects fraught with dangerous controversy. This version of what would now be *Five Dissertations* existed in a manuscript which is now lost, although the book was set up and printed, some copies falling into public hands. However, the two latter subjects were finally dropped thanks to Hume's 'abundant prudence' and the relevant pages were simply cut out of the book. The two essays would not be published until after Hume's death. When copies of the reprinted book went into circulation, a less contentious essay, *Of the Standard of Taste*, was bound in at the end. To complicate matters even further Hume dedicated the book to his clergyman cousin John Home, who had written the tragedy *Douglas*. The idea of a minister writing for the theatre had caused a scandal which Hume sought to defuse by writing a defence of the play in his dedication. Then he prevaricated and Millar published 800 copies without the dedication. Hume had 'not been so heartily vexed at any accident of a long time', and the *Dissertations* were finally published in January 1757. Only a few months later the essays were republished in a new edition of *Essays and Treatises on several Subjects*. The *Four Dissertations* were never republished as such.

The Dedication is 'to the reverend Mr Hume, author of *Douglas*, a tragedy'. Hume was still embroiled in controversy thanks to his connection to this cousin John. John, a supporter of the Hanoverian side during the '45, was taken prisoner after the battle of Falkirk, escaped from Doune castle and was appointed as minister of Athelstaneford in 1747. Here he wrote a classical verse drama, *Agis,* which was turned down by Garrick for performance in London, 'the best actor, but the worst critic in the world', according to Hume, but was eventually performed at Rich's Covent Garden theatre in March 1757.

He then adapted an old Scottish ballad on Gil Morrice into a new play, *Douglas.* Hume had had sight of this play by October 1754 when he wrote to a Professor Spence of Oxford that it was 'a new tragedy on a subject of invention; here he [Home] appears a true disciple of Sophocles and Racine. I hope in time he will vindicate the English stage from the reproach of barbarism'. But David Garrick remained on the side of the barbarians and rejected this play also. The Lords Elibank and Kames, plus Hume, suggested rewrites and the play was made ready for production in Edinburgh by December 1756. The theatre was in Playhouse Close in the Canongate, not far from Hume's lodging in Jack's Land, and the production was in the hands of West Digges. Mrs Sarah Warde was one of Digges' company and a rehearsed reading of the play took place in her lodgings with David in the role of the hero, Glenalvon, with Jupiter Carlyle, John Home himself, and Adam Ferguson also in the cast. Elibank, Kames, and others of the Select Society formed an enthusiastic audience, and after the reading the company moved to the nearby Erskine Club for claret and griskins (roast sucking-pig). Hume was duly satirised and lampooned for his support of his clergyman cousin:

A report prevails that no persons will be admitted into the theatre on the 14th instant, but clergymen, at which rumour many other persons are offended; he thinks it his duty to acquaint the public that the pit alone is particularly kept by order for the fraternity. The boxes are already let to ladies (except the box prepared for the Moderator); and there will be several vacant places in them, which will no doubt be filled by gentlemen who do not belong to that ancient and venerable society . . . Tickets printed for the occasion to be had at the lodgings of D.H. Esq; and no other tickets will be received at the door, nor will any money be taken there.[21]

The play, performed on 14th December 1756, was a huge success in Edinburgh, at the conclusion of the première one member of the audience reputedly calling out, 'Whaur's your Wullie Shakespeare noo?' Garrick belatedly climbed onto the bandwagon of Home's success to produce *Agis* and his next play *The Siege of Aquilea*. Home was given a pension of £330 annually and a sinecure of the same amount but he was forced to resign his ministry in 1757.

Hume and his cousin carried on a good-natured dispute for their lifetime as to the spelling of Home/Hume, David finally suggesting that they draw lots for it. When referring to John in his letters, he spells it 'Hume'. With his cousin, unlike the General Assembly, he finds:

> these differences of opinion I have only found to enliven our conversation; while our common passion for science and letters served as a cement to our friendship. I still admired your genius, even when I imagined that you lay under the influence of prejudice; and you sometimes told me that you excused my errors on account of the candour and sincerity which you thought accompanied them.[22]

He then praises *Douglas* to the skies:

> The unfeigned tears which flowed from every eye in the numerous representations of it that were made of it on this theatre; the unparalleled command which you appeared to have over every affection of the human breast: these are incontestible proofs that you possess the true theatric genius of Shakespeare and Otway, refined from the unhappy barbarism of the one and the licentiousness of the other.[23]

Three years previously, in the *History*, Hume said that Shakespeare had 'a total ignorance of theatrical art and conduct' but he did exist as a theatrical yardstick against which everyone had to be measured. Hume is also human and favours his relative well beyond the strictures of criticism.

The Natural History of Religion can be seen as forming an unholy quartet with the three posthumous works, *Of Suicide, Of the Immortality of the Soul,* and the *Dialogues concerning Natural Religion,* and these three works will be considered later when summing up Hume's religious position. However, *The Natural History of Religion* begins with Hume posing two questions, 'to wit that concerning its foundation in reason and that concerning its origin in human nature'. The first question he dismisses out of hand: 'no rational enquirer can, after serious reflection, suspend his belief a moment with regard to the primary principles of genuine theism and religion'. Hume felt that his views on this were so inflammatory that they were published posthumously as *Dialogues on Natural Religion.*

He examines history to find that 'the most ancient records of human race still present us with polytheism as the popular and established system'. The origin of all religion arises from a fear of the unknown, of 'events seeming then the most unkown and unaccountable'. But giving rise to 'Madness, fury, rage, and inflamed imagination, thought they sink men to the level of the beasts, are for a like reason, often supposed to be the only dispositions in which we can have direct communication with the deity'. These are, of course, 'dispositions' that were anathema to the eighteenth century mind. 'While one sole object of devotion is acknowledged the worship of other deities is regarded as impious and absurd.' This, given human nature, means giving *carte blanche* to bigotry and persecution. His conclusions are truly shocking, 'Ignorance is the mother of devotion . . . the whole is a riddle, an enigma, an inexplicable mystery. Doubt, uncertainty, suspense of judgement appear the only result of our most accurate scrutiny concerning this subject.' Thus religious belief is driven by the passions. This directly relates to the precepts in the *Treatise* which Hume was, very often unknowingly, continually restating.

In this case Hume was making a more direct reference since *Of the Passions* consists of a literal reworking of Part II of the *Treatise.* In that he defined the passions:

> Of the first kind is the sense of beauty and deformity in action, composition and external objects. Of the second are the passions of love and hatred, grief and joy, pride and humility . . . When we take a survey of those passions there occurs a division of them into direct and indirect. Under the indirect passions I comprehend pride, humility, ambition, vanity, love, hatred, envy, pity, malice, generosity, with their dependents. And under the direct passions [I comprehend] desire, aversion, grief, joy, hope, fear, despair and security.

But now he changes the order and deals first with the direct passions, especially hope and fear, these having been the originating features in the birth of religion. The two passions can exist simultaneously as when a virgin bride is full of fear but hopeful of pleasure, and he delays explaining 'the effect of a mixture of passions, when one of them is predominant and swallows up the other'. This he does in Section VI: 'the predominant passion swallows up the inferior and converts it into itself. Thus the more the bride is hopeful the less she will be fearful and *vice versa*'. He moves the argument to a conclusion:

> It is remarkable that lively passions commonly attend a lively imagination. In this respect, as well as others, the force of the passion depends as much on the temper of the person, as on the nature or situation of the object.[24]

This almost acts as an introduction to the third dissertation *Of Tragedy*.

It cannot be denied that Hume, no avid theatregoer, was writing about his observations on *Douglas* and generalised from them. The paradox of being entertained while being made to weep interested him greatly:

> It seems an unaccountable pleasure which the spectators of a well made tragedy receive from sorrow, terror, anxiety and other passions which are in themselves disagreeable and uneasy. The more they are touched and affected, the more they are delighted with the spectacle and as soon as the uneasy passions cease to operate, the piece is at an end.[25]

He concludes that because the audience know the events to be fictional, they allow the eloquence, or art, of the dramatist to smother the horror and give satisfaction to the onlookers. This was true in Sophocles and is still true in Spielberg.

In *Of the Standard of Taste* Hume sets out four standards of taste, 'a delicacy of imagination, which is requisite to convey a sensibility of those finer motions: the frequent survey or contemplation of a particular species of beauty: comparisons between the several species and degrees of excellency: and finally, freedom from prejudice'. All this is a far cry from the 'enthusiasm' and 'superstition' of religious belief and forms a picture of the ordered mind Hume strove to possess. Just as *My Own Life* sums up Hume's literary career, *Of the Standard of Taste* shows us a vision of Hume at his mature prime.

In his will Hume gave permission for the two suppressed essays to be attached to his *Dialogues concerning Natural Religion* and, although this was not done, they were published separately and anonymously in 1777, a year after his death.

There was controversy enough in 1757 when the *Natural History of*

Religion came under fire from Hume's old enemy William Warburton, he of the vitriolic review of the *Treatise* in the *History of the Learned.*

Warburton published his attack, purporting to be letters of Warburton edited by the Reverend Richard Hurd. It was pure spleen, describing Hume as 'a puny dialectician from the North'. Hume, true to his intentions, kept above the fray. 'Anything so low as Warburton or his flatterers I should certainly be ashamed to engage with.' Hume continued to lampoon Warburton, claiming at one point that he had been circumcised and turned Mahometan. 'I saw him yesterday in the Mall with his turban, which really becomes him very well.'

The suppressed essays had leaked as far as France and were in translation there in 1770, but before that the storm clouds that had gathered in Edinburgh were about to burst.

The Church of Scotland had travelled far since the reforming days of John Knox, but the second reformation after the suppression of the Covenanters had driven it into a stern, unforgiving and fundamentalist mode; while a group inside the Church, the 'Moderates', were trying to accommodate the liberal views of the Enlightenment, the 'High Flyers' were moving backwards into severe Calvinism. Not for the last time, the Church was in schism, and, to this day, a fundamentalist minority still exists in the more remote parts of the country.

One of these Highflyers, the Reverend George Anderson, published *An Estimate of the Profit and Loss of Religion* in 1753, in which he mentions Bayle's proposition that 'There is one first universal and eternal cause which exists necessarily and should be called God'.[26] His view is a totality, even warning sceptics that they may turn to atheism. Of the Deists, 'I am confident, the orthodox will admit, that all attributes ascribed to God, which sap and undermine the foundations of religion must pass for atheism'. He attacks 'Sopho', a pen name of Kames: 'The more I examine Sopho's essays, the hotter and ranker the scent of atheism grows'. Hume is accused, in the same chapter, of saying in *Of Human Understanding* that we have no foundation for ascribing any attribute to the Deity, but what is precisely commensurate with the imperfection of the world. Therefore, he says, Hume means 'that this cannot afford us reason to conclude any perfection in the maker of the world'. Anderson has the closed mind of one who believes that any criticism of Christian belief is an attack on the whole and that, if you are not wholly committed, you are automatically atheist. As all of his kind will, he finally, with relish, turns to punishment:

The professors of the natural and revealed religion are under no obligation to use atheists and infidels as brethren in religious belief, and the christians, in particular, are obliged to exclude them from their communion and fellowship, not only in sacred things, but likeways all unnecessary conversation upon other subjects.[27]

He promises a lengthier work on excommunication, excuses Jews and Mahumetans (sic) since they never were Christians but asks for judgement from the supreme church judicature, quoting Paul to the Corinthians: 'Now I have written unto you not to keep company, if any man that is called a brother be a fornicator, or covetous, or idolator, or a railer or a drunkard, or an extortioner, with such an one, no, not to eat'. No one could doubt that the attack was directly asking for excommunication of Hume and Kames. Twenty years earlier, in 1733, Anderson had published an extensive pamphlet, *A Reinforcement of the Reasons proving that the Stage is an unchristian Diversion,* in which he had referred to 'some *esprits forts* or bold wits having got it into their heads that they were accountable only, (if accountable at all) to their own notions and principles'.[28] He quotes Peter and Paul as authorities forbidding stage plays, although he does admit that this is a consequential, and not an express condemnation of the theatre. Finally he quotes the *Admonition* of the Presbytery of Edinburgh of 30th November 1727 condemning a play, 'filled with horrid swearing, obscenity and expressions of a double meaning, tending to corrupt the minds of the spectators and to the practice of the grossest immoralities'. The play was *The Minor,* featuring Samuel Foote. Then, in 1755, a pamphlet by the Reverend John Bonar was published. It was *An Analysis of the Moral and Religious Sentiments contained in the Writings of Sopho and David Hume, esq.* This pamphlet was addressed to the members of the General Assembly and the attack was now direct. He draws the attention of the members of the Assembly to the 'poison contained in these volumes'. He does admit that one of these gentlemen is a 'fine writer and a subtle disputant' (Hume) while the 'latter holds a place of great importance in this country and even bears an office in your church' (Kames). In attacking Hume he throws Hume's writing on miracles back in his face: 'That the very positions are such as ought to be sufficient for all men of sense not only to make them be rejected, but rejected without further examination'.[29] He then quotes extensively from both authors those passages he considers impious or heretical and concludes with a peroration worthy of the most doctrinaire pedagogues:

> Thus, gentlemen, I have laid before you a few of the many passages which occur in the works of these two authors, and which at first view strike at the foundations of all virtue and religion, both natural and revealed. That the promoters of such impious opinions deserve the very highest censures is beyond dispute. What you shall think proper to do in this assembly, a short time will discover . . . some of you at least live in the greatest intimacy with one who represents the blessed Saviour as an impostor, and his religion as a cunningly devised fable. May your conduct be such as fully to wipe off all these reproaches; and testify to the world that you will have no society with the workers of iniquity.[30]

This was worthy of a Grand Inquisitor, but a reply came from the more liberally minded Hugh Blair in the form of *Observations on a Pamphlet*:

> The author's zeal for religion would deserve the highest commendation, if in some instances, it did not seem to be misguided, in others to exceed the bounds of piety . . . Every fair reader must admit, with regret, that there are to be found in the writings of this elegant author [Hume] some principles by no means consistent with sound doctrine. There was therefore no necessity for ascribing to him positions which he does not advance, in order to support the charge of irreligion against him. The conduct of the author of the *Analysis* can scarcely be accounted for; as it manifestly leads to do harm rather than good to the cause he pretends to support . . . Justice demands this acknowledgement as due to an elegant and agreeable writer, even though a free thinker; and it must at the same time be observed that it appears very like a contradiction to accuse a man on one page of scepticism and infidelity and in the following page to tax him with an attachment to Popery and superstition.[31]

So Hume and Kames had one friend at least, but Anderson was arguing for the excommunication of both men at the General Assembly. Though the sanction did not carry the heavy penalty of religious and social exclusion as experienced in former times, in the comparatively small society of Edinburgh it would have caused the two men severe difficulties.

Kames could not have sat on the bench and his legal practice would cease immediately; Hume would have found it more difficult to be published and would be shunned by polite society, so it was not altogether an empty threat.

Hume wrote to Allan Ramsay, talking at first of Kames:

> They will not at once go to extremities with him, and deliver him over to Satan without any preparation or precaution. They intend to make him be prayed for in all the churches of Scotland during six months, after which, if he do not give signs of repentance he is to be held as *anathema maranatha*. Meanwhile I am preparing for the Day of Wrath, and have already bespoken a number of discreet families, who have promised to admit me after I shall be excommunicated . . .
>
> You may tell that reverend gentleman the Pope that there are many here who rail at him, and yet would be much greater persecutors had they equal power. The last Assembly sat on me. They did not propose to burn me, because they cannot. But they intend to give me over to Satan, which they think they have the power of doing. My friends, however, prevailed and my damnation is postponed for a twelvemonth. But next assembly will surely be upon me. Anderson, the godly, spiteful, pious, splenetic, charitable, unrelenting, meek, persecuting, Christian, inhuman, peace-making, furious Anderson, is at present very hot in pursuit of Lord Kames.[32]

Kames used his considerable influence to have the whole affair dropped but the Assembly of 1756 had to debate a motion proposing the excommunication of Hume. The Moderates formed an impressive caucus, meeting at the Carrier's Inn and instructing the landlord to lay in a gross of claret. The inn became known as the *Diversorium*. But, wisely, the assembly rejected the motion and Anderson died in the same year.

The affair exposed the bigotry of the High Flyers who had simply followed others in branding Hume an atheist, even although nowhere in his writing does he ever maintain that God does not exist. But for the High Flyers doubt was denial and actually reading Hume's work would only confuse the issue, so he was to carry the label of atheist for life. Hume would have been glad to find a proof for God's existence. One clear beautiful night when Adam Ferguson, his successor at the Advocates' Library, and he were walking home, he suddenly stopped, looked up at the starlit sky, and

exclaimed, 'Oh, Adam, can anyone contemplate the wonders of the firma-
ment and not believe in a God!'[33] But, like many of Hume's statements on
the subject, it can be read in two different ways. However, the Moderates
were now, as a reaction to Anderson's vitriol, or, perhaps, as a result of the
claret at the *Diversorium,* endorsing the liberalism of the Enlightenment.
Even the reactionary rump realised also that excommunicating Hume
would have given the Enlightenment its first martyr and made Scotland
the laughing stock of Europe. Although Hume treated the matter with stoic
humour, it was another irritation. He often had thoughts of retiring to a
small village in France, having calculated that his investments brought him
an income of 1800 livres a year, 'The pay of two French captains', but he
needed the libraries and publishers of Edinburgh:

> Scotland suits my fortune best and is the seat of my principal
> friendships, but it is too narrow a place for me and it mortifies me
> that I sometimes hurt my friends.[34]

The furore over *Douglas* had brought the High Flyers into dispute again
with the Moderates with a narrow victory for the latter, although the
reputation of Scotland had not emerged unscathed. The last word was a
pamphlet of 11th January 1757 satirising the Presbytery of Edinburgh
entitled *Votes of the P . . . y of E . . . h*:

> Resolved;   That Learning, Genius and Merit are the Bane of
>   Society and ought to be discouraged.
>
> Resolved;   That Ignorance, Dullness, and Demerit are the Glory of
>   this covenanted Church, and ought, therefore, to be
>   encouraged.
>
> Resolved;   That every Proposition which silly people alone maintain,
>   is true.
>
> Resolved;   That Improvements of all sorts are hurtful to Society.
>
> Resolved;   That no alteration be ever attempted to be made of the
>   Principles, the Customs, and the Manners of men.
>
> Resolved;   That the Poets are public Nuisances and ought, like
>   noxious Weeds, to be extirpated.
>
> Resolved;   That the present time is the same as that of the
>   Covenant.
>
> Ordered: That the People of Scotland remain forever in
>   Barbarity.[35]

Hume had managed to keep his head below the parapet while these religious death throes of the Middle Ages were taking place, and on 15th May 1757 he wrote to Strahan:

> I have begun a new work some time ago though I did not fix my resolutions of persevering till I should find that I was pleased with it. It is the writing of the History of England from the accession of Henry VII. I wish I had from the first begun with that period. It really is the commencement of modern history: and I should have obviated many objections to my history of the Stuarts by taking matters so high. However this retograde [sic] motion is not unusual . . . I do not however preclude myself from the purpose of writing the period after the Revolution, by my undertaking this work; but shall be somewhat advanced before I go to London. I have more command of books here, than I could easily have had in that place, at least such books as suit this subject. For it is much to be lamented that there are no public libraries in London.[36]

Historians were busy in Edinburgh at this time since William Robertson was now well advanced with his *History of Scotland* which would be published with great success in 1759. Robertson was a friend of Hume's and had led the Moderates in the General Assembly opposing Hume's excommunication:

> it is admirable how many men of genius this country produces at present. Is it not strange that at a time when we have lost our princes, our parliaments, our independent government, even the presence of our chief nobility, are unhappy in our accent and pronunciation, speak a very corrupt dialect of the tongue we make use of; is it not strange, I say, that in these circumstances we should really be the people most distinguished for literature in Europe?'[37]

Hume's work was already well known in Europe and by the winter of 1758 the first volume of his *History* would appear in France. He was assiduous in sending copies to the Abbé Le Blanc and also sent him a copy of *Douglas*. Hume spent great efforts in advancing the work of his friends and colleagues and his letters abound with recommendations for the work of Blacklock, the impoverished blind poet he had befriended.

By August 1757 the *History* had reached the Reformation but writing the *History* in the reactionary atmosphere of Edinburgh was tiring him and he wrote to John Clephane on 3rd September contradicting his views of the spring:

> I shall certainly be in London next summer and probably to remain there during life, at least if I can settle myself to my mind, which I beg you to have an eye to. A room in a sober discreet family who would not be averse to a sober, discreet, virtuous, frugal, regular, quiet, good-natured man of bad character: such a room, I say, would suit me extremely, especially if I could take most of my meals in the family: and, more especially still, if it was not far distant from Dr Clephane's . . . I am resolved to write no more. I shall read and correct, and chat and be idle, the rest of my life.[38]

His intention to give up writing must be taken with a pinch of salt but only a month later he wrote to Captain James Edmonstone, a L'Orient colleague:

> I am engaged in writing a new volume of history from the beginning of Henry the VII till the accession of James I. It will probably be published the winter after the next. I believe I shall write no more history, but proceed directly to attack the Lord's Prayer and the Ten Commandments and the single Cat. And to recommend suicide and adultery, and so persist till it shall please the Lord to take me to himself.[39] [The 'Cat' was the Catechism]

Meanwhile Hume carried on with the completion of the *History*, however deep his feelings of depression at the pervading narrowness of some aspects of Edinburgh society.

While London supported several literary reviews, Scotland had none although *The Edinburgh Review* would set about remedying the lack in 1755. Alexander Wedderburn, a Moderate and friend of Hume's, wrote a telling preface:

> The design of this work is to lay before the public from time to time a view of the progressive state of learning in this country. The great number of performances of this nature, which, for almost a century past have appeared in almost every part of Europe, where knowledge is held in esteem sufficiently proves that they have been found useful.
>
> Upon the first revival of letters in Europe [a reference to the

Reformation] their progress in Scotland was very rapid and very remarkable . . . Scotland might well have flattered herself with hopes of attaining a distinguished rank in the literary world. But those happy prospects soon gave place to the melancholy scene of disorder and violence that civil dissensions produced . . . nor could the arts of peace flourish in a country averse to industry and rent with divisions. Upon the accession of James VI to the crown of England the minds of men were entirely occupied with that event. The advancement of their own fortune became an object of attention to very many . . . if countries have their ages with respect to improvement, North Britain may be considered as in a state of early youth, guided and supported by the more mature strength of her kindred country . . . it is proposed to give a full account of all books published within Scotland within the compass of half a year, and to take notice of such books published elsewhere as are most read in this country.[40]

By its own definition, the *Edinburgh Review* remained firmly parochial and lasted for only two issues, to be re-founded, and afterwards to achieve lasting fame, by Francis Jeffrey, Henry Brougham and the Reverend Sidney Smith in 1802.

But the expansion of thought encouraged by the Moderates and the thinkers of the Enlightenment did bring about an examination of Scottish identity. It took the unlikely form of setting about to destroy the Scots dialects which had been in question ever since the Act of Union of 1707 when Scotland became North Britain and England declined to become South Britain. Scottish members of both houses of Parliament were derided for their seemingly impenetrable accents and the English lampooned the Scots with the same degree of violence as the Lowland Scots showed towards the Highlanders. David Hume spoke a Lowland Scots which was perfectly acceptable among the highest society in Edinburgh but defeated Bristol merchants; it was a dialect with a wide vocabulary and a distinctive accent, differing from the dialects of north-eastern or south-western Scotland, for example, but understandable by their inhabitants. Outside the Highlands and Western Isles very few Scotsmen spoke Gaelic, a complete and entire language, related to the Celtic languages spoken by peoples northwards from Galicia, through Brittany, Cornwall and Wales to Ireland and Scotland. Hume claimed his speech was 'totally desperate and irredeemable' although his prose was elegantly correct; that is to say, it obeyed the Classical rules of syntax and grammar with only occasional Scots words or phrases. He also spoke Latin, Greek and French with perfect grammar and a strong Scots accent. The Scots felt they had to set about the Anglification of their dialect, a process of destruction which continued through the best efforts of the BBC up to the present times. The presence of a quasi-independent Parliament once again in Edinburgh has started to put the process into reverse after three hundred years, with regional accents and even occasional dialect words now appearing in the broadcast and print media.

The process of Anglification started in 1761 when the Select Society had invited Thomas Sheridan to give a course of lectures on English speech. He was an Irish opportunist, an actor, the author of *A Plan of Education for the young Nobility and Gentry of Great Britain,* a lecturer on elocution and the father of the actor, playwright and politician Richard Brinsley Sheridan. In 1780 he even published a pronouncing Dictionary, causing Boswell to complain justifiably, 'What entitles Sheridan to fix the pronunciation of English?':

> At St Paul's chapel. June 16 1761. Mr Sheridan proposes to read two courses of lectures; the first, on elocution, the second on the English tongue, consisting of eight lectures each.
>
> In the first he will treat of everything necessary to a good delivery, under the following heads, articulation, pronunciation, accent, emphasis, pauses or stops, pitch and management of the voice, tones and gesture.
>
> In the second, he will examine the whole state and constitution of the English tongue, so far as relates to sound, in which he will point out its peculiar genius and properties, and specific difference from others, both ancient and modern.[41]

The tickets were a guinea each and the lectures were attended by more than '300 gentlemen'. They were repeated on 18th July 'for the ladies', missing out the classical references. Many of those who attended also subscribed at the door to his forthcoming book for half a guinea. Kames subscribed, but his name is misspelt and Sheridan points out that the many misspellings were due to the hasty notes, and he apologises in advance. Lord Auchinleck, James Boswell's father, bought two copies.

The lectures were printed by Strahan for Millar and were a great success, being reprinted ten times. Sheridan ventures into philosophy, 'the variety of treatises which have lately been published on the passions, and the number of essays on taste; in which the writers widely differ from each other in their principles'. But, 'the rising generation so instructed would be uniform in their use of words, and would be able to communicate their ideas to each other with ease and perspicuity'. The uniformity he found essential since:

> Not only the Scotch, Irish, and Welsh have each their own idioms which uniformly prevail in those countries but almost every county in England has its peculiar dialect. Nay in the very metropolis two different modes of pronunciation prevail, by which the inhabitants of one part of the town are distinguished from those of the other. One is current in the city and is called the cockney the other at the court end and is called the polite.[42]

Naturally Sheridan preferred the 'polite', and felt that:

> It cannot be denied that an uniformity of pronunciation throughout Scotland, Ireland and Wales, as well as throughout the several counties of England would be a point much to be wished; as it might in a great measure contribute to destroy those odious distinctions between subjects of the same king, and members of the same community which are ever attended by ill consequences.[43]

In Edinburgh, the Select Society was so impressed by Sheridan's lectures that it set out an ambitious, if unpatriotic, ambition:

> As the intercourse between this part of Great Britain and the capital daily increases, both on account of business and amusement, and must still go on increasing, gentlemen educated in Scotland have long been sensible of the disadvantages under which they labour from their improper knowledge of the ENGLISH TONGUE [sic] and the impropriety with which they speak it.
>
> Experience hath convinced Scotsmen that it is not impossible for persons born and educated in this country to acquire such knowledge of the English tongue as to write it with some tolerable purity.

They set about this project with a will, and a board of directors took subscriptions from the usual enthusiasts. Lords Elibank and Kames, Blair,

Robertson and Ferguson all wanted to sound like Englishmen and signed up, while still speaking Scots in court, university and their clubs. This particular project was doomed and took the Select Society to its death, but up to a few years ago Scots children spoke English in the classroom and Scots in the playground. Hugh Blair, who had supported Hume against the High Flyers of the Assembly, was appointed as Regius Professor of Rhetoric and Belles Lettres at Edinburgh University. The University now had chairs in Latin, Greek and, for the first time in Britain, English. When Robertson's *History of Scotland* was published in 1759, Hume sent him a letter of congratulation and told him that all London thought that, since his English was so good, he must be an Oxford-educated writer.

Hume, while keen to avoid Scotticisms in his prose, took no part in these somewhat ridiculous affairs, although a search for such words and phrases took place with the *Scots Magazine* of 1760 offering, in an Appendix, helpful suggestions: 'These Scotticisms . . . may be useful to such of our countrymen as would avoid Scotticisms in speaking or writing'. It defined the difference between will and shall, etc; preferred 'conformable to' to 'conform to'. The article recommended 'discretion' not 'civility', 'call him' not 'cry him', 'with regard to' not 'anent'. Johnsonian definitions of behove, narrate (a word then only used in Scotland), notwithstanding, prejudge, prejudice, succumb, were given – Johnson's *Dictionary* had been published in 1755 – and on 31st March 1764 the magazine printed a letter from a London correspondent listing more Scotticisms:

The great source of Scotticisms is mispronunciation, whether by false sounds or false stresses; a source however copious more to be regretted than reproached considering the distance of Scotland from that capital which centers [sic] the propriety of the English language.

Even in England spelling was undergoing changes, with some changes that seem to have emigrated to America at birth:

Our reformers in the art of spelling, who at present chiefly confine themselves to one class of words: to substantive nouns and verbs derived from the Latin, such as honour, favour, labour, which they write as honor, favor, and labor, increase the distance between the writing and the pronunciation.[44]

Being aware of the changes that were taking place as speech and spelling were codified and homogenised, Hume had written to Millar in June

1758, while the first part of the *History* was being reprinted, telling the printer to follow his own method of spelling and not to make amendments. On 5th August he wrote to Strahan that on the 15th:

> the manuscript copy of my new volume will be put into the stage coach in two white iron boxes, directed to you. As there are in the same boxes a few papers on private business will you please leave the boxes unopened till I come to London which will probably be about the end of this month or the beginning of the next. I go up on horseback which is the reason why I send the manuscript before me.[45]

Hume arrived in London shortly after the death of John Clephane and he would be in the capital until October 1759, living in Lisle Street, now in the heart of London's Chinatown, but then beside Leicester Fields. He lodged with a Miss Anne Elliot who, with her sister Peggy, ran a boarding establishment for visiting Scotsmen. It was from here that he oversaw the publication of the *Tudors*. This work was made easier by the opening of the Reading Room at the British Museum to the public on 15 January 1759, and by 3 March 1760 he held a reader's ticket valid for six months. In fact he renewed his readership a full year later and his name is entered as a reader just below that of Samuel Johnson.

On 12 March 1759 *The History of England under the Tudors* was published in two quarto volumes. It is highly readable, as one would expect, elegantly and with comparatively little bias, thus managing to offend the partisans of both sides of any argument at some point or other. But Hume could not hide his own opinions. For example, of Henry VII:

> his capacity was excellent but somewhat contracted by the narrowness of his heart . . . he neglected to conciliate the affections of his people, he often felt the danger of resting his authority on their fear and reverence . . . avarice was, on the whole his ruling passion. [After the Wars of the Roses] . . . these seem the chief causes which at this time bestowed on the crown so considerable an addition of prerogative, and rendered the present reign a kind of epoch in the English constitution.

He is, however, capable of schoolboy howlers in dealing with events for which he had no references:

On the second of August 1492 a little before the sun set, that Christopher Columbus, a Florentine, set out from Cadiz on his memorable voyage of the discovery of the western world.

Columbus was from Genoa and he set sail from near Huelva.

The defeat of the Scots at Flodden is dealt with matter-of-factly without any trace of condemnation for Scottish inefficiency or regret at the slaughter of the nation's nobility.

He does have sympathy for Anne Boleyn and her misfortunes, but feels that she displayed too much haughty grandeur. However, she did not deserve her final fate: 'her body was negligently thrown into a common chest of elm-wood, made to hold arrows, and was buried in the tower'.

He is ambivalent over Henry VIII:

> The absolute uncontrolled authority which he maintained at home, and the regard which he acquired among foreign nations are circumstances which entitle him to the appellation of a great prince; while his tyranny and cruelty seem to exclude him from the character of a good one. His exterior qualities were advantageous and fit to captivate the multitude . . . it may be said with truth that the English in that age were so thoroughly subdued that, like eastern slaves, they were inclined to admire even those acts of violence and tyranny which were exercised over themselves, and at their own expense.

Edward VI was a beloved bigot, but since Protestant bigots are less severe than Catholic ones, 'all English historians dwell with pleasure on the excellencies of this young prince'.

Mary Tudor, however,

> possessed few qualities either estimable or amiable, and her person was as little engaging as her behaviour and address. Obstinacy, bigotry, violence, cruelty, malignity, revenge, tyranny, every circumstance of her character took a tincture from her bad temper and understanding.

The second volume was devoted entirely to the reign of Elizabeth I, and this allows him to deal extensively with Mary, Queen of Scots. He tries to be even-handed about any dispute between the two queens, but finally absolves Elizabeth of any lack of justice.

He points up Mary's difficulties on arrival when she met the full bigotry of the Scottish Reformation and puts the case for Mary's claim to Elizabeth's throne. This however would be thwarted by Elizabeth's firm grasp on sovereignty:

> What is most singular in the conduct and character of Elizabeth is that though she was determined never to have any heir of her own body, she was not only extremely averse to fix any successor to the crown; but seems also to have resolved, as far as lay in her power, that no one, who had pretensions to the succession should ever have any heirs or successors.

As to the 'casket letters' used to condemn Mary, Hume says: 'we shall not enter into a long discussion of the authenticity of these letters', and he then gives us a three-page-long footnote advocating their authenticity. Here he is heavily biased in favour of Elizabeth, although 'an excellent hypocrite', and her case against Mary as, at first a dupe of the Guise faction, and finally as a centre for Catholic plots. Of Walsingham he says:

> The great character indeed, which Sir Francis Walsingham bears for probity and honour, should remove from him all suspicion of such base arts as forgery and subornation; arts which even the most corrupt ministers in the most corrupt times would scruple to employ.

This of a man taken, even by the most enthusiastic supporters of Elizabeth, as the founder of the British secret service, a master of codes and spies, as well as turning a blind eye to the use of torture. Hume glosses over the entrapment by Walsingham of Mary in the Babington plot. He concludes of the two queens:

> Mary is a princess of great accomplishments, both of body and mind, natural as well as acquired, but unhappy in her life, and during one period, very unhappy in her conduct.

Of Elizabeth:

> There are few great personages in history who have been more exposed to the calumny of enemies and the adulation of friends than Queen Elizabeth. We may find it difficult to reconcile our fancy to her as a wife or a mistress; but her qualities as a sovereign,

though with some considerable exceptions, are the object of undisputed applause and approbation. No woman was ever more conceited of her beauty, nor more desirous of making impression on the hearts of beholders, no one ever went to a greater extravagance in apparel.

Though, surprisingly, and on no evidence whatsoever, he found her chastity 'very much to be suspected'.

The literature of the time did not suit Hume's Augustan tastes and he viewed its love of history with the same distaste he had shown as a student at Edinburgh. Spencer's 'pencil' was employed in drawing the affectations and conceits and fopperies of chivalry.

The reception by the public was not good and he was particularly attacked for his support of Elizabeth, but:

I was now callous against the impressions of public folly, and continued very peaceably and contentedly in my retreat in Edinburgh. To finish in two volumes the more early part of the English History.[46]

Then by April 1759 the *Tudors* was being translated into French by the Abbé Prévost, probably best known as the author of *Manon Lescaut*. His reputation in Paris was now very high and a friend, John Stewart, a wine merchant, wrote to him telling how a visit by Hume would give 'a most general and unfeigned satisfaction to a great number of people' including one young nobleman who had learnt English simply to read Hume in the original. Stewart also requests two copies of Robertson's *History*. This caused Hume to write jokingly to Robertson, 'here I sat near the historical summit of Parnassus, immediately under Dr Smollett; and you have the impudence to squeeze yourself by me, and place yourself under his feet. (In 1757 Smollett had published a four volume *History of England*.)

Hume was still reading as widely as ever and he told Adam Smith: I am afraid of Kames' *Law Tracts*. A man might as well think of making a fine sauce by a mixture of wormwood and aloes as an agreeable composition by joining metaphysics and Scots law.[47]

His spirits were high and he was enjoying his success:

I signed yesterday an agreement with Mr Millar, where I mention that I proposed to write a History of England from the beginning to the accession of Henry VII, and he engages to give me £1400 for the copy. This is the first previous agreement ever I made with a bookseller. I shall execute this work at leisure without fatiguing myself by such ardent application as I have hitherto employed. It is chiefly as a resource against idleness that I shall undertake this work: for as to money I have enough: and, as to reputation, what I have wrote already will be sufficient, if it be good; if not, it is not now likely that I shall write better.[48]

Since £1,400 was a vast amount of money, Hume was now a demonstrably bestselling author.

He returned to Edinburgh at the end of October to add the references to the *Tudors*, but he set about the earlier history, with the intention of visiting the British Museum for further research. Hume's reference to 'the beginning' was to mean from the invasion by Julius Caesar in 55 BC. However he undertook the work, it was at a furious pace, often fourteen hours at a time, with letters requesting books or information being fired off to all and sundry. One letter to Millar on 22 March 1760 lists twenty-seven books. There was no time to attend Sheridan's lectures, even if Hume had had the inclination to sound like an Englishman. Which he emphatically did not.

He was far too busy correcting proofs, sometimes belatedly, and writing the *History of England from the Invasion of Julius Caesar to the Accession of Henry VII*.

Inevitably the pre-Roman civilisation is treated harshly while that of the Romans brings the first lights of civilisation to Britain:

No species of superstition was ever more terrible than that of the Druids . . . [and the Romans] were at last obliged to abolish it by penal statutes, a violence, which had never in any other instance been practised by these tolerating conquerors.

The only source for the period of Roman occupation quoted by Hume is the historian Tacitus. Since he was the son-in-law of the conquering Roman general Agricola it is, unsurprisingly, complimentary to the invaders. Anarchy returned with the departure of Rome, and the An-glo-Saxons were:

in general a rude uncultivated people, ignorant of letters, unskilful in the mechanical arts, untamed to submission under law and government, addicted to intemperance riot and disorder . . . the Conquest put the people in a situation of receiving slowly from abroad the rudiments of science and cultivation, and of correcting their rough and licentious manners.

Hume's eighteenth-century mind rejected everything but law and the proper order of the realm. Thomas à Becket was a 'prelate of the most lofty intrepid and inflexible spirit who was able to cover to the world and, probably to himself, the enterprises of pride and ambition, under the disguise of sanctity and of zeal for the interests of piety and religion'. While Henry II was the greatest prince of his time for wisdom, virtue and ability. Richard I brought a reign that was oppressive, and, anyway, he passed only four months of his reign in England with arbitrary high taxes, and his brother John was no better as a successor, 'a complication of vices, equally mean and odious, ruinous to himself and injurious to his people'. Hume would disagree that Magna Carta, which he Anglicised as the Great Charter, benefited only the nobles and clergy and he goes into detail over the gains made by the people. The ideas of chivalry were, one feels, much to Hume's relief, 'in a great degree, banished by the revival of learning; they left modern gallantry and the point of honour, which still maintain their influence, and are the genuine offspring of those ancient affectations'.

In Volume Two his view of William Wallace is surprisingly contemporary. He was a man 'whose valorous exploits are the object of just admiration, but have been much exaggerated by the traditions of his countrymen'. But his fate was 'unworthy of a hero'.

Hume covers the wars with France dispassionately, although 'Henry V was somewhat above middle size, his countenance beautiful, his limbs genteel and slender, but full of vigour, and he excelled in all warlike and manly exercises'. Finally, Richard III 'was of a small stature, hump-backed and had a very harsh disagreeable visage, so that his body was in every particular no less deformed than his mind'. Hume is definite that Richard did order the murder of the Princes in the Tower, but then his source for Richard's reign is Henry VII's Chancellor and apologist, Sir Thomas More.

The *History* taken as a whole is an extraordinary work. It deals only with mankind and commences only when written records exist. Most previous histories had started with the creation of the world, but Hume rejected the Pentateuch utterly:

> . . . a book presented to us by a barbarous and ignorant people,
> written in an age when they were still more barbarous, and in all
> probability long after the facts which it relates, corroborated by no
> concurring testimony, and resembling those fabulous accounts which
> every nation gives of its origin.[49]

Until the later Middle Ages Hume is unhappy with man's place in the
order of things:

> The Christian centuries preceding the Renaissance were still for
> him 'The Dark Ages' during which religion and reason did violence
> to one another, to their mutual detriment. [But] Hume, as the
> reader will have observed, has been careful to avoid attacking
> religion directly, he professes to be attacking only what he describes
> as being its popular, superstitious, fanatical forms.[50]

The *History* is written throughout in an elegant, clear and easily readable
English, with a few anachronistic spellings. The text itself is a continuous
narrative, uninterrupted by statistics or attempts to find contemporary
relevances. There are remarkably few dates, except in the marginalia, and
his character summaries are, while judgemental, as even-handed as he
could make them. This, of course, was a sure way of offending everybody
and the reception of the *History* was not enthusiastic critically, despite
increasingly good sales. The clergy, especially, were, as they expected to be,
offended by the work. Hume had treated all religious movements as
unreasoning hindrances to the onward flow of rational government.
Fifteen years later Edward Gibbon would publish his *Decline and Fall
of the Roman Empire* and treat Christianity as just another of the many sects
flourishing in the first millennium. The belief that all philosophy or history
must have a basis in religious faith and its interpretation was reluctant to
die and all those who even questioned it were immediately dubbed atheists.
Hume's *History* was seen as more pernicious since it was easy to read and
would, thus, be available to more people than his philosophy. But it too was
immediately translated into French and his 'back-list' of *Essays* in their
various editions was still selling well. All except the *Treatise*, that is:

> But notwithstanding this variety of winds and seasons to which my
> writings have been exposed, they had still been making such
> advances that my copy money, given me by booksellers, much
> exceeded anything formerly known in England. I was become not

only independent, but opulent. I retired to my native country of Scotland, determined never more to set my foot out of it: and retaining the satisfaction of never having preferred a request to one great man or even making advances of friendship to any of them. As I was now turned of fifty I thought of passing all the rest of my life in this philosophical manner.[51]

He could not have been more wrong.

ELEVEN

A Quiet Manner of Sliding Through Life

H ume may have chosen this point in his life to say goodbye to the world and retire to scholarly affluence in Edinburgh, but the world was not yet ready to say goodbye to David Hume.

He had been living in London to see his *History* through the press and was enjoying its atmosphere less and less. This atmosphere in London had changed none too subtly. French imperial ambitions were coming to an end with Wolfe's conquest of Canada and Clive's successful campaigns in India. George III had acceded to the throne in 1760, and the Earl of Bute, backed by William Pitt, was Prime Minister. English pride of nationhood was at its height and Bute's filling his government with Scottish placemen made London an uncomfortable place for Scotsmen. But Hume had become friendly with the Earl of Shelbourne who included him among his circle of literati at his Mayfair house. It was probably there that Hume first met Benjamin Franklin. Hume could have relied on Shelbourne's future patronage and by keeping a low profile could have stayed on quite comfortably in London. After all, he had no intention to write any further works. But Hume disliked patronage as being inimical to free expression and he intended to return to Scotland in due course. On 12th December 1761 he wrote to Shelborne:

> An accident, a little unexpected, has hastened my journey to Scotland a little sooner than I expected. I was offered a chaise that sets out tomorrow morning, where I could sit alone and loiter and muse for the length of four hundred miles. Your Lordship may judge, by this specimen of my character, how unfit I am to mingle in such an active and sprightly society as that of which your Lordship invited me to partake, and that in reality a book and a fireside, are the only scenes for which I am now qualified . . . I remember to have seen a picture in your Lordship's house of a Hottentot who fled from a cultivated life to his companions in the woods and left behind him all his fine accoutrements and attire. I

compare not my case to his for I return to a very sociable, civilised people.[1]

He had already said that 'Edinburgh was too narrow for me', and that London was inhabited by 'the barbarians on the banks of the Thames'. So this is Hume atypically sounding dog-in-the-manger. His fame seemed to him to be based on criticism, and he had, as far as he was concerned, completed his writing with the *History*. He was, however, rich and could return to Edinburgh in some style:

> I have hitherto been a wanderer on the face of the earth without any abiding city; but now I have at last purchased a house, [to] which I am repairing, though I cannot say that I have any fixed property in the earth, but only in the air; for it is the third story of James's Court, and it cost me five hundred pounds. It is somewhat dear, but I shall be exceedingly well lodged.[2]

In May 1762 he moved house to James's Court at the top of the Lawnmarket, almost exactly opposite his previous lodging at Riddel's Close and only a few yards from the house in which he had been born. It had been built by James Brownhill in 1725 and was one of the most fashionable addresses in the city. Kames had been one of its residents. Hume's apartment, in the western half of the court, consisted of four or five rooms, as well as a kitchen and, given the steepness of the ridge on which it perched near the Castle, the house was on the third floor, facing south, and on the sixth floor, facing north. Sadly, this part of the court followed the Edinburgh tradition and burnt down in 1857 to be rebuilt in Victorian style. But Hume had views to the south over Edinburgh as well as looking north across the Forth estuary to Fife. He reminded Adam Smith that he could see Kirkcaldy from his window. James's Court was – and still is – a courtyard with many dwellings forming their own community and the inhabitants holding their own assemblies and balls. Today the courtyard even sports a tree – a rarity in Edinburgh's Old Town. The problem of nightly waste disposal was solved for them by employing their own sweepers and it was, in fact, a cross between an early form of tenants' association and a privately serviced apartment block. Into this came sister Katherine and the ever-loyal Peggy Irvine who furnished the apartments in stylish comfort. When Boswell visited him in November 1762, he found him in his house in James's Court, in a good room newly fitted up, hung round with Strange's prints. He was sitting at his ease reading Homer.[3]

He was within easy walking distance of his clubs or of friendly tea tables for whist. His eccentric thought and dangerous atheism would be tolerated in most nearby taverns. He certainly felt himself to be settled at last.

Hume had always been a keen student of French thought and his work had been translated into French with great success not only by Le Blanc but also by the Abbé Prévost. Reports had reached Hume that he was an object of discussion and admiration to the *philosphes* of Paris, and he had received a letter from a *salonaire,* one of the great hostesses of Paris. Written on 13th March, it was from the Comtesse de Boufflers, 'the most amiable and accomplished lady in this kingdom, or indeed any other'. A diplomat remarked, 'I never saw so much wit grace and beauty united in one person . . . justly esteemed as the most admirable woman of her time'. She was Marie-Charlotte-Hippolyte de Campet de Saujeon, Comtesse de Boufflers, born on 14th September 1725. Curiously enough her grandmother was Scots, Jean Margaret Murray.

Marie-Charlotte was brought up as lady-in-waiting to the Duchess of Chartres, whose husband was a cousin of Louis XV, and on 15th February 1746 she made a conventional marriage to Edouard, Marquis de Boufles-Rouveret, a morose cavalry officer of limited intelligence. She dutifully bore him a son while he pursued a doggedly dull military career and the couple were, to all intents and purposes, separated. Her father had been a military governor and it was said that, for her, the two words – 'military career' – were synonymous with boredom, and Marie-Charlotte was never bored. Lacking any maternal advice, or perhaps in spite of it, she immediately entered the somewhat racy circle of the Maréchal de Luxembourg who, in turn, introduced her to another cousin of Louis XV, the extremely rich Louis François de Bourbon, Prince de Conti. Apart from his personal fortune, which was vast, he received a personal pension from the King which, in 1760, was worth £2,625 annually (roughly £212, 625 in today's money). She was described as 'somewhat frail' but beautiful at twenty-seven, while he was a vigorous thirty-four. But she found in this cousin of the king the qualities lacking in her husband and he was captivated by her. He had been a successful soldier and diplomat of liberal principles. He maintained Abbé Prévost as his chaplain, but, since the Prince was a sceptic, the Abbé was forbidden to say Mass. Conti was Grand Prior of the Knights of St John of Malta and, as such, had a Paris residence in the Temple district of Paris, as well as his country estate at L'Isle Adam on the banks of the Oise some fifteen miles to the north-west of the capital. He also owned vineyards and estates all over France as well as various properties in Paris. 'He liked pleasure as well as power and took a ring from everyone to whom he made love. When he died his executors found 4000 of them – each labelled with a different name.'[4]

But the Comtesse de Boufflers was no fly-by-night conquest and the Prince installed her in his town house near the Temple on the north side of the Rue Notre-Dame de Nazareth as his *maitresse en titre*. It was said of her that:

> She was a voracious reader and paradoxes did not frighten her. She enunciated, in a firm and decisive tone, indisputable judgements, but with such a persuasive and soft delivery that she entranced all hearts.[5]

She made a note to herself, 'In discussion – clarity, truth and precision!'[6] In her correspondence with Hume she even wrote, 'Believe I have a tender heart, well meaning, sensitive and loving! One must be very ill at ease with the world not to wish to die. This truly smacks of a paradox!'[7] This intellectual Queen of Paris went on:

> For a long, time, Sir, I have struggled with conflicting sentiments. The admiration which your sublime work has awakened in me and the esteem with which it has inspired me for your person, your talents and your virtue, have frequently aroused the desire of writing to you, that I might express these sentiments with which I am so deeply smitten.[8]

And, possibly remembering that her grandmother was a Murray, she told Hume that she had read his *History of the Stuarts* in the original. In her effusive letter to Hume she admits to contrary impulses. His 'sublime work' has made her realise her comparative insignificance. Then she quotes from the *History*: 'Men's views of things are the result of their understanding alone: their conduct is regulated by their understanding, their temper and their passions'.[9] A quotation which so encapsulates Hume's thinking in the *Treatise* that he would have been flattered beyond thought:

I was ravished by the clarity, the majesty, and the touching simplicity of your style. Its beauty is so striking, that it could not escape me, even with my lack of fluency in English. You are, sir, an admirable painter. Your pictures have a grace, a naturalness and an energy which surpasses anything one could imagine.[10]

She adds a postscript hoping that Hume will visit Paris at the conclusion of the war – it would end in the Peace of Paris in 1763, with Britain victorious – and that she will be able to make his visit pleasant.

Hume was, predictably, overwhelmed by this unexpected letter and replied on 15th May, confessing to having indulged himself in 'agreeable visions of vanity'. With typical generosity he recommends that she read Robertson's *History of Scotland*, praising particularly his even-handedness in dealing with Mary, Queen of Scots. Finally he tells her that he hopes to visit Paris at the conclusion of the war and, given that his command of the language has 'rusted among books and study', will gladly place himself under her protection. Understandably cautious of unexpectedly returning to this foreign country, he was polite but uncommittal.

His recommendation that she read Robertson was doubly generous since both men were being attacked in a pamphlet – published anonymously, but in reality the work of William Tytler – denying Mary's involvement in Darnley's murder. The dispute placed Hume's friendship with Lord Elibank under pressure, and the doubts can still cause heated exchanges even today.

Controversy of a more serious nature affected Hume in Edinburgh with the publication by James Macpherson of *Fingal* and *Temora*, two epic poems composed by 'Ossian' and 'translated' from the original Gaelic by Macpherson. Scotland felt it had found its Homer or, at least its *Beowulf*. Macpherson refused to produce the original manuscripts but, in spite of this, the publication was supported by no less a figure than Lord Bute. English literary society immediately smelt a rat and Scotland felt that this response impugned its national honesty. The stage was set for a major dispute, involving Hume from the outset, since he had recommended Macpherson to his publisher Millar.

Hume was always sceptical as to the authenticity of the poems and, for once, agreed with Samuel Johnson that the poems were, in all probability, forgeries. He concluded by saying that the Highlanders had such a need for a cultural heritage that they would easily be deceived. He also felt their literary status was not as high as their own status as rarities in the civilised world of the eighteenth century.

All of this, along with the continuing label of 'atheist', combined to isolate Hume from the literary establishment of Scotland. He was the tolerated eccentric radical – possibly dangerous, sometimes amusing, certainly convivial company and an excellent companion – but outside the mainstream. When the post of Historiographer Royal for Scotland was revived in 1763 it was not Hume but Robertson who was appointed. Carlyle noted that Hume was 'a little hurt'. The Comtesse de Boufflers' letter must have shone in his heart.

He continued his correspondence with the Comtesse de Boufflers and she managed to get hold of the latest volumes of his *History*. His attempts to send them to her personally had been foiled by the continuing war, but by May 1762 she was writing in praise of them. She also sought Hume's aid in easing the plight of Jean-Jaques Rousseau who was in political exile for his writings. She admitted that Rousseau was easily misunderstood but possessed a pure, constant virtue.

Hume was appalled at this news and wrote at once to Rousseau assuring him of all the help he could arrange. Hume then wrote to Elliot of Minto asking him to apprise Lord Bute and even George III of the philosopher's plight, as well as trying to persuade Millar to act as a publisher for any new work that Rousseau might produce.

Rousseau was, in fact, in Neuchâtel under the protection of George Keith on behalf of Frederick the Great. Keith was an exiled Jacobite, but for all that a great admirer of Hume, and he hoped, in vain, that he, Rousseau and Hume would set up a philosophic commume at Keith Hall near Aberdeen. Nothing came of this scheme, nor was Hume able, at this point, to help Rousseau.

The Comtesse wrote (in English) thanking Hume and he responded, praising her English, though unaware that her companion and secretary was, in fact, an Englishwoman, Lydia Becquet. He also repeated his intention of visiting Paris, but stressed that this would have to be a visit of long duration and that it would have to suffer a temporary delay. A friend of Hume's, Andrew Stuart, had been in Paris and reported to another colleague:

> When you have occasion to see our friend David Hume tell him he
> is so much worshipped here that he must be void of all passions if

he does not immediately take post for Paris. In most houses where I am acquainted here one of the first questions is, 'Do you know Monsieur David Hume whom we all admire so much?'[11]

But if the mountain would not come to Mahomet, then the Comtesse had no compunction in coming to it and she left Paris for London on 17 April 1763. She was accompanied by Hume's friend Lord Elibank, who as Patrick Murray was her cousin. On arrival he was sent ahead to arrange a meeting with the historian. This he failed to do.

However, such was Mme. de Boufflers' reputation as the hostess of the most celebrated salon in Paris that she was fêted by the nobility and literati alike. The inveterate gossip Horace Walpole entertained her at Strawberry Hill, his fantasy house in Twickenham. He had rejected the Classicism of the times and, as the Goths had sacked Rome, the new style was 'Gothic'. On 30th April he wrote:

> Last Saturday arrived a Mme. de Boufflers, *sçavante, galante*, a great friend of the Prince of Conti and a passionate admirer *de nous autres Anglois*. My poor niece has taken a house here . . . Mme. de Boufflers has heard so much of her beauty that she told me she would be glad to peep trough a grate anywhere to get a glimpse of her.[12]

Within a month the hectic sightseeing and socialising was beginning to take its toll, for when she came again to Strawberry Hill on 17th May:

> Mme. de Boufflers I think will die a martyr to a taste which she fancied she had and finds she has not. Never having stirred ten miles from Paris, and having only rolled in an easy coach from one hotel to another on a gliding pavement, she is already worn out with being hurried from morning to night from one sight to another. She rises every morning fatigued with the toils of the preceding day that she has not the strength, if she had the inclination, to observe the least, or the finest thing she sees. She came hither today to a great breakfast I had prepared for her with eyes a foot deep in her head her hands dangling and scarce able to support her knotting bag. She had been yesterday to see a ship launched, and went from Greenwich by water to Ranelagh . . . We breakfasted in the great parlour and I had filled the hall and large cloister by turns with French horns and clarionets. As the French

ladies had never seen a printing house I carried them into mine;
they found something already set, and desiring to see what it was, it
proved as follows

For Mme. de Boufflers

The graceful fair who loves to know
Nor dreads the north's inclement snow
Who bids her polished accent wear
The British diction's harder air;
Shall read her praise in every clime
Where types can speak or poets rhyme.

This little *gentilesse* pleased.[13]

Her party were given a fête champêtre at Esher by Fanny Pelham with
more bad verse. Walpole, on this occasion, found her agreeable but lacking
in vivacity. 'She has an unrelaxed attention to applause; you would think
she was always sitting for her picture to her biographer.' But the celebrity
sightseeing was far from over, and even if she was not to meet her idol,
Hume, there was one sight of London not to be missed.

Topham Beauclerk told Boswell that when Mme. de Boufflers was
first in England she was desirous to see Johnson, I accordingly went
with her to his chambers in the Temple, where she was entertained
with his conversation for some time. When our visit was over, she
and I left him and were got into Inner Temple Lane, when all at
once I heard a voice like thunder. This was occasioned by Johnson,
who, it seems, upon a little reflection had taken it into his head
that he ought to have done the honours of his literary residence to
a foreign lady of quality, and eager to show himself a man of
gallantry was hurrying down the staircase in violent agitation. He
overtook us before we reached the Temple Gate, and, brushing
between me and Mme. de Boufflers, seized her hand and conducted
her to her coach. His dress was a rusty brown morning suit, a pair
of old shoes by way of slippers, a little shrivelled wig on the top of
his head, and the sleeves of his shirt and the knees of his breeches
hanging loose. A considerable crowd of people gathered round and
were not a little struck by this singular appearance.[14]

Mme de Boufflers, or, according to George Selwyn, 'Mme. Blewflower, as
our mob calls her, has been at Woburn'.[15] She also visited Wakefield,

Sion, and Yorkshire before leaving for Paris on 23rd July. She had failed to meet her idol, Hume, and was now, unsurprisingly for one 'a little frail', exhausted.

Lord Elibank had written to Hume in May, realising that he had missed him either in Edinburgh or at Ninewells:

> . . . I assure you from Mme. de Boufflers that her only errand to England, where I had the happiness to attend her from Paris, was the hopes of meeting you in London. You cannot in decency neglect the opportunity of gratifying this flattering curiosity, perhaps passion, of this most amiable of God's creation . . . I should only add that no author ever yet attained to that degree of reputation in his own lifetime that you are now in possession of at Paris . . .[16]

Hume, in fact, was visiting Harrogate and Knaresborough in Yorkshire and had returned to Edinburgh by July. From there he wrote to Mme de Boufflers:

> Being engaged in a party to a remote corner of the country, I was informed very late of the visit with which your ladyship has been pleased to favour this island, and after Lord Elibank was so good as to give me intelligence of it, I delayed for some time paying my respects to your ladyship by letter in hopes that I might possibly be able to do it in person, and thereby to gratify that desire by which I have long been possessed, of making myself known to a lady so universally valued, and who has done me so much honour, by giving me marks of her attention. But the reasons which detain me in this country are so powerful, that I find I must lay aside for the present so flattering a project, and must reserve that happiness to a time, which I shall always keep in my eye, when I may be able to pay my respects to your ladyship in Paris. Meanwhile, it gives me pleasure to hear that the English nation have shown themselves sensible of the honour you have done them by this visit, and have endeavoured to express their regard in the best manner which the custom and manners of the country would permit. I am only afraid that, to a person acquainted with the sociable and conversible parties of France, the showy and dazzling crowds of London assemblies would afford but an indifferent entertainment, and that

the love of retreat and solitude, with which the English are reproached, never appears more conspicuously than when they draw together a multitude of five hundred persons.[17]

It might be thought that Hume would have made every effort to facilitate Mme de Boufflers' much desired meeting, but instead he made no such effort and even despatched the above letter to Paris.

He was fifty-two years old, comfortably wealthy, and settled as part of Edinburgh society. He had been badly bruised by the adverse reception of his work in London and Edinburgh, and was permanently branded as an atheist. He had confused the party loyalists by embracing the parliamentary principles of Whiggism, and at the same time, condemning their political jobbery. He felt that it was time to lower his head from the parapet and retire into the circle of his friends in Edinburgh. Always ill at ease in large gatherings, he dreaded the thought of Strawberry Hill's French horns and clarionets, as well as the prospect of being derided by fashionable London for his Scots accent, where he would be lionised only by proxy as one famous in Paris. Also, given his tendency to procrastinate and linger on the high diving board, he must have breathed a sigh of relief when he heard that Mme de Boufflers was safely back in Paris and the relationship would again be confined to letter-writing. His relief was short-lived.

As happened so often in Hume's life, a summons from the aristocracy changed all his plans and set him, even at fifty-two, on a new course of action:

I have got an invitation, accompanied with great prospects and in expectations from Lord Hartford [sic] if I would accompany him, tho' without any character, in his embassy to Paris. I hesitated much on the acceptance of this offer, tho' in appearance very inviting; and I thought it ridiculous, at my years, to be entering on a new scene and to put myself in the lists as a candidate to fortune. But I reflected that I had in a manner abjured all literary occupations, that I resolved to give up my future life to amusements, that there could not be a better pastime than such a journey, especially with a man of Lord Hertford's character, and that it would be easy to prevent my acceptance from having the least appearance of dependence. For these reasons, and the advice of every friend whom I consulted, I at last agreed to accompany his Lordship, and I set out tomorrow for London.[18]

Hume wrote this to his old friend Adam Smith, whom he had clearly not consulted, on 9th August 1763, immediately before his departure. A comment in *My Own Life* gives a strong clue as to his reluctance to accept the post as well as to his avoidance of Mme de Boufflers: 'I was reluctant to begin connexions with the great, and because I was afraid that the civilities and gay company of Paris would prove disagreeable to a person of my age and humour'.

Francis Conway, Earl of Hertford, could hardly be described as a fellow spirit of David Hume's. He was known to be a respectable churchgoer, ploddingly efficient and with a marked lack of personality. The father of thirteen children and somewhat tight-fisted, he was unlikely to be acceptable to the 'gay company of Paris'. George III had already appointed as secretary to the embassy one Charles Bunbury, a notorious rake of no intellect whatever but with useful connexions in the royal circle. Bunbury would continue to draw his salary of £1,000 a year without ever leaving England, while being ignored by Hertford who wanted his own man in place. Hertford was the cousin of Horace Walpole and must have known of Hume's reputation in France, possibly even from Mme de Boufflers herself. Hume also had many influential friends in London and, as soon as Hertford's decision to appoint a secretary became known, they would have lobbied for his appointment.

Hume denied the use of his network of friends to Mure of Caldwell:

> I was now a person clean and white as the driven snow, and that were I to be proposed for the see of Lambeth, no objections can henceforth be made to me. What makes the matter more extraordinary is that the idea first came into my patron's head without the suggestion of any one mortal.[19]

Hume also gathered that Hertford felt Hume to be a suitable tutor to his twenty-year-old son, Lord Beauchamp, who was thought of as 'very amiable and promising'. Until he took up his post in Paris Hume would not meet Lord Beauchamp who had gone ahead of the ambassadorial party, which could not leave until the Ambassador from France, le Comte de Guerchy, arrived in London. An anonymous letter appeared criticising Hertford's appointment of a Scot, but the printers were sentenced to a fine of £100. Mure of Caldwell told Hume, 'I was in London when a man was fined £100 for taking your name in vain'.[20]

Meanwhile, Hume summoned up his courage and wrote to Mme de Boufflers since it was now inevitable that they should meet. He thanks

Lord Hertford, 'the most amiable nobleman in the court of England', for rousing himself from 'a state of indolence and sloth which I falsely dignified with the name of philosophy'. He assures her she will not find him 'wanting in my regard and attachment towards you' and promises to calm a growing row between Rousseau and the Countess. Hume seems not to have realised yet that Rousseau, 'our savage philosopher', was in a state of permanent dispute with whoever tried to help him, but he ends by hoping that the Comte de Guerchy will arrive in London soon so that Hume will have the opportunity of throwing himself at Mme de Boufflers' feet. On 15th October he sailed for Paris.

In December he let James's Court to the Reverend Hugh Blair and sent him instructions which emphasise Hume's enthusiasm for house-keeping:

> You have got an excellent house for its size. It was perfectly clean of vermin when I left it and I hope you will find it so. I would advise you not to put a bed in the little closet near the kitchen; it would be stifling to a servant and certainly would encourage bugs. The garret is neatly fitted up for a manservant; and the other closet will suffice for two maids. Never put a fire in the south room with the red paper: it is so warm of itself, that all last winter, which was a very severe one, I lay with a single blanket; and frequently upon coming in at midnight, starving with cold, have sat down and read for an hour as if there were a stove in the room. The fires of your neighbours will save you the expense of a fire in that room. You have an excellent cellar for wine, but there is a little inconvenience about having your coals and small beer in it at the same time, which my sister will explain to you.[21]

It does seem as if Katherine and Peggy Irvine were remaining in Edinburgh as housekeepers for Hugh Blair. Hume had purchased a chaise before he left for Paris and this also stayed behind to become part of the household. Many times in France, being entertained by the *haut monde*, Hume longed to return to his quiet settled life in Edinburgh.

His life in France would be anything but quiet or settled, arriving first at Boulogne, thanks to contrary winds in the Channel, thus disappointing the officials waiting in Calais to give the formal welcome due to an ambassador. But by 18th October 1763 they were in Paris.

Unlike today there was no official embassy residence and the first residence of Lord Hertford was at the Hôtel de Grimberg in the fashionable Rue St Dominique, on the left bank of the Seine conveniently opposite the Louvre. But Lord Beauchamp, who had preceded the party, was keen to show off his celebrated tutor, and Hume had scarcely time to catch his breath when:

> Lord Beauchamp told me that I must go instantly with him to the Duchess de la Valière's: when I excused myself on account of dress, he told me that he had her orders, though I were in boots. I accordingly went with him in a travelling frock, where I saw a very fine lady reclining on a sofa, who made me speeches and compliments without bounds. The style of panegyric was then taken up by a fat gentleman, whom I cast my eyes upon and observed him to wear a star of the richest diamonds: it was the Duke of Orleans. The duchess told me that she was engaged to sup in President Hainaut's,* but that she would not part with me: I must go along with her. The good President received me with open arms and told me among other fine things that the day before the Dauphin said to him etc., etc. Such instance of attention I found very frequent and even daily.[22]

This rushed visit into celebrity was an accurate foretaste of Hume's time in Paris. When the American President John F. Kennedy made an official visit to Paris with his fashion-conscious wife Jackie, he remarked that he would be remembered as 'the man who accompanied Jackie Kennedy to Paris'. It could also be said that Hertford's embassy is remembered as having taken place during Hume's stay in the capital. Given the centralist/monarchist regime created by Louis XIV, Paris was, to a large extent, France. Power was concentrated in the king's law-making powers but:

> The edicts of the kings of France have not the force of laws until they are registered by the *parlement* of Paris . . . this show of liberty serves the people instead of the reality, they are satisfied with daring to oppose, where, in effect, opposition is of no effect, for the king holds a bed of justice.[23]

These *parlements* in Paris and the regional cities were, in fact, starting to flex their muscles, especially in managing to bring about the suppression of the Jesuit order, but the true control was still at the centre and the centre

* He was president of the *Parlement de Paris*.

was Louis XV, in Paris, Versailles, Fontainebleau, or Compiègne where, of course, Hertford and Hume would attend. The common people of France were still, almost mystically, attached to their *roi-père*. At the battle of Dettingen in 1743, a dying French soldier asked a passing Englishman who had won the battle. When he was told it was England and her allies, the Frenchman expired saying, 'Ah! Mon pauvre roi!' Only fifty years later the common people would cut off the king's head.

The Peace of Paris in 1763 had meant a total humiliation for France and massive supremacy for Britain. France lost Canada, India, and Senegal, Minorca was restored to Spain which also gained Louisiana as a sop for the loss of Florida. In the Caribbean only Martinique, St Pierre Miquelon and Guadeloupe remained to France, while France managed to retain some limited fishing rights around Newfoundland. A contemporary warned, 'the dexterity of the French to gain by negotiation what they lose by war is indeed remarkable', but here it was the losses which were remarkable. Thanks to these losses and the expense of the wars of Spanish and Austrian Succession as well as the, for France, disastrous Seven Years War, the country was now on the verge of bankruptcy. A bankruptcy which, Professor Roger Price says in his *Concise History of France,* would bring on the Revolution in 1789. The nobility, however, centred on Paris, still enjoyed the last years of wealth and society: 'The manners of that celebrated metropolis (I mean among the better rank) are of the agreeable voluptuous kind and lulls them into the most effeminate softness'.[24] In common with the intelligentsia the nobility had had little or no interest in the wars of colonial conquest, except on the rare occasions when some financial gain might present itself. National hubris had excluded the intellectuals from pan-European contact except by correspondence, and now that travel was again possible they welcomed visitors from abroad, especially those from England, which to them included Scotland, and that meant, above all, David Hume.

But scarcely had he unpacked and caught his breath from his visit to the Duchesse de la Valière when he received a most unwelcome letter from Mme. de Boufflers, written on the 16th in English by Lydia Becquet:

Scarce recovered from the measles I cannot, sir, write myself, am obliged to use another hand, the same reason prevents my being at Paris on your arrival which was my intention. It gives me great concern to be hindered from giving you that proof of my esteem

and regard, and doing myself the honour of being the first in the
kingdom who pays what is due to so illustrious a man. My situation
will not allow me to answer your letter more particularly, I
postpone it till we meet; please, sir, to present my compliments to
Lord and Lady Hertford.[25]

The letter ends with a rather shaky signature 'H de Saujon, ptessse de
Boufflers' and had been written at L'Isle Adam.

It is a mark of the intensity of gossip in these circles that her measles
were still being discussed in October 1765 when Voltaire wrote to Mme
du Deffand, 'I know the history of the Duchesse de Bouffler's pox. If she
had been inoculated she would have been secure'.[26] The measles were now
smallpox and she had been promoted to a Duchess.

Back in 1764, however, Hume responded at once:

It was with much regret I received the letter with which your
Ladyship was pleased to honour me. Your Ladyship was the first
person to whom I had proposed to pay my respects at Paris, and I
found myself disappointed, for some time, of so flattering an
expectation; but I was still more afflicted to hear of your bad health
which had detained you in the country . . . I have as yet had but
two days' experience of this city, but have great reason already to
praise its politeness and hospitality, for which it is so famous. A
more quiet manner of sliding through life would perhaps suit better
my habits and turn of mind.[27]

Between now and the end of 1765 Hume wrote to Adam Smith, Adam
Ferguson, Alexander Wedderburn, and to Robertson, Millar and Blair,
among others, giving an account of his life. It was an uninterrupted paean
of praise. 'I eat nothing but ambrosia, drink nothing but nectar, breathe
nothing but incense, and tread on nothing but flowers.' In the course of his
diplomatic duties he met the entire royal family and was so bold as to
address the King directly. Louis XV never replied to Hume and Hume was
mortified until he was told that the King never spoke to anyone on first
acquaintance. Mme de Pompadour made up for this, as did the Duc de
Berry, later Louis XVI, and a gaggle of royal children down to and
including the future Charles X, now only five years old, but quite clearly
heard to utter the word 'Histoire' as well as 'other terms of panegyric'. The
Dauphin was reported to be 'very strongly in my favour'.

'The compliments of Dukes and Marischals of France and foreign ambassadors go for nothing with me at present. I retain a relish for no kind of flattery but that which comes from the ladies.'[28] This was the unqualified praise Hume had sought since the publication of the *Treatise*. But for all that he was now a superstar he sometimes longed for 'the plain roughness of the Poker . . . to qualify such lusciousness'. He acquired a lady translator for the *History*, Octavie Belot, 'a woman of merit', and in the Scots College he found fourteen volumes of the Memoirs of James II, which he told Millar would cause some revisions in a new edition of the *History* which 'I fancy will not be soon'. The limits of his diplomatic duties are seen in the letter to Hugh Blair in December:

> He [Lord Hertford] has got an opinion, very well founded, that the more acquaintance I make and the greater intimacies I form with the French, the more I am enabled to be of service to him. So he exacts no attendance from me, and is well pleased to find me carried into all kinds of company. He tells me that if he did not meet me by chance in third places we should go out of acquaintance. Thus you see my present plan of life sketched out.[29]

The ambassador was, in fact, so pleased with Hume as a kind of Cultural Attaché at large that he set about gaining Hume the full position of Secretary with a salary and pension of £1,000 a year for life. Needless to say this was subject to the usual delays in turning good intentions into hard cash. Six months later Hume wrote to Mure of Caldwell:

> I seem every moment to be touching on the time when I am to receive my credential letter of Secretary to the Embassy, with a thousand a year of appointments. The King has promised it – all the ministers have promised it – Lord Hertford earnestly solicits it – the plainest common sense and justice seem to require it – yet I have been in this condition above six months, and I never trouble my head about the matter, and have rather laid my account that there is to be no such thing.[30]

Outside the nobility were the men of letters, all equally keen to meet Hume:

> Those whose persons and conversations I like best are D'Alembert, Buffon, Marmontel, Diderot, Helvetius and old President Henault,

who, though now decaying retains that character that made him once the delight of France. He had always the best cook and the best company in Paris. But though I know you will laugh at me, as they do, I must confess that I am more carried away from their society than I should be, by the great ladies, with whom I became acquainted at my first introduction to court and whom my connexions with the English ambassador will not allow me to drop.[31]

This is a particularly feeble excuse for Hume to indulge in what Hume delighted in.

Mure of Caldwell gives us a picture of the adulation which was meted out to Hume when he quotes from a letter by Andrew Stewart. Hume had replied to a letter of Stewart's casually using an invitation from the Duchess D'Aiguillon as scrap paper:

This is but a small circumstance, if you knew the immense court that is paid to him from all quarters of this country. All ranks of people – courtiers, ladies young and old, wits and savants, vie with each other in the incense they offer up to the célèbre Monsieur Hume. Amidst all this intoxicating worship, he preserves his own natural style and simplicity of manners; and deigns to be cheerful and jolly as if no such things had happened to him. His manner though differing in some respects from the French, does not fail, however, to succeed with them. It must be owned that some of his admirers were at first a good deal surprised with the largeness of his figure. They had generally, in idea, clothed him with a person very little encumbered with matter. Diderot, among others, was in this mistake, and told Mr Hume at their first interview, that in place of taking him for the author of his works, he would have taken him for, 'un gros Bernardin bien nourri'. [32]

Being mistaken for a well-nourished priest is hardly flattery, but Hume and Diderot became great friends. Denis Diderot's father was a master cutler but disowned his literary son. His marriage also failed and Diderot became, for a time, a serial philanderer. His *Pensées Philosophiques* was burned by the authorities and his *Lettre sur les Aveugles* earned him a spell in prison. Asked to edit Chambers' *Cyclopedia*, he set about composing the *Encyclopédie*, a summary of all human knowledge. Inevitably he became the guest of Catherine the Great, wrote novels and plays and finally settled in Paris with Sophie Volland, his final and devoted mistress. Hume was now mixing in extremely vivid company.

Hume's fame was so widespread that the wit Nicolas Chamfort remarked that he thought David Hume must be dead since he had only met him three times that day, and it is to Lord Hertford's credit that he did not feel any jealousy, but continued to encourage the social life of his secretary:

> I was carried about six weeks ago to a masquerade by Lord Hertford; we both went unmasked, and we had scarce entered the room when a lady in mask came up to me and exclaimed, 'Oh, Monsieur Hume, you do well to come here unmasked. You will be showered with praises and honours. You will be able to tell from all this how much France has taken you to its heart.' This prologue was not a little encouraging, but as we advanced through the hall, it is difficult to imagine the caresses, civilities and panegyrics which poured on me from all sides: you would have thought that everyone had taken advantage of his mask to speak his mind with impunity. I could observe that the ladies were rather the most liberal on this occasion, but what gave me great pleasure was to find that most of the elogiums bestowed on me turned on my personal character; my naiveté and simplicity of manners, the candour and mildness of my disposition, etc. *Non sunt mihi cornea fibra* [I am not worthy of such praise]. I shall not deny that my heart felt a sensible satisfaction from this general effusion of good will, and Lord Hertford was much pleased and even surprised; Though he said that he thought he had known before upon what footing I stood with the good company of Paris.[33]

The ambassador clearly felt towards his somewhat self-satisfied secretary what the American President was to feel towards his couture-conscious wife. But popularity provokes jealousy and that inveterate gossip Horace Walpole, who was in Paris at this time and was the cousin of Lord Hertford, comments on Hume's success:

> Everything English is in fashion [and] our bad French is accepted into the bargain. Many of us are received everywhere; Mr Hume is fashion itself although his French is as unintelligible as his

English . . . [Hume] is treated here with perfect veneration. His
History, so falsified in many points, so partial in as many, so very
unequal in its parts, is thought the standard of writing. Five or six
of the women that I have seen already are very sensible. The men
in general are much inferior . . . the style of conversation is solemn,
pedantic, and seldom animated, but by a dispute. I was expressing
my aversion to disputes: Mr Hume, who very gratefully admires the
tone of Paris, having never known any other tone, said with great
surprise, 'why what do you like, if you hate both disputes and
whisk?'* . . . Mr Hume who is the only thing in the world that
they believe implicitly; which they must do for I defy them to
understand any language that he speaks. If I could divest myself of
my wicked and unphilosophic bent to laughing, I should do very
well.[34]

Walpole did have the grace to admit that Mme du Deffand said he had *le
feu moqueur*. Although Walpole was not alone in commenting on Hume's
accent, which he accepted was atrocious, and he even considered resigning
his post as a result of his grammatically correct but almost unintelligible
French. Walpole's French was ungrammatical, but well accented. However, John Moore noted in 1779:

Politeness and good manners, indeed, may be traced, though in
different proportions, through every rank from the greatest of the
nobility to the lowest mechanic.

A stranger . . . whose accent is uncouth and ridiculous in the ears
of the French . . . is heard with the most serious attention. [But]
What Frenchmen consider good manners many Englishmen would
call flattery, perhaps fawning.[35]

Hume had made the same observations himself, when living in Reims.
But Moore went on to comment on the women Hume was so anxious to
meet:

. . . an admirable mixture of agreeable women who . . . joined in
the conversation even when it turned to subjects of literature, upon
which occasions English ladies generally imagine it becomes them
to remain silent. But here they took their share without scruple or

* An early name for whist

hesitation. Those who understood anything of the subject delivered their sentiments with great precision, and more grace than the men. Those who knew nothing of the matter rallied their own ignorance in such a sprightly manner as convinced everybody that knowledge is not necessary to render a woman exceedingly agreeable in society.[36]

And their interests were not confined to the arts:

They dabbled in science as in philosophy, and rustled into lecture rooms where Abbé Nollet discoursed on chemistry, and fancied they were scientific because they enjoyed an 'experiment' and greeting every explosion of fetid gas with pretty little screams and terror-stricken 'ahs' with dainty handkerchiefs at their noses, they pronounced the whole thing charming. Such were the fashionable amusements of society, from the farmer-general's wife to the scion of royalty, the Dauphin and future Louis XVI, for whom the courtier physician in 1744 prefaced his performances, 'the oxygen and hydrogen will now have the honour of amalgamating before your Royal Highness'.[37]

It was into this society that Hume was now pitched and all the great hostesses, as well as Mme de Boufflers, vied with each other for his company.

The doyenne of the great ladies was probably Marie-Thérèse Rodet Geoffrin, nicknamed the Tsarina of Paris. She was born in 1699, the orphan daughter of a valet of the Dauphine, had married well at fourteen and inherited her husband's vast fortune. This rich, hardly educated widow was the only *salonaire* outside the nobility but her generosity and the warmth of her personality made her popular with all the intellectuals of the day. An enthusiastic autodidact, her favourite author was said to be the daunting Protestant Bayle. Her Monday salon, clashing with Mme de Boufflers', allowed no conversation except on art, 'her house on the Rue St. Honoré filled with painters, sculptors, architects, engravers'. Friedrich Grimm, the German critic, delivered a long list of the topics forbidden by Mme Geoffrin at her Monday salon. Wednesday, however, was a more general salon for men of letters and David Hume was welcome there. With Mme de Boufflers still convalescent in the country, he probably visited Mme Geoffrin first. William Cole, an English visitor to her salon, gives a vivid picture of the procedure:

Mme Geoffrin, . . . when she came in, she immediately flung
herself carelessly into an elbow chair, almost half reclined, with one
leg thrown over the knee of another, and so she sat for two or three
hours, and being without stays, in the loose, easy and negligent
dress of the Frenchwomen, she had more the appearance of a
person just having got out of bed, with a nightgown flung hastily
over her, than a person dressed to make a visit in an evening.[38]

He noticed the absence of stays among the hostesses as a rarity compared
to England. He was also astonished that when they sat to dinner a servant
would place a pot of hot coals beneath them, and they would spread their
skirts over the pot and dine in warmth:

I came into the room where there were ten or twelve people who
dined with Mme Geoffrin every Wednesday. The dinner was
excellent. The mistress of the house did not serve, but talked with
her friends. During my time in France I never found such
generosity, such simplicity and such a relaxed atmosphere. The
other guests seemed to me to be friendly and at their ease together.
The open and contented air of Mme Geoffrin surrounded everyone.
We withdrew where there was a table set for us to serve ourselves
with coffee, but it was the mistress who took care of us. We all sat
round a table with our cups which Mme Geoffrin filled from a
cafetière; there was a jug of cream which many of us took; an abbé
beside me stirred some cream into his coffee, tasted it slowly and
said to Mme Geoffrin, 'Madame,' he said said with more affection
than criticism, 'everything which we eat here, everything we take
here, is absolutely at the peak of perfection, but this cream is sour.'
'I know', said Mme Geoffrin, 'But I am forced to serve it. The
woman who sells me the cream is mortified by the death of her
cow. How can I abandon her? Is it not better to have bad cream?'[39]

She was much loved, and Hume, twelve years her junior, was always her
'fat rascal', while she rose above the jealousies that beset the other
hostesses who treated their special guests as personal possessions. She
did, however, quarrel with Mme de Belot, Hume's translator, over some
unknown subject. Hume remained friends with her, sending her a
specially bound copy of the *History*, which Mme Geoffrin claimed shamed
all the other books in her library.

The hostesses guarded their celebrity guests as today football mangers guard their star players, and the most formidable of those ladies was the 68-year-old Marie de Vichy-Champrond, Marquise du Deffand. She kept a suite of rooms at the convent of St Joseph in the Rue St Dominique, on the left bank, not far from Hertford's Embassy and now housing the French Ministry of War. Stricken with blindness, the Marquise lived in some state with a salon decorated in buttercup-coloured watered silk, with two maids and two footmen as well as a secretary, Wiard, and more importantly, as time would show, a companion, Julie de Lespinasse. She described herself as 'the most lively corpse in Paris' and was seen at operas, plays and suppers across the town. She was also an enthusiastic correspondent. Her blindness allowed her to reverse the day and she never rose until the afternoon, forbidding her guests to leave before she tired, usually at five or six the following morning. Horace Walpole said of her, 'Her soul is immortal and forces her body to keep it company'. To Hume's dismay it was said of her that the only difference between her cook and a notorious poisoner was their intentions.

When Hume joined her circle it was dominated by Jean le Rond D'Alembert, a philosopher and mathematician. D'Alembert, born in 1717, was a foundling who had been adopted by a lieutenant-general of artillery. By 21 he was a professor of mathematics and by 1745 he had a pension of 500 livres. By October 1748 he was the 'petit ami' of Mme du Deffand. He was also a close friend of Diderot and wrote most of the mathematical entries in the *Encyclopédie*, as well as writing an introductory essay on the relationships between mathematics and philosophy. He was offered a life of luxury by Catherine the Great, and Frederick the Great offered him the Presidency of the Academy in Berlin, but D'Alembert refused to leave Paris.

Voltaire had been a regular guest of Mme du Deffand's before his departure for Prussia in 1753 and talked of the discussions, enthusiasms, wit, and eloquence he found there. Thereafter he corresponded regularly with Mme du Deffand. It is interesting that of all Hume's correspondence with the French *philosophes* – and it was extensive – he never had any direct dealing with Voltaire. Voltaire, living a stone's throw from the Swiss border at Ferney, told Mme du Deffand 'You have only to send him to me; I will speak to him, and above all, listen to him'. Hume claimed that diplomatic business confined him to Paris and the two never met. Mme du Deffand, on the other hand, supplied him with Hume's works and acted as a go-between. She wrote to Voltaire on 25 June 1764:

This evening I will charm M Hume by reading your letter to him.
[He had written praising Hume's history and philosophy on 20
June.] You are happy with his work, you praise his personality; he is
gay simple and good. In my opinion the English wits are worth
more than ours; I never find a dogmatic or imperative tone; They
speak the truth more strongly than we, but never simply to gain
celebrity.[40]

But her emotional world was torn apart when, joining her guests
unexpectedly early one evening, she found them already entranced in
the company of her attractive and much younger companion Julie de
Lespinasse. This confrontation led to Lespinasse leaving Mme du Duf-
fand to establish her own salon, taking with her the star of Mme du
Deffand, Jean D'Alembert. Writing to Voltaire on 3 March 1766, he said,
'Between us there is no marriage, no love, but reciprocal esteem and all the
sweetness of friendship'. A comment which could have fitted Hume's
relationship with Mme de Boufflers.

The stable of encyclopaedists, wits, and writers Mme du Deffand
had so carefully tended also left her and her salon was now composed
only of the high aristocracy and diplomats. There were no more dawn
departures from the Convent of St Joseph. She became bitter against
her sister hostesses, for example, and not surprisingly, Mme de
Boufflers: 'That idol of the Temple, is a vanity ridden woman,
concerned only with outward effect'. She remained friends with
Walpole but her friendship with Hume did not survive the rupture
of 1763. In 1766 he wrote to her justifying his attempt to remain
friends with both ladies:

I find adopting animosities repugnant. I beg you, dear lady, to
weigh once more these feelings on the scales of your exquisite
judgement and, considering the course of normal behaviour, even if
the side these scales come down on is not the most favourable to
me, believe in my ardent desire to regain your friendship.[41]

They never corresponded again and Mme du Deffand outlived Hume
by four years to die at eighty-one. In her final letter to Walpole, she
told him she had no regrets and left him her only legacy – her dog,
Tonton.

The third rival to Mme de Boufflers for Hume's attention was, indeed,

Julie de Lespinasse. Thirty-one years old, tall and well built, but without conventional beauty, her charm captured everyone. Schooled in conversation in the salon of Mme du Deffand, after she left, an implacable hatred existed between the two women for the rest of their lives. Mlle de Lespinasse took a modest house opposite the convent of Bellechasse, insultingly near that of Mme du Deffand. One can guess at the gleefully spiteful reactions of the other hostesses in that her furnishings were provided by Mme de Boufflers and Mme Geoffrin among others. Unfortunately, on setting up her new establishment she fell ill with smallpox to be nursed devotedly by D'Alembert. She recovered but the cost was high: she was pockmarked and swollen. Her intellect, however, was still attractive to men. She was certainly attractive to D'Alembert, who fell ill in his turn while she nursed him in his garret room. On recovery he left his hermit-like existence and moved into her apartment. Rumours of their marriage flew but were never substantiated, and Paris revelled in the couple's delicious immorality, while the pair were still to be seen on Mondays and Wednesdays at Mme Geoffrin's salon.

Hume, who presumed she was D'Alembert's mistress, which she probably was not, called her, 'really one of the most sensible women in Paris'. He was a constant visitor at a time when:

> Anglomania consisted of three things, whist, *Clarissa Harlowe*,* and Hume. Historian and philosopher, a distinguished wit in spite of his bulk and vulgarity, sympathetic in spite of his silences, Hume received a thousand kindnesses from Julie.[42]

When she died in 1776 her salon ceased. 'When the Lord struck the shepherd the flock dispersed', but D'Alembert lived on until 1783.

It is extraordinary that a fat, middle-aged, clumsy Scotsman speaking good French with an impenetrable accent was not only welcomed by these great ladies, but was allowed to visit more than one salon. This amounted almost to marital infidelity and was equivalent to a football player playing for two rival teams in the same week. But he was *le bon David* and as an exotic stranger and diplomat was not expected to understand the rigid protocols of the *grandes dames*. So he was forgiven his transgressions. He dressed expensively, was witty and a celebrity diplomat, so his long conversational gaps and clumsily swept aside teacups were excused on

* A novel By Samuel Richardson

the grounds of genius. They flocked to see him as 'a rhinoceros at a fair'. The ladies made the rules of the game, and David Hume was a star player.

Of these ladies he said, 'You would take them all for Vestals by the decency of their behaviour in company. Scarce a double entendre ever to be heard, scarce a free joke; What lies beneath this veil is not commonly supposed to be so pure'.[43] No such accusation had been made against the 'Idol of the Temple', Mme de Boufflers.

On Mondays she entertained at the Rue Nôtre Dame de Nazareth. The Prince's own private quarters were in the Temple itself and he maintained a town house beside Mme de Boufflers' residence. The fact that these establishments were within a few hundred yards of each other reflects the bizarre structures operating during the *ancien régime*. When the Count was in the Temple, he was the Grand Prior of the Knights of St John, and could not possibly have a mistress. In the Rue Nôtre Dame de Nazareth, the Prince could behave as a bachelor, and when he was with Mme de Boufflers, he was simply living with his Mâitresse en Titre. Mercifully for etiquette, the Prince maintained only one mistress at a time, and after his quarrel with his previous lady, Mme de Arty, Mme de Boufflers occupied the title. The formal reception would include fifty to a hundred people, the ladies seated with their escorts hovering nearby. A more informal, but much more exclusive, gathering would take place in the Salon de Quatre Glaces. Here the guests were of the noblest, 'higher in rank than those of the Marquise du Deffand . . . no encyclopaedists (even though Mme de Boufflers mixed with them) and no one from commerce or finance'.[44] But David Hume was welcome. 'In the salons, the irony of Mme de Deffand, the sentimentality of Lespinasse tired him. The soirées of the Temple were perfect.'[45]

In a painting by Michel-Barthelémy Ollivier of the salon in May 1766, the ladies serve the tea and cakes without servants in what they take to be the English style, the gentlemen read or talk, while the Prince himself in a rather dated wig, 'more the style of Louis XIV than Louis XV', has his back to the small boy who is playing the harpsichord. The small boy is Mozart. The most prized accomplishment at these gatherings was conversation. It had to be witty, informed, challenging and, above all, to inspire and display intelligence. This was a period when thought as much as dress had ever changing fashions and the scepticism of Hume was the highest fashion. He was the greatest prize of Mme de Boufflers, who 'one imagined could equally seduce and infuriate by her brilliant and extravagant conversation'.[46] Her wit could certainly bite, although on one occasion she was struck by a riposte. She had described Mme de Pompadour as no more than the 'first whore of the kingdom'. Mme de Mirepoix, friend to both ladies, responded, 'Do not ask me to count up to three'.

We are, in the painting by Ollivier, given a glimpse of 'these charming inhabitants of a vanishing world, dancing in the golden mist of afternoon tea, unaware that night is falling . . . in the distance at the other end of Paris [is] a vision of a scaffold erected in the square which is no longer the Place Louis XV'.[47]

Hume and Mme de Boufflers had been corresponding for some time and now, after her recovery from measles, were able to meet regularly. Their relationship went beyond friendship but stopped well short of romantic love. At first she called Hume her *petit ministre*, a joking reference to his diplomatic position, before they began to exchange views on philosophy, when he became *cher mâitre*. She is definite in her views – the theatre bores her – but Hume's letters make her laugh and she wishes to divert him, stressing that he is welcome to call at the Temple. Hume sent her reports on the gossip of the court, since he was in attendance, which echo Cyrano de Bergerac's comic *Gazette* in Rostand's play. But he did feel that the relationship was in danger of moving on to a more emotional plane than he wished, and that he was in danger of an unwarranted attachment. On 6th July 1764 he wrote to her from Compiègne:

> I have had a great inclination for some days past to pay my addresses to you, but have restrained myself from reason, as I imagined, but really I believe from pride and humour surely the most misplaced in the world . . . I make advantage of the ten leagues of interval that lie between us, and feel already some progress in the noble resolution I have formed of forgetting you entirely before the end of summer . . . to cut things short, I kiss your hands most humbly and devoutly and bid you adieu.[48]

Her reply is dated 6th July but this is quite possibly a mistake. Her letters show her impulsive nature – the crossing of a 't' extends across an entire page, inks and pens change frequently – and her handwriting speaks of great haste. The letter, however, is a model of tact and consideration. Hume had, out of normal loyalty, sent her a copy of *Douglas* and she starts with a long critique of the play ending with an elegant rejection:

you are my master of philosophy and morals, and I have often said to you that if, on those subjects I had ideas at least as true and sophisticated I would be under an obligation to develop them. But to diminish the overweening pride that knowing this must inspire you to see in me, and having been your disciple I would like to give lessons to you in my turn in a war in which speculation does not have the capacity for enmity that other debates can engender. My dear Master, I therefore say to you freely but with regret that the tragedy of your friend [Douglas] did not please me, and more than that I have read the works of your writers which merely confirms that the tragic muse is not to my taste.[49]

She rather mockingly complained that the folio format of his *Essays* made it inconvenient to read either in bed, or more picturesquely, in the sunshine by the banks of the Oise, the river running through the Prince's estate at L'Isle Adam, some twenty miles east of Paris. The centre of this estate was the Prince's hunting lodge, a vast elegant building occupying the entire island of the Prieuré in the river which had been in his family since 1691. The Prince's hospitality was lavish with each guest being provided with a coach and horses as well as a personal train of servants. The ladies, and we presume Hume, remained among the willows and poplars on the island while the Prince supervised the hunt, until riding out to greet his return. The cellar was stocked with the entire output of the vineyard of Romanée Conti – still one of the most prized of all wines – and in the stables over a hundred horses were in permanent readiness for the Prince in his buff and blue hunting colours to choose from. There was presumably a selection of quiet horses for Mme de Boufflers, who was a poor rider. The building was destroyed in the Revolution, rebuilt, destroyed again in the Franco-Prussian War and is now a modest nineteenth-century villa, available for conferences and receptions. The island is also smaller now since the Oise has been widened to accommodate commercial barge traffic. But at the time when David Hume was a frequent guest it was the epitome of aristocratic elegance and a far cry from Ninewells. Mme de Boufflers was mistress of all this and her letter to Hume continues, not in the manner of a sophisticated Queen of the Salons, but in the tone of an aggrieved lover:

You wish to part from me, for what motive I cannot tell, but I know very well that I am likewise obliged to part from you. It is not with ill-will and it is not hard for me to say that you have an authority and a goodness of heart that I esteem and a genius that I admire, and a wit that pleases me, and that you are a foreigner and will soon leave, and that when you visit, early or late, you do not disgust me as do most of the people I am forced to live amongst . . . but I cannot maintain either a simple esteem or an objective admiration.[50]

She goes on to say that, for her, such admiration leads to such affection that she has had, in the past, to break off several friendships and describes herself as:

a feeble bush who has spread its roots too wide and so is exposed to all kinds of injuries and risks.

Then, finally, comes a great contradiction:

Adieu, mon cher Mâitre, I hasten to love you no more and to have no shame to be the last to finish this affair. But as I have not yet started it, I allow myself today to assure you <u>that I love you with all my heart</u>' [my underline].

It is easy to understand how Mme de Boufflers acquired her reputation for paradoxes. Hume's reply reveals that he, at least, is indulging in a courtly dance of emotions and he acknowledges the danger of unrestrained affection. But, 'who would not drink up the poison with joy and satisfaction?' He knew of her unstable emotional background and that she had threatened suicide more then once – the thought of it is 'a poignard at my heart' – and then briskly returns to a defence of *Douglas*! Finally he bids her good-bye and hopes she will be in Paris by August so that he may enjoy her company. Without any such statement having been made, the rules had been established, and to reinforce them Mme de Boufflers wrote on the 21st asking rhetorically if he thought she had a heart capable of tenderness, charity, and sensitive to friendship. Presuming that he agrees, she tells him that she has a sacred duty which leaves little affection for others and that he is asking her to spread herself too thinly, but that she can control the greater part of her time and give it to Hume. She flatters herself that he will like this letter better than her last one and adds that she would have to have had little skill as a letter-writer to have badly expressed a friendship which her heart felt so vividly. Hume replied, rather churlishly, that he supposed she would have to continue her loyalty to the Prince, but that his regard for her is unalterable, and that she has saved him 'from a total indifference towards everything in human life'. She was furious at his seeming half-heartedness. 'Your letter arrived this morning, but do you think I am happy with it? You reply in two pages and I wrote you eight! . . . I waited a long time for your letter, I waited impatiently for it, and I am not at all satisfied with it! We shall see what excuse you will give me!' Her fury was, somewhat, a studied part of the dance since she also invited Hume to accompany the Prince and herself to the country with a party of others. Hume wrote back in delight that she could cut him limb from limb, but like 'those pertinacious animals of my country', fleas, he would expire still attached to her. This was one of those times when Hume showed that he lacked the true romantic touch. 'Now, I throw myself at your feet, and give you nothing but marks of patience and long-suffering and submission. But I own, that matters are at present on a more proper and more natural footing, and long may they remain so.' The priggish schoolboy who had poured such scorn on cavaliers and their romantic fantasies was now a man of fifty-three trying to control his own fantasies. But it is difficult to believe that Hume was involved in anything more than a delicious game of dalliance. He ended by saying, 'I will not begin a new sheet, lest I be tempted to give you eight pages'. They could now continue in safety and with a friendship that would last their respective lifetimes. At L'Isle Adam they could walk by the banks of the Oise, unencumbered by outside opinion and tolerated by the Prince. In Paris he was her expected companion and Mme du Deffand now referred to Hume as the High Priest of the Idol of the Temple.

However much Hume's behaviour was tolerated, and even envied in Paris, and however much his Francophile behaviour was constructive in raising the French regard for England, there was always the risk that he could be seen by outsiders as 'having gone native'. This is exemplified by an exchange of letters between Hume and Gilbert Elliot of Minto who had visited Paris in 1764 to arrange schooling for his sons. Business took Elliot back home before the matter could be concluded and he left the final arrangements to Hume. A stiff-necked civil servant, he saw Hume relaxed in French society and wrote from Brussels on 15th September voicing his criticisms:

> Allow me in friendship also, to tell you, I think I see you at present upon the brink of a precipice. One cannot too much clear the mind

of little prejudices, but partiality to one's country is not a prejudice. Love the French as much as you will, many of the individuals are surely the proper objects of affection, but above all still continue an Englishman.[51]

He then has the arrogance to continue his advice in French: 'Habite l'univers, mais aime sa patrie'. Minto had been a fellow-student of Hume's at Edinburgh University and had risen to be first Lord of the Admiralty, but his letter is a model of pomposity. He admits, patronisingly, that the French are loveable little rascals and one must not be prejudiced, and then reminds Hume that he is, after all, English! Though Hume was no Scottish Nationalist – he approved of the Act of Union – and had many reservations about his native country, he was defiantly not an Englishman and made this totally clear in his furious reply to Minto: 'I cannot imagine what you mean by saying that I am on the brink of a precipice'. He goes on to say that he will probably be abandoned by the government at the conclusion of Hertford's embassy:

I shall be obliged to leave Paris, which I confess I shall turn my back on with regret. I shall go to Toulouse [Adam Smith was in Toulouse] or Montauban, or some provincial town in the South of France, where I shall spend, contented, the rest of my life with more money, under a finer sky, and in better company than I was born to enjoy. From what motive or consideration can I prefer living in England to that in foreign countries? I believe, taking the continent of Europe from St Petersburg to Lisbon, and from Bergen to Naples, there is not that ever heard my name, who has not heard of it with advantage, both in point of morals and genius. I do not believe there is one Englishman in fifty who, if he heard that I had broke my neck tonight, would not be rejoiced in it. Some hate me because I am not a Tory, some because I am not a Whig, some because I am not a Christian, and all because I am a Scotsman. Can you seriously talk of my continuing an Englishman? Am I, or are you, an Englishman? Will they allow us to be so? Do they not treat with derision our pretensions to that name, and with hatred our pretensions to surpass and govern them? I am a citizen of the world; but if I were to adopt any country, it would be that in which I live at present, from which I am determined never to depart, unless a war drive me into Switzerland or Italy.[52]

Allowing for a certain degree of conceit, brought on by plentiful Romanée Conti and every salon in Paris inflating his ego, Hume felt justifiably neglected by both Scotland and England. He voices the complaint, still heard today, that the English are not properly grateful for the Scots running their country for them, and quite reasonably prefers the laissez-faire intellect of France to the rigid factionalism of England. He is adamant that the weather in the south of France is preferable to that in Scotland – no one would argue with this – and the living is cheaper, but atypically fails to mention the food. Some of these are still the core arguments for British expatriates. Surprisingly he remained friends with Minto and did arrange for the placement of his sons in a Paris school, but the subject of nationalism was avoided by both of them, and two years later Hume left France never to return.

But he was not only the darling of the salons, he was welcome at the tables of the *philosophes*. As we have seen, philosophy was fashionable and the spirit of inquiry that had produced the *Encyclopédie* as well as, incidentally, the Philosophical and Select societies in Edinburgh, was still burning brightly. One of the greatest of the great tables of Paris was in the Rue Royale, at the Butte St Roche, where Paul-Henry Thiry, Baron d'Holbach, presided over philosophical evenings always accompanied by exquisite food and rare wines: David Hume's idea of perfection. Holbach was a German-born philosopher who had taken French citizenship. He was comfortably rich with a château at Grandval which became a country refuge for the *philosophes*. He was described as the '*Amphitryon des philosophes*', but since Amphitryon was cuckolded by Zeus to become foster father to Hercules, it is difficult to see why. He contributed 438 articles, mainly scientific, to the *Encyclopédie*, and was author of the *Système de la Nature*, a 'systematic defence of atheistic materialism'. This took Locke's idea of humanity as a machine into almost total atheism, but embraced Hume's thought that man's pursuit of his own good needed the cooperation of others and so contributed to the ultimate good of all mankind. Government, therefore, needed to foster this enthusiasm and relied on its authority for the happiness of the individual. Needless to say, this rejected monarchy, aristocracy and the church, God being the creature imagined by man to explain the inexplicable. Diderot said that Holbach felt 'it is not enough to be a savant, one must have goodness'. Like so many in Paris, Holbach had been agog to meet Hume and he was made welcome at the sumptuous dinners on Sundays and Thursdays. Mme D'Holbach

was thoroughly bored by these events but the conversation was enthusiastically followed by D'Holbach's aged mother, the still lively Mme
d'Aine. Here, as at Mlle de Lespinasse's, Hume would have met D'Alembert who was to become one of his greatest friends, although, astonishingly, Hume admits to not having read all of D'Alembert's works,
certainly not those regarding geometry and algebra:

> In other respects, D'Alembert is a very agreeable companion and of
> irreproachable morals . . . He lives in an agreeable retreat, suitable
> to a man of letters. He has five pensions . . . the whole amount of
> these is not 6000 livres a year, on the half of which he lives
> decently and gives the other half to poor people with whom he is
> connected. In a word, I scarce know a man who, with some
> exceptions (for there must always be exceptions), is a better model
> of a virtuous and philosophical character.[53]

D'Alembert was enough of a personal friend to be able to tell Hume to
modify his habit of staring glassily at whoever was speaking to him. It was
to no avail and Hume even terrified Rousseau by staring at him.

D'Alembert, a distinguished mathematician, was co-editor with Denis
Diderot of the *Encyclopédie*, contributing the articles on mathematics. He
also contributed to Rousseau's article on Geneva which infuriated Voltaire
– it didn't take much to infuriate Voltaire – resulting in Voltaire's
resignation as a contributor to the *Encyclopédie*. Diderot himself was a
regular at Holbach's well-laden table and it was an exclusive group all of a
similar mind, something which astonished Hume, more used to the range
of differing opinions in the Edinburgh clubs. Hume's friend Andrew
Stuart, a temporary guest of the Baron's, attempted to disagree with the
assertion that Christianity would be abolished in Europe by the end of the
eighteenth century, and was duly laughed at for his pains. They nicknamed him 'the immortal soul'.[54]

Hume, himself unused to such solidarity, put the Deist point of view,
saying that he had never seen any true atheists. Holbach told him that of
the eighteen dining at the table, fifteen were convinced atheists, while the
other three were as yet undecided.

There are three elements which separate Hume's position from that of
the *philosophes*. They had all grown up under the teachings of the Catholic
Church which they now rejected with certainty. Hume, under the
influence of Bayle, rejected all certainties. He felt that their certainty

was a kind of aristocratic arrogance. Secondly they connected atheism with the concept of the universe as a machine without any proof and, lastly, they accepted life as it existed without any attempt to look for causes in the past or projections into the future.

But all of the *philosophes* risked imprisonment or exile if their published writings became too blatant. The *parlements* were quick to find fault and book burnings were common. However, since the police or soldiery who were despatched to collect the offending works from the publishers were more often than not illiterate, the publishers usually gave them the remaindered copies of unsold works and continued to sell the banned works on the black market: for a greatly increased price.

It is tempting to think that it was at dinners such as these that the basic intellectual theses for the Revolution were established, but this was clearly not so. These intellectuals felt themselves above the common people, about whose happiness they philosophised with no idea of practical application. They were committed to endorsing utilitarian philosophy, and to measuring the efficacy of governments by results, but they made no calls to man the barricades. They had little concept of the conditions under which the common people of France suffered, especially outside the large towns. The one *philosophe* whose writings were to be a basis of the Revolution was Jean-Jacques Rousseau, but he was in more or less permanent exile and, anyway, was not socially acceptable in Parisian circles. The *philosophes* were also remote from the aristocratic power base that surrounded the Court. That group was enclosed and arrogantly non-intellectual. Carlyle overheard Hume saying that he had asked Baron d'Holbach if he thought there would soon be a revolution favourable to liberty in France. D'Holbach, perhaps disillusioned with everything and presuming that any movement would start with the Court, answered, 'No, for the noblesse had all become poltroons'.[55] Interestingly, Hume and Diderot would have dined often in the restaurant Le Procope. It was in the Rue de L'Ancienne Comédie, thus close to Hume's lodgings. But it was also near the Rue Jacob and the Jacobin Club so fifty years later the restaurant would become the favourite meeting place for Robespierre and Danton. However, in 1765 Hume thought that, notwithstanding the knavery of the aristocracy, and the ivory towers of the intellectuals, something was bound to change soon.

Oddly enough, twenty years after his death, Hume was quoted as an authority doubting the wisdom of executing a sovereign. Joseph, Comte

de Maistre, a counter-revolutionary, published *Considérations sur la France*
which contained an essay unjustifiably entitled *Reflections on the French
Revolution by David Hume*. It contained a quotation from Hume's
comments on the execution of Charles I purporting to argue against
'breaking the supple chain from the throne of the Supreme Being'.
Posthumous fame can be unreliable.

One element in French life had changed, however, and that was the
power of the church. The Jesuit order had been suppressed in 1762 and the
intellectuals had, long since, rejected its teachings. Over a century previously, Edmond Richer, a doctor of the Sorbonne, had preached against
their power – 'the scourge of the French church and universities' – and had
moved the loyalty of the lower clergy away from subjection to Rome while
the higher reaches of the hierarchy simply looked to their aristocratic
connections for preferment. For the bulk of the people the French church
was a Gallic church dependent on internal politics, which were, supposedly, the affair of the *parlements*. But the *parlements* were themselves
ignored by the aristocracy who surrounded Louis XV. Hume met no
church leaders and his contact with the aristocracy was limited, and yet he
suspected that the edifice was liable to crumble.

There had been sporadic discontent in Geneva since 1763 and there
would be peasant risings in Russia in 1774, in Bohemia in 1775, and in
Hungary in 1790. The Irish Volunteers and the Dutch Patriots were in
arms in the 1770s, while in America a revolution against unjust taxation
grew, through incompetence, into a War of Independence. Britain had
managed a deft change in government at home in 1688 which neutered
revolt and took the unwarranted name of the Bloodless Revolution, but
France sleepwalked until 1792 when the lid blew off the pressure cooker
and national debt, widespread poverty, overseen by a corrupt and worthless administration, exploded as nowhere else. Since Louis XIV's time the
head of all government had been the king, and when the government
failed Louis XVI paid for that failure under the guillotine. In 1763 only
Hume's head was far enough out of the sand to see the danger approaching.

This peaceful co-existence of conversation in the salons and vigorous
discussions with the *philosophes* continued unruffled. Laurence Sterne
visited Paris, and Hume entertained a party at the Embassy where, among
others, Diderot and d'Holbach were entertained by his delivering a
satirical sermon. Afterwards, 'David was disposed to make a little merry

with the parson and in return the parson was equally disposed to make a little merry with the infidel'.[56]

Then in October 1764 an event occurred to cause a change in the status of the relationship with Mme de Boufflers. Hume heard of the death of the Marquis de Boufflers and wrote at once:

> The late incident, which commonly is of such moment with your sex, seems so little to affect your situation either as to happiness or misery, that I might have spared you the trouble of receiving my compliments upon it; but being glad of taking any opportunity to express my most sincere wishes for your welfare, I would not neglect an occasion which custom has authorised.
>
> Receive then with your usual, I cannot say constant, goodness the prayers of one of your most devoted friends and servants. I hope that every change of situation will turn out to your advantage. In vain would I assume somewhat of the dignity of anger when you neglect me; I find that this wish still returns to me with equal ardour.
>
> I hear . . . that you are to be in Paris on Saturday. I shall be there about that day se'nnight: I hope that your etiquette, which allows you to receive relations and particular friends opens a wide enough door for my admission.[57]

This is an extraordinary letter in which Hume does not know whether to chide her for laxity in correspondence, to offer a formal note of condolence, or to ask if the rules for aristocratic mourning allow the admission of fat friends. The resulting composition is unsatisfactory and unpleasant. Mme de Boufflers wrote back to Hume on 2nd November with a concise summary of her situation:

> I have been ill and I have been plunged into deep grief which has deprived me of the courage to write. The death of M. de Boufflers has forced me to take stock of my affairs. The first decision I have made is favourable to you. I shall be in Paris until Thursday. If you could call I would be indebted . . . never doubt my friendship.[58]

Now Paris society had only one topic of conversation. Would the Prince marry Mme de Boufflers? She would lose her freedom of action as a *salonaire,* being then the wife of a Prince of the blood. For a society drenched in the niceties of etiquette the opportunities for gossip were endless and Hume's appearances at other salons would have been greeted by a gasp, not because he was committing a *faux pas,* but because everyone present hoped he might have news and be prepared to share it.

Elizabeth Percy, Duchess of Northumberland, was a prize gossip and wrote in her diary:

> At the latter end of the year the news of Paris was that the Prince of Conti was certainly to marry Mme de Boufflers whom I had seen before in England. People thought it very extraordinary in every way as the Princes of the blood seldom marry women so much their inferiors, and still more extraordinary that any man would marry a woman who was once his mistress and who he had quitted as such for the last seven years. It is true that his friendship has always appeared to continue in the strongest manner but it is seldom people marry for friendship. Her character was very high at Paris in all other respects, and that was a blemish easily excused there. Her husband was so complaisant as to die about six weeks before this report prevailed and gave her a chance to be raised to a very high station . . . However, at last prudence prevailed, and, as the Prince of Conti as Grand Prieur de Malta would have lost £15000 sterling a year of his income and the palace in which he resided by the marriage he and the lady agreed it to be better to live on upon the foot of friendship as they have continued to do ever since.[59]

The duchess was clearly a great loss to the tabloid press, exaggerating the Prince's income and, with no justification, asserting that the relationship had been non-sexual for seven years, but it was a remarkably accurate summary of the situation.

Hume wrote on 28th November that he had taken the temperature of opinion and felt that the marriage was expected to take place, but that the Comtesse should expect censure if only from jealous acquaintances, so she should expect 'much honour and much vexation' although the 'former is never compensation for the latter'. He only wants to see her 'alive and healthy and gay in any fortune'. It was never even imagined that she might form an alliance with Hume.

Lydia Becquet wrote on the Comtesse's behalf on 4th December inviting Hume to call, when he did his best to console her and to calm her after her now dashed expectations. He summed all of this up in the longest letter he ever wrote to her on 10th December. He tells her that the Prince, like all men of his rank, cannot 'be activated by private regards', reinforcing the Duchess of Newcastle's view that 'a long and sincere attachment, passing from love to friendship', has lost none of its warmth. He assures her that he feels, and 'with the most pungent sensation', the cruelty of her situation. His advice, finally, is to let her involvement with the Prince slowly decline and 'betake yourself, to a private and sociable, and independent life at Paris'. He assures her that she will still be the centre of a vivid and stimulating circle and ends by suggesting, clumsily, that he might accompany her on a visit to Italy.

In fact Mme de Boufflers disregarded this advice and continued her friendship with the Prince, using Hume as her confidant and '*cher Maître*'. The Prince at the same time leant on Hume to dissuade Mme de Boufflers from the hopes of a marriage. He was now suffering a loss himself as Mme de Arty, his previous mistress, was dying, and in March Hume called at the Rue Notre Dame de Nazareth to deliver his condolences to the Prince and Mme de Boufflers.

Hume did not have his own troubles to seek at this time since he was still not confirmed in the post he had been occupying for nineteen months. Lord Hertford now received a letter from George Greville absolutely forbidding Hume to be appointed. Hume can only have presumed that Greville had recently read the more anti-Whig aspects in his *History* and continued with his duties at the embassy without interruption.

But Mme de Boufflers was still in considerable distress. She visited England but found no cure there and returned to Paris. Astonishingly, probably due to lobbying by Mme de Boufflers in London, Hume was finally confirmed by Greville as secretary in June:

> So in spite of atheism and deism, of Whiggism and Toryism, of Scotticism and Philosophy, I am now in possession of an office of credit, and of £1200 a year, without dedication or application, from the favour alone of a person, whom I can perfectly love and respect.[60]

As so often happened to Hume, whenever calm descended on his life, circumstances changed to disrupt it. He gave the news to brother John at Ninewells on 14 July:

> Lord Hertford goes Lord Lieutenant to Ireland, and there is an end of the ambassador, and probably of the secretary . . . all is turned

topsy-turvy, and before next winter perhaps I am at your fireside
without office or employment. Here indeed I allow you to say; so
much the better. For I never had much ambition, I mean, for
Power and Dignity, and I am heartily cured of the little I had. I
believe a fireside and a book the best things in the world for my
age and disposition.[61]

It would be some time before he could indulge himself in the pleasures of
'a fireside and a book' since Lord Hertford had asked Hume to accompany
him to Ireland, and had even furnished an apartment for him in Dublin.
Hume was reluctant to take up the appointment. 'It is like stepping out of
light into darkness to exchange Paris for Dublin', and opinion in London
was hostile to more Scotsmen being placed in Government positions. Also
John Trail, once chaplain to the Paris Embassy and now bishop of Down
and Connor, wrote advising Hume to reject the secretaryship on account
of his treatment of Ireland and the Stewarts in his *History*. Trail felt that
Hertford might have to lay 'an absolute embargo on him [Hume] and his
philosophy'. Probably for the first time in his life his unsought reputation
was actually reinforcing his personal wishes. Hertford did obtain a lifetime
pension for Hume of £400 a year, and until the arrival of the new
ambassador, the Duke of Richmond, Hume was Chargé d'Affaires for
the English interest in France.

Hume now had to deal with the various diplomatic disputes still
unresolved as a result of the Treaty of Paris. The French were obliged to
dismantle the fortifications of Dunkirk, to indemnify the Canadians
holding French Bills of Exchange, and to enforce fishing limitations
around Newfoundland. Hume was, needless to say, assiduous, though
limited by being a commoner while dealing with the aristocrats of the
French Government. The Duc de Choiseul, a minister of Louis XV,
remarked to Mme du Deffand that Hume was 'not effective in affairs of
state', but then these affairs were labyrinthine. Dunkirk was not deforti-
fied until 1783, and the Canadian repayments were made the next year,
but the Newfoundland fishing dispute lingered until 1904. The government circles were happy to allow Hume to grace the salons of the
hostesses and to adorn the tables of the *philosphes* but affairs of state
were reserved for their own kind. Opening their eyes would take a little
more time.

Hume was, meanwhile, considering where he would live next:

Paris is the most agreeable town in Europe, and suits me best, but it is in a foreign country. London is the capital of my own country, but it never pleased me much. Letters are there held in no honour: Scotsmen are hated: superstition and ignorance gain ground daily. Edinburgh has many objections and allurements. My present mind . . . is to return to France.[62]

He was invited by Mme de Boufflers to visit herself and the Prince at L'Isle Adam. She was 'in despair at the thought of your leaving. You gave the most brilliant prosperity to society'. His mind was confused and he extended the sub-lease on his Edinburgh house, while at the same time he leased and then abandoned apartments in Paris. But, finally, he had to go to London to give an account of his stewardship of the Embassy:

Nothing is so agreeable to an irresolute man as a measure which dispenses him from taking an immediate resolution. I am exactly in the case.[63]

TWELVE

No Scene of My Life Was Ever More Affecting

U nfortunately, David Hume was not to return to England without
bringing a complication with him. The complication, which would
become extremely serious, was Jean-Jacques Rousseau.

Rousseau was born in Geneva in 1712 where his mother died within a
few days of his birth, leaving him to be brought up by his watchmaker
father without any formal education. At the age of fifteen he was sent as a
page into the household of a Mme de Warens who introduced him to
sexuality and Catholicism, ensuring his lifelong attachments to Venus and
the Christian Deity:

> For the rest of his life Rousseau was to call Mme de Warens his
> *maman* ascribing to her those qualities of sweetness, grace, and
> beauty, which, as a motherless child, he longed to find in all the
> women under whose spell he was later to fall.[1]

He was appointed as secretary to the French Embassy in Venice where he
discovered that 'everything depends entirely upon politics', and 'a people is
everywhere nothing but what its government makes of it'. On his return to
Paris he entered a prize essay competition on the impact of the arts and
sciences on the moral state of mankind. This essay laid the foundation for
all his later thought and, although it won Rousseau the competition, it
flew in the face of the Encyclopaedists by declaring that knowledge, of
itself, corrupts the intrinsic virtue of the uneducated savage. This opinion
and his now overweening self-righteousness managed to alienate all his
supporters and, not for the last time, he went into rural exile, this time in
the forest of Montmorency and under the patronage of Mme d'Epinay.

While in Paris he had begun a lifelong association with a maid at his
lodgings, Thérèse Levasseur, who was neither physically attractive nor
even literate. Since Rousseau insisted that she be included in all social
invitations and sat at table with him at all times, she was a considerable
embarrassment to his friends and automatically excluded him from the
tables of the *philosophes*. She did, however, bear him five children, all of

whom Rousseau took from Thérèse at birth and gave to a foundling hospital. Rousseau claimed, in appalling self-justification, that Thérèse was incapable of caring for children, but more probably his own deprived childhood had turned him against the concept of a family.

The Encyclopaedists rounded on him, feeding his already virulent paranoia, and Voltaire's *Candide* was a satire on the gullibility of Rousseau's uncorrupted innocent. Since Rousseau had no sense of humour whatsoever, he took this as an attack on himself. During this exile with Mme d'Epinay he wrote *The New Héloise*, a novel of love and rural simplicity. It was an international bestseller and Rousseau followed it with *Émile*. This, continuing his thought from his initial premises of undefiled simplicity, included an endorsement for a system of education which allowed natural development rather than disciplined instruction. This scandalised rigorously minded French society, although later it would become the basis for the twentieth-century educational theories of Froebel and Pestalozzi. In 1762, in exile in Luxembourg, after the now inevitable quarrel with Mme d'Epinay, he published the *Social Contract*, with its startling opening sentence, 'Man is born free, and everywhere he is in chains'. Its principles of liberty, equality and fraternity became the slogan of the Revolution and Rousseau advocated a society in which the individual is obedient to laws which express the collective will of the people. Montesquieu and Voltaire had praised the British Constitution but for Rousseau the British Parliament was undemocratic. He was promptly denounced, yet again, in France and fled to Môtiers-Travers, in Neuchâtel, where he was under the benign protection of Frederick the Great. French philosophers in exile were not uncommon in the eighteenth century and Frederick had sheltered Voltaire from 1749 until 1753; even Diderot would have to flee to St Petersburg and Catherine the Great in 1773.

Neuchâtel was an independent principality and its Governor was George Keith, a Jacobite Scot, exiled since 1715, but still hereditary Earl Marischal of Scotland. But Hume's first contact with Rousseau had been through Mme de Boufflers who had also provided the quarrelsome philosopher with a refuge in the luxury of L'Isle Adam. For her pains she was given a complimentary copy of *La Nouvelle Héloïse*.

The relationship between the two men eventually became such a matter of public acrimony that in 1766 Hume was to publish an account of the whole affair, first edited and published in French by D'Alembert, who was

not always literally correct in his translation. Hume prefaced the pamphlet: 'It was with great reluctance that a man possessed of such pacific
disposition could be brought to consent to the publication of the following
piece. He was very sensible that the quarrels among men of letters are a
scandal to philosophy; nor was any person in the world less formed for
giving occasion to a scandal, so consolatory to blockheads. But the
circumstances were such as to draw him into it'.[2]

Hume now picks up the story from the beginning:

> My connection with M. Rousseau began in 1762, when the
> Parlement of Paris had issued an arrest for apprehending him on
> account of his *Émile*. I was at this time at Edinburgh. A person of
> great worth wrote to me from Paris [Mme de Boufflers] that M.
> Rousseau intended to seek an asylum in England and desired I
> would do him all the good offices in my power. As I conceived M.
> Rousseau had actually put his design in execution, I wrote to several
> of my friends in London, recommending the celebrated exile to
> their favour. I wrote also immediately to M. Rousseau himself,
> assuring him of my desire to oblige and readiness to serve him. At
> the same time I invited him to come to Edinburgh, if the situation
> would be agreeable, and offered him a retreat in my own house, so
> long as he should please to partake of it . . . the following is the
> answer I received.
>
> Môtiers-Travers [near Neuchatel], Feb 19 1763
>
> My Lord Marischal, in acquainting me that the amiableness was
> still greater than the sublimity of your genius, rendered a
> correspondence with you every day more desirable, and cherished in
> me those wishes which he inspired of ending my days near you. Oh
> Sir!, that a better state of health and more convenient
> circumstances, would but enable me to take such a journey in the
> manner I could like! . . . What transports should I not exclaim, on
> setting foot in that happy country which gave birth to David Hume
> and the Lord Marshal of Scotland![3]

What state of health was referred to is unclear since Rousseau was a
lifetime hypochondriac. He claimed to be stricken in his 'nether parts'
with an unspecified affliction so that he could wear neither underclothes
nor breeches and was normally dressed in an Armenian-style fur-lined
robe.

The matter might have rested there, but Hume was genuinely distressed at the plight of his fellow philosopher. Mme de Boufflers would have told him that Rousseau thought Hume was 'the truest philosopher that I know and the only historian to write with impartiality'. Rousseau was now claiming not only persecution, which was true, but also poverty which was not. Rousseau was trying to sell his *Dictionnaire de Musique* and Hume tried to rally support for this scheme. Later he saw the truth:

> I now know of a certainty that this affectation of extreme poverty and distress was a mere pretence, a petty kind of imposture which M. Rousseau successfully employed to excite the compassion of the public.[4]

In October 1765, however, Rousseau was driven out of Neuchâtel after booby-trapped boulders were hung over his front door and even the Swiss women threatened to cut his throat. Hume, appalled at this and at the bidding of Mme de Verdelin, another of Rousseau's female champions, wrote a letter regretting that they could not meet until the summer but, in the meantime, recommending him to travel to England where he would be welcomed by Gilbert Elliot and where he hoped he might find peace and happiness. Hume tells us that he wrote to John Stewart, the wine merchant, of Buckingham Street:

> Stewart was to look out for some honest discreet farmer who might be willing to lodge and board M. Rousseau and his Gouvernante – Thérèse Levasseur – in a very decent and plentiful manner at a pension which Stewart might settle at fifty or sixty pounds a year; the farmer to keep such agreement a profound secret, and to receive from M. Rousseau only twenty or twenty-five pounds a year. I engaging to supply the difference.[5]

Rousseau replied from Strasbourg where he was following Marischal Keith to the court of Frederick the Great:

> Your goodness affects me as much as it does me honour. The best reply I can make to your offers is to accept them, which I do. I shall set out in five or six days to throw myself into your arms. Such is the advice of the Lord Marshal, my protector friend and father, it is the advice also of Mme de Verdelin . . . I may say it is the advice of my own heart, which takes a pleasure in being

indebted to the most illustrious of my contemporaries, to a man whose goodness surpasses his glory. I sigh after a solitary and free retirement, wherein I might finish my days in peace.[6]

But Hume was delayed and on 16 December Rousseau was in Paris and accommodated thanks to the generosity of the Prince de Conti. He was, of course, an object of fascination to the sensation-hungry Parisians and Hume, innocently, put all of this curiosity down to affection. 'His very dog, which is no better than a collie, has a name and reputation in the world.' Rousseau insisted that his dog, Sultan, was allowed to accompany him everywhere. His mistress Levasseur was still in Switzerland.

With the blinkered vision of the recently infatuated Hume was blind to all warnings. 'The philosophers of Paris foretold to me that I could not conduct him to Calais without a quarrel, but I think I could live with him all my life.' Hume was directly warned against Rousseau by Baron d'Holbach: 'You are warming a viper in your bosom. You don't know your man, David, you don't know your man'. Horace Walpole, who loathed all philosophers, was bitterly envious of the fame Rousseau was enjoying and set about 'a little raillery' by concocting a false letter, purporting to be from Frederick of Prussia:

My dear Jean-Jacques,
You have renounced Geneva, your native soil. You have been driven from Switzerland, a country of which you have made such boast in your writings. In France you are outlawed: come then to me. I admire your talents and amuse myself with your reveries; on which however, by the way, you bestow too much time and attention. It is high time to grow prudent and happy; you have made yourself sufficiently talked of for singularities little becoming a great man; show your enemies that you have sometimes common sense, this will vex them without hurting you. My dominions afford you a peaceful retreat: I am desirous to do you good, and will do it, if you can but think it such. But if you are determined to refuse my assistance, you may expect that I shall not say a word about it to anyone. If you persist in perplexing your brains to find out new misfortunes, choose such as you like best; I am a king and can make you as miserable as you can wish: at the same time, I will engage to do that which your

enemies never will, I will cease to persecute you, when you are
no longer vain of persecution.
Your sincere friend,
Frederic.[7]

Walpole first recited this fairly feeble joke at Mme de Geoffrin's salon and
was so pleased with its reception that he wrote it out with corrections to
the French by Helvétius and others. He repeated it in Hume's presence at
a dinner party, but, since Hume was decidedly unamused by its schoolboy
tone, never showed him the written version. Walpole was inordinately
proud of the stir his letter caused. *'Me voici à la mode!'* It is a mark of the
underlying triviality of the *salonaires* and even of the *philosophes* that if you
were not socially acceptable, or if your work was too violently provocative,
you were instantly cast as a figure of fun.

But leaving the barely suppressed giggling and with dire warnings
behind them, on 4 January 1766 the unlikely pair left Paris, arriving in
Calais on the 8th to be detained by contrary winds. During the journey
and at Calais Hume used the time to ask Rousseau if he would think of
writing his memoirs, to be told that he had already done this and did
intend to publish them. Writing from London to Mme de Boufflers,
Hume says that Rousseau intends to paint himself in his true colours, but
has serious doubts as to his ability to do that:

> With regard to his health, a point in which few people can be
> mistaken, he is very fanciful. He imagines himself very infirm. He
> is one of the most robust men I have ever known. He passed ten
> hours in the night-time above deck in the most severe weather,
> when all the seamen were almost frozen to death, and he caught no
> harm. He says that his infirmity always increases on a journey, yet it
> was almost imperceptible on the road from Paris to London.[8]

Hume also asked Rousseau if he would accept a pension from George III.
Rousseau said he would consult his 'father', meaning the Lord Marischal.
Hume presumed this would be approved of and contacted General
Conway, Hertford's brother and a leading Whig minister. Word also
reached Rousseau at Calais of Walpole's letter, but Rousseau dismissed it,
thinking to be a lampoon by Voltaire.

Finding accommodation for Rousseau was proving difficult due to his
insisting of having deference paid to Levasseur which many respectable

Englishmen, and, more especially, respectable Englishwomen, found unacceptable. Hume had yet to meet her, but had been amply informed of her ignorance and of her unaccountable influence over Rousseau. 'In her absence his dog has acquired that ascendant. His affection for that creature is beyond all expression or conception.' At one time the dog got lost and advertisements were placed in all the newspapers as were notices of good fortune when the dog was found. When invited by Garrick to attend a performance, Rousseau refused to leave Sultan alone in his lodgings. 'He howled and made a noise', and Rousseau said that, if a stranger called, then Sultan might panic and run into the street. Finally Hume persuaded the dog-loving philosopher to leave his charge. In the theatre Garrick sat him in a box opposite the King and Queen, and the royal couple were said to have watched Rousseau more intently than they watched Garrick. In *Lettre à M D'Alembert sur les spectacles* in 1758 Rousseau had found the theatre a corrupting influence, likely to debase the audience, also his contribution to the entry in the *Encyclopédie* for 'Geneva' gives his views more clearly. 'There is no theatre in Geneva. Not that plays themselves are disapproved of; but one fears the taste for extravagant finery and the dissipation and libertinage which troops of actors spread amongst the young.' He asks for stricter control of actors' conduct and perhaps then the plays will educate the populace into finer tastes and a delicacy of senti-ment. He would like to see greater censorship spread across Europe.[9] Clearly he was an exception to his own rule.

Rousseau was now in temporary lodgings with Mr Pulleyn, a good-natured grocer in Chiswick, and eagerly awaiting the arrival of Levasseur. She had left Paris in the company of James Boswell, 'a young gentleman, very good humoured, very agreeable and very mad', but Hume dreaded some event fatal to Rousseau's honour during the journey. His fears were well founded since Boswell, ever eager for yet another conquest, seduced Levasseur between Paris and Calais without much difficulty. She, twenty years Boswell's senior, told him, 'I allow that you are a hardy and vigorous lover, but you have no art'. On the next night she gave him lessons and rode him, 'like a bad rider going downhill'.[10] Boswell then delivered her to Rousseau, who fortunately was none the wiser, at Chiswick. Her presence meant that Rousseau had to decline an invitation to dine with General Conway, who had now gained agreement from the King for Rousseau to receive a pension of a hundred pounds a year. Hume had also finally arranged for Rousseau and Levasseur to live with one Richard Davenport in his house at Wooton in Staffordshire about one hundred and fifty miles north-west of London. He had written to ask about the suitability of Davenport's house on 4th March 1766:

1. Is there wood and hills about M Davenport's house?
2. Cannot M. Rousseau, if he should afterwards think proper, find a means to boil a pot, or roast a piece of meat in Mr. Davenport's house, so as to be perfectly at home?
3. Will Mr. Davenport, in that case, be so good as to accept a small rent for an apartment; for this circumstance, I find, is necessary.
4. Can M. Rousseau set out presently and take possession of his habitation?[11]

Hume was now back in his lodgings in Lisle Street but did not find this 'new scene much to my taste'. On 12th January he told Mme de Boufflers:

The method of living is not near so agreeable in London as Paris. The best company are usually, and more so at present, in a flame of politics: the men of letters are few, and not very sociable: the women in general are not very conversible. Many a sigh escapes me for your sweet and amiable conversation: I paint you to myself all serenity, and cannot believe that ever I had the misfortune to displease you. I often steal an hour's chat with you; *Sic mihi contigat vivere, sicque mori* [Thus I am fated to live and thus I die]. As often as I see Lady Hervey, or Lord Tavistock, or the Holdernesse family, I have the satisfaction of hearing your name mentioned, which is some consolation in this land of banishment, Adieu, my amiable friend![12]

Finally all arrangements for Rousseau's departure to Wooton were in place and he and Levasseur came to lodge with Hume at Lisle Street overnight. Davenport had found a chaise that was returning empty to Staffordshire and had booked places for the pair on it, thus saving Rousseau half the fare. With his startling aptitude for savaging the hand of friendship, Rousseau decided that Davenport, with the connivance of Hume, was patronising him with charity and flew into a sulk. Then he objected to Hume's staring at him:

As we were sitting one evening after supper, silent by the fireside, I caught his eyes intently fixed on mine, as indeed happened very often, and that in a manner of which it is very difficult to give an idea; at that time he gave me a steadfast piercing look, mixed with a sneer, which greatly disturbed me. To get rid of the embarrassment I lay under, I endeavoured to look full at him in my turn; but in fixing my eyes against his, I felt the most inexpressible terror, and was obliged soon to turn away. The speech and physiognomy of the good David is that of an honest man; but where, great God! did this good man borrow those eyes he fixes so sternly and unaccountably on those of his friends! The impression of this look remained with me, and gave me great uneasiness. My trouble increased even to a degree of fainting; and had I not been relieved by an effusion of tears, I had been suffocated. Presently after this I was seized with the most violent remorse; I even despised myself; still, at length, in a transport, which I still remember with delight, I sprang on his neck, embraced him eagerly; while almost choked with sobbing, I cried out, in broken accents, 'No, no. David Hume cannot be treacherous; if he be not the best of men, he must be the basest of mankind.' David Hume politely returned my embraces, and gently tapping me on the back, repeated several times, in a good-natured and easy tone, 'Why, what my dear sir! Nay, my dear sir! Oh, my dear sir!' He said nothing more.[13]

Hume was deeply upset by this episode and confided to Hugh Blair, 'I think no scene of my life was ever so affecting'. However, Hume commented wisely, 'Capricious men, like forward children, should be left to kick against the pricks and vent their spleen unnoticed'. At least they would now be unnoticed by Hume as he and Rousseau never met again.

They did, however, correspond in what became one of the most celebrated epistolary rows of the eighteenth century. Rousseau had no intention of becoming friendly with his somewhat bucolic neighbours who were keen to call on the famous exile. He wrote to Hume:

Wooton March 29 1766
The minister of the parish came to see me yesterday who, finding that I spoke to him only in French, would not speak to me in English, so that our interview was almost a silent one. I have taken a great fancy to this expedient, and shall make use of it with all my neighbours, if I have any. Nay should I even learn to speak English,

I would converse with them only in French, especially if I were so happy as to find that they did not understand a word of that language. [However] I had rather lodge in the hollow trunk of an old tree in this country than in the most superb apartment in London.[14]

Hume had been accused of tampering with Rousseau's correspondence while in Chiswick. He had brought Rousseau a parcel of mail, on which he had paid the charges due. Rousseau told him to take them back to the postal office. But, Hume pointed out, this would make them the property of the clerks, who, knowing the famous addressee, would certainly open them. Rousseau said he was indifferent:

I began to be afraid, from what I observed of M. Rousseau's disposition and character that his natural restlessness of mind would prevent enjoyment of that repose to which the hospitality and security he found in England invited him. I saw, with infinite regret, that he was born for storms and tumults, and the disgust which might succeed the peaceful enjoyment of solitude and tranquillity would soon render him a burden to himself and everybody about him. But, as I lived at the distance of a hundred and fifty miles from the place of residence, and was constantly employed in doing him good offices, I did not expect that I myself should be the victim of this unhappy disposition.[15]

Hume was still keen to excuse Rousseau and he told Hugh Blair:

He has read very little during the course of his life, and has now totally renounced all reading: he has seen very little and has no curiosity to see or remark; he has reflected, properly speaking, and studied very little; and has not, indeed very much knowledge; he has only felt, during the whole course of his life; and, in this respect, his sensibility rises to a pitch beyond what I have seen any example of; but it still gives him a more acute feeling of pain rather than pleasure. He is like a man who were stripped not only of his clothes but of his skin, and turned out in that situation to combat with the rude and boisterous elements.[16]

Over-sensitivity turned to fury when the *St James's Chronicle* published the Walpole squib anonymously. Rousseau, now convinced that it had been written by D'Alembert at Hume's urging, wrote to the paper denying its contents and stating that 'the imposter has his accomplices in England'. Hume was astonished and deeply hurt by this turn of affairs:

> . . . I am, of a sudden, the first man, not only suspected, but certainly concluded to be the publisher; I am, without further enquiry or explication, intentionally insulted in a public paper; I am from a dearest friend converted into a treacherous and malignant enemy; and all my present and past devices are at one stroke very artfully cancelled. Were it not ridiculous to employ reasoning on such a subject, I might ask M. Rousseau, 'Why am I supposed to have any malignity against him?' . . . I pursued my usual train, by serving my friend in the least doubtful manner, I renewed my application to General Conway, as soon as the state of that gentleman's health permitted it: the General applies again to his Majesty: his Majesty's consent is renewed, the Marquis of Rockingham, first commissioner of the treasury is also applied to; the whole affair is happily finished, and, full of joy, I convey the intelligence to my friend.[17]

Rousseau responded that his present troubles deprived him of the ease and presence of mind to direct his conduct. He could not accept the pension if it was to be given secretly so Hume and Conway took the letter to be a refusal on those grounds and set about to get the secrecy clause revoked:

> As to the deep distress which he mentions to General Conway, and which he says, deprives him of his reason, I was set very much at ease on that head by receiving a letter from Mr. Davenport who told me that his guest was, at that very time, extremely happy, easy, cheerful and even sociable . . . His pretence of an extreme sensibility had been too frequently repeated to have any effect on a Man who was so well acquainted with them.[18]

Hume's requests to get the secrecy condition removed were successful and he wrote to ask if Rousseau would now accept it. However, Rousseau's reply sidestepped the issue:

Wooton, 23rd June 1766
I imagined, sir, that my silence, truly interpreted by your own conscience, had said enough; but since you have some design in not understanding me, I shall speak.

You have but ill disguised yourself. I know you and you are not ignorant of it. Before we had any personal connections, quarrels or disputes; while we knew each other only by literary reputation, you affectionately made me the offer of the good offices of yourself and friends. Affected by this generosity, I threw myself into your arms; you brought me to England, apparently to procure me an asylum, but in fact to bring me dishonour. You applied to this noble work, with a zeal worthy of your heart and a success worthy of your abilities. You needed not have taken so much pains; you live and converse with the world; I with my solitude. The public love to be deceived and you were born to deceive them. I know one man, however, whom you cannot deceive; I mean yourself. You know with what horror my heart rejected the first suspicion of your designs. You know I embraced you with tears in my eyes, and told you, if you were not the best of men, you must be the blackest of mankind. In reflecting on your private conduct, you must say to yourself sometimes, you are not the best of men: under which conviction, I doubt you will ever be the happiest.

I leave your friends and you to carry on your schemes as you please; giving up to you, without regret, my reputation during life; certain that sooner or later justice will be done to that of both. As to your good offices in matters of interest, which you have made use of as a mask, I thank you for them and shall dispense with profiting by them. I ought not to hold a correspondence with you any longer, or to accept it to my advantage in any affair in which you are to be the mediator. Adieu, sir, I wish you the truest happiness; but as we ought not to have anything to say to each other for the future, this is the last letter you will receive from me.[19]

Hume was stunned by this reply and, probably unwisely, demanded Rousseau's reasons for this attack and got a reply on 10th July. Rousseau stated that he was ill and 'little able to write', and then in eighteen pages goes on to say that he is 'an enemy to every kind of artifice' and relates his version of the relationship autobiographically with Hume in the third person. He hints that Hume might have been jealous of the 'favourable reception I met with from a great Prince'. He ridicules Hume, 'a man apt to throw away his money', for commissioning a portrait of Rousseau from

Allan Ramsay, and Hume, in a footnote, points out that it was, in fact, a sketch given to him by Ramsay. He praises Hume for his efforts but asserts that he did not need the pension, could have come to England by his own efforts and was quite capable of earning a living himself. Plenty of people would have offered him accommodation, and he now accuses Hume of alienating him from Davenport. Hume's footnote points out that, in spite of this attack, he has asked Davenport to 'continue his kindness to his unhappy guest'. As to his enemies in England, Hume says, 'If Mr Rousseau could have seen things exactly as they are, he would have seen that he had no other friend in England but me and no other enemy but himself'. The translator of the English version cannot restrain himself and adds a footnote, 'General opinion indeed, was that he had too much philosophy to be very devout and too much devotion to have much philosophy.' Rousseau accuses Hume of questioning his Gouvernante secretly about his affairs and now openly includes D'Alembert in the plot over the false letter, so that Hume and Walpole had used him to discredit Rousseau. His paranoia reaches classical heights when he accuses Hume of preparing a secret letter of defamation to be used if Rousseau had accepted the Royal pension. Then, for no discernible reason, he reminisces that once when they were travelling from Paris and sleeping in the same room he heard Hume cry out 'Je tiens, Jean-Jacques Rousseau'. Hume, in a note, admits to not knowing if he dreams in French. He ends: 'if you are innocent, deign to justify yourself, if you are not, adieu forever'.

In reply, twelve days later, a now enraged Hume wrote:

> I enjoyed about a month ago an uncommon pleasure, when I
> reflected that through many difficulties and by moist arduous care
> and pains, I had, beyond my most sanguine expectations, provided
> for your repose honour and fortune. But I soon felt a very sensible
> uneasiness when I found that you had wantonly and voluntarily
> thrown away all those advantages, and was [sic] become the enemy
> of your own repose, fortune and honour. I cannot be surprised after
> this that you are my enemy. Adieu, and for ever.[20]

In the published *Concise Account* D'Alembert denies any complicity in the composition of the letter, or of any hatred of Rousseau. He laments 'his having so little confidence in the probity of mankind, and particularly that of Mr Hume'.

Hume had sent copies of the correspondence to Mme de Boufflers who was equally outraged by it, finding Rousseau's conduct incomprehensible. She also begged Hume not to publish his account of the affair, but the matter was taken out of Hume's hands by D'Alembert who published the *Exposé Succint*. This caused a minor row in France as, subsequently, several articles were published in favour of Rousseau only to be proscribed in their turn by royal command.[21] In September Mme du Deffand wrote to Voltaire wondering if there existed anywhere in the world such a sad madman as Jean-Jacques. When, in November, an English version of Hume's account appeared, the translator prefaced the pamphlet, 'The facts are all laid before the public, and M. Hume submits his cause to the determination of every man of sense and probity'. Hume, probably with some relief, deposited all the letters in the British Museum: 'be so good as to give them the corner of any drawer, I fancy few people will trouble you by desiring to see them'; but atypically for a curator, Dr Matthew Maty, the under-librarian, felt the papers properly belonged in Edinburgh and they became the property of the Royal Society of Edinburgh which has, in turn, deposited them with the National Library of Scotland. The affair had also detained him, unnecessarily, in London until September when what he really wanted was to return to a quiet life in Edinburgh. Mme de Boufflers wrote to him on 6th May 1766 that the Prince had given Hume an apartment in the Temple:

> You may arrive whenever you want. Your room is totally furnished, gay and pretty and comfortable. You have the best of rooms. There is a well stocked library and if you do not work it will be your own fault.

But he resisted the temptation to return. He had been determined from his arrival in Britain to quit London. He had terminated the lease of the Rev Blair on James's Court and Katharine had made it ready for his return. On 1st February an old friend and near neighbour had written to him:

> I am glad to hear from your sister, there is no ifs of your coming to Scotland. I am glad, even that you, infidel as you are, have chased the gospel out of James's Court. But what shall we do with you? You are spoiled; it's impossible for me to retain you. I am a Christian. I neither paint nor fricassée. My wit is much abated, but I can play at quadrille and sleep with you. Will that do? Lord bless you, bring Rousseau here. Trees to shelter him? Such nonsense,

there's as many trees in Scotland as will hang all the rogues in
England, every man his tree. Tell him that and he won't be afraid
of want of shelter.[22]

Clearly Hume's correspondent only knew of Rousseau's philosophical
reputation and presumably intended to doze quietly in an armchair across
the fireplace from Hume. She was Mrs Alison Cockburn, a widow, two
years younger than Hume and a lively Edinburgh hostess. Tall and
prepossessing, she was said to resemble Queen Elizabeth I. Her house
in Blair's Close was only twenty or so yards from James's Court and Hume
was a frequent visitor:

Hume often went to tea with Mrs. Cockburn and was often late
when the choicest delicacies had been eaten, but said, 'Trouble
yourself very little about what you have or how it appears, you
know I am no epicure but only a glutton.' A tipsy relative locked up
the cloakroom with the walking habiliments and borrowing from
neighbours took place. Those which fell to Mr Hume's lot
happened to produce a peculiarly ludicrous effect.[23]

She was happy when Hume was once more back in James's Court, 'I am
truly glad to get David home again; he's a very old friend, and I've long had
a habit of liking him and being diverted with him.' She was amused, rather
than shocked, by Hume's scepticism and regarded him as an adornment to
Edinburgh and, therefore, a welcome guest in her house. She thought he
really did not understand his own personality:

I really believe Nature, in forming you, (for ye know God did not
make you) took such just proportions of matter and such a due
mixture of passions and appetites as just served the purpose of one
another; and all this you impute to reason, who has nothing to do
in the matter.[24]

This slightly guarded Scots affection was entirely different from the hot-
house adulation he had experienced in Paris and Hume found it very
welcome. He did, however, continue his correspondence with Mme de
Boufflers:

But I am now in Edinburgh [in February 1767], and finding myself
at my own fireside, amid my books, conversing with company who
are both estimable and agreeable, my former passion for study,

derived from nature and habit, has seized me with greater violence
after so long an interruption and I so occupied with present things,
that I form no distant resolution: at least none that I shall speak of,
lest I should not be believed, and lest my not executing it should
expose me to the reproach of levity.[25]

He goes on ask Mme de Boufflers, 'with your usual eloquence', to thank
the Prince for all his kindness in having arranged accommodation for
Hume in Paris. But he still has a pang of regret: 'I am almost vexed to find
that my Fridays are too well supplied and still more that I myself cannot
enjoy the good company which assemble with you on that day', and he asks
to be remembered to 'all and sundry of them'. He would continue to
correspond with Mme de Boufflers for the rest of his life but it is clear
from this letter that Hume knew they would never meet again. In *My Own
Life* he says:

I left Paris and next summer went to Edinburgh, with the same
view as formerly of burying myself in a philosophical retreat. I
returned to that place, not richer, but with much more money and a
much larger income by means of Lord Hertford's friendship.[26]

Lord Hertford's friendship was to mean that David Hume was now to
start on yet another career as a civil servant. Lord Hertford had resigned
his Lord Lieutenancy of Ireland and returned to London as Lord
Chamberlain. At the same time his brother, General Conway, had taken
over the secretaryship of the Northern Department dealing with home
and foreign affairs in all countries north of France. Naturally this included
North Britain, or, rather, Scotland, but Conway lacked an under-secretary. Both men knew and respected Hume, a Scot and an ex-Chargé
d'Affaires, so the offer was made. Hume was astonished and by 20th
February 1767 he was back in London:

I was surprised by a letter from Lord Hertford, urging me to come
to London and accept the office of Depute Secretary of State under
his brother. As my Lord knows that this step was contrary to the
maxims I had laid down to myself, he engaged Lady Hertford to
write me at the same time, and inform me how much she and my
Lord desired my compliance. I sat down. Once or twice to excuse
myself; but I could not find terms to express my refusal of a request
made by persons to whose friendship I had been so much

obliged . . . I feel at present like a banished man in a strange
country: I mean, not as I was while with you at Paris, but as I
should be at Westphalia or Lithuania, or any place the least to my
fancy in the world.[27]

He felt that he had, 'from a philosopher, degenerated into a petty
statesman, and am entirely occupied in politics. I am too well acquainted
with our usual fluctuations and revolutions to believe that this avocation
will be durable'.[28]

Hume had corresponded with Conway when he was in the Paris
Embassy over naval actions against pirates on the coast of West Africa,
and he had also given him detailed reports on the French destruction of
the fortifications of Dunkirk received at the embassy from the Duc de
Praslin, the French Foreign Secretary. He had reported on the continuing
negotiations for the payment of Canadian bills and showed his house-
keeping skills in negotiating just rates of exchange. In 1765 complaints
against French fishermen in Newfoundland had continued and he had
coped with French complaints over English armed incursions in the West
Indies. He also delivered detailed reports of the clergy's assemblies, their
treatment of the Bull *Ugenitus*, the Dauphin's poor health, and the general
gossip of the French court. Although Conway had complained that Hume
was treated as an inferior by the aristocratic French Foreign Office, he had
been a conscientious Chargé d'Affaires.

Ironically, one of Hume's first duties was to advise Conway as to
whether the much disputed pension should be paid to Rousseau. Hume
promptly agreed and Davenport was informed but Rousseau had fled with
Levasseur and a little luggage, claiming he was heading for Dover and a
return to France. Since he had written from Spalding in Lincolnshire, his
geography was not of the best. He had travelled due east instead of south,
and was claiming that Conway had made him a prisoner of state. He
promised not to publish his memoirs and claimed he would never speak of
Hume or at least would never do him dishonour. Hume said 'this poor
man is absolutely lunatic and consequently cannot be the object of any
laws or civil punishment . . . If he could be settled in any safe and quiet
retreat, under a discreet keeper, he has wherewithal to bear all charges'. He
put much of the blame on Levasseur, 'It is suspected that she has
nourished all his chimeras in order to chase him out of a country where,
having no person to speak to, she tired most desperately'.[29]

Hume wrote to Mme de Boufflers, hoping that she might be able to help this 'real and complete madman', and when Rousseau returned to Paris it was under the forgiving shelter of the Prince de Conti. Eventually he took the patronage of the Marquis de Girardin at Ermenonville where he died of a thrombosis on 2nd July 1778. His most famous work, the *Confessions*, was published posthumously in 1781 and it carries no reference to his quarrel with Hume. He was an extreme example of the auto-didact who defends his hard-won thoughts from wholly ima-ginary attacks. He counter-attacked when there had been no direct attack except in his own imagination. However, aspects of his political and social thinking are in the bases of all subsequent radical theories and he exemplifies the man who is his 'own worst enemy'. Lacking any social skills, he rejected society as his imagined enemy and drove himself further and further into bitterness and hatred. David Hume, who had a benign view of his fellow men – at least in practice – was at first baffled and then infuriated by having the hand he had offered in selfless friendship severely bitten. He makes no mention of the affair in *My Own Life*, and Hume was happy to have the matter closed. He was 'heartily tired of the subject . . . and here I shall take my leave of it, I hope for ever'.

Hume's post in the government was, like many others, unpaid and it was expected that he would take a share in the fees and charges imposed by the department. By July he could tell his brother that his income was £1,100 a year, and since the figure was so precise, unaffected by the vagaries of the markets, we may take it that it was based on his expected share. His post was not in any way onerous and bordered on that of a sinecure. 'Under-secretaries were of very little importance until the nine-teenth century and even in that century not of very great importance . . . Lord Palmerston, you know, never consults an under-secretary.'[30]

The Foreign Office, in its modern existence, dates only from 1782, and up to that time foreign affairs were dealt with by the secretaries of the two departments, Northern and Southern. They had no permanent Cabinet position and were called to attend as and when foreign affairs were thought by the Prime Minister or the King to demand their attention. George III was still trying to run the Cabinet personally, and with Pitt, now the Earl of Chatham, desperately ill in semi-retirement, the forces were more or less equally matched between the Tories, who were shedding their Jacobite allegiances, and the Whigs, of whom Conway was a prominent member. France's imperial ambitions continued to decline as Britain took a firmer and firmer hold on Canada and India, while America's problems were being studiously ignored in the hope that they would go away.

In December, while still in Edinburgh, Hume had received a letter from John Crawford, nicknamed 'Fish' since he was slippery and never still. He had been a friend of Hume's in Paris where he circulated in the company of Walpole and Mme du Deffand. Crawford's rakish behaviour had plunged him into parental hot water and Hume had managed to extricate him. Crawford said:

> I know not if you remember that you gave me permission to propose you as a member of a very infamous society in Pall Mall. In spite of all that has been said against this society there was too much taste and sense in it for one black ball to appear against you.[31]

Hume was delighted and replied:

> I am very sensible of the honour which has been done me by your society. I desire you to express to them my sentiments on this head and to notify my acceptance. There are surely some dues to pay, which I desire you to advance for me, and to inform me of the amount of them. I shall now think myself secure of good company when any accident brings me to London.[32]

The club in question was the notorious Almack's, founded in 1764 by one McCall with twenty-seven other founder members of whom Crawford was one. Its entire purpose was to play for high stakes at any one of several card games, with members who would turn their coats inside out for luck and wear leather wristbands to protect their lace cuffs, while playing in masks to conceal their emotions. Entire fortunes would be won or lost on the turn of a card or the roll of the dice. Although Hume was not in the same category as the young aristocrats who readily mortgaged their expected inheritances, he was well enough respected as a whist player to have the offer of £1,000 annual stake made to him in return for a percentage of his winnings. Hume refused to be 'a pickpocket for hire'. But he was always a keen player, sometimes to the embarrassment of his neighbours, as Mure of Caldwell recalls:

> On the floor below Hume in James's Court was Mrs Campbell of Succoth, mother of the Lord President. One Sunday evening Hume,

who was on friendly habits with Mrs Campbell's family, stepping down to take tea with her, found assembled a party of pious elderly ladies met to converse on topics suitable to the day. David's unexpected entrance on such an occasion caused some dismay on the part of the landlady and her guests; but he sat down and chatted in so easy and appropriate a style, that all embarrassment soon disappeared. On removal of the tea things, however, he gravely said to his hostess, 'Well, Mrs Campbell, where are the cards?' 'The cards, Mr Hume, surely you forget what day it is?' 'Not at all, madam,' he replied, 'you know we often have a quiet rubber on a Sunday evening.' After vainly endeavouring to make him retract this calumny she said to him, 'Now, David, you'll just be pleased to walk out of my house, for you're not fit company in it tonight.'[33]

However, his playing was not without its critics, and much later in his life:

David could not bear criticism of his play and my mother was used to find fault with him *à tort et à travers*. One night, playing at Abbey Hill late, she and Hume got into a warm discussion on his play and the philosopher lost his temper. He took up his hat and calling to a pretty Pomeranian dog that always accompanied him, 'Come away, Foxey' walked out of the house in the middle of the rubber . . . David, who lived in St Andrew's Square, a good mile distant, was at the door before breakfast, hat in hand, with an apology.[34]

Hume was now living in Brewer Street, Golden Square – the Misses Elliot having moved from Lisle Street, and now being helped out by Peggy Irvine – on the edge of what is now Soho, and he was able to live the life of a man of fashion, with his servant, William Boyd. He also kept a friendly eye on the children of Baron Mure, who were being educated near London. They noted Hume's fashionable appearance:

I remember as a boy being much struck by the French cut of their laced coats and bags and especially with the philosopher's ponderous uncouth person, equipped in a bright yellow coat spotted with black.[35]

Young Mure was taken to St Paul's by Hume when, seeing the poor attendance, and hoping to curry favour with 'our sceptical friend', he said he thought it was foolish 'to lay out a million on a thing so useless'. Hume said:

Never give an opinion on subjects of which you are too young to judge. St Paul's, as a monument of the religious feeling and taste of the country, does it honour and will endure. We have wasted millions on a single campaign in Flanders, and without any good resulting from it.[36]

His work as an under-secretary was not demanding: attending from ten in the morning until three in the afternoon, with very little pressure on him. He could read, write letters or entertain friends during his office hours and there was little to tax his powers. Very little official correspondence survives from Hume's tenure as an under-secretary. He composed covering letters for Conway's correspondence, and he did exert himself in an attempt to gain a consulship for Tobias Smollett. Smollett favoured Nice or Leghorn as possible postings but, since Smollett had published his vitriolic account of *Travels in France and Italy*, he was loathed in both countries and Hume tried to persuade him to apply elsewhere. The attempt came to nothing.

One task fell to Hume that did allow him to show some influence for, in May 1767, the General Assembly of the Church of Scotland met and would receive a Royal Address delivered by the High Commissioner, John, Earl of Glasgow. The speech was signed by Conway, but it was an open secret that the author was David Hume. The Assembly had considered excommunicating Kames and Hume in 1756, but now the Moderates held sway and a ringing royal endorsement of their policies would be appreciated. It was subsequently printed, after two letters supporting taxation in the American colonies, in the *Edinburgh Evening Courant* of 3rd May:

Right reverend and well beloved we greet you, etc . . . We take this opportunity of repeating to you those assurances of our Royal support and authority, which you have so truly and deservedly merited by your steady adherence to the discouragement of vice and immorality, and to the advancement of true religion so essential to the welfare and prosperity of our people.

Convinced, as we are, of your prudence and firm resolution to concur in whatever may promote the happiness of our subjects, it is unnecessary for us to recommend to you to contentious and unedifying debates, as well as to avoid every thing that may tend to disturb that harmony and tranquillity which is so effectual in

councils solely calculated for the suppression of every species of
irreligion, immorality and vice. As we have the firmest reliance on
your zeal in support of the Christian faith, as well as in the wisdom
and prudence of your councils. We are thoroughly assured that they
will be directed to such purposes as may best tend to enforce a
conscientious observance of all those duties which the true religion
and laws of these kingdoms require, and on which the felicity of
every individual depends.

. . . We are convinced that the same wise conduct which has
often manifested itself in your former meetings will be exerted on
the present occasion, and that cordiality, unanimity, and brotherly
love will attend all your proceedings, and be the means of securing
a happy and satisfactory conclusion of the present meeting of the
general assembly. And so we bid you heartily farewell.
By his Majesty's command,
Conway.[37]

Blair and Robertson were duly grateful.

Hume had plenty of time to socialise and, thanks to his continued
friendship with Hertford and Conway, found himself a guest at the best
tables in the best houses. One such was Conway's at Park Place near Henley-
on-Thames. Hume visited there often and, thanks to a dedicated diarist, the
forty-one-year-old widow, Lady Mary Coke, there is a charming record of a
week in July 1767 when she was a guest. Her father was the 2nd Duke of
Argyll, briefly also Duke of Greenwich, and she maintained some state at
her house in Notting Hill, London. She had visited Paris and had met Mmes
du Deffand and de Boufflers in the company of Horace Walpole. Walpole's
constant presence with her in Paris probably explains why she made no
record of meeting Hume. But now they were both present in the rural idyll:

> 'Tis a delightful place, but to be sure the hills are very steep. After
> talking a long walk, we played at bowls; 'tis a great while since I
> played, yet I think they agreed I was one of the best of the party.
> When it grew dark we came in, and finished the evening with Pope
> Joan.* I won eighteen shillings . . .

* A game involving a circular board and a pack of cards from which the eight of diamonds
(Pope Joan or the Curse of Scotland) has been removed and stakes are laid against
markings on the board. Whoever manages to play a card according to the markings wins
the stake.

Friday. In the evening we played at Pope Joan and I lost five guineas and a shilling . . .

Saturday. Mr Hume does not like Shakespeare. Would you have thought it possible that a man of genius should not be able to discover the beauties of that admirable writer? We are all out against him. I won thirteen guineas, which was lost among three so nobody was ruined.

Sunday 17th You know Mr Hume is a great infidel: 'tis the only thing I dislike in him. I have had some conversation with him, but I have no hopes of converting him from his erroneous way of thinking, and, thank God, his infidelity does not invalidate my belief. I was the only one of the company that went to church; it rained terribly . . . I lost thirty shillings.

Wed 20th We had a noble haunch of venison for dinner . . . Mr Hume has a violent stomach, and General Conway eats heartily.[38]

On the Thursday Hume left with Conway for London. This is the first mention of Hume's 'violent' stomach which would now plague him to the end of his life. Conway gave up his secretaryship on 20 January 1768 and Hume's post ceased. He was now free to return to Edinburgh, but the inevitable Humean delay took place. In October 1768:

I form schemes every day of retiring to Edinburgh, and of drinking my claret and spending my latter days among my friends: but it requires more resolution than I am master of to remove from one place and go to another. No man has been so tossed about than I have been, and no man has more reluctance to changes. Had I been born to a small estate in Scotland of a hundred a year, I should have remained at home all my life, planted and improved my fields, read my book, and wrote philosophy: but living among the great and composing history has been the lot of the later part of my life. I believe, however, that I shall write no more history, though some people pretend to urge me to it, and I find no obstacle but indolence with the want of any proper object as a motive. I have had such reason to entertain such contempt for the public, as not to think their approbation a motive to renounce the pleasures of sauntering and idleness: and my experience of the little addition which riches give to happiness makes that view still more contemptible. You will think me, however, somewhat inconsistent when I tell you that one reason for my remaining in London is the correcting of a new edition of my *History* . . . I can only say that I do it for myself and it amuses me.[39]

He was seriously looking to his resettlement in Edinburgh, however. He told Hugh Blair that he had taken 'one of Allan Ramsay's houses, but gave it up again on the representation of some of my friends in Edinburgh'. This had been the redoubtable Alison Cockburn who wrote to him on 16 December 1768:

I went over that moment to the house you mentioned; it has a good aspect and a bad, a very bad aspect. It has a bank of earth before it and the sun – no windows to the west – nothing but the cold north, with distant views of verdure and sunshine, which it can never hope to partake of. In short I would as soon be the soul of an unburied sinner wandering about the river Styx as live in one of these houses. They have one poor parlour and a tolerable room off a floor. £73! I would not take one of them gratis . . . they are bad unwholesome houses.[40]

The house was in Ramsay Garden, one of a speculative development there by Allan Ramsay. Its eccentric many-turreted roof led to its nickname of 'Goose-pie House'. It is now one of the most sought-after addresses in Edinburgh.

Still in London, Hume continued to enjoy good food, wine, and conversational company. 'I continue my parasitical practices, that is, of dining at all the great tables that remain in London.' Alexander 'Jupiter' Carlyle visited London in 1769 and dined with Mrs Walkinshaw, housekeeper for the Princess Dowager of Wales, mother of the King. She was also the elder sister of Clementina Walkinshaw, reputed mistress of Bonnie Prince Charlie. Hume was also of the company:

The conversation was lively and agreeable, but we were much amused with observing how much the thoughts and conversation of all those the least connected were taken up with every trifling circumstance that related to the court . . . It was truly amusing to observe how much David Hume's strong and capacious mind was filled with infantine [sic] anecdotes of nurses and children.[41]

His 'strong and capacious mind' had been much exercised by the Douglas Cause. In 1761 the Marquess of Hamilton had died childless and intestate, leaving Archibald-Steuart Douglas, the Marquess's nephew, to fight for the vast estate. The contestant was the young Duke of Hamilton, the next male heir. Hamilton could not believe that Lady Jane, the Marquess's sister, could have borne a son at the age of fifty-one, and Hume had been convinced of the validity of the Hamilton claim since his Paris days when he had known the boy's guardians. On 15 July 1767 the Court of Session in Edinburgh found in Hamilton's favour, only by the casting vote of the Lord President, and Hume wrote to Mure, one of the Hamilton boy's guardians, 'you may easily conceive my satisfaction on Hamilton's victory'. He expected that the decision would be challenged in the House of Lords but, 'I think you run very little chance to lose it'. However, on 27 February 1769 the House of Lords overturned the verdict. Hume was incandescent with rage at the injustice and let his views be known around London and to Baron Mure:

> No body, my dear Baron, can be more sensible than I am of the vexation which you must feel from this unfortunate issue of your labours and from the insolent triumph of your enemies; and I heartily sympathise with you on it. But I own, there is another person, whose condition affects me still more sensibly, it is that of poor Andrew Stuart, who had conducted this affair with singular integrity and ability, and who yet must lie under such unmerited reproach, and for aught that I can see without remedy.[42]

Stuart, a lawyer, had jeopardised his future in defending his cause and Lord Chief Justice Mansfield had been vicious in his treatment of the boy in court, accusing his witnesses of perjury. Victory may have gone to Stuart but his name was blackened and the victory was Pyrrhic indeed. Mure replied on 17 May 1769:

> You may believe it gave me the highest satisfaction to find your feelings, with regard to the determination of that cause, corresponding so perfectly with my own. You were present at all the proceedings and heard every argument . . . Poor Andrew Stuart, his treatment, in the same way as it does you, touches me more than all the rest. I can't express how much I feel for him. He is soon to be

down among us. I long to embrace him . . . I rejoice to hear that you too, my dear David are soon to be with us. I shall long to embrace you also. There are daily fewer men on whom one would choose to confer that mark of kindness.[43]

Lady Mary Coke felt Hume had hurt himself with his part in the affair. He had been an outspoken critic of Lord Chief Justice Mansfield and his part in the House of Lords appeal. Having, at first, supported the Hamilton claim, he now felt for the underdog and was appalled at the treatment young Stuart had received from Mansfield.

He was also much moved by the John Wilkes affair. Wilkes, an agitator for greater liberty, was first imprisoned, then elected Member of Parliament for Middlesex, and then became the idol of the mob and enemy of Bute and, thus by implication, all Scots. Hume had always been on the side of greater liberty but had been a lifelong opponent of the mob. 'This madness about Wilkes excited first indignation, then apprehension; but has gone to such a height that all other sentiments with me are buried in ridicule.' The balance of his views, which had resulted in his *History* being castigated by both sides, now meant that he supported liberty but only when curtailed by liberal authority. This was dangerously suspect since the fervent partisanship of the late eighteenth century did not allow one to see both sides of a question.

His views were now a subject of scandal for an under-secretary, running counter to the policies of government:

Oh! How I long to see America and the East Indies revolted totally and finally, the revenue reduced to half, public credit fully discredited by bankruptcy, the third of London in ruins, and the rascally mob subdued. I think I am not too old to despair of being witness to all these blessings.[44]

He did oversee a complete eight-volume edition of his *History*, but by August 1769 he was back in James's Court, Edinburgh, with a view of Kirkcaldy and, by inference, of Adam Smith from his windows. His correspondence with Mme de Boufflers came to a temporary halt and he abandoned any idea of visiting her, or even of settling in small-town France, if that had ever been more than a pipe dream. He had been reviled and adulated. He had been poor and was now, thanks to various government pensions and the works of his pen, very rich. He had been shunned by polite society in Edinburgh and lionised in the drawing rooms of Paris. Philosopher, soldier, historian, diplomat and civil servant, he was coming home. David Hume was tired. He was also, although he did not know it, suffering from the onset of the disease that would kill him.

THIRTEEN

To Have Done With All Ambition

H ume had spent the five months from October 1766 to February 1767
in Edinburgh but, apart from that comparatively short visit, had not
lived in the city since 1763, a gap of some six years. During this time the city
had 'expanded itself prodigiously' beyond the mediaeval spine of the High
Street. The first major building moves had been made to the south of the Old
Town where Lady Nicolson had built a street of detached houses and twenty-
seven acres of land were being surrounded by the building of George Square.
The square was soon to become 'a sought after address for leading men of law
and as town houses for lairds whose estates lay in that direction'.[1] Little of it
remains today since it was vandalised by Edinburgh University's rebuilding
in the 1960s. To the north of the city, the old Nor' Loch had been drained,
leaving a noxious swamp, and access to the north was by a way of a mound of
spoil from building across the valley. This was the 'bank of earth' Alison
Cockburn had told Hume about after her visit to Ramsay Garden. Another
route for crossing the swamp of the drained loch was by the new North
Bridge, which had unfortunately collapsed in 1769, killing five people.

But James Craig's plan for a New Town to be built on the north side of
the drained loch was progressing with an elegant grid of three wide
avenues, Princes, George and Queen Streets, running between two
squares, St George's (later changed to Charlotte) and St Andrew's,
and intersected by seven smaller streets. Alison Cockburn recommended
two properties in George Street, which:

> lie in the eye of the sun . . . easy access for carriages . . . you have
> many acquaintances in that street . . . I think I will take Scot of
> Hondon's [?] house for you directly. It has a garden, coach house,
> etc. and then your avarice will speak for itself. I shall also secure
> you in a wife without putting you to any trouble about resolving.[2]

Hume had other ideas and evidently thought himself rich enough to
acquire a plot of land for himself on the south-west corner of St Andrew's
Square, the more easterly of the squares:

I returned to Edinburgh in 1769, very opulent (for I possessed an income of £1000 a year) healthy, and though somewhat stricken in years, with the prospect of enjoying long my ease and of seeing the increase of my reputation.[3]

The plot had cost him £165 4s 11d with an annual 'feu duty', or ground rent, of £2 18s and was large enough to allow for a dwelling house, coach-house and stables with open views to the south. These open views became a matter for dispute in October 1771 when it became clear that building was to start on the south side of Princes Street at Hume's back door. To prevent this, he, with other feuars, took the case to the Court of Session who promptly threw out their claim, but, six months later the House of Lords reversed their decision and, to this day, Princes Street has buildings only on its north side.

But in October 1769 he was quite simply glad to be back in James' Court:

I have been settled here two months and am here body and soul without casting the least thought of regret to London, or even to Paris. I think it improbable that I shall ever in my life cross the Tweed, except perhaps a jaunt to the North of England for health or amusement. I live still, and must for a twelvemonth, in my old house in James's Court, which is very cheerful and even elegant, but too small to display my great talent for cookery, the science to which I intend to addict the remaining years of my life; I have just now lying on the table before me a receipt for making *Soupe à la Reine**, copied with my own hand. For beef and cabbage (a charming dish) and old mutton and old claret, no body excels me. I make also a sheep's head broth in a manner that Mr Keith speaks of it for eight days after, and the Duc de Nivernois would bind himself apprentice to my lass to learn it.[4]

Hume had, with epicurean forethought, brought several 'receipts' or recipes back from France, including the *soupe à la reine* from Mme de Boufflers, and the long-suffering Peggy Irvine had successfully mastered

---

* This soup was a favourite with Queen Marguerite d'Anjou (1553–1615) and was served every Thursday at Court. It consisted of pounded roast chicken breasts in consommé with breadcrumbs, almonds, hard-boiled eggs and cream. Hume could also have used pigeons or partridges. (*Larousse Gastronomique*, p. 911, London 1976)

them so that Hume's table had the reputation of being one of the most sophisticated in the capital:

> Those few dishes he made the old woman the complete mistress of, and satisfied himself with this knowledge in her, following his friend A. Smith's principle of division of labour, limiting her success to those few articles.[5]

Likewise his cellar was amply stocked with the finest claret, and the Edinburgh *Literati* who flocked to James's Court were renamed the *Eaterati*. Perhaps conspicuous by his absence from the circle was Adam Smith who was busily writing the *Wealth of Nations*. Although Hume always kept a room ready for his old friend, he seldom visited Edinburgh and when he did Hume would rebuke him for the shortness of his stay. For his part Hume, remembering too many nauseous English Channel crossings, seldom crossed the Firth of Forth.

He now had no wish to write any further or to enhance his reputation:

> It is impossible for me to forget that a man who is in his 59th year has not many more years to live, and that it is time for him, if he has any common sense, to have done with all ambition. My ambition was always moderate and confined entirely to letters; but it has been my misfortune to write in the language of the most stupid and factious barbarians in the world, and it is long since that I have renounced all desire of their approbation, which indeed could no longer give me either pleasure or vanity.[6]

It might be thought that Hume was becoming more misanthropic with age, and, while overseeing a revised edition of his *History*, was expunging 'many villainous seditious Whig strokes'. There is no doubt that his various experiences of political life had disenchanted him greatly. Henry Mackenzie, who knew him well, said:

> He was not at all the Jacobite or Tory which he was sometimes accused of being, and as his *History* was supposed to evince. He had an indolent gentleness in his nature which was averse to enthusiasm and perhaps unfriendly to bold ideas and expression. He loved the moderate, the temperate in everything, and from that disposition as well as his propensity to disbelief he had an aversion to the fanatics and Cromwellian partisans of the Commonwealth.[7]

Hume was now planning his retirement and, even if he was not con-
sciously aware of it, was choosing the place in which he would die in peace.
New editions of his *History* and of his *Essays,* both bestsellers, demanded
his constant attention, and his correspondence with Strahan in London
was prodigious. He told Strahan, 'I am building a small house, I mean a
large house for an author'. Strahan suggested a visit to London, but
builders being what they were in 1770 – they seem to have changed little
over the intervening years – Hume was required to remain in Edinburgh
and explained the situation to Mure of Caldwell:

> By being present I have already prevented two capital mistakes
> which the mason was falling into; and I shall be apprehensive of his
> falling into more, were I to be at a distance.[8]

Hume's daily visits to inspect the building of his house took him across the
swamp of the now drained Nor' Loch, which had only the vaguest of
paths, and on one occasion he slipped and fell into the bog. For a man of
Hume's bulk and lack of agility this was extremely dangerous and he
managed to attract the attention of some passing fishwives, themselves
taking a short cut from the Old Town to Newhaven, as he called
desperately for help. But they, recognising the near-to-drowning philosopher, told him that helping atheists, such as he, was certainly not their
intention. Hume countered that all good Christians should help whoever
they can, even those thought to be their enemies. Unconvinced, the
fishwives refused to help until Hume became a Christian and recited the
Lord's Prayer and the Creed then and there. Hume, being a scholar and
not a bigot, knew both texts – he probably knew them in several languages
– and promptly obeyed as strong arms deposited the floundering but
grateful man on the grassy path. Hume always admitted that Edinburgh
fishwives were the most acute theologians he had ever met.[9]

He had also told Mure that: I am engaged in building a house, which is
the second great operation in human life : for the taking of a wife is the
first, which I hope will come in time'.[10] Alison Cockburn had told Hume
that she would 'secure you in a wife without putting you to any trouble' but
he had made no reply. It was natural to a widow of middle years that such
an eminent figure as Hume, now that his travels seemed to be over, would
be in search of a wife to preside as hostess in his new establishment. Henry
Mackenzie was in no doubt that Hume was highly enamoured of Nancy
Ord. She was an English lady of half Hume's age and the daughter of

Robert Ord, Lord Chief Baron of the Scottish Exchequer, reputedly witty, beautiful and possibly a previous recipient of Hume's suit. The rumour that Hume was about to marry was powerful:

> March 21st 1770
> A report has spread abroad and has even reached this far distant shore! That Mr Hume is to quit his immortal mistress, his historical muse, for a mere mortal! For a wife. What a pity! . . . is it possible, can a man quit the applause and adulation of the whole world – and become the property of one female. Oh fie, let us not hear of it. Or in the Boswellian manner let us have every circumstance, every motive in the newspapers that produced so strange a catastrophe. If the writer of this had a pen that would write, the writer would argue much against marriage, a vile institution below the native dignity and liberty of man![11]

This anonymous letter is preserved by the National Library of Scotland in the sequence following the signed letters of Alison Cockburn, whose name has been added to the cover by a later hand. It is inconceivable that the widow who had offered to find Hume a wife should so inveigh against marriage. The tone is too flippant for Mme de Boufflers, although the rumour had reached Mme du Deffand, but the writer of the letter has carefully concealed the gender. We shall probably never know the true author.

Hume was, however, a close friend of Nancy Ord, although his existing correspondence to her is slight. In August 1770 he had written her a long and elaborately humorous apology for having made off with six gambling chips from her father's table and she was undoubtedly one of Hume's female friends in Edinburgh. But he had many such friends and conversation with young ladies was one of his greatest joys:

> . . . he never introduced in conversation his abstruse or sceptical speculations: that . . . his sentiments were moral and natural and pleasing, and even playful in the extreme. This is evinced by his letters, which are perfect in their kind. He could bring himself down without effort to the most familiar playfulness with young persons, and particularly delighted in the conversations of youthful females. Mr Hume was one of our constant visitors – making, as was the custom of those days, tea-time his hour of calling. In the

summer he would often stroll to my father's beautiful villa of North Merchiston. On one occasion – I was then a boy of thirteen – he, missing my mother, made his tea-drinking good with two or three young ladies of eighteen or nineteen (his acquaintances) who were my mother's guests. I recollect perfectly how he talked to them; and my recollection has been rendered permanent by an occurrence which caused some mirth and no mischief. When the philosopher was amusing himself in conversation with the young ladies, the chair began to give way under him, and gradually brought him to the floor. The damsels were both alarmed and amused, when Mr Hume, recovering himself and getting upon his legs, said in his broad Scotch tone, but in English words (for he never used Scotch), 'Young ladies, you must tell Mr Adam to keep stronger chairs for heavy philosophers.'

This simple story is a good specimen of the man. He was above all affectation.[12]

His conversation was reported by Mrs Ann Murray Keith:

men who like David Hume can relish an intercourse that without cant or pretensions of Platonism has all the arguments of the ridiculous system. My sisters and I were of that circle where D. Hume lived intimately with, and a most pleasant companion he was! His conversation never turned on those subjects which gave offence in his writings – he was one of the sweetest tempered men and the most benevolent that ever was born – his early studies had turned very much on the dreadful effects of enthusiasm, and that led him too far in his endeavours to correct the errors which had exited his horror. There was a simplicity and pleasantness of manners about him that was delightful in society – he was a charm in domestic life! In short he was one of the most worthy and agreeable men I ever knew. I was not in Edinburgh when he died, but my sisters got a farewell visit from him ten days before his death – I fancy he saw they could not have stood anything that came too near the subject, so he avoided anything particular and endeavoured to make the conversation as cheerful as possible, he paid the same compliment to all these ladies with whom he lived in intimacy . . . I never heard that he had through the whole course of his life any one particular attachment.[13]

Hume had made a spectacularly unsuccessful attempt at paying suit to a countess in Turin and was deeply involved with Mme de Boufflers while in Paris. The first occurrence was almost certainly masculine bravado while the second was an attraction of minds which grew into a profound affection. Hume's friendship was easily gained and he made great efforts to help his friends whenever he could, but domestically his establishment of sister Katherine along with Peggy Irvine as cook/housekeeper remained stable. He clearly had great charm, if also a disconcerting gaze, and could be relied on to amuse. In Edinburgh there was a certain *frisson* in entertaining the Great Infidel, while safe in the knowledge that he would never shock domestically, beyond suggesting whist on the Sabbath. His early 'disease of the learned' had been conquered by him in solitude at Ninewells, and ever since then his deepest emotions had remained closely wrapped. While there was ready access to friendship and affection – even love in a Platonic sense – there was no such access to physical love or to lifelong commitments. Hume was that person, so sought after by hostesses even today, the witty and entertaining, well-informed, confirmed bachelor.

A mixture of Peggy's recently learned cooking skills and Hume's conversational and debating powers meant that his table at James' Court, and later in the new house, was well attended by distinguished company, both lay and divine. His old friend Kames would mix with John Bruce, Professor of Logic, and Joseph Black, Professor of Chemistry, as well as Principal Robertson. The traditional church still viewed him with suspicion and, lacking any sense of humour, occasionally walked out of Hume's house. He was, however, tolerated, if only for his wit:

> One Sunday morning, Hume met Sir James Hunter, an eminent banker, with his wife, on their way to church and was asked to accompany them. 'What, go to church with you? With publicans and money changers; the same that were driven with scourges out of the temple!! No, no, I'll never be seen entering a church in such company.[14]

Having let James' Court to James Boswell, Hume moved to his new house in May 1771, and he was hugely proud of it. He wished Strahan could see it: 'You would not wonder that I have abjured London for ever'. Although it is now in the centre of the city, in Hume's day it was still on the northernmost limits and the street it stood in had not even been named.

The frequently repeated story is that Nancy Ord was leaving Hume one day and, on the side of his house, chalked 'St David's Street'. Peggy Irvine was about to wash off the graffito when Hume stopped her: 'Never mind lassie, many a better man has been made a saint of before'. The street is still called St David's Street. Why a lady of quality was carrying a piece of chalk is probably a question that should not be asked, but, apart from St Andrew, St David is the only British patron saint in the New Town. The story is simply too good to be denied.

One of Hume's most famous guests in St David's Street was Benjamin Franklin. Franklin had come to Britain in 1764 as agent for the Pennsylvania Assembly to contest the right of London to impose taxes without allowing representation by the colonists. He had met Hume in London and had visited Edinburgh in 1759 and had presented papers to the Select Society. Now he could not fail to notice the changes to the city since, on this visit, he found only temporary lodgings. The inn in which he had lodged previously had been demolished to make way for the reconstructed North Bridge:

> If on that first morning Mr Franklin leaned on the parapet of the new bridge and looked curiously across at the expansion of the town west of the Calton Hill, he might have observed a recently finished house in St David Street south of St Andrew's Square, a structure which bore a singular resemblance to his own dwelling in Philadelphia.[15]

This was 27th October 1771 and Franklin wrote:

> Dear Friend,
> Through storms and floods I arrived here on Saturday night, late and was lodged miserably at an inn. But that excellent Christian David Hume, agreeable to the precepts of the Gospel, has received the stranger and I now live with him at his house in the New Town most happily.[16]

Henry Marchant, a New England lawyer and friend of Franklin's, was also in Edinburgh and Principal Robertson took him to dine, 'with much free sociablity', at Hume's. Frankilin visited the west of Scotland with Marchant and returned to Hume in November when Hume gave a dinner for both of them with Kames, two professors from the university, Black, Russell, of the chair of Physics, and Adam Ferguson. Marchant, who was not a natural enthusiast, went so far as to say, 'In such company I could not fail to be entertained'.

Although Hume was a firm believer in the independence of the American colonies, Franklin and he were not always in accord, since Franklin's vehemence made him uneasy. 'I always knew him to be a factious man and faction next to fanaticism is of all passions the most destructive of philosophy.'[17] Hume thought that the 'colonies are no longer in their infancy. But yet I say to you, they are still in their nonage, and Dr Franklyns [sic] wishes to emancipate them too soon from their mother country'.[18] Mr Allen, Justice-General of Pennsylvania, thought Franklin was 'so turbulent and such a plotter as to be able to embroil three kingdoms, if he ever has an opportunity'.[19]

Franklin left Edinburgh in January 1772 and Hume wrote to him in February:

> I was very glad to hear of your safe arrival in London, after being exposed to as many perils as St Paul, by land and by water, though to no perils among false brethren: for the good wishes of all your brother philosophers in this place attend you heartily and sincerely, together with much regret that your business would not allow to pass more time among them.[20]

Hume's brother John had moved from Ninewells to James's Court to oversee his son's education while David was in London. David proved himself a good uncle when, in December 1770, he bought John's eldest son, Joseph, but always known as 'Josey', a commission in the 2nd Dragoon Guards. Josey was eighteen years old and already David thought him to be 'clever, though a little giddy'. According to Hill Burton, 'he indulged in many of the eccentricities and peculiarities so often exhibited by the Scottish gentry'. Apart from drinking, whoring and incurring debts, Josey also appeared to undergo total Anglification:

> Dear Josey alias Joe.
> I give you thanks and at the same time ask pardon: I give you thanks for your letter, and ask your pardon for being so late in answering it. But if you knew the occupation which proceeds from flitting, or, as you Englishmen call it, removing, you would excuse my delay in writing . . . We are now almost fully settled in our new house in St Andrews Square and your aunt and I are very happy in

our situation. Your friend Peggy alone seems to agree ill with it in point of health, I suppose because of the sudden change from a close suffocating air to a free and open one. Your family move at the end of this week; and your Pappa seems to be as happy in the prospect of his situation. His new house is indeed very agreeable and agreeably situated.[21]

Hume hoped he would take pleasure in his sword, cockade and well-trained horse and beseeched him not to neglect learning English pronunciation. 'It is an agreeable quality and easily carried about with you. I was too negligent in that quality when I was of your age.' But by October of that year Hume wrote to Josey, secretly offering him money. The secret was to be kept from John since the money was to refund Josey's expenses in his treatment for gonhorrea: a 'peculiarity so often exhibited by the Scottish Gentry'.

By January of 1772 Hume broke a long silence and wrote to Mme de Boufflers. The silence had been mutual and without rancour for it was difficult, given the past intensity of the relationship, to continue as they had. The gap had allowed the temperature to cool and now they could continue as occasional correspondents. Mme de Boufflers had broken the silence first with a now non-existent letter. Hume thanks her for her news and then:

> For my part, I have totally and finally retired from the world, with a resolution never more to appear on the scene in any shape. This purpose arose, not from discontent, but from safety. I have now no object but to
>
> > Sit down and think, and die in peace –
>
> What other object can a man of my age entertain? Happily I found my taste for reading return, even with greater avidity, after a pretty long interruption: but I guard myself carefully from the temptation of writing any more; and though I have had great encouragement to continue my history, I am resolved never again to expose myself to the censure of such factious and passionate readers as this country abounds with. There are some people here conversible enough: their society, together with my books, fills up my time sufficiently, so as not to leave any vacancy; and I have lately added the amusement of building, which has given me some occupation.
>
> I hearken attentively to the hopes you give me of seeing you once

more before I die. I think it becomes me to meet you in London; and though I have frequently declared that I should never more see that place, such an incident as your arrival there would be sufficient to break all my resolutions.[22]

One resolution that Hume had made was never to answer his critics, and in the past he had allowed the limited criticism of the *Treatise* to go more or less unchallenged. He had carried on a correspondence in a more or less light-hearted vein with Robert Reid of Aberdeen. Reid was a year older than Hume, married with nine children, a minister at New Machar and a regent in King's College, Aberdeen. 'Reid took Hume's work (the *Treatise*) to have proven that the major assumption of Berkeley's philosophy, that what is before the mind is always some idea, would lead to absurdity'.[23] He formed the Aberdeen Philosophical Society and in 1763 wrote to Hume:

When you have seen the whole of my performance, I shall take it as a very great favour to have your opinion of it, from which I make no doubt of receiving light, whether I receive conviction or no . . . a little philosophical society here . . . is much indebted to you for all its entertainment . . . If you write no more in morals, politics, or metaphysics, I am afraid we shall be at a loss for subjects.[24]

By 1764 Reid had the chair of Moral Philosophy at Old College, Glasgow. According to Reid, Descartes, Locke, Berkeley and Hume stated that the immediate object of thought is always some impression or idea. He calls this the *ideal* theory. Hume showed, according to Reid, that this leads to scepticism and an absurd philosophy of the mind. His appeal to common sense is inspired by Locke. Contrary to this is the need to postulate innate conceptual principles and this is a direct consequence of Hume's arguments. 'What is immediately before the mind is always some impression of idea', and Hume argued this to an extreme conclusion. Reid turned to Berkeley in that we have a notion of mind as an active power, to Locke in that we perceive the primary qualities of matter, and to Descartes in that our basic conceptions arise, not from experience but from innate principles. Reid was committed to empiricism and common sense. We conceive of the existence of the qualities of external objects since they arise from the innate principles of the mind. Innate since they are the gift of God. These convictions need no justification because they are self-evident without the use of reasoning. In America Thomas Jefferson was an admirer of Robert Reid. 'It was very probably from Reid that he borrowed the idea of 'self-evident truths' for the Declaration of Independence. He also put Reid at the centre of his planned curriculum for the University of Virginia. (Hume was very carefully left out.)'[25]

Hume and Reid had, over the years, agreed to differ, but not so James Beattie. He was also from Aberdeen where he was Professor of Moral Philosophy and Logic at Marischal College and in 1770 he had published *An Essay on the Nature and Immutability of Truth; in opposition to Sophistry and Scepticism.* He characterised Hume's works as 'Those unnatural productions, the vile effusion of a hard and stupid heart, that mistakes its own restlessness for the activity of a genius, and its own captiousness for sagacity of understanding'. He was 'imposed on by words not well understood'. 'The style of the *Treatise* is obscure and uninteresting.'

He quotes Hume as having himself quoted the titles of the chapters in Aristotle's *Ethics* to show that, for example, he valued manly freedom among the virtues. Beattie accuses Hume of mistranslation, being 'misled by etymology', and wishes 'our learned metaphysician had extended his researches a little beyond the titles of those chapters'.[26]

Beattie visited London in 1773 and his visit as recorded by him reads like a triumphal progress. On 8th May the Archbishop of York told Beattie that the King had spoken to him suggesting a scheme to get him a professorship in Edinburgh, 'but I had many enemies there'. The King replied, 'Everybody who is a friend to Hume must be his enemy, but he has cut Mr Hume up by the roots'.[27] The likelihood of this appointment was based on what turned out to be a false rumour. But he was promised, and received, a pension of £200 a year. Then on 16th May Strahan told him that his book had boosted the sales of Hume's *Essays,* and that Hume had become 'a little peevish'. Strahan also said that Hume had been jealous of Robertson's success with his history and that he 'was obliged to print some editions of Robertson's history without alteration of date, as Hume could not bear to think that the sale of that work had been so extensive as it really was.'[28]

Hume had, in fact, angered Strahan in March 1773 with a silly dispute over how many copies of the octavo edition of the *Essays* were left but had poured oil on troubled letters in a letter of apology, and it may well be that even by May his pride was still hurt. On 3rd June Beattie records: 'Garrick had been praising it highly [the *Essay*] as a most excellent work (which he always does when speaking of it)'. Johnson seconded him warmly: 'Why sir, there is in it a depth of reasoning, and a splendour of language which makes it one of the first rate productions of the age'.[29] Beattie had a private audience of the King who praised the book 'I never stole a book but one, said His Majesty, and that was yours. I stole it from the Queen and gave it to Lord Hertford to read',[30] and on 9th July Beattie was admitted as LLD at Oxford.

He was also celebrated for having written *The Minstrel,* a long tedious Spenserian poem. However, the relative reputations of Hume and Beattie were put into perspective in Hume's obituary in the *Annual Register* for 1777:

> This work [the *Treatise*] though not inferior to anything of the moral or metaphysical kind in any language was entirely overlooked, or decried at the time of publication, except by a few liberal minded men, who had courage to throw aside their popular and literary prejudices and follow sound reasoning, without being afraid of any dangerous conclusion, or fatal discovery. Dr Beattie has been so successful as to obtain a pension by his *Essay on the Immutability of Truth;* in which he discovers all the violence of a sectary, and all the illiberality of a pedant, and abuses rather than refutes Mr Hume.[31]

Hume had managed, just, to adhere to his lifelong resolution never to engage in public controversy over his work, but he did insert a preface to future editions of the *Essays,* in which he accuses his critics of founding their attacks on the thought contained in the *Treatise*, which he dismisses as 'a juvenile work, which the author never acknowledged'. He advises future critics to read the *Essays* only and hopes that the *Advertisement* was 'a complete answer to Dr Reid and that bigoted silly fellow Beattie'. The rejection of the *Treatise,* some thirty-four years earlier, still rankled.

It is extraordinarily sad that the author of a work which changed philosophy so radically should, in the final years of his life, despairingly disown his most influential work. He had achieved fame for works of history and politics, but his reconsideration of metaphysics brought him nothing but chagrin. The edition was still unsold at his death, but as this is written, the *Treatise* is available in countless editions, in as many languages, and learned commentaries on it occupy considerable lengths of shelving in most libraries. Hume would have shrugged resignedly.

Still seeing to his own comfort, he was decorating his now two-year-old home and had commissioned the ever faithful Nancy Ord to help him, and wrote to her panicking on 12th April 1773. He had made a mistake in his measuring of the height of his ceilings. They were, in fact, nine feet eight inches high. He salutes her and prays heartily for her return.[32]

A literary review, called the *Edinburgh Magazine and Review*, had been founded in 1773 by Gilbert Stuart. Stuart was thirty-one years old and a hack writer – 'a young man who promised much and performed little of value'[33] – who had written an essay on the *Antiquity of the British Constitution* which he had sent to Hume in July 1763 and which Hume had praised out of a feeling of kindness. He told Elliot of Minto that his comments were 'calculated to encourage a young man of merit',[34] and now he would repay this early encouragement. But he had misjudged Stuart and gave him advice:

> It were better, however, for him, and everybody, to pursue, in
> preference to the idle trade of writing, some other lawful
> occupation, such as cheating like an attorney, quacking like a
> physician, canting and hypocratising like a parson etc., etc. etc.[35]
> His habits were irregular and his passions fierce . . . his mind was
> diseased with envious rancour . . . his numerous critical labours
> were directed to annihilate all the genius of his country.[36]

The row continued when, in August 1770, Hume wrote to Strahan and to Cadell urging the publication of a *History of Great Britain* by one Robert Henry. Hume thought it 'writ with perspicuity and propriety of style . . . but neither sprightly nor elegant, and it is judicious but not curious'.[37] It was also very long. Henry was a minister of Moderate views and the incumbent of the New Greyfriars Church in Edinburgh whence he had come from Berwick-on-Tweed and had his ear well to the literary ground of Edinburgh. Stuart was keen to establish himself as the scourge of the previous generation and had already attacked Kames and Monboddo although the first volume of Henry's *History* had met with praise. Henry was certain that Stuart would launch an attack on the second volume and asked Hume to intervene. This he did by submitting a review of his own to Stuart. While hardly praising the work to the skies, it was laudatory enough, especially in its moral guidance. On 13th December 1773 Stuart, astonishingly, altered this subtly into comic irony and transformed the review into one of comic dismissal. Hume restored his original tone in the proofs and resubmitted the review. Stuart said, 'David Hume wants to review Henry but that task is so precious that I will undertake it myself'. Hume's review was never published – Stuart 'kept a copy of it in his cabinet, for the amusement of friends' – and the final printed review was devastating. Hume became an enemy of Stuart's who lost no opportunity of deriding his work in later issues of the *Edinburgh Magazine*:

> Hume has behaved ill in this affair and I am preparing to chastise him. You may expect a series of papers in this magazine, pointing out a multitude of errors, and ascertaining his ignorance of English history. It was too much for my temper to be assailed by both infidels and believers.[38]

Stuart's assault on the *literati* of Edinburgh was spectacularly unsuccessful and in the summer of 1774 wrote: 'I am sorry now that I left London and the moment I have money enough to carry me back to it, I shall set off. I mortally abhor and detest this place and every body in it. Never was there a city where there was so much pretension to knowledge and so little of it'.[39]

He took to a life of bitterness and alcohol in London, only to return to his native country to die of dropsy in August 1786. 'Gilbert Stuart, it seems, suffered most of the miseries of unsuccessful authorship and paid dearly for talents misapplied.'[40]

Since David Hume was the Great Infidel, it was clear to the narrow minds operating in Edinburgh that the ministry was, for him, packed with religious zealots to whom he was, without exception, bitterly opposed. We have seen his wry amusement that the Whigs thought his *History* a work of Tory propaganda – since it criticised Whigs – just as the Tories thought him Whig for the reverse reason. Since he criticised some aspects of the Church he was, therefore, a blanket anti-clerical. Such liberalism is deeply troubling to the bigot, and the fact of his supporting a minister of the Church, such as Henry, was met with equal hostility.

It had happened previously in a major way when he was in dispute with Robert Wallace in 1751. In a lengthy footnote to his essay *Of National Characters*, published in 1748, Hume attacked the over-zealous clergymen:

> The ambition of the clergy can often be satisfied only by promoting ignorance and superstition and implicit faith and pious frauds . . . most men have an overweening conceit of themselves: but these

have a peculiar temptation to that vice, who are regarded with such veneration, and are even deemed sacred by the ignorant multitude.[41]

It was not a screaming denunciation, but, rather, a good-humoured admonition. By way of reply Wallace wrote a *Letter from a Moderate Thinker*. This was an equally temperate piece pointing out that in attacking the zealots, or High Flyers, Hume was making the mistake of presuming the whole from a study of a part. Wallace, a member of the Rankenian and Philosophical Societies, had met Hume by 1751 and the two men had become friends. There had been another response to Hume's essay by Professor Alexander Gerard of Aberdeen —'one of a group of ministers at Aberdeen called by Hume "my friendly adversaries"'.[42] Wallace felt it was needless to publish his *Letter from a Moderate Thinker* and the two men stayed in close contact. They had a lively dispute over Hume's essay, *Of the Populousness of Ancient Nations,* conducted, according to Ramsay of Ochtertyre, 'with great ability and good temper'. Also, in 1756 Wallace was a strong supporter of the Moderates when the General Assembly tried to excommunicate Hume. Even-handedness and open-mindedness did exist where the Enlightenment had shone, but there were still many dark corners.

James Boswell, for example, found it difficult to reconcile the fact that he admired both Hume and Johnson, whose views were diametrically opposed to each other. It is one of the tragedies of the eighteenth century that the two men never met in debate with Boswell sitting ready to record the exchange: Johnson, a Scotophobe, Jacobite and high Tory advocate of the Church of England, and David Hume, a rational freethinker and sceptic of simple faith. But since Johnson 'talked for victory' in a con-versation and Hume for enlightenment, perhaps it is as well the two never met. Boswell had a simple belief in the efficacy of church attendance, even if, like Samuel Pepys a century before, it was also a convenient place to form attachments with the other sex. Boswell also had a firm belief in the immortality of the soul, possibly since he believed that someone as splendid as himself must continue for ever, and was horrified that Hume not only denied it in conversation but would publish a posthumous refutation.

But as the dust of the dispute with Stuart settled, Hume continued his domestic life surrounded by his friends. Then on 15th March 1773 he invited his nephew Josey to stay with him – 'as your furlough will last a twelvemonth after which your regiment is to be here, you may about two years hence have collected some money, and what is better, some wit, before you visit foreign countries'.[43]

Whether Josey gathered any wit or not by April 1775, he was ready to go to France *en route* for a posting to Metz. David paid him £120 to buy his lieutenancy – it was ratified in the spring – and to finance his time in Paris on the way to Metz. To further facilitate this visit he wrote to Mme de Boufflers asking that she receive him:

> He has as you will see, an agreeable figure, and if he could speak the language his behaviour and conversation is very good so that I doubt not that he will be acceptable to the good company of the place.[44]

How acceptable a young cavalry officer would find a 51-year-old Countess is another matter, but Hume asked Mme de Boufflers to give Josey letters of introduction to the Governors of Metz and its surrounding province. He also wrote to Josey advising him on lodgings:

> I would have you drive to the Hotel de Tours, Rue Paon, Faubourg St Germain as a creditable place at which I have known several of my friends to lodge. Enquire the price of apartments before you fix on any. The landlord will provide you with a valet de place, and you may probably dine every day at the Table d'Hote in good company.[45]

He suggests getting a good tailor and attending the theatre before waiting on Mme de Boufflers and Baron d'Holbach among others. It is a typical uncle's letter hoping for a young man to follow in his footsteps.

In his letter to Mme de Boufflers Hume complains about the Scottish climate and says that he sometimes entertains the notion of returning to France, but knows that he will probably never carry the idea into execution. She promptly replies that his return would make her the happiest person in the world and that there is a beautiful house, with a garden, in the Temple which he could rent. It is separated from her garden by a wall through which a gate might be made so that they could meet and dine together daily. She adds that he is alone through choice. He never subsequently referred to the idea and he would only write to her once more to say good-bye from his deathbed, but the idea of the two ageing savants living out the remainder of their lives in adjacent houses separated only by a garden wall, like Pyramus and Thisbe, is a very touching one. But it was not to be.

Hume remained in his new house receiving guests, inevitably including the fame-hungry James Boswell. Boswell had Johnson in London and Hume in Edinburgh, but could never understand how David Hume could so differ from him in religion and yet remain so agreeable:

Sunday, December 17 1775
After church called on David Hume and found him sitting after dinner with his sister and youngest nephew. He had on a white nightcap and a hat above it. He called for a fresh bottle of port which he and I drank all but a single glass which his nephew took. I indeed took the largest share. Then we drank tea. Mr Hume said he had not met with the encouragement which he deserved as a man of genius, for Mr Hume had known several men of letters who had never heard of him . . . I also thought of writing his life . . . It was curious to see David such a civil, sensible, comfortable looking man and to recollect, 'This is the Great Infidel'. Belief or want of belief is not absolutely connected with practice. How many surly men are teachers of the gospel of peace![46]

Hume clearly had occasional moments of depression, but in the spring of 1776 two books were published to his great joy. The first, published on 20th February, was the opening volume of Edward Gibbon's *Decline and Fall of the Roman Empire.* Hume had met Gibbon in Edinburgh in 1758, Gibbon anticipating in a letter that he would meet 'the great David Hume', and the two men had corresponded occasionally since then, but Hume's reaction on reading the first volume was ecstatic:

As I ran through your volume of history with a great deal of avidity and impatience, I cannot forbear discovering somewhat of the same impatience in returning you thanks for your agreeable present, and expressing the satisfaction which the performance has given me. Whether I consider the dignity of your style, the depth of your matter, or the extensiveness of your learning, I must regard the work as equally the object of esteem; and, I own that if I had not previously had the happiness of your personal acquaintance, such a performance, from an Englishman in our age would have given me some surprise. You may smile at this sentiment; but it seems to me that your countrymen, for almost a whole generation, have given themselves up to barbarous and absurd faction, and have totally neglected all polite letters, I no longer expected any valuable production to come from them. I know it will give you pleasure, as it did me, to find that all the men of letters in this place concur in their admiration of your work, and in the anxious desire of your continuing it.

When I heard of your undertaking (which was some time ago), I own I was a little curious to see how you would extricate yourself from the subject of your last two chapters. I think you have observed a very prudent temperament, but it was impossible to treat the subject so as not to give grounds of suspicion against you and you may expect that a clamour will arise. This, if anything, will retard your success with the public; for in every other respect your work is calculated to be popular. But, among many other marks of decline, the prevalence of superstition in England prognosticates the fall of philosophy and decay of taste, and though no body be more capable than you to revive them, you will probably find a struggle in your first advances.[47]

The two last chapters of this first volume dealt with 'a candid but rational inquiry into the progress and establishment of Christianity'. Gibbon appalled his readers by treating Christianity as merely another sect of dubious origins: 'the theologian may indulge the pleasing task of describing religion as she descended from heaven, arrayed in her native purity. A more melancholy duty is imposed on the historian'.[48] Then, having reviewed the growth of the sect with facts rather than faith, he concludes, 'on the subject of martyrdoms, it must still be acknowledged that the Christians, in the course of their intestine discussions, have inflicted far greater severities on each other that they had experienced from the zeal of infidels'.[49] Gibbon is still censured for his objectivity even today.

In his letter Hume also agreed with Gibbon that Macpherson's *Ossian* was a forgery, but goes further:

It is, indeed, strange that any men of sense could have imagined it possible that about twenty thousand verses, along with numberless historical facts, could have been preserved by oral tradition during fifty generations, by the rudest, perhaps of all European nations; the most necessitous, the most turbulent and the most unsettled.[50]

He concludes by telling Gibbon that the second volume is eagerly awaited, but 'I cannot expect to live so long as to see the publication of it'. Gibbon said that this letter 'overpaid the labour of ten years'.

The controversy over *Ossian* also arose on 6 March 1775. In his *Journal* James Boswell records:

> Drank tea with David Hume, having half a year's rent of his house to pay him. He spoke of Mr Johnson's *Journey* in terms so slighting that it could have no effect but to show his resentment. He however agreed with him perfectly about Ossian. But then he disbelieved not so much for want of testimony, as from the nature of the thing, according to his apprehension. He said if fifty bare-arsed Highlanders should say that *Fingal* was an ancient poem, he would not believe them. He said it was not to be believed that a people who were continually concerned to keep themselves from starving or from being hanged should preserve in their memories a poem in six books. He said that Homer had once been written which made a great difference. He said that the extensive fame of Ossian was owing to the notion that the poems were so ancient; that, if Macpherson had given them as his own, nobody would have read them to an end. He acknowledged that there were some good passages in them, and perhaps there might be some small parts ancient. He said the Highlanders who have been famed as a warlike people, were so much flattered to have it thought that they had a great poet among them and they all tried to support the fact, and their wish to have it so made them even ready to persuade themselves into it.[51]

Hume's scathing views of the Highlanders have already been noted and were not uncommon in the eighteenth century. The Jacobite Risings and a system of agriculture superseded in the South combined with a separate language to make Scotland north-west of Stirling into an alien land. The Highlanders themselves did little to contradict the Lowland stereotyping of their culture, clinging to high-sounding titles and chieftainships based on no more than oral tradition. The Romantic Revival and the Victorian enthusiasm for the Highlands would have to wait until the next century.

The second volume to be praised by Hume was his friend Adam Smith's *An Inquiry into the Nature and Causes of the Wealth of Nations*, published on 9th March:

Euge! Belle! Dear Mr Smith; I am much pleased with your
performance and the perusal of it has taken me from a state of
great anxiety . . . it has depth and solidity and acuteness, and is so
much illustrated by curious facts, that it must at last take the public
attention . . . but these and a hundred other points are fit only to
be discussed in conversation, which till you tell me the contrary, I
shall flatter myself with soon. I hope it will be soon: for I am in a
very bad state of health and cannot afford a long delay.[52]

He ends by telling Smith of the death of Mure of Caldwell, 'one of the
oldest and best friends I had in the world'.

It was at this time that Hume wrote *My Own Life* and in it looks
forward to his own end:

In spring 1775, I was struck with a disorder in my bowels which at
first gave me no alarm, but has since, as I apprehend it, become
mortal and incurable. I now reckon on a speedy dissolution. I have
suffered very little pain from my disorder: and what is more strange,
have, notwithstanding the great decline of my person, never suffered
a moment's abatement of my spirits; insomuch, that were I to name
the period of my life which I should most choose to pass over
again, I might be tempted to point to this later period. I possess
the same ardour as ever in study, and the same gaiety in company. I
consider besides, that a man of sixty five, by dying, cuts off only a
few years of infirmities: and though I see many symptoms of my
literary reputation's breaking out at last with additional lustre, I
know that I had but a few years to enjoy it. It is difficult to be
more detached from life than I am at present.[53]

His friends were extremely worried and on 11 April 1776 Adam Ferguson
wrote to John Hume:

David, I am afraid, loses ground. He is cheerful and in good spirits
as usual, but I confess that any hopes, from the effects of the turn
of the season towards spring, have very much abated. A journey to
the South, particularly to Bath, has been mentioned to him; but the
thoughts of being from home, hurried at inns, and exposed to
irregular meals, are very disagreeable to him. Black is of the opinion
that he ought not to expose himself to anything that is so, and that
for his complaints, the tranquillity and usual amusements of his

own fireside with proper diet, is his best regimen, so that I think the thoughts of any journey are at present laid aside.[54]

Joseph Black was not only the Professor of Chemistry but also of Medicine at Edinburgh University and one of the leading physicians of his day. Similarly so was Sir John Pringle in London who advised Hume to visit him before making a journey to Bath, and Hume went against Black's advice and set out for London on 21 April. He was accompanied by Colin Ross, the manservant to the late Mure of Caldwell, and his cousin the Rev. John Home travelled north with Adam Smith to meet him and then return south with the invalid. They met at Morpeth in Northumberland and John Home noted:

They came to Morpeth on 23rd April 1776 and would have passed Mr David Hume, if they had not seen his servant Colin, standing at the gate of an inn. Mr Home thinks that his friend, Mr David Hume, is much better than he expected to find him. His spirits are astonishing, he talks of his illness, of his death, as matters of no moment, and gives an account of what passed between him and his physicians since his illness began, with the usual wit, or with more wit than usual. He acquainted Mr Smith and me that Dr Black had not concealed the opinion he had of the desperateness of his condition and was rather averse to his setting out, 'Have you no reason against it' said David, 'but an apprehension that it may make me die sooner? That is no reason at all.' I never saw him more cheerful or in more perfect possession of all his faculties his memory his understanding, his wit. It is agreed that Smith shall go on to Scotland and that I should proceed to Bath with David. We are to travel one stage before dinner and one stage after. Colin tells me that he thinks Mr Hume better than when we left Edinburgh. We had a fine evening as we went from Morpeth to Newcastle. David, seeing a pair of pistols in the chaise, said, that as he had very little at stake, he would indulge me in my humour of fighting the highwaymen. Whilst supper was getting ready at the inn, Mr Hume and I played an hour at picquet. Mr David was very keen about his card playing.[55]

However, on the next morning:

Mr Hume not quite so well in the morning. We talked about national affairs and Mr Hume commented that it was to be regretted that the two most civilised nations, the English and the French, should be on the decline; and the barbarous, the Goths and Vandals, of Germany and Russia, should be rising in power and renown.[56]

By the 26th Home notices that Hume is now so thin that he sits on a cushion and their chaise has to travel slowly to avoid shaking the passengers. But Hume had a more dispassionate view of his condition:

My friend has written both to London and Edinburgh that I am a great deal better, and will shortly be quite better. His notion is founded on my good spirits a circumstance somewhat fallacious. However I am sensibly better, but the root of the distemper still remains, and discovers itself by a heavy dull pain, about the pit of my stomach, which appears more evidently distinct from a colical pain since my journey. My friends tell me that Sir John Pringle, from his present notion of my case is resolved to send me to Bath which will not be disagreeable to me.[57]

On the 28th:

Mr Hume this day told me that he had bought a piece of ground; and when I seemed surprised that I had never heard of it, he said it was in the new church yard on the Calton Hill, for a burying place; that he meant to have a small monument erected, not to exceed in expense a hundred pounds, that the inscription should be:-

DAVID HUME[58]

The day before they arrived in London Hume complained of the cold and asked for a second coverlet at night. Since he had intermittent fevers and could only bear a thin mattress and a single sheet, everyone was heartened by the passing of the fever. Home found him 'wonderfully well'. Hume thought 'it was a good thing to be like other people'.

In London he lodged again in Brewer Street, with a Mrs Perkins, 'few doors from Miss Elliots', and immediately consulted Sir John Pringle who saw nothing alarming in Hume's case. The town was full of approbation for Adam Smith's *Wealth of Nations* and Hume was ready to set out for Bath, making arrangements for a new servant, Hugh Semple, to be sent ahead of him. Sir John diagnosed a contraction in the colon and, feeling much better, Hume set out for Bath, arriving for consultations with Dr Gustard. He was an Edinburgh minister's son with a 'winning address' and a 'very good business'.

The journey from Morpeth and then to Bath was, thanks to the company of John Hume, totally enjoyable:

> Never was there a more friendly action, nor better placed: for what between conversation and gaming (not to mention sometimes squabbling) I did not pass a languid moment; and his company, I am certain, was the chief cause why my journey had such a good effect.[59]

Bath had grown into a fashionable, and scandalous, resort under the 'reign' of Richard 'Beau' Nash who had died fourteen years earlier. Alexander Carlyle, more recently, had found:

> Bath is beautifully built, and situated in a vale surrounded with small hills cultivated to the top; and being built of beautifully polished stone, in warm weather it is intolerably hot . . . The only thing about it which is not agreeable to the eye is the dirty ditch of a river which runs through it.[60]

Hume would not, on this occasion, visit the gaming houses, with stakes as high as at Almack's, or even attend the balls held every evening. He would avoid the sexual adventures of mixed bathing in the Cross-Bath, but confine himself to the invalid routine of 'taking the waters':

> Dr Gustard, with whom I am much taken, says that he never saw a case so much what may be called a Bath case, and in which he is more assured of the patients recovery. To tell the truth, I feel myself so much relieved that, for the first time these several months, I have today begun to open my mind to the expectations of seeing a few more years: but whether this be very desirable at my age I shall not determine. I have not ventured to write anything to Sir John Pringle till we have made a further trial.[61]

Hume was becoming frustrated with his medical experts, Black having diagnosed a haemorrhage of the intestine, Pringle a stricture of the colon, and Gustard claiming it was merely a bilious upset certain to be cleared up by the Bath waters. Whether it was this dissatisfaction or simply an advance of his condition, by 8th June he wrote to Katharine with some despondency:

My dear Katy

I know you will be much afflicted when I tell you that all the good accounts which I gave you of my recovery are overthrown. The Bath waters which I thought were agreeing with me have done me hurt, and all my bad symptoms have recurred. I believe that Sir John Pringle will be for sending me to Bristol or Spain, or God knows where, but I consider all these experiments as vexatious and troublesome, as well as fruitless and I have reason to think that Dr Black alone has conjectured the true ground and issue of my distemper . . . I have now done what my friends insisted on so earnestly, though I myself had never any hopes from it. I shall not probably stir any more from my house during the remainder of my life, which however may be longer than I shall have reason to wish it . . . my distemper may prove of a more lingering nature . . . I have a good appetite and digestion – sleep tolerably – keep my spirits, so that I may still last a long while, too long I am afraid.[62]

On 10th June he wrote to his brother:

John Hunter . . . coming accidentally to town, and expressing a very friendly concern about me, Dr Gusthart [sic] proposed that I should be examined by him; he felt very sensibly a tumour or swelling in my liver, and this fact, not drawn by reasoning, but obvious to the senses, and perceived by the greatest anatomist in Europe, must be admitted as unquestionable, and will alone account for my situation. They kept, very foolishly, this opinion of Mr Hunter's a secret from me till yesterday; and now they pretend that the tumour, being small may be discussed [dissolved] by medicines and regimen: a very silly expectation that an inveterate disease of long standing and in a vital part, will yield to their feeble remedies in a man of my years.[63]

Hume was able to feel the tumour for himself, 'about the bigness of an egg and is flat and round', and, always trusting to experience as the best tutor: 'Even St Thomas, the infidel apostle, desired no better authority than his fingers'. With this in mind he left Bath in June, planning to meet John 'Fish' Crawford in Coventry for a tour of Wales, while Hume would confidently impoverish him every evening at games of picquet. This was not to be since, before the appointed rendezvous, Hume was back in St David's Street. He would never travel again:

I had yesterday a Grand Jury of physicians who sat upon me, the Drs Cullen, Black and Home. They all agree declare the opinions of the English physicians absurd and erroneous. They own a small tumour in my liver, but so small and trivial that it could never do me material injury, and they say I might have lived twenty years with it and never have felt any inconvenience from it . . . They have thoroughly persuaded me to be of their opinion; and, according to their sentiments my distemper is now a haemorrhage as before, which is an illness that I had as lief die of as any other.[64]

It is clearly difficult for modern medicine to make a more thorough diagnosis of Hume's condition. A contemporary physician has drawn up a summary.

Medical Attendant	Diagnosis	Prognosis
Joseph Black	Intestinal haemorrhage with colic and diarrhoea	fatal
Sir John Pringle	Intestinal stricture	excellent
John Gustard	Common bilious complaint	excellent
Black, Cullen and Home	Intestinal haemorrhage and Liver tumour[65]	fatal

Another summarises:

The common factor in all the five diagnoses of Hume's physicians is that they are all affections of the digestive system and in particular of the intestine and liver. The anatomical diagnosis of the disease from which Hume died is therefore that it arose from the intestine and the liver . . . the condition of ulcerative colitis was not recognised in Hume's day . . . it is well recognised that carcinoma of the large intestine may supervene on ulcerative colitis . . . Our conclusion must be that the existence of ulcerative colitis prior to the onset of carcinoma of the large intestine in Hume's case is possible but not proved.[66]

Hume wrote to his brother on 18th July:

At present I find it almost impracticable for me to bear a chaise, and my physicians are not in the least surprised at it. It is the natural effect of the progress of my distemper, or I should have said distempers: for I certainly have both a disorder in my bowels and in my liver; though all my physicians here agree in treating the latter as a very slight malady in comparison of the former. The one, however, prevents any effectual trial of a remedy for the other: mercurial preparations would be the proper remedy for the Schirrus [a hard swelling] but dare not be given while my bowels are in such disorder – and while my liver is in a diseased state, it prevents any hopes of a cure to my bowels. Between both I am in a bad way, and may draw out to a greater length than I could wish it.[67]

Hume did not want a protracted death and had, in any case, made arrangements for his departure. He had drawn up a will on 4th January with a codicil on 15th April. His brother was to be his inheritor and executor, or, in the case of his earlier death, his second son David. Hume thought Josey too unreliable to be an executor and he was, in any case, in poor health. Katherine would inherit £1,200 and have the lease of James's Court, or, if it was sold, £20 a year for her life. In the first will she was given all English books, but this was later changed to a 'hundred red books of her own choice'. This is our only clue that Katherine was a reader and would have taken an interest in Hume's work. Peggy Irvine, now well on in years, would receive three years' salary and his other servants were bequeathed a year's wages. There were other small bequests to nephews of £1,000 each and £50 to his nieces, nephew David's £1,000 being specifically for his education. This was a fruitful investment since he rose to become became Baron Hume, Professor of Scots Law at Edinburgh University where he was tutor to Walter Scott. Ferguson and D'Alembert were to get £200 each, with a similar bequest to Adam Smith after he had overseen posthumous publication of the *Dialogues concerning Natural Religion*. Finally Edinburgh Infirmary was given £50. Having already purchased a plot for burial, he made clear arrangements:

If I shall die anywhere in Scotland, I shall be buried in a private manner in the Calton Church Yard, the South side of it, and a Monument be built over my body at an expense not exceeding a hundred pounds with an inscription containing only my name with the year of my birth and death, leaving it to posterity to add the rest.

This echoes what he had told John Home in the chaise from Morpeth.

Smith was uneasy about the task of literary executor and on 7th August Hume solved the problem with a codicil leaving his manuscripts to Strahan with instructions to publish within two years of his death. 'I desire that *My Own Life* be prefixed to the first edition of any works printed after my death, which will probably be the ones at present in the press. I desire that my brother may suppress all my other manuscripts.' In October 1776 Adam Smith refused the bequest of £200 since he had not taken charge of the manuscripts. This codicil also gave Anne Ord ten guineas to buy a ring, 'as a memorial of my friendship and attachment to so amiable and accomplished a person'. More light-heartedly:

> I leave to my friend, Mr John Home of Kilduff, ten dozen of my
> old claret at his choice; and one single bottle of that other liquor
> called port. I also leave to him six dozen of port, provided that he
> attests under his hand, signed John Hume, that he himself has
> himself alone finished that bottle at two sittings; by this concession
> he will at once terminate the only two differences that ever arose
> between us concerning temporal matters.[68]

The differences were over the spelling of the family name. Hume had offered to cast lots with John Home as to the spelling of their names. Home refused: 'Nay, that is a most extraordinary proposal indeed, Mr Philosopher. For if you lose you take your own name, and if I lose, I take another man's'.[69] Josey was given £50 to repair the drains at Ninewells, and if he had not managed to do this within the year, then the money would go to the Chirnside poor.[70]

The precise disposition of Hume's literary estate was more complicated. Still unpublished were the *Dialogues concerning Natural Religion* and two essays, *On Suicide* and *Of the Immortality of the Soul*. The *Dialogues* were written about the same time and had been revised frequently since, but Hume was, rightly, afraid of the controversy which would follow their publication:

> Some of my friends flatter me that it is the best thing that I ever
> wrote. I have hitherto forborne to publish it, because I was of late
> desirous to live quietly, and keep remote from all clamour.[71]

On 7th August Hume added the codicil leaving his manuscripts to Strahan:

> I also ordain, that if my *Dialogues,* from whatever cause, be not
> published within two years and a half of my death, as also the
> account of my life, the property shall return to my nephew David,
> whose duty, in publishing them, as the last request of his uncle,
> must be approved of by all the world.[72]

However, back in July, Hume was patently declining in health and his desire to be remote from all clamour was thwarted when James Boswell called on the 7th. In his journal Boswell records a conversation which must rank as one of the most tactless ever held, also as an outstanding record of how to bring the least comfort to an invalid:

> Thought I would go and see Mr David Hume who was returned
> from London and Bath, just a-dying. I found him alone, in a
> reclining posture in his drawing room. He was lean, ghastly, and
> quite of an earthy appearance. He was dressed in a suit of grey
> cloth with white metal buttons, and a kind of scratch wig. He
> was quite different from the plump figure which he used to
> represent. He had before him Dr Campbell's *Philosophy of
> Rhetoric.* He seemed to be placid and even cheerful. He said he
> was just approaching his end. I think those were his words. I
> know not how I managed to get the subject of immortality
> introduced. He said he had never entertained any thought of
> religion since he had read Locke and Clarke. I asked him if he
> was not religious when he was young. He said he was and he
> used to read *The Whole Duty of Man*: that he made an abstract
> from the catalogue of vices at the end of it, and examined himself
> by this, leaving out murder and theft and such vices as he had no
> chance of committing, having no inclination of committing . . .
> He then said flatly that the morality of every religion was bad,
> and, I really thought, was not jocular when he said that when he
> heard a man was religious, he concluded he was a rascal, though
> he had known some instances of very good men being
> religious . . . I had a strong curiosity to be satisfied if he persisted
> in disbelieving a future state even when he had death before his
> eyes . . . I asked him if it were not possible that there might be a

future state. He answered that it was possible that a piece of coal put upon the fire would not burn; and he added that it was a most unreasonable fancy that we should exist forever. That immortality, if it were at all, must be general, that a great proportion of the human race has hardly any intellectual qualities; that a great proportion of the human race dies in infancy before being possessed of reason; yet all these must be immortal; that a porter who gets drunk by ten o'clock with gin must be immortal; that the trash of every age must be preserved, and that new universes must be created to contain such infinite numbers. This appeared to be an unphilosophical objection, and I said, 'Mr Hume, you know spirit does not take up space'. I asked him if the thought of annihilation never gave him any uneasiness. He said not the least; no more than the thought that he had not been. 'Well,' said I, 'Mr Hume, I hope to triumph over you when I meet you in a future state, and remember you are not to pretend that you was joking with all this infidelity.' 'No, no', said he, 'But I shall have been so long there before you come that it will be nothing new.' In this style of good humour and levity did I conduct the conversation. Perhaps it was wrong on so awful a subject. But as nobody was present, I thought it could have no bad effect . . . the truth is that Mr Hume's pleasantry was such that there was no solemnity in the scene and death for the time did not seem dismal . . . Mr Lauder, his surgeon came in for a little and Mr Mure, the Baron's son, for another small interval. He was, as far as I could judge, quite easy with both. He said he had no pain, but was wasting away. I left him with impressions which disturbed me for some time . . . He said, 'If there were a future state, Mr. Boswell, I think I could give as good account of my life as most people.'[73]

While this tells us much about Boswell's sense of self-importance, it also shows Hume's toleration of other points of view.

He was now almost housebound, his absence of pain, almost certainly, being achieved by an intake of laudanum, and could only make short journeys in a sedan chair. He was, in his own words, 'going as fast as his enemies could wish and as easily as his friends could desire'. While sending Strahan the inevitable corrections to the *Essays* he said, 'my physicians say everywhere that they have cured me, which is very agreeable intelligence, though somewhat new to me'.[74] What was less welcome was the fact that Katherine was also unwell. On 25th July, 'Our sister has become very infirm She keeps to bed this day from a slight fever', and four days later Katherine has 'lost her judgement' and he is 'obliged to put a keeper upon her'. Other deaths were coming close to him, and on 20th August he wrote one of his most poignant letters. It was to Mme de Boufflers:

> Though I am certainly within a few weeks, dear Madam, and perhaps within a few days, of my own death, I could not forbear being struck with the death of the Prince de Conti – so great a loss in every particular. My reflection carried me immediately to your situation in this melancholy incident. What a difference to you in your whole plan of life! Pray write me some particulars; but in such terms that you need not care, in case of decease, into whose hands your letter may fall. My distemper is a diarrhoea, or disorder in my bowels, which has been gradually undermining me these two years; but, within these last six months, has been visibly hastening me to my end. I see death approach gradually, without any anxiety or regret. I salute you, with great affection and regard, for the last time.[76]

There is no record of a reply to this letter. By this time Mme de Boufflers had become the mistress of Gustav III of Sweden, and at his death in 1792 she returned to France. After a brief exile and arrest during the Revolution she died in 1800 at the age of seventy-five.

Hume was visited by Katherine Muir, widow of John, and he presented her with a copy of his *History*. She was grateful for the gift but fearful for his reputation: 'O David, that's a book you may well be proud of. But before you dee you should burn all your wee bookies'. Hume managed to raise himself on his elbow and fix her with a questioning eye: 'And what for should I burn all my wee bookies?' She left before the debate could take place.[77]

Adam Smith visited Hume and hoped for a recovery, but Hume told him:

> Your hopes are groundless. An habitual diarrhoea of more than a year's standing would be a very bad disease at any age; at my age it is a mortal one. When I lie down in the evening I feel myself

weaker than when I rose in the morning; and when I rise in the morning weaker than when I lay down in the evening. I am sensible, besides, that some of my vital parts are affected, so that I must soon die.[78]

He fantasised to Smith as to how he would delay getting into Charon's boat, claiming that he had urgent corrections to make to his works and that he would 'open the eyes of the public'. He even might see the downfall of some of the prevailing systems of superstition. But Charon, he thought, would be adamant: 'Get into the boat this instant, you lazy loitering rogue'. Naturally he would soon pass into the Classical Hades, with no sign of St Peter and the gates of Heaven.

His nephew, John, came to be with Hume on the 20th and his last letter, on the 23rd, was written by John at Hume's dictation. It was to Adam Smith concerning the fate of his manuscripts and advising Smith that, as he was now only conscious for a few hours daily, there was no point in visiting him.

Joseph Black, Hume's physician, broke the news of his death to Adam Smith on Monday, 26th August:

Yesterday about 4 o'clock Mr Hume expired. The immediate approach of his death became evident in the night between Thursday and Friday when the looseness became very excessive and was attended with vomiting now and then and this continued the greater part of the time that remained and so weakened him that he could no longer rise out of his bed. He continued to the last perfectly sensible and free from pain or feelings of distress. He never dropped the smallest expression of impatience but when he had occasion to speak to the people about him always did it with affection and tenderness. I thought it improper to write to bring you over, especially as I had heard that he had dictated a letter to you on Thursday or Wednesday desiring you not to come. When he became very weak it cost him an effort to speak and he died in such a happy composure of mind that nothing could have made it better.[79]

Neither the *Caledonian Mercury* nor the *Edinburgh Evening Courant* noted Hume's death, preferring news from the newly declared independent America. The *Scots Magazine,* however, did carry an obituary, noting that the philosopher had died after:

a tedious illness . . . the region of metaphysics he soon looked through and abandoned. The laurels he duly valued were in another soil – in both lines after ages will extol and admire the author. They behold in his character the most agreeable contradictions. The virtues of humanity, unshaken by the most absolute scepticism: the moral duties of this life flourishing under a total disregard of another, and even the graces and temper of a Christian, in an avowed enemy of the Christian faith.[80]

On Thursday 29th the funeral took place with a large crowd braving a heavy rainstorm. One of two legends tells that one man in the crowd called out, 'Ye ken he was an atheist!' to which someone else replied, 'Aye, but he was honest!' The other legend is that some of the crowd waited in the graveyard, fearfully crouched behind gravestones, to see if the devil would appear to carry off the Great Infidel's soul. They got fruitlessly soaked for their pains. James Boswell certainly records that he watched the interment while concealed behind a wall. He then went to the Advocates' Library and read some of Hume's essays, 'somewhat dejected in mind'. Hume's family wisely employed two guards to prevent desecration of the grave.

In February of 1776 'a lair four yards by five' had been bought by Hume for £4 and in 1778 John Hume had bought additional ground. Robert Adam set about sketching a 'severe Roman drum' and the verso of his sketch in 1776 shows a pencil projection of the tomb atop the Calton Hill. Workshop drawings followed but the sketch 'Type VI' is an octagon on a square base in Adam's own hand with some additional enthusiastic vegetation.[81] The final result is merely the drum without the octagon. 'Was it just that Uncle David had left only £100 for the purpose and arches and octagons were awfully expensive?'[82]

The monument was duly built by Robert Adam in 1777. Adam Smith thought it a piece of atypical vanity and today it is surrounded by the unsavoury litter of drug addiction. Hume, however, cannot be blamed for the truly appalling statue recently erected outside the Sheriff Court in Edinburgh. He is portrayed, seated, half clad in a toga, holding, but not reading, a book. As a portrayal of a voracious reader and a fashionable dresser it does nothing to embody the spirit of one of the greatest of Edinburgh's men of genius.

FOURTEEN

The Legacy

A lthough David Hume's body lay in the Calton burial ground, his acquaintanceship with controversy was by no means over since *My Own Life, Of Suicide, Of the Immortality of the Soul* and the *Dialogues Concerning Natural Religion* still remained in Strahan's hands unpublished.

Now, in accordance with Hume's will, the *Dialogues* and *My Own Life* were to be published. *My Own Life* would create no controversy but the *Dialogues* had been read by Adam Smith who had severe reservations about the wisdom of publication, 'The latter, though finely written, I could have wished remained in manuscript to be communicated only to a few people'.[1] Hugh Blair had read the *Dialogues* in 1763, when Hume was about to leave for Paris, and made his views clear:

As far [as] your present journey, though I with the rest of your friends most sincerely regret your absence, yet I entirely approve of it. You are going to a country where you will want nothing of being worshipped, except bowing the knee to you . . . in several Poker clubs in Paris your statue would have been erected. If you show them the MSS of certain dialogues perhaps this honour may still be done you. But, for God's sake, let that be a posthumous work, if ever it shall see the light – though I really think it had better not.[2]

Also in 1763 Hume had admonished Elliot of Minto:

Is it not hard and tyrannical in you, more tyrannical than any Act of the Stuarts, not to allow me to publish my Dialogues? Pray, do you not think that a proper dedication may atone for what is exceptionable in them?[3]

Hume has his tongue in his cheek here and, in any case, loathed dedications. But the roguish tone hides the fact that he knew the *Dialogues* would place him once more in the jaws of controversy.

In 1777 Strahan took the plunge and the two essays, at least, were published simply as *Two Essays* but with the names of neither the author nor the publisher on the title page. The manuscript of *Of Suicide* has numerous corrections and revisions, but the published work contains none of these revisions. Fortunately for contemporary readers, the version published by the Liberty Fund in 1987 uses the corrected manuscript version in the National Library of Scotland.

It is not hard to find the reason for everyone's caution about publication, and the very first sentence was bound to offend:

> One considerable advantage that arises from philosophy consists in the sovereign antidote which it affords to superstition and false religion. All other remedies against that pestilential distemper are vain, or at least, uncertain.[4]

If we believe that every event was predestined by God, then it follows that suicide must be part of the divine plan:

> Is it because human life is of so great importance that it is a presumption for human prudence to dispose of it? But the life of a man is of no greater importance to the universe than the life of an oyster.[5]

He cannot but see suicide as a perfectly valid choice when 'the horror of pain prevails over the love of life'. If the sin in suicide is taken as wilfully disturbing God's work, then, logically, it is an equal sin to divert a river for irrigation purposes or, even, pluck wild fruit. He ends with an exhortation which would have sent the conservative clergy into paroxysms of rage:

> If suicide be considered a crime, 'tis only cowardice can impel us to it. If it be no crime, both prudence and courage should engage us to rid ourselves at once of existence when it becomes a burden. 'Tis the only way that we can be useful to society, by setting an example, which, if imitated, would preserve to every one his chances for happiness in life, and would effectually free him from all danger of misery.[6]

He continues in a footnote:

> There is not a single text of scripture which prohibits it [suicide] . . . Resignation to providence is, indeed, recommended in scripture; but that implies only submission to ills which are unavoidable, not to such as may be remedied by prudence or courage.[7]

In other words, the strictures against suicide are entirely man-made without any scriptural authority and without any basis in reason. If your emotions tell you that life is truly unbearable, you should have the courage to end it. 'Reason is, or should be, the slave of the passions.'

In *Of the Immortality of the Soul* Hume finds the arguments for immortality beyond reason and all the justifications for the soul's existence false:

> The arguments for it are commonly derived either from
> metaphysical topics, or moral or physical. But in reality, it is the
> gospel, and the gospel alone, that has brought life and immortality
> to light.[8]

Here there is scriptural authority and Hume deals briskly with the metaphysical belief that the soul is immaterial and that it is impossible for thought to belong to a material substance. But, as Hume proved in the *Treatise,* abstract reason alone cannot establish a fact. Also, if the soul is immortal, it existed before our birth, and since we know nothing of our life before birth we can presume nothing as to the existence of a life after death. The moral argument is based largely on the concept of reward or punishment after death, but, if everything is ordained by God, then he cannot judge men for carrying out what, after all, was his will. Physically, mankind is conditioned to fear death, but if there is immortality, then there is no death and nature has cheated itself:

> All doctrines are to be suspected which are favoured by our
> passions. And the hopes and fears which give rise to this doctrine
> are very obvious . . . Nothing could set in a fuller light the infinite
> obligations which mankind have to divine revelation: since we find
> that no other medium could ascertain this great and important
> truth.[9]

The passions, untrammelled by their slave, reason, cannot be trusted and men have therefore backed them up by ascribing their knowledge of immortality to divine revelation. As John Calvin said of the arguments surrounding the problem of predestination, 'It is a mystery known only to God!' and Hume could not diminish man's powers of reason by accepting divine revelation as such a catch-all answer. The controversy continues to this day with no less a figure than Doctor Tom Wright, Bishop of Durham, denying the immortality of the soul.

Reaction to these essays was slow in coming but in 1783 the works were republished, this time naming Hume as the author, with a violent rebuttal. This was the somewhat ponderously titled *Essays on Suicide and the Immortality of the Soul ascribed to the late David Hume, never before published with remarks intended as an Antidote to the poisons contained in their Performances.*

The essays were reprinted in this volume and were followed by the anonymous article *Anti Suicide* which starts with an attack on philosophy itself: 'It is indeed hard to say what reason might do were it freed from all restraints'.[10] Presumably reason controlled by the passions was too horrifying to be contemplated, and since philosophers were forever improving on one another, matters could only get worse. The author was writing from behind the selective filters of Highflying clerical rigidity. 'Neither priestcraft nor magisterial power cramped the progress of improving reason or baffled the genius of enquiring man.'[11] Presumably neither the persecution of Galileo nor Socrates' death sentence ever took place. The author asserts that liberality of thought has led to disaster, but that the remedy is at hand. 'Mankind are certainly at present in a state of deepest corruption and depravity, and at the same time apt to continue strangely insensible of the misery and dangers to which, under the government of infinite wisdom, it necessarily renders them . . . A steadfast belief of religion is, in truth, the best antidote or remedy for each of them.'[12] Having freed the world from the pernicious evils of philosophy, the rules are established. 'It seems to be a maxim in human existence that no creature has a right to decide peremptorily on the importance, utility, or necessity of his own being . . . It is the prerogative of Heaven alone to kill and make alive'.[13] The attack on the validity of suicide ends by stating that the idea that orthodoxy can be challenged clearly arises from ignorance. 'This impious slander on the Christian faith is the obvious consequence of the grossest inattention to its nature and tendency.'[14]

Turning to the *Immortality of the Soul,* the author sets the tone from the start with some contorted English: 'The ingenuity of Scepticism has been long admired but here the author boldly outdoes all his former outdoings'.[15] Hume's statement that a life filled with the fear of death is contrary to a belief in immortality is reversed by orthodoxy. 'Strange that in the view, and even in the arms of an infinite power and goodness, a dawn so fair and promising, should at once be clouded with all the horrors of eternal night? Such a supposition would be contrary to the whole conduct and the laws of nature.'[16] The work ends by reprinting an exchange of letters from Rousseau's *Nouvelle Héloise* containing the arguments for and against suicide.

The refutation is neither witty nor fresh and merely restates orthodoxy but it is interesting that it was published six years after the *Essays* appeared. While Hume was alive, the attack would have been immediate and aimed directly at the man himself. Now it is merely a long-forgotten comment on the writings of a dead philosopher.

Strahan still had the manuscript of the *Dialogues* in his possession but was even more reluctant to publish that work. He vacillated for two years, finally returning the text to Hume's nephew David who courageously did publish it in Edinburgh as a single volume in 1779.

Hume starts the work with a justification for using the form of dialogue to present it. There were already distinguished forerunners to the dialogue form with Cicero's *De Natura Deorum* and Galileo's *Dialogue concerning the two chief World Systems*. Hume had used it himself in *A Dialogue*, published in 1751 with *An Enquiry concerning the Principles of Morals*. Now he admits that a system of philosophy delivered as a conversation is scarcely natural, but that a one-to-one dialogue, such as that of Socrates and Plato, simply conveys the image of pedagogue and pupil. Here the subject is obvious, and, at the same time, important, so:

> the vivacity of conversation may enforce the precept, and where the variety of lights, presented by various personages and characters, may appear neither tedious nor redundant.[17]

However, Professor Mossner suggested another possible reason:

> Even in the relatively tolerant intellectual society of eighteenth century Britain, prudence demanded that any attack on religion, natural or revealed, especially natural *and* revealed as in the present case, had better be written by indirection, that is, ironically.[18]

But, as we have seen, society was not altogether tolerant and Hume had already established the setting of the work in a dialogue some time in 1751 when he explained his ideas to Elliot of Minto. The *Dialogues* were to examine 'natural' religion, that is, the religion that is inherent in us and put there by God. In effect the discussion strayed into an examination of 'revealed' religion, where faith inspires belief. There were to be two principal characters, Cleanthes, the philosophical theist, and Philo the sceptic. Hume felt that Minto might do well as a model for Cleanthes with Hume himself as Philo. A character called Demea interjects from time to time as a convinced natural theist and, as his model, Hume probably had Samuel Clarke in mind. Clarke felt that moral judgements could be as certain as those in mathematics and that a proof of God's existence could be found by the use of mathematics. The readers of the *Dialogues* would have no difficulty in recognising the views of Philo as Hume's own, and therefore Hume, with his tongue firmly in his cheek, lets Cleanthes win the argument. Hume has refined his authorial skills to the point where he now creates fully three-dimensional characters.

The book opens with, for Hume, an ideal circumstance: learned men encountering each other in a library to debate with Pamphilus acting as commentator. Demea sets out his idea for a system of philosophic education, with the study of natural theology only being attempted when there is a mind 'enriched with all the other sciences'. The young mind must be 'seasoned with early piety' when studying the 'strange ridiculous conclusions which some of the greatest geniuses have derived from the principles of mere human reason'. Philo appears to agree and now argues, heavy with Humean irony, for an examination of this 'frail faculty of reason'. Both Demea and Cleanthes agree to hear this, Demea believing Philo will endorse his argument, while Cleanthes smiles at the coming trap. He expects Philo will show that through scepticism at its most extreme man can believe nothing whatsoever.

Philo says that 'the larger experience we acquire, and the stronger reason we are endowed with, we always render our principles the more general and comprehensive: and that [which] we call philosophy is nothing more but a more regular and methodical operation of the same kind'. Cleanthes then proposes that the sceptics believe so little and can disprove so much that they are left with a need for a higher certainty and 'tend to the confirmation of true religion, and serve to confound the cavils of atheists, libertines, and freethinkers of all denominations'.

At the start of Part II Demea is delighted by this apparent, if negative, proof of God's existence by Cleanthes and wants to move to an examination of the nature of so self-evident a God, while Cleanthes gives what has become known as the Argument from Design. The world is one great machine with infinite subdivisions, much as though designed by man. This was very close to some of the theories Hume met while he was dining with the *philosophes*. The author of nature is, therefore, possessed of an intelligence analogous to man's. But, argues Philo, there can be no proof of the cause of anything created. However, Cleanthes goes on to argue that scepticism strengthens the argument for religion since the sceptic tries to trace causes from effects and his greatest errors proceed from 'too luxuriant a fertility [of thought] which suppresses your animal good sense'.

Philo is confounded by this and Demea interjects that since God's ways are not our ways and 'his attributes are perfect, but incomprehensible . . . and that the infirmities of our nature do not permit us to reach any ideas which in the least correspond to the ineffable sublimity of the divine attributes', God will inevitably defy description. This puzzles Cleanthes who asks Demea how he can conceive of a God who is so unlike man in thought and accuses him of mysticism. Angered by this, Demea counters that the soul of man is a composition of distinct faculties, while God is all things for all times, unchanging and complete. Cleanthes says that a god like this, simple and immutable, has no thought, no will and is no mind at all. Therefore mystics are, in fact, atheists.

Philo, sensing that the argument is becoming heated, changes course to look at the cause of creation, as judged by its effects. 'A mental world, or universe of ideas requires a cause as much as does a material world or a universe of objects.' But then what was the cause of the cause – and so on *ad infinitum* back to the mind of the Supreme Being where different ideas fall into order or their own volition? So why can we not allow that this applies also to the material world? Cleanthes interrupts Philo 'You ask me "what is the cause of the cause?" I know not, I care not; that concerns not me. I have found a deity, and here I stop my enquiry. Let those go further, who are wiser or more enterprising'. Philo accuses him of being vague and tells him that he cannot believe that 'so wild and unsettled a system of theology is, in any respect, preferable to none at all'. But, says Cleanthes, causes imply design and there must, therefore, be a designer 'and to this concession I adhere steadily and this I regard as a sufficient foundation for religion'.

At this point:

> The only position we have so far is the anthropomorphic theism
> proposed by Cleanthes. It is the one we are being asked to accept
> in lieu of any better system of thought. This is the provisional
> conclusion which Hume had in mind, doubtless when he spoke to
> Elliot of making Cleanthes the hero of his argument.[19]

Part VI starts with Philo decrying Cleanthes for his weak grasp of faith and Philo argues that the universe is the sum of its parts and is like an animal with the deity as its soul. Also if one asserts that our limited experience is an unequal standard by which to judge the unlimited extent of nature, the absolute incomprehensibility of the divine nature is, in itself, a proof of its existence. Cleanthes cannot at first reply to this sophistry, but then says that, since the world has no organs of sense and no origin of motion, it is more like a vegetable than an animal and so cannot have a soul. He also cannot maintain a belief in the eternity of the world. There would have to be 'total convulsion of the elements'. Philo cannot see why there should have been such 'convulsions' in the past, but 'Chance has no place on any hypothesis, sceptical or religious. Everything is surely governed by steady, inviolable laws. And were the inmost essence of things laid open to us, we should then discover a scene, of which at present, we can have no idea'.

This seems to lead us towards Stephen Hawking's dream of 'knowing the mind of God'.

In Part VIII Philo asks whether an altogether different and unfamiliar cause rather than a simulacrum of human intelligence could have made the world as it is. Cleanthes dismisses this, saying that while such whimsies may puzzle us, they will never convince us. Philo proposes that rather than intelligence there is a system of natural selection which has produced the present state of existence. There are, in fact, so many possible explanations that a total suspense of judgement is the only reasonable resource. While theologians have fixed and contradictory ideas, the free thinker 'who remains, with all mankind, on the offensive' must prevail. The idea is that God is faintly analogous to human intelligence, and that our possessing such intelligence leads to the belief in the existence of God. But pure intelligence cannot have a moral sense:

> So the conduct of human life remains as it did. The religious
> hypothesis is impotent. There is no natural religion. Revealed
> religion is sanctioned only by faith which is a miracle and
> unphilosophical. What remains? Man, intrepid and enlightened
> man, stands starkly alone to fend for himself in an indifferent
> nature.[20]

This was, in fact, a direct refutation of Hutcheson's idea of a God-given sense of moral good:

Hume's analysis of 'natural' religion had the effect of destroying a whole tradition of theological reflection. That is not to say, of course, that no examples of this tradition survive; they do and they always will. It is to say that Hume discredited this tradition utterly.[21]

Demea clearly feels that the argument is getting away from its purpose and suggests that instead of arguing *a posteriori*, it would be more fruitful to examine the case *a priori*. His argument is exactly that of Samuel Clarke in his Boyle lectures of 1704 and 1705 when he published them as *A discourse concerning the Being and Attributes of God*. Hume had read this and rejected its arguments when a student. To recap, the argument is that the universe exists now and must have evolved from something – nothing can evolve from nothing – therefore there is an infinitely existent Being, that is, God. This is pounced on by Cleanthes:

Nothing is demonstrable unless the contrary implies a contradiction. Nothing that is distinctly conceivable implies a contradiction. Whatever we conceive as existent, we can also conceive as non-existent. There is no Being, therefore, whose non-existence implies a contradiction. Consequently there is no Being whose existence is demonstrable. I propose this argument as entirely decisive, and am willing to rest the whole controversy upon it.

Philo agrees wholeheartedly with this argument, claiming that the *a priori* argument has only ever pleased 'people of a metaphysical head' and that most people find their religion in other sources.

Demea shifts ground again, weakly arguing that all men look forward to futurity and appeasing unknown powers. Part X deals with the three problems of 'Is God willing to prevent evil, but not able? Why, if God can prevent evil, he allows so much of it to exist? Whence then is evil?' The scholar William H. Capitan describes this as a 'trilemma' put by Philo. 'He is demolishing natural religion, not by disproving God's existence, but by invalidating the argument to God's moral attributes.'[22] This goes far to destroy the argument of God as an omnipotent 'designer' and leaves Cleanthes 'resting the whole system of religion on a point which, from its very nature, must be forever uncertain [and so] you tacitly confess that that system is equally uncertain'; here Philo rests his case and challenges Cleanthes. 'It is your turn now to tug the labouring oar, and to support your philosophical subtilities against the dictates of plain reason and experience.'

Cleanthes says that to drop the analogy with humanity is to abandon all religion, but that an abstract benevolence, regulated by wisdom and limited by necessity, may produce such a world as at present. Following this, Philo asks if this world is what a reasonable man might expect from an abstract benevolent deity and delineates the four circumstances on which depend all our ills. Firstly, pains, as well as pleasures, excite all creatures to action in the great work of self-preservation; secondly, the world is ruled by general, not particular, laws; thirdly, all particular beings are equipped with only the powers they need for existence; fourthly, the system by which all of these factors coincide is extremely inaccurate and seemingly random – rain brings fertility but also floods, winds allow us to navigate but can become destructive hurricanes. Could a beneficient and omnipotent Being have created the world as it is? Here Philo drops his pretence and offers a bleak and rational view of the world:

> The only method of supporting divine benevolence (and that is what I willingly embrace) is to deny absolutely the misery and wickedness of man . . . Look round this universe. What an immense profusion of beings, animated and organised, sensible and active! You admire this prodigious variety and fecundity. But inspect a little more narrowly these living existences, the only beings worth regarding. How hostile and destructive to each other! How insufficient all of them for their own happiness! How contemptible or odious to the spectator! The whole presents nothing but the idea of a blind nature, impregnated by a great vivifying principle, and pouring forth from her lap, without discernment or parental care, her maimed and abortive children.

He is interrupted by Demea, who at last sees that Philo and Cleanthes are on the same side. Cleanthes tells him that, far from being an ally, Philo has been amusing himself at their expense. He has led them into voicing the extreme views of learned divines. Philo asks Cleanthes to show some admiration for these divines who can change their views so easily. Demea is furious that he has been the victim of a trick and storms off.

In the last part of the *Dialogues* Cleanthes, who is clearly exhausted by the whole affair, says that he will never again debate with Philo and Demea together and Philo apologises for his extreme stance:

. . . in proportion to my veneration for true religion, is my
abhorrence of vulgar superstitions: and I indulge a peculiar pleasure,
I confess, in pushing such principles, sometimes into absurdity,
sometimes into impiety. And you are sensible that all bigots,
notwithstanding their great aversion to the latter above the former,
are commonly equally guilty of both.

Cleanthes disagrees: 'Religion, however corrupted, is better than no
religion at all'. Philo points out the horrors from history committed in
the name of religion and Cleanthes tells him that they were the base acts
of men committed under the cloak of religion. Philo answers that, except
for philosophical and rational religion, all other kinds of religion will be
used similarly. 'Take care, Philo, replied Cleanthes, take care: push not
matters too far: allow not your zeal against false religion to undermine
your veneration for the true.' Philo accepts that he must be guided by
reason and that, 'to be a philosophic sceptic is, in a man of letters, the first
and most essential step towards being a sound, believing Christian'. He
adds ambivalently, 'the whole of natural theology . . . resolves itself into
one simple, though somewhat ambiguous, at least undefined proposition
that the cause or causes of order in the universe probably bear some remote
analogy to human intelligence'. Hume concludes, 'I cannot but think that
Philo's principles are more probable than Demea's, but those of Cleanthes
approach still nearer the truth'.

The result of the debate is a draw, or that purely Scottish legal verdict,
'not proven'. It is true that the *Dialogues* prove neither the existence nor
non-existence of God, either in the sense of a true divinity or in the Deist
construct of a Supreme Being created by mankind. But running through
all of it is the belief that the difficulties of life, war, cruelty, greed, etc.,
have been caused by man himself and can be solved only by man. Natural
hazards, earthquakes, famines, etc., occur by chance and must be borne by
mankind as best they can. It is up to man to shine a light into the darkness
and to deal with what he finds there:

This enlightened, Humean way of life may appropriately, albeit
ironically, be named the *religion of man*. Call this creative scepticism
and declaration of independence, humanism, or naturalism, or
neopaganism, or secularism, or positivism, or pragmatism, or
agnosticism, or what you will, it is a serene and confident
affirmation, in the most authentic voice of the Enlightenment, of

the perennial theme of the dignity of man, his dignity in living and his dignity in dying. In the most profound sense, this ironic insight into the *religion of man* 'philosophical and rational' is the legacy out of the grave, as it were, of David Hume's *Dialogues of Natural Religion*.[23]

And:

As far as revealed religion is concerned Hume's judgement is wholly negative. It is indeed veiled in irony, but the irony is thin, the animus is clear and his contempt total . . . Two hundred years before its appointed time and in the idiom of its own day, Hume has made clear to us the doctrinal emptiness of secularised Christianity.[24]

Given that in *Of Miracles* Hume had argued that, to be miraculous, events had to be impossible and were, therefore, illusory; that in *Of the Immortality of the Soul* he had denied the concept of immortality and the existence of a soul; and that in the *Dialogues* he disproved the existence of natural religion and allowed that acceptance of revealed religion needed a miraculous event – faith over reason – why did he take so much time and trouble to write what, after all, would only bring opprobrium?

Hume's childhood education was clerically dominated. He was taught, either by his uncle, the minister of Chirnside, or by a teacher working closely with the minister. The family at Ninewells, indeed the house itself, were in the shadow of the kirk, and the attitude of the countryside was one of subservience to the teaching of the church. At university in Edinburgh Hume would have been exposed to the first hints of radical thought. There was a groundswell of debate which included examinations of church teaching, but deference was still paid, at least in public, to traditional views. From Europe Descartes, Spinoza, and, above all, Bayle would have been studied, even if covertly, by the student body and the works of British thinkers such as Hobbes, Locke and Berkeley would have circulated. The student clubs were notorious for free thinking and the radicalism endemic in universities flourished. The professors, largely, regarded this as a healthy student fad which would pass, and as 'Jupiter' Carlyle commented, most of the student body went on to be God-fearing lawyers or even ministers. But the fad did not pass for David Hume, and during his time of mental anguish at Ninewells between 1727 and 1734 he rejected the accepted teachings of the church:

> His thoughts on religion were 'a perpetual struggle of a restless imagination against inclination, perhaps over reason'. But it seems likely that the struggle was over by the time Hume was eighteen . . . and Hume never again lapsed into orthodoxy.[25]

In all probability Hume did not make his views too stridently clear to his family and he found the effort bordering on hypocrisy. Thirty years later he summed up his views on hypocrisy:

> Is it putting too great a respect on the vulgar, and on their superstitions, to pique one's self on sincerity with regard to them? Did one ever make it a point of honour to speak truth to children or madmen? . . . I wish it were still in my power to be a hypocrite in this particular. The common duties of society usually require it; and the ecclesiastical profession only adds a little more to an innocent dissimulation, or rather simulation, without which it is impossible to pass through the world. Am I a liar, because I order my servant to say, I am not at home, when I do not wish to see company?[26]

Religious thought was still as dogmatic as it ever had been and the teaching of it was vulgarised in order to be intelligible to all:

> What characterised the dominant religious thought of the period was a sustained attempt to secure for the propositions of religion a firm foundation which could make them acceptable to any man of sound mind and common sense.[27]

The Shorter Catechism, in which the basic tenets of Christianity were set out as questions with indisputable answers, was taught to all children. Argument was severely discouraged, so that dogma became part of life and believers felt that either they had discovered religious truth for themselves or that it had been God-given from birth:

> Eventually in *The Natural History of Religion* Hume fused his hypothesis of hypocrisy and delusion into a theory of self-deception which explained the religious believer as a victim of his own habit of dissimulation.[28]

Hume had little regard for the intellectual capacity of the 'religious believer' whom he believed had not the capability to embrace philosophy:

> The vulgar – a densely populated class in Hume's estimate – would find little satisfaction in so spare a doctrine and some inconvenience in performing real rather than ceremonial duties.[29]

> We may conclude, therefore, upon the whole, that, since the vulgar, in nations, which have embraced the doctrine of theism, still build it upon irrational and superstitious principles, they are never led into that opinion by any process of argument, but by a certain train of thinking, more suited to their genius and capacity.[30]

Also since Christianity was based on a miraculous event, itself an impossibility, and not on the truth achievable only by philosophy, it was proscribed by his old mentor, Bayle:

> In short, there's so much probability, any worship which subsists upon a falsehood will one time or another degenerate, that we should never give quarter to error on what pretences soever . . . But there's no prescribing against truth, 'twas the highest injustice to leave it continually buried in obscurity, on pretence it had never seen the light.[31]

Where Hume examined religions for himself he found, firstly and unsurprisingly, that he held a grudging preference for the Classical Gods in that they only indulged in lust, incest and adultery, while the Christian God deals out cruelty, wrath, fury, vengeances and 'all the blackest vices'. He had a dislike of exalting a fount of vengeance, albeit one held to be divine:

> Popular religions are really, in the conception of the more vulgar votaries, a species of daemonism; and the higher the deity is exalted in power and knowledge, the lower of course is he depressed in goodness and benevolence.[32]

And he is disgusted with the unintellectual acceptance of such dogma:

> Survey most nations and most ages. Examine the religious principles which have, in fact, prevailed in the world. You will scarcely be persuaded they are anything but sick men's dreams: or perhaps will regard them as the playsome whimsies of monkeys in human shape,

than the serious positive, dogmatical asseverations of a being who dignifies himself the name of rational.[33]

He knew he was attacking one of the principal branches of the establishment and decrying much of the world's beliefs. He had excused himself in 1741 in the essay *Of the Dignity or Meanness of Human Nature,* 'I am sensible that a delicate sense of morals, especially when attended by a splenetic temper, is apt to give man a disgust of the world'.[34] Except when being criticised for his whist playing tactics, I can find no trace of a 'splenetic temper' – but no matter.

Taking the *Dialogues* and the *Natural History* together, Charles Hendel summed up, saying:

> . . . religion when not infected by superstition and fanaticism, yields no inference that can be the source of any action, or forbearance, and no motives superior to, or additional to, the motives proper to ordinary everyday morality . . . Hume's attitude to true religion can therefore be summed up in the threefold thesis: (1) that it consists exclusively in intellectual assent to the 'somewhat ambiguous, at least undefined' proposition – God exists; (2) that the God here affirmed is not the God as ordinarily understood; and (3) as a corollary from (1) and (2) that religion ought not to have, and when 'true' and 'genuine' does not have, any influence on human conduct – beyond, that is to say, its intellectual effects, as rendering the mind immune to superstition and fanaticism. Hume attacks not religion, but superstition and idolatry, he questions not the existence of God, but only the mistaken arguments for such existence, and the unworthy modes of conception in which they result.[35]

Hendel also asserts that Hume was, in the *Dialogues,* dramatising the inner conflict of his own mind. It does, however, seem more likely that this conflict was long over. 'Once he had succeeded in formulating the general lines of his own philosophy, he had quite definitely concluded that religion is not merely an ambiguous but in the main a malign influence.'[36] This is the more likely view of Kemp Smith, echoed by James Noxon: 'It was the challenge of explaining the religious beliefs professed by others, I suggest, that sustained Hume's interest in religion long after he had lost his own belief in it'.[37] Hume himself set out his views on religion in *Of Miracles,* written in 1737:

> . . . we may conclude, that the Christian religion not only was first
> attended with miracles, but even at this day cannot be believed by
> any reasonable person without one. Mere reason is insufficient to
> convince us of its veracity: And whoever is moved by faith to assent
> to it, is conscious of a continued miracle in his own person, which
> subverts all the principles of his understanding, and gives him a
> determination to believe what is most contrary to custom and
> experience.[38]

For Hume custom and experience led to human understanding, and, 'it is
precisely because he bases morality upon human nature that he divorces
morality from the religion of his time'.[39] His God was the human intellect:

> Of course the God whom Hume accepts is not the traditional
> Judeo-Christian God, for Hume does not believe that we know
> anything about the deity. This God is the God of the philosophers,
> a kind of principle of order, although we really do not, and
> probably never will, fully comprehend it.[40]

Many critics have accused Hume of abandoning philosophy after the
reception of his *Treatise* and some have accused Hume of writing about
religion only to advance his career. Since three of his works were
posthumous it is difficult to see how this could advance his career. But
academics have continued to attack Hume's motives even up to recent
times. In 1930 Vinding Kruse, the Danish scholar, accused him of not
seeking philosophical, but literary, fame and suppressing his most radical
ideas for public appreciation. Kruse gives us no clue as to how he
discovered Hume's suppressed ideas, and since Hume regarded the public
as his 'supreme court', this theory is unlikely. Professor J.H. Randall
attacked him for writing for fame and to make money, presumably from
the point of view of one holding academic tenure and having no need to
earn a living from his pen.

Hume's discussion of religion in all its aspects is, in fact, thoroughly
philosophical and in his time no serious thinker could fail to debate the
accepted belief that God exists and gives us an innate belief in morality:

> Two motives inspire this argument about the nature of the deity.
> One is our human interest. We cannot restrain our inquiry about
> what God is, even though we meet with results unsatisfactory to us.
> We feel a necessity to believe something on this sign. But we also

encounter in ourselves another kind of necessity. Whatever we believe must be consistent with itself, or with our beliefs, so as stand undoubted and certain. If we find no such stable position, we ought to hold aloof from all commitments. And this is the truly sceptical attitude, in conflict here with the initial attitude of dogmatism.[41]

Hume was a true sceptic, who could not resolve his doubt by argument. He could neither prove nor disprove the existence of God by reason. In 1870 Thomas Huxley coined the word 'agnostic' which has come to mean one who can neither believe nor disbelieve, and perhaps Hume's debate on God's existence ends there.

Hume's true belief was in the existence of reason which, as a slave controlling the passions, would lead man to create a world which operated entirely to his own advantage – and since that advantage could only come to fruition in peace and amity, he would behave in such a manner as to foster the peace and amity needed.

If any phrase can be coined to define the Enlightenment, it is that this period, starting with Bayle in France, saw the start of the ascendancy of reason over faith. The results were as diverse as, for example, James Hutton laying down the principles of 'seminal variation' on which Darwin would base his theory of natural selection and Adam Smith founding the modern science of economics. It can be maintained that our modern world started here and David Hume's philosophy, far from falling 'dead-born from the press', was at its root.

As a man he was as ungainly physically as he was nimble mentally, with few social graces, although he was devotedly conventional in his manners, adjusting his conversation to his company and always capable of enchanting his hostess. That is, when he remembered what day of the week it was. In conversation he was given to long silences with that unsettling steady regard, but enjoyed the intellectual table-talk of the *philosophes*. He was, probably, at his happiest during the embassy to Paris where he lived in a totally artificial world at the head of which was the Comtesse de Boufflers. She, while admitting that she could never be his intellectual equal, was a gentle admirer. Their relationship was one verging on romantic love but without final commitment. Her position as a *Maitresse en Titre* forbade it for her, and Hume was emotionally incapable of such a relationship, attempting in July 1764 to bring the friendship to a stop. His inexpert courting of the Comtesse de Duvernon in Turin had clearly hurt him deeply, and afterwards his relations with females were polite but reserved with only Boufflers melting that reserve. He had a dislike of public speaking and was no orator, talking to partake and learn, rather than adopting the Johnsonian conversational style of seeking crushing victories.

It is at university that we first see him diverging from the expected path of life, and during his attack of the 'Disease of the Learned' this divergence became an unbridgeable intellectual gulf. For the rest of his life Hume was an outsider and observer, his intellect creating a critical view of his surroundings, and his shy personality never allowing him fully to become a part of it. He found Edinburgh too narrow (but it held most of his friends), London too barbaric even allowing for the excellence of its libraries, and Paris too precious, although he could have found seclusion as a neighbour of the Comtesse de Boufflers. His ideal, it seemed, was a small university town in provincial France, giving access to a library – and, probably, a good tailor. An equivalent to Voltaire's exile at Ferney would have been Hume's idea of peace.

The most suitable epitaph for David Hume is that written by Adam Smith to Strahan in November 1776. It is worth quoting in full:

> Thus died our most excellent and never to be forgotten friend; concerning whose philosophical opinions men will no doubt judge variously, every one approving or condemning them according as they happen to coincide or disagree with his own; but concerning whose conduct there can scarce be a difference of opinion. His temper, indeed, seemed to be more happily balanced, if I may be allowed such an expression, than that perhaps of any other man I have ever known. Even in the lowest state of his fortune, his great and necessary frugality never hindered him from exercising, upon proper occasions, acts of both of charity and generosity. It was a frugality founded not upon avarice, but upon the love of independency. The extreme gentleness of his nature never weakened either the firmness of his mind, or the steadiness of his resolutions. His constant pleasantry was the genuine effusion of good nature and good humour, tempered with delicacy and modesty, and without even the slightest tincture of malignity, so frequently the disagreeable source of what is called wit in other men. It never was the meaning of his raillery to mortify; and therefore, far from

offending, it seldom failed to please and delight those who were the objects of it. To his friends, who were frequently the objects of it, there was not perhaps any one of all his great and amiable qualities which contributed more to endear his conversation. And that gaiety of temper, so agreeable to society, but which is so often accompanied with frivolous and superficial qualities, was in him certainly attended with the most severe application, the most extensive learning, the greatest depth of thought, and a capacity in every respect the most comprehensive. Upon the whole, I have always considered him, both in his lifetime, and since his death, as approaching as nearly to the idea of a perfectly wise and virtuous man, as perhaps the frailty of human nature will admit.[42]

My Own Life

18 April 1776

It is difficult for a man to speak long of himself without vanity: therefore I shall be short. It may be thought an instance of vanity, that I pretend at all to write my life: but this narrative will contain little more than the history of my writings; as indeed, almost all my life has been spent in literary pursuits and occupations. The first success of most of my writings was not such as to be an object of vanity.

I was born the 26 of April 1711, Old Style, at Edinburgh. I was of a good family, both by father and mother. My father's family is a branch of the Earl of Home's or Hume's; and my ancestors had been proprietors of the estate which my brother possesses, for several generations. My mother was the daughter of Sir David Falconar, President of the College of Justice: the title of Lord Halkerton came by succession to her brother.

My family, however, were not rich; and being myself a younger brother, my patrimony, according to the mode of my country, was of course very slender. My father, who passed for a man of parts, died, when I was an infant; leaving me, with an elder brother and a sister under the care of our mother, a woman of singular merit, who, though young and handsome, devoted herself entirely to the rearing and educating of her children. I passed through the ordinary course of education with success; and was seized very early with a passion for literature which has been the ruling passion of my life and the great source of my enjoyments. My studious disposition, my sobriety, and my industry gave my family a notion that the law was a proper profession for me: but I found an unsurmountable aversion to every thing but the pursuit of philosophy and general learning: and while they imagined I was poring over Voet and Vinnius, Cicero and Virgil were the authors which I was secretly enjoying.

My very slender fortune, however, being unsuitable to this plan of life, and my health being a little broken by my ardent application, I was tempted or rather forced to make a very feeble trial for entering into a more active scene of life, In 1734, I went to Bristol with some recommendations to eminent merchants; but in a few months found that scene totally unsuitable to me. I went over to France, with a view to prosecuting my studies in a country retreat; and there I laid that plan of life which I have steadily and successfully pursued: I resolved to make a very rigid frugality supply my deficiency of fortune, to maintain unimpaired by independency, and to regard every object as contemptible, except the improvement of my talents in literature.

During my retreat in France, first at Reims, but chiefly at La Flèche in Anjou I composed my *Treatise of Human Nature*. After passing three years very agreeably in that country, I came over to London in 1737. In the end of 1738 I published my *Treatise*; and immediately went down to my mother and brother, who lived at his country house and was employing himself very judiciously and successfully in the improvement of his fortune.

Never literary attempt was more unfortunate then my Treatise of human nature. It *fell dead born from the press* [Hume's italics]; without reaching such distinction as even to excite a murmur among the zealots. But being naturally of a cheerful and sanguine temper, I soon recovered from the blow, and prosecuted with great ardour my studies in the country. In 1742, I printed at Edinburgh the first part of my Essays: the work was favourably received, and soon made me entirely forget my former disappointment. I continued with my mother and brother in the country; and in that time, recovered the knowledge of the Greek language, which I had too much neglected in my early youth.

In 1745 I received a letter from the Marquess of Annandale, inviting me to come and live with him in England: I found also that the friends and family of that young nobleman were desirous of putting him under my care and direction: for the state of his mind and health required it. I lived with him a twelvemonth: my appointments during that time made a considerable accession to my small fortune. I then received an invitation from General St Clair to attend him as secretary to his expedition, which was first meant against Canada, but ended in an incursion on the coast of France: next year, to wit 1747, I received an invitation from the general to attend him in the same station in his military embassy to the courts of Vienna and Turin. I there wore the uniform of an officer; and was introduced at these courts as Aide-de-camp to the General, along with Harry Erskine and Capt. Grant, now General Grant. These two years were almost the only interruptions which my studies have received in the course of my life: I passed them agreeably and in good company: and my appointments, with my frugality, had made me reach a fortune, which I called independent, though most of my friends were inclined to smile when I said so: in short I was now master of near a thousand pound.

I had always entertained a notion that my want of success in publishing the Treatise of Human Nature had proceeded more from the manner than the matter; and that I had been guilty of a very usual indiscretion, in going to the press too early. I therefore cast the first part of the work anew in the Enquiry concerning Human Understanding, which was published while I was at Turin. But this piece was at first but little more successful than the Treatise of human nature. On my return from Italy, I had the mortification to find all England in a ferment on account of Dr Middleton's Free Enquiry; while my performance was entirely overlooked and neglected. A new edition which had been published at London of my Essays, moral and political, met not with a much better reception.

Such is the force of natural temper, that these disappointments made little or no impression on me. I went down in 1749 and lived two years with my brother at his country house; for my mother was now dead. I there composed the second part of my Essays, which I called Political Discourses; and also my Enquiry concerning the Principles of Morals, which is another part of my Treatise that I cast anew. Mean-while my bookseller, A. Millar, informed me that my former publications (all but the unfortunate Treatise) were beginning to be the subject of conversation, that the sale of them was gradually encreasing [sic] and that new editions were demanded. Answers, by Reverends and Right Reverends, came out two or three in a year: and I found by Dr Warburton's railing that the books were beginning to be esteemed in good company. However, I had fixed a resolution, which I inflexibly maintained, never to reply to any-body: and not being very irascible in my temper, I have easily kept myself clear of all literary squabbles. These symptoms of a rising reputation gave me encouragement as I was ever more disposed to see the favourable than unfavourable side of things; a turn of mind, which is more happy to possess than to be born with an estate of ten thousand a year.

In 1751 I removed from the country to the town; the true scene for a man of letters. In 1752 were published at Edinburgh, where I then lived, my Political Discourses, the only work of mine that was successful on the first publication: it was well received abroad and at home. In the same year was published at London my Enquiry concerning the Principles of

Morals, which, in my opinion (who ought not judge on that subject) is of all my writings, historical, philosophical, or literary, incomparably the best: it came unnoticed and unobserved into the world.

In 1752, the faculty of Advocates chose me as their librarian, an office from which I received little or no emolument, but gave me command of a large library. I then formed a plan of writing a History of England; but being frightened with the notion of continuing a narrative, through a period of 1700 years, I commenced with the accession of the House of Stuart; an epoch when, I thought, the misrepresentations of faction began chiefly to take place. I was, I own, sanguine in my expectations of the success of this work. I thought, that I was the only historian, that had at once neglected present power, interest, and authority, and the cry of popular prejudices; and as the subject was suited to every capacity, I expected proportional applause: but miserable was my disappointment: I was assailed by one cry of reproach, disapprobation, and even detestation: English, Scotch and Irish; Whig and Tory; churchman and sectary, free-thinker and religionist; patriot and courtier united in their rage against the man who had presumed to shed a generous tear for the fate of Charles I and the Earl of Strafford: and after the ebullitions of this fury were over, what was still more mortifying, the book seemed to sink into oblivion. Mr Millar told me that in a twelvemonth he sold only forty five copies of it. I scarcely heard of one man in the three kingdoms, considerable for rank and or letters, that could tolerate the book. I must only except the Primate of England, Dr Herring, and the Primate of Ireland, Dr Stone; which seem two odd exceptions. These dignified prelates separately sent me messages not to be discouraged.

I was, however, I confess, discouraged; and had not the war been at that time breaking out between France and England, I had certainly retired to some provincial town of the former kingdom, have changed my name, and never more have returned to my native country. But as this scheme was not now practicable, and the subsequent volume was considerably advanced, I resolved to pick up courage and start again.

In this interval I published at London my Natural History of Religion along with some other small pieces: its public entry was rather obscure, except only that Dr Hurd wrote a pamphlet against it, with all the illiberal petulance, arrogance, and scurrility which distinguishes the Warburtonian school. This pamphlet gave me some consolation for the otherwise indifferent reception of my performance.

In 1756, two years after the fall of the first volume, was published the second volume of my History, containing the period from the death of Charles I till the Revolution. This performance happened to give less displeasure to the Whigs and was better received. It not only rose itself; but helped to buoy up its unfortunate brother.

But though I had been taught by experience that the Whig party were in possession of bestowing all places, both in the state and in literature, I was so little inclined to yield to their senseless clamour, that in above a hundred alterations which farther study, reading, or reflection engaged me to make in the reigns of the first two Stuarts, I have made them all invariably to the Tory side. It is ridiculous to consider the English constitution before that time as a regular plan of liberty.

In 1759 I published my history of the House of Tudor. The clamour against this performance was almost equal to that against the History of the first two Stuarts. The reign of Elizabeth was particularly obnoxious. But I was now callous against the impressions of public folly; and continued very peaceably and contentedly in my retreat at Edinburgh, to finish in two volumes the more early part of the English History; which I gave to the public in 1761 with tolerable, and but tolerable success.

But notwithstanding this variety of winds and seasons to which my writings had been exposed, they had still been making such advances that my copy money, given me by the booksellers, much exceeded anything formerly known in England: I was become not only independent, but opulent. I retired to my native country of Scotland, determined never more to set foot out of it; and retaining the satisfaction of never having preferred a request to one great man or even making advances of friendship to any of them. As I was now turned of fifty, I thought of passing the rest of my life in this philosophical manner; when I received in 1763 an invitation from Lord Hertford, with whom I was not in the least acquainted, to attend him on his embassy to Paris, with a near prospect of being appointed Secretary to the Embassy, and, in the meanwhile, of performing the functions of that office. This offer, however inviting, I first declined: both because I was reluctant to begin connections with the great, and because I was afraid that the civilities and gay company of Paris would prove disagreeable to a person of my age and humour: but on his Lordship's repeating the offer, I accepted of it. I have every reason, both of pleasure and interest to think myself happy in my connections with that nobleman; as well as afterwards with his brother, General Conway.

Those who have not seen the strange effect of modes will never imagine the reception I met with at Paris from men and women of all ranks and stations. The more I recoiled from their civilities, the more I was loaded with them. There is, however, a real satisfaction in living at Paris from the great number of sensible, knowing and polite company with which the city abounds above all places in the universe. I thought once of settling there for life.

I was appointed Secretary to the Embassy, and in summer 1765, Lord Hertford left me being appointed Lord Lieutenant of Ireland. I was *chargé d'affaires* till the arrival of the Duke of Richmond towards the end of the year. In the beginning of 1766, I left Paris and next summer went to Edinburgh, with the same view as formerly of burying myself in a philosophical retreat. I returned to that place, not richer, but with much more money and a larger income by means of Lord Hertford's friendship, than I left it: and I was desirous of trying what superfluity could produce, as I had formerly made of a competency. But in 1767 I received from Mr Conway an invitation to be Under-Secretary; and this invitation, both the character of the person, and my connexions with Lord Hertford, prevented me from declining. I returned to Edinburgh in 1769, very opulent (for I possessed a revenue of 1000 pounds a year) healthy, and though somewhat stricken in years, with the prospect of enjoying long my ease and of seeing the increase of my reputation.

In spring 1775 I was struck with a disorder in my bowels which at first gave me no alarm, but has since, as I apprehend it, become mortal and incurable. I now reckon on a speedy dissolution. I have suffered very little pain from my disorder; and what is more strange, have, notwithstanding the great decline in my person, never suffered a moment's abatement of my spirits: insomuch that were I to name the period of my life that I should most like to pass over again I might be tempted to point to this later period. I possess the same ardour as ever in study, and the same gaiety in company. I consider besides, that a man of sixty five, by dying, cuts off only a few years of infirmities: and though I see many symptoms of my literary reputation's breaking out at last with additional lustre, I know that I had but a few years to enjoy it. It is difficult to be more detached from life than I am at present.

To conclude historically with my own character – I am, or rather was (for that is the style I must now use in speaking of myself; which emboldens me the more to speak my sentiments) I was, I say, a man of mild dispositions, of command of temper, of an open social and cheerful humour, capable of attachment, but little susceptible of enmity, and of great moderation in all my passions. Even my love of literary fame, my ruling passion, never soured my humour, notwithstanding my frequent disappointments. My company was not unacceptable to the young and careless, as well as to the studious and literary: and as I took a particular pleasure in the company of modest women, I had no reason to be displeased with the reception I met with from them. In a word, though many men in any wise eminent have found reason to complain of calumny, I never was touched, or even attacked by her baleful tooth: and though I wantonly exposed myself to the rage of both civil and religious factions, they seemed to be disarmed in my behalf of their wonted fury: my friends never had occasion to vindicate any one circumstance of my character and conduct: not that but the zealots, we may well suppose, would have been glad to invent and propagate any story to my disadvantage, but they could never find any which, they thought, would wear the face of probability. I cannot say there is no trace of vanity in making this funeral oration of myself; but I hope it is not a misplaced one; and this is a matter of fact which is easily cleared and ascertained.

*The Banned Books**

Roger de Rabutin, Conte de Bussy-Rabutin was born on 3 April 1618. Destined for a life as a soldier, he joined the Regiment de Bussy on 6 August 1634 as a commander of light horse artillery and took part in various sieges. By 12 March 1638 he was made a colonel of foot and was presented at court where he fought a duel resulting in a hasty return to the colours as Garrison Commander at Moulins, where he had an ill-advised affair with the Comtesse de Busset. The result of the affair was disgrace and he was sent to the Bastille while his regiment was disbanded. On his release on 28 April 1643 he married Gabrielle de Toulageon who was, conveniently, very rich and the couple moved to Burgundy, near his cousin Mme de Sévigny. With his wife's money he restarted his military career, buying himself a lieutenantcy in his old division of the light horse artillery and rose to be lieutenant general and eventually state councillor. In 1646 his wife died leaving him three daughters. In a moment of complete madness he physically attempted to carry off Mme de Miramion, a nineteen-year-old widow, who resisted loudly and forcefully, resulting in Bussy-Rabutin having to pay her 6000 livres in indemnity. He returned to court and there became the lover of the Marquise de Montglas. He spent what was left of his fortune, was turned down for a loan by Mme de Sévigné but bailed out of debt by Montglas. Ill and back at court, he wrote scandalous portraits of the ladies and 'obscene hallelujahs' for Easter 1659 but a 'party of pleasure' at Roissy caused the King to exile him to Burgundy until November of that year. He wrote a book of *Amorous Proverbs* which pleased the king and gave him some protection. He became an academician in 1665, and the *Amorous history of the Gauls* was published in Liége. It is written as an Arcadian frolic of uninhibited heroes:

> In the reign of Theodate, the war which lasted above twenty years did not hinder the making of love sometimes; but as the Court was filled with old insensible cavaliers or young people born amidst the

* See page 208 and Plate 10.

noise of arms, and whom that trade had rendered brutal, this had made most of the ladies a little less modest than formerly and, as they must have languished in idleness if they had not made advances, or at least if they had been cruel, many of them were tender hearted and some of them impudent. Ardelite was one of the latter . . .'.

Towards the end of the work the mask of anonymity is beginning to slip and Rabutin wanders into autobiography, ending with a biography of Madame de Sévigné. In case no one had realised who these thinly disguised characters were, he then pulls aside the veil of classical names by providing a key to the real names of his principal characters: Theodate was Louis XIV and Ardelite – tender-hearted and impudent – was Mme d'Olonne. The King tried to buy up all copies but a black market soon flourished in Paris. On account of this latest scandal he was again sent to the Bastille for thirteen months, then exiled to Bussy where he expected to live out his life in the Burgundian countryside with the Marquise de Montglas. But on his arrival at the chateau he found that Montglas had lost patience and abandoned him. He redecorated the chateau, one room filled with bad portraits of the military heroes he had never equalled. They range widely to include Oliver Cromwell and Gustavus Vasa, and are carefully labelled, since otherwise they would be completely unidentifiable. His bedroom has slightly better portraits of famous mistresses, presumably to console himself for the lack of one for himself. He was allowed back to Versailles in 1688 with a pension of 4000 livres but died of a stroke at Autun on 9 April 1693. *The Amorous History of the Gauls* was translated into English in 1725. 'The original has been the delight of the gay, the witty, the polite and the learned for above half a century.' The translation obligingly uses the real names without Rabutin's flimsy disguise. He was a tragi-comic character whose writings nowadays might appear in *Private Eye*. Censoring him so publicly – and unnecessarily – was one of the less enlightened moments of the eighteenth century.

Prosper Jolyot de Crébillon, the father of the author of *L'Ecumoire*, was born in Dijon on 13 January 1674. A Jesuit-educated lawyer, he wrote the *Death of the Children of Brutus* (unperformed) and *Idomeneo*, which was performed in 1705 to bad reviews. He promptly rewrote it overnight and it then achieved a mild success. He speculated wildly in dangerous investments and impoverished himself, living in a scarcely furnished apartment infested with cats and dogs. Writing more historical tragedies between 1707 and 1726 brought him success at last and he was elected to the Académie in 1731. He became police censor for belles-lettres and history and Mme de Pompadour gave him a pension of 1000 livres in 1745. He was also appointed as curator of the Royal Library. His more celebrated son was born on 14 February 1707, and grew up in this theatrical and literary world, although educated by Jesuits. In 1734 he wrote *L'Ecumoire, ou Tanzai et Néardané, histoire Japonais,* one of twenty pseudo-oriental works published in that decade. It was a heavy-handed version of a traditional fairy story about an enchanted spoon. It is given to Tanzai before his wedding to Néardané, and licking it causes him to be impotent on his wedding night. While he searches for a cure for his impotence his country descends into anarchy. Néardané also licks the spoon but is cured by a libertine, losing her virginity the while. The couple are reunited and vow to rule justly without any further complications. This fanciful plot gave Crébillon scope for bawdy humour and social comment. The spoon stands for the Bull *Unigenitus* of 1713, which condemned Jansenism, and activating it let loose untold horrors on France. It was also a scandalous *roman à clef,* involving the Cardinals de Noailles and de Rohan as the high priest, and the Duchesse de Maine as a wicked witch. Unlikely to cause riotous dissipation in Edinburgh, the book had landed Crébillon in the Château de Vincennes, although his friend the Duchesse de Conti obtained his release after a few days. It was read enthusiastically by Voltaire, Marivaux and Prévost. Crébillon went on to write a number of mildly scandalous works all set in fictional far-off places. In March 1742 Cardinal Fleury exiled him to thirty leagues beyond Paris but by July he was back with a pardon. Astonishingly, in 1759 he got his father's job as censor and his writing became gloomier. He died in poverty in April 1777. So the work by a censor, from a family of censors, was censored by the advocates of Edinburgh.

Jean de La Fontaine was born in Château-Tierry on 8 July 1621. He entered an Oratory at twenty in 'a moment of fervour' and formed an attachment to the Classics before returning to Château-Thierry to help his father as a forestry administrator. Then in 1654 he translated Terence's *Eunuch.* It was a total failure. However, he was taken up as a private laureate by Mme de Sévigné for whom he wrote celebratory poems.

During this time he learnt to write with a literary gallantry capable of sugaring the bitterest pill while carousing in the bars of the bohemian Temple quarter of Paris. He defended Fouquet after his fall from grace at the accession of Louis XIV in the *Elegy to the nymphs of Vaux*. Then between 1664 and 1685 he wrote the *Contes et Nouvelles en vers*. These were short verse stories from Boccaccio and Margaret of Navarre, or even Ariosto and Rabelais. In their bawdy depictions of sexual appetite old men were cuckolded, randy priests pursued nymphomaniac parishioners and gallants surprised eager ladies during their toilettes. They were a huge success and nothing he wrote subsequently lived up to them. His *Fables* were re-workings of Aesop and other children's tales. He was rejected for membership by the Académie and died in April 1695. The good advocates must have neglected to notice that La Fontaine's principal sources, Boccaccio's *Decameron,* and Margaret of Navarre's *Heptameron,* were all already on their shelves and, in any case, had been previously plundered by Geoffrey Chaucer.

Notes

Principal abbreviations:
BL British Library
EUL Edinburgh University Library
NAS National Archives of Scotland
NLS National Library of Scotland

PREFACE

1. Smout, T.C. *Paper at Prato Conference,* 1978, quoted by Braudel, Fernand in *Civilisation and Capitalism* Vol. III, p. 372, London 1984.
2. Hume, David, *Dialogues Concerning Natural Religion,* p. 3, ed. Norman Kemp Smith, Edinburgh 1947.
3. Tuchman, Barbara, *Bible and Sword,* p. 148 Papermac 1982.

CHAPTER ONE

1. *Parochial registers,* County of Edinburgh, B.1704/1714, Vol. 685 (i), No 15 Frame 4216.
2. Hume, David, *A True Account of the Behaviour and Conduct of Archibald Stewart, Esq., Late Lord Provost of Edinburgh,* p.10, London 1748.
3. Drummond Henry, *Histories of Noble British Families,*Vol II, London 1846.
4. Hume, David, 'My Own Life', NLS, MSS 23159, p23. It is also reprinted in Appendix I to this volume.
5. Mossner, E.C., *The Life of David Hume,* p. 24, Oxford 1980.
6. Boswell, James, *Edinburgh Journals,* p. 99, Edinburgh 2001.
7. Hume, David, *A True Account, Op Cit.,* p. 11.
8. *My Own Life.*
9. Graham, Henry Grey, *The Social Life of Scotland in the Eighteenth Century* p. 25, London 1928.
10. Graham Roderick, *John Knox, Democrat,* p. 189, London 2001.
11. Ramsay of Ochtertyre, James, *Scotland and Scotsmen in the Eighteenth Century,* p. 57, Theommes Press 1996.
12. Binnie, G.A.C., *Churches and Graveyards of Berwickshire,* 1995.
13. Ramsay, *Op. Cit.,* p. 226.
14. *Ibid.,* p. 231.

15. Horn, D.B., *A Short History of the University of Edinburgh*, p. 36, Edinburgh, 1967.
16. Clarke, Samuel, *A Demonstration of the being and attributes of God.* Ed. Enzio Valiati, Cambridge 1998.
17. Ramsay, *Op. Cit.*, p. 8n.
18. Broadie, Alexander, *The Scottish Enlightenment*, p. 26, Edinburgh 2001.
19. Quoted by Arthur Herman in *The Scottish Enlightenment*, p. 2, London, 2002.
20. Wodrow, *Analecta* (December 1724) Maitland Club 1843.
21. Ramsay, *Op. Cit.*, p. 195.
22. Wodrow, *Op. Cit.*
23. Ramsay, *Op. Cit.*, p. 273.
24. Simson, John, *The Case of Mr John Simson*, Edinburgh 1715.
25. Hog, James, *A letter to a gentleman detecting the gangrene of some errors vented at this time.* Edinburgh 1716.
26. Wodrow, *Op. Cit.*
27. Carlyle, Alexander, *Autobiography*, p. 94, London 1910.
28. Leechman, William, *Some account of the life of Francis Hutcheson.* A foreword to, Hutcheson, Francis, *A system of Moral Philosophy*, pp. xvii, xxxiii, Glasgow 1755.
29. *My Own Life.*
30. Hume, David, NLS, MS 23159, Vol IX p.4 (Also reprinted in Mossner, E.C., *David Hume's Essay on 'Chivalry and Modern Honour, Modern Philology* Vol 45, pp. 54/60, Chicago 1947.)
31. Mossner, E.C., *Ibid.*, pp. 54/60, Chicago 1947.
32. Carlyle, *Op. Cit.*, p. 94.

CHAPTER TWO

1. *My Own Life.*
2. *Ibid.*
3. Quoted by Herman, Arthur, in *How the Scots invented the modern World*, p.80, New York 2001.
4. Hancock, P.D., *A Short History of Edinburgh University Library*, Edinburgh 1980.
5. *My Own Life.*
6. Hume, David, *Letters*, NLS MS 23152, p17.
7. *Letters of David Hume*, ed. J.Y.T. Greig, Vol I, p.9, Oxford 1932 (subsequently referred to as *Letters*).
8. *Ibid.*, p.9.
9. *Ibid.*, p.154.
10. DuBos, Abbé, *Critical reflections on Poetry and Art*, trans. Nugent,Vol. II, p.64, London 1748.
11. *Letters*, Vol. I, p. 9.
12. Hill Burton, J., *Life and Correspondence of David Hume*, Vol. I, p.45,n.2, Edinburgh 1846.

13. Dubos, Abbé, *Op. Cit.*, pp.5/9, London 1748.
14. *Ibid.*, pp.4,18,66,332.
15. Cobban, Alfred, *A History of Modern France*, Vol. I, p.83, Pelican 1965.
16. Bayle, Pierre, *The Dictionary Historical and Critical*, London 1738.
17. *Ibid.*
18. *Ibid.*
19. Hume, NLS MS 23159 Vol. IX, p.14.
20. Fénelon, François de Salignac de la Mothe, *The Difference between a Philosopher and a Christian,* from *Five pieces on the evidence for the existence of God.* Supposedly trans. by Bishop Barclay, *passim*, London 1779.
21. *My Own Life.*
22. Buchan, William, *Domestic Medicine,* Edinburgh 1769.
23. *Letters*, Vol. I, p.15.
24. *Ibid.*, p.15.
25. Mure, William, *Caldwell Papers, Part II. Vol. II*, p.178, Maitland Club, Glasgow 1854.
26. *Letters*,Vol. I, p.13.
27. *Ibid.*, p.13.
28. Mossner, E.C., *Life of David Hume, Op. Cit.*, p.84.
29. Cheyne, George, *The English Malady*, London 1733.
30. *Letters,* Vol. I, p.17.
31. DuBos, Abbé, *Op. Cit.*, Vol. II, p.64, London 1748.
32. Fénelon, François de Salignac de la Mothe, *Advice and Consolation for a Person in Distress, passim*, Glasgow 1750.
33. Strathern, Paul, *Hume in 90 Minutes*, p.12, London 1996.

CHAPTER THREE

1. Minutes of the presbytery of Chirnside 1713–1734, quoted by Mossner, E.C. *The Life of David Hume*, p. 81 n.,Oxford 1980.
2. Defoe, Daniel, *A Tour through the whole Island of Great Britain,* London 1975.
3. Latimer, John, *Annals of Bristol in the 18th Century*, p. 190, Bristol 1893.
4. Cave, C.H., *A History of Banking in Bristol*, p.66, Bristol 1899.
5. Montagu, Lady Mary Wortley, *Selected Letters*, p.116 ed. Robert Halsband, 1970.
6. Tytler and Alison, *Travels in France*, Vol II, p.220, Edinburgh 1816.
7. Lauder, Sir John, Lord Fountainhall, *Journals*, p.5, Scottish History Society, Edinburgh 1900.
8. Montagu, Lady Mary Wortley, *Op Cit.*, p.117.
9. Cobban, Alfred, *Op. Cit.*, p.29.
10. Chambers, Robert, *A Biographical Dictionary of Eminent Scotsmen*,1875.
11. EUL *Laing MSS*, II, 301.
12. *Letters*, Vol. I, p.22.
13. Hume, David, *Essays and Treatises,Vol. II*, pp. 124/125, Oxford 1962.

14. *Letters*, Vol. I, p.22.
15. *Ibid.*, Vol. I, pp.19–21.
16. Meyer, P.H., Hume in 18th Century France, Unpublished PhD thesis, Columbia University, 1954.
17. Loriquet, Charles, Lecture in *Travaux de l'academie de Reims*, pp.202/213, Vol. 22, Reims 1855.
18. Morrisoe, Michael, 'Did Hume read Barclay?', *Philological Quarterly*, No. 53, p.314, University of Iowa, 1973.
19. Bazin, Hippolyte, *Une Vieille Cité de France*, Vol. II, p.370, Reims 1900.
20. *Catalogues de Bibliothèque Jésuite*, Bibliothèque Patrimoine de Reims, MS 2007/2008, *passim*.
21. *My Own Life*.
22. Hume, *An Unpublished Letter*, ed. Mossner, p.32, *The University of Texas Studies in English*, xxxvii, 1958.
23. Balfour, Sir Andrew, *Letters writ to a Friend*, p.30, Edinburgh 1700.
24. Petit, Claude, *Un Écossais à la Flèche, Cahiers Flèchois*.
25. Hume, *Treatise of Human Nature*, ed L. A. Selby-Bigge, p.190, Oxford 1998. (All subsequent references are given as *Treatise*.).
26. Hume, *An Unpublished Letter*, ed. Mossner, *The University of Texas Studies in English*, xxxvii (1958), p. 32. On the cover of the copy in the National Library of Scotland is a manuscript dedication by Mossner himself to Professor William Beattie, of the Institute for Advanced Studies in the Humanities of the University of Edinburgh, with the comment, 'note the low opinion Hume has of professors!!!'.
27. *Letters*, Vol. I, p.361.
28. Hume, David, *Essays and Treatises*, Vol. II, pp.115/116, Oxford 1962.
29. Desgraves, Louis, *Revue Française de l'Histoire de la Livre*, No. 55, p.192, June 1987.
30. Mossner, *Life of Hume, Op. Cit.*, p.627.
31. *Ibid.*, p.627.
32. EUL Laing MSS, *Ibid.*, p.627.
33. *Ibid.*, p.627.
34. *Ibid.*, p.301.

CHAPTER FOUR

1. Freeman, Charles, *The Closing of the Western Mind*, p.341, London 2003.
2. Strathern Paul, *Locke in 90 Minutes*, p.9, London 1996.
3. Locke, John, *Essay Concerning Human Undertsanding*, p.49,Wordsworth Classics 1998.
4. *Ibid.*, p.7.
5. Warnock, G.J., *The Oxford Companion to Philosophy*, p.89, Oxford 1995.
6. Wain, John, *Samuel Johnson*, p. 198, London 1974.
7. Voltaire, *Oeuvres*, Vol XVIII, p.274, Paris 1821.
8. Hill Burton, J. *Op. Cit.*, pp.64/69.

9. *Treatise, Op Cit.* (To avoid tedious repetition of notes, quotations from this work in this chapter are not footnoted.)

10. Ayer, A.J., *Hume*, p.54, Oxford 1980.

11. Ayer, *Op. Cit.*, p.60.

12. Hume, David, *History of England*, pp.137/8, London 1754.

13. Ayer, *Op. Cit.*, p.66.

14. NLS, Acc 10805, c1739/40.

15. Stewart, M.A. and Wright, J. P., *Hume and Hume's connexions*, pp.160/161 Edinburgh 1995.

16. Berlin, Isaiah, *The Age of Enlightenment*, p.190, Oxford 1979.

17. Pope, Alexander, *Essay on Man, Epistle II*, ed. J. Ryland, 1900.

18. Flew, Andrew, *Introduction to An Enquiry Concerning Human Understanding*, p.vii, Chicago 1988.

CHAPTER FIVE

1. Hume, David, *Of Civil Liberty, Essays*, p.87, ed. E.F.Miller, Indianapolis 1985. (Hereafter quoted as *Essays.*).

2. Branston, James, *The art of politics*, 1729.

3. Hume, *A Concise and Genuine Account of the dispute between Mr Hume and M. Rousseau*, p.9, London 1766.

4. Hume, *New Letters*, ed. Klibansky and Mossner, p.2, Oxford 1954. (Hereafter quoted as *New Letters.*)

5. *Letters*, Vol. I, p.25.

6. Turnbull, George, *The Principles of Moral Philosophy, an Enquiry into the Wise and Good Government of the Moral World*, Vol. II, endpapers, London 1740.

7. NLS MSS 23159 p.5, Articles of agreement between David Hume of Lancaster Court and John Noon of Cheapside, Bookseller.

8. *The London Stage*, ed. A.H. Scouten, Part 3, pp.731–733, Illinois 1941.

9. *Letters*, Vol. I, p.20.

10. *Treatise, Op. Cit.*, pp.264/265.

11. *My Own Life.*

12. *Ibid.*

13. *New Letters of David Hume*, pp.3/5.

14. *Letters*, Vol. I, pp.30/31.

15. Mossner, E.C., *The Continental Reception of Hume's Treatise, Mind*, Vol LVI, p.33, Edinburgh 1947.

16. Boswell, James, *Private Papers from Malahide Castle*, pp.273/4, privately printed, 1932.

17. *The Edinburgh Amusement*, July 11, 1771, pp.99/100.

18. Stewart, Dugald, *Biographical Memoirs of Adam Smith, William Robertson, and Thomas Reid*, Edinburgh 1811.

19. *Letters*, Vol. I, pp.30/31.

20. Mossner, E.C., *Life, Op. Cit.*, p.33.

21. *Ibid.*, p.33.

22. *The History of the Works of the Learned* (1739), pp.353/404 *passim*, London 1793.
23. *Ibid.*
24. Mossner, *Life, Op. Cit.*, p.617.
25. *Letters*, Vol. I, pp.38/39.
26. Norton, David Fate, 'More Evidence that Hume wrote the Abstract', *Hume Studies*, Vol. XIX, p.218, University of Utah 1993.
27. *Common-Sense or the Englishman's Journal*, July 5 1740, London.
28. Smith, Adam, *The Wealth of Nations*, ed. J.R. McCulloch, p.ii, Edinburgh 1872.
29. *Edinburgh Amusement*, July 11, 1771, pp.51/52.
30. *Ibid.* July 25, pp.99/100.
31. *Annual Register,* chapter on *Characters*, pp.27/32.

CHAPTER SIX

1. Carlyle, *Op. Cit.,* pp.94/95.
2. *Letters*, Vol. I, pp.26/27.
3. Leechman, William, in Foreword to *A System of Moral Philosophy*, by Francis Hutcheson, pp. xx, xxv, xxxiiii, Glasgow 1755.
4. *Journal of the History of Philosophy*, Vol. IV, pp.69/72, 1966 University of California.
5. *Letters*, Vol. I, p.32.
6. Hume, David, *An Enquiry concerning Human Understanding*, p.57, ed. Antony Flew, Chicago 1988.
7. *Treatise*, p.470.
8. *Letters*, Vol. I, p.33.
9. *Ibid.*, pp.34/5.
10. *Treatise*, pp.454, 456.
11. *Letters*, Vol. I, p.37.
12. *Ibid.*, p.38.
13. *Ibid.*, p.40.
14. *Ibid.*, p.36,n.
15. *Ibid.*, p.36.
16. Hilson, J., 'An Early Account of David Hume', *Hume Studies*, pp.78/80, Vol. I, University of Western Ontario.
17. Miller, Eugene F., Foreword to *Essays, moral and political of David Hume*, p.xvii, Indianapolis, 1985.
18. Winchester, Simon, *The Meaning of Everything*, pp.20/26, Oxford 2003
19. Quoted by Williams, Basil, *Oxford History of England*, Vol. XI, p.172, Oxford 1949.
20. *The Scots Magazine*, Vol. IV, 1742, p.119.
21. *Memorials of James Oswald,* Preface, Edinburgh 1825.
22. NAS, Abercairny Papers, GD 24/1/554.
23. *Letters*, Vol. I, p.48.
24. *Caldwell Papers,* Vol. II, p.69, Maitland Club.

25. *Letters*, Vol. I, pp.44/45.
26. *My Own Life*.
27. *Letters*, Vol. I, p.43.

CHAPTER SEVEN

1. Carlyle, *Op. Cit.*, pp.54/55.
2. *Letters*, Vol. I, pp.56/57.
3. *Ibid.*, p.58.
4. *London Chronicle*, November 1776, p.444.
5. *Letter to a Gentleman*, pp.24/25, ed.Mossner and Price, Edinburgh 1967.
6. *Letters*, Vol. I, p.62.
7. *My Own Life*.
8. Fraser, William, *The Annandale Family Book*, p. cccxxxvi.
9. Wood, *Peerage of Scotland*, Vol. I, p.77.
10. *Letters*, Vol. I, p.60.
11. *Ibid.*, pp.60/61.
12. *Ibid.*, p.64.
13. *Ibid.*, p.65.
14. *Ibid.*, p.68.
15. *Ibid.*, p.70.
16. *Ibid.*, p.75.
17. *Ibid.*, p.79.
18. Murray, Thomas, *Letters of David Hume*, p.50, Edinburgh 1841.
19. *Ibid.*, p.56.
20. *Letters*, Vol. I, pp.87/89.
21. *New Letters of David Hume*, p.17.
22. Carlyle, Alexander, *Op. Cit.*, pp.286/7.
23. Hume, David, *A true account of the behaviour and conduct of Archibald Stewart*, *Op. Cit.* p.6.
24. *Ibid.*, p.11.
25. Home, Henry, *Essays on several subjects concerning British Antiquities*, pp.216/217, Edinburgh 1747.
26. *Ibid.*, p.199.
27. Maitland Club, *Caldwell Papers*, Vol. I, p.73.
28. Hume, David, *A true account of the behaviour and conduct of Archibald Stewart*, *Op. Cit.*, p.20.
29. Mackenzie, Henry, *Anecdotes and Egotisms*, p.172, Oxford 1927.
30. *Letters*, Vol. I, p.92.
31. *Ibid.*, p.91,n.
32. *Ibid.*, p.93.
33. *Ibid.*, p.90.
34. *New Letters*, pp.18/20.
35. Hume, MS 23159, p.27 NLS, also printed in Hill Burton, *Op. Cit.*, Vol. I, p.444 ff.

36. *Ibid.*, p.27.
37. Fortescue, J.W., *A Side-show of the Eighteenth Century*, p.332, *Blackwood's Magazine*, Edinburgh 1933.
38. Richmond, H.W., *The Navy in the War of 1739–45*, Vol. III, p.26, Cambridge 1920.
39. NLS, MS 23159.
40. NLS, MS 25688, memorandum of Aug 27th.
41. NLS MS 25688, p.13.
42. *Ibid.*
43. *Letters*, Vol. I, p.94.
44. BL Add MS 26638.
45. NLS MS 23159, p.170.
46. NLS MS 23159, pp.137–163.
47. NLS MS 23159, p.171.
48. *New Letters*, pp.24/26.
49. NLS MS 23159, p.174.
50. *Ibid.*, p.175.
51. *Ibid.*, p.175.
52. *Ibid.*, p.176.
53. *Ibid.*, p.176.
54. *Ibid.*, p.176.
55. *Ibid.*, p.176.
56. NLS MS 23159, p.176.
57. BL Add MS 26638, p.9 (verso).
58. *Letters*, Vol. I, p.99.
59. *New Letters*, pp.24–26.
60. *Letters*, Vol. I, p.113.
61. *Essays*, p.199.
62. *Ibid.*, p.200.
63. *Ibid.*, p.201.
64. *Ibid.*, p.208.
65. *Ibid.*, p.208.
66. *Ibid.*, p.215.
67. *Ibid.*, pp.486/7.
68. *Ibid.*, p.492.

CHAPTER EIGHT

1. *Letters*, Vol. I, p.112.
2. *Ibid.*, p.109.
3. All quotations from the account of his journey are from *Letters*, Vol. I, pp.114–133.
4. Morris, Constance Lily, *Maria Theresa*, London 1938.
5. Hardy, Francis, *Memoirs of James Caulfield, Earl of Charlemont*, pp.13/14, London 1812.

6. *Ibid.*, pp.14/16.
7. *Ibid.*, p.17.
8. Craig, Maurice James, *The Volunteer Earl*, p.43, London 1948.
9. Hardy, Francis, *Op. Cit.*, p.44.
10. *Ibid.*, p.45.
11. *Edinburgh Magazine*, June 1802, pp.430/431.
12. *My Own Life*.
13. Erickson, Carolly, *Bonnie Prince Charlie*, p.246, Robson Books, 2001.
14. *Edinburgh Magazine*, January 1802.
15. *Letters*, Vol. I, p.132.
16. *My Own Life*.
17. *Letters*, Vol. I, p.106.
18. *Enquiry concerning Human Understanding*, p.165, ed. L.A. Selby-Bigge, Oxford 1961.
19. *Ibid.*, p.115, n.
20. *Ibid.*, p.161.
21. *My Own Life*.
22. *Letters*, Vol. II, p.340.
23. *Scotch Haggis*, pp.187/191, Edinburgh 1822.
24. All quotations are from *An Enquiry concerning the Principles of Morals*, ed. L.A. Selby-Bigge, Oxford 1961.
25. NLS MS 25163, p.38.
26. *My Own Life*.
27. *Letters*, Vol. I, p.158.
28. *Ibid.*, p.159.
29. *Ibid.*, p.159.
30. *Ibid.*, p.294.
31. *Ibid.*, pp.161/162.
32. Quotations from these essays are from the relevant titles in *Essays, Moral, Political and Literary, Op. Cit.*
33. *Monthly Review*, Jan. 1752, p.19.
34. *Ibid.*, p.20.
35. *Ibid.*, p.71.
36. Dubos, Abbé, *Critical reflections on Poetry and Art*, trans. Nugent, Vol. II, *Op. Cit.*, p.64.
37. *Letters*, Vol. I, p.192.
38. *Letters*, Vol. I, p.168.

CHAPTER NINE

1. *Letters*, Vol. I, p.164.
2. *Minute Book of the Faculty of Advocates*, pp.14/15, The Stair Society 1999.
3. *Letters*, Vol. I, pp.166/167.
4. *Minute Book of the Faculty of Advocates*, pp.14/15, *Op. Cit.*
5. Mackenzie, Alexander, *Anecdotes and Egotisms, Op. Cit.*, p.171.

6. *Letters*, Vol. I, p.170.
7. Minto, Sir Gilbert Elliot, *Proposals for carrying on certain public works in the city of Edinburgh*, pp.7/33, Edinburgh 1982.
8. Topham, Edward, *Edinburgh Life in the 18th Century*, p. 7, Glasgow 1989.
9. Grant, *Old and New Edinburgh*, Vol. II, p.17, London 1883.
10. Burt, Edward, *Letters from a Gentleman in the North of Scotland*, pp.3/17–19, London 1815.
11. Topham, *Op. Cit.*, p.10.
12. *Ibid.*, p.12.
13. Carlyle, Alexander, Letter to Ebenezer Marshall of Cockpen, EUL, Dc.4.41/96.
14. Topham, *Op. Cit.*, p.12.
15. Houston, R.A., *Social Change in the Age of Enlightenment*, p.285n., Oxford 1994.
16. Houston, R.A., *Op. Cit.*, p.200.
17. Graham, H.G., *Social Life in Scotland in the Eighteenth Century*, p.501, London 1950.
18. Houston, R.A., *Op. Cit.*, p.384.
19. *My Own Life*.
20. *Letters*, Vol. I, pp.211/212.
21. *Ibid.*, p.212.
22. Carlyle, *Op. Cit.*, pp.17/18.
23. Chambers, Robert, *Traditions of Edinburgh*, p.155, Edinburgh 1980.
24. *Essays and Observations, physical and literary*, Edinburgh 1754.
25. McElroy, David D., 'A Century of Scottish Clubs' (unpublished thesis), Vol. I, Edinburgh University 1969, p.68/3.
26. Stewart Dugald, *Biographical Memoir of William Robertson*, p.314, Edinburgh 1811.
27. *Letters*, Vol. I, pp.220/221.
28. *Letters*, Vol. I, pp.219.
29. Stewart, Dugald, *Op. Cit.*, p.316.
30. *Book of the Old Edinburgh Club*, Vol. III, p.148, Edinburgh 1910.
31. *Boswell's Edinburgh Journals*, *Op. Cit.*, p.17.
32. EUL MS Dc.4.41/96.
33. Carlye, *Op. Cit.*, p.287.
34. NLS MS 23159, p.14.
35. *Notes and Queries*, p.561, December 1979.
36. *Letters*, Vol. I, p.170.
37. *Letters*, Vol. I, p.258.
38. *Boswelliana*, p.263, Grampian Club.
39. *Ibid.*, p.221,.
40. *Letters*, Vol. I, p.180.
41. *Letters of David Hume to William Strahan*, p.3, n.2, ed. G. Birkbeck Hill, Oxford 1888.

42. *Letters,* Vol. I, p.193.

43. *Ibid.,* p.214.

44. *My Own Life.*

CHAPTER TEN

1. Hume, David, *History of England,* p.7, London 1754/6.

2. MacQueen, Daniel, *Letters on Mr Hume's History of Great Britain,* pp.4/5, Edinburgh 1756.

3. Mossner, E. C., 'An Apology for Hume, the Historian', *Publications of the Modern Language Association of America,* Vol. LVI, September 1941.

4. *Letters,* Vol. I, p.237.

5. Brown, John, *An Estimate of the Manners and Morals of the Times,* Vol. I, p.15, London 1757.

6. *Ibid.,* pp.58,59.

7. *Ibid.,* Vol. II, p.87.

8. *Letters,* Vol. I, p.249.

9. *History* (to avoid tedious repetition of notes all subsequent quotations are from *The History of England,* David Hume, Indianapolis, 1983 and are not noted).

10. *Letters,* Vol. I, p.185.

11. *Ibid.,* p.217.

12. *Ibid.,* p.221/222.

13. *My Own Life.*

14. Wexlar, Victor G., *David Hume and the History of England,* p.33, Philadelphia 1979.

15. *Ibid.,* p.337 n..

16. *Ibid.,* p.290.

17. *Essays,* p.494.

18. *Ibid.,* p.499.

19. *Ibid.,* p.501.

20. *Letters,* Vol. I, p.223.

21. *Theatre,* Anon, Edinburgh 1756.

22. Hume, David, *Four Dissertations* p.iii, Thoemmes Press, 1995 (reprint of the 1757 edition), p.vi.

23. *Ibid,,* p.xix.

24. *Ibid.,* p.180.

25. *Ibid.,* p.185.

26. Anderson, George, *An Estimate of the Profit and Loss of Religion,* Edinburgh 1753.

27. *Ibid.,* pp.389/390.

28. Anderson, George, *A Reinforcement of the Reasons proving that the Stage is an unchristian Diversion,* p.7, Edinburgh 1733.

29. Bonar, John, *An Analysis of the Moral and Religious Sentiments contained in the Writings of Sopho and David Hume, esq,* p.2, Edinburgh 1755.

30. *Ibid.*, pp.48/49.
31. Blair, Hugh, *Observations on a Pamphlet,* pp.1/23, Edinburgh 1755.
32. *Letters,* Vol. I, p.224.
33. Graham, Henry Grey, *Scottish Men of Letters,* p.42, London 1901.
34. *Ibid.*, p.314.
35. *Votes of the P . . . y of E . . . h, Die Mercurii, die 29no Dec 1756,* Edinburgh, 1757?.
36. *Letters,* Vol. I, p.251.
37. *Ibid.*, p.255.
38. *Ibid.*, p.264.
39. *New Hume Letters, Op. Cit.,* p.43.
40. *Edinburgh Review,* pp.i/iii, 1755.
41. *The Scots Magazine,* Vol. xxiii, 1761, p.389.
42. Sheridan, Thomas, *A Course of Lectures on Elocution,* London 1762, *passim,* reprint Scolar Press 1968.
43. *Ibid.*, p.206.
44. Temple, Launcelot, *Sketches on Various Subjects,* p.19, London 1758.
45. *Letters,* Vol. I, p.286.
46. *My Own Life.*
47. *Letters,* Vol. I. p.304.
48. *Ibid.*, p.314.
49. *Of Miracles, Op. Cit.,* p.188.
50. *Dialogues Concerning Natural Religion, Op. Cit.,* pp.14–19.
51. *My Own Life.*

CHAPTER ELEVEN

1. *Letters,* Vol. I, p.348.
2. *Letters,* Vol. I, p.367.
3. Boswell, *Op. Cit.,* p. 25.
4. Mansell, Philip, *Prince of Europe,* p.52, London 2003.
5. Schazmann, P.-E., *La Comtesse de Boufflers,* p.29, Paris 1933.
6. NLS MS 23153, p.75.
7. *Ibid.*, p.76.
8. *Ibid.*, p.76.
9. *Ibid.*, p.76.
10. *Ibid.*, p.76 .
11. *Letters,* Vol.1 p.374,n. .
12. Walpole, Horace, *Letters,* Vol. V, p.314, ed. Paget, Oxford 1903.
13. *Ibid.*, p.327.
14. Jesse, John Heneage, *Geoge Selwyn and his Contemporaries,* p.233, London 1843.
15. *Ibid.*, p.242.
16. *Letters,* Vol. I, p.388, n.1.
17. *Ibid.*, p.387/388.

18. *Ibid.*, p.392.
19. *Ibid.*, p.393.
20. *Caldwell Papers*, p.251, *Op. Cit.*
21. *Letters*, Vol. I, p.420.
22. *Ibid.*, p.498.
23. Young, Arthur, *Letters concerning the present state of the French nation*, p.142, London 1769.
24. *Ibid.*, p.146.
25. NLS MS 23153, p.71.
26. Deffand, Mme du, *Correspondence complète*, p.328, Paris 1865.
27. *Letters*, Vol. I, pp.406/7.
28. *Ibid.*, p.407.
29. *Ibid.*, p.420.
30. *Caldwell Papers*, I, Vol II, p.255, *Op. Cit.*
31. *Ibid.*, pp.419/420.
32. *Caldwell Papers*, II, Vol I, p.255, *Op. Cit.*
33. *Letters*, Vol. I, p.437.
34. Walpole, *Letters*, Vol. VI, pp.298, 301, 309, 332, *Op. Cit.*
35. Moore, John, M.D., *A view of Society and manners in France, Switzerland and Germany, Vol. I*, pp.29, 30, 68, London 1779.
36. *Ibid.*, p.25.
37. *Caldwell Papers*, p.45, Op. Cit.
38. Cole ,William, *A Journal of my Journey to Paris in 1765*, p.82, ed. F.G. Stokes, London 1931.
39. *Ibid.*, p.128.
40. Deffand, p.305, *Op. Cit.*
41. *Letters*, Vol. II, p.72.
42. Glotz et Maire, *Salons du XVIIIe Siècle*, p.240, Paris 1949.
43. *Letters*,Vol. I, p.431.
44. Glotz et Maire, p.142, *Op. Cit.*
45. Schazmann, p.69, *Op. Cit.*
46. Glotz et Maire, p.147, *Op. Cit.*
47. *Ibid.*, p.157.
48. *Letters*, Vol. I, pp.450–452.
49. NLS, MS 23153, p.75 et seq.
50. *Ibid.*, p.76.
51. NLS MS 23155.
52. *Letters*, Vol. I, p.470.
53. *Letters*, Vol. II, p.110.
54. Carlyle, p.292, *Op. Cit.*
55. *Ibid*, p.292.
56. Texte, Joseph, *Jean-Jacques Rousseau and the cosmopolitan spirit*, p.280, London 1899.
57. *Letters*,Vol. I, p.476.

58. NLS MS 23153, p.82.
59. Percy, Elizabeth, Duchess of Northumberland, *Extracts from her diaries*, p.61, ed. Greig, J., London 1926.
60. *Letters*, Vol. I, p510.
61. *Ibid.*, p.512.
62. *Ibid.*, p.521.
63. *Ibid.*, p.532.

CHAPTER TWELVE

1. Wokler, Robert, *Rousseau*, p.3, Oxford 1995.
2. Hume, David, *A Concise and Genuine account of the dispute between M. Rousseau*, p.iv, London 1766 (subsequently *Concise Account*).
3. *Ibid.*, p.3/4.
4. *Ibid.*, p.8.
5. *Ibid.*, p.11.
6. *Ibid.*, pp.6/7.
7. *Ibid.*, pp.20/21.
8. *Letters*, Vol. II, p.2.
9. Lough, J., *Encyclopédie, Selected Articles*, p.90, Cambridge 1954.
10. *Boswell on the Grand Tour*, pp.293/294, London, 1955.
11. *New Hume Letters*, p.133, *Op. Cit.*
12. *Letters*, Vol. II, p.11.
13. *Concise Account*, pp.52/54.
14. *Ibid.*, pp.16/17.
15. *Ibid.*, p.19.
16. *Letters*, Vol. II, p.29.
17. *Concise Account*, pp.23/24.
18. *Ibid.*, p.27.
19. *Ibid.*, pp.29/30.
20. *Ibid.*, pp.31/87.
21. *Caldwell Papers*, Pt. II, Vol. II, p.109, *Op. Cit.*
22. Cockburn, Alison, *Letters and a Memoir*, pp.45/46, ed. T. Craig Brown, Edinburgh 1899.
23. *Ibid.*, p.42.
24. *Ibid.*, p.71.
25. *Letters*, Vol. II, p.119.
26. *My Own Life*.
27. *Letters*, Vol. II, pp.123/4.
28. *Ibid.*, p.128.
29. *Ibid.*, p.139.
30. Tilley, John, *The Foreign Office*, p.3, London 1933.
31. *Letters*, Vol. II, p.203n.
32. *New Hume Letters*, p.155, *Op. Cit.*
33. *Caldwell Papers*, Vol. I p.41n, *Op. Cit.*

34. *Ibid.,* p.39.
35. *Ibid.,* p.39.
36. *Ibid.,* p.38.
37. *Edinburgh Evening Courant,* 3rd May 1767.
38. *Letters and Journals of Lady Mary Coke,* ed. J.A. Home, Vol. II, pp.312/316, Bath 1970.
39. *Letters,* Vol. II, p. 188.
40. Cockburn, Alison, p.72, *Op. Cit,* and NLS MS 23154, p.31.
41. Carlyle, *Autobiography,* p.545, *Op. Cit.*
42. *Letters,* Vol. II, p.200.
43. *Caldwll Papers,* II, pp.155/156, *Op. Cit.*
44. *Letters,* II, p.184.

CHAPTER THIRTEEN

1. Cosh, Mary, *Edinburgh, The Golden Age,* p.3, Edinburgh 2003.
2. NLS MS 23154, p.32.
3. *My Own Life.*
4. *Letters,* Vol. II, p.208.
5. Mackenzie, Henry, p.172, *Op. Cit.*
6. *Letters,* Vol. II, p.209.
7. Mackenzie, Henry, p.169, *Op Cit.*
8. *Letters,* Vol. II, p.232.
9. Caldwell, p.177n., *Op. Cit.*
10. *Letters,* Vol. II, p.232.
11. NLS MS 23154, p.32.
12. Adam, William, *Sequel to the Gift of a Grandfather,* pp.21/22, Blair Adam Press, 1836.
13. NLS MS 3524, p.71.
14. *Caldwell Papers,* I, p.40. *Op. Cit.*
15. Nolan, J. Bennet, *Benjamin Franklin in Scotland and Ireland,* p.172, University of Pennsylvania 1938.
16. *Ibid.,* p.172.
17. *Letters,* Vol. II, p.286.
18. *Ibid.,* p.287.
19. Carlyle, *Autobiography,* p.458 *Op. Cit.*
20. *Letters,* Vol. II, p.257.
21. Hume, David, *Some Unpublished Letters,* ed. Geoffrey Hunter, pp.6/8 University of Leeds 1960. (These are copies of lost originals made by John Turnbull W.S. which he found in the papers of Joseph Hume of Horndean, Josey's grandson.)
22. *Letters,* Vol. II, p.255.
23. Lehrer, Keith *Thomas Reid,* p.3, London 1989.
24. *Ibid.,* p.3.
25. Herman, Arthur, p.223. *Op. Cit.*

26. Beattie, James, *An Essay on the Nature and Immutability of Truth*, p.440, New York 1983.
27. *Ibid.*, p.42.
28. Beattie, James, *London Diary*, p.35, ed. Ralph Walker, Aberdeen 1956.
29. *Ibid.*, p.47.
30. *Ibid.*, p.86.
31. *Annual Register*, 1777, chapter on *Characters*, pp.27/32.
32. NLS MS 9427, p.24.
33. *Letters*, Vol. II, p.184n.
34. *Ibid.*, p.184.
35. Disraeli, Isaac, *Calamities of Authors*, Vol. II, p.51, London 1812.
36. *Ibid.*, p.234.
37. *Ibid.*, pp. 65/70 *passim*.
38. *Ibid.*, p.60.
39. *Ibid.*, p.74.
40. *Biographical Dictionary of Eminent Scotsmen*, p.420, Edinburgh 1875.
41. *Essays*, p.200n.
42. Mossner, E.C., *The Forgotten Hume*, p.111, New York 1943.
43. *Some Unpublished Letters*, p.13, *Op. Cit.*
44. *Letters*,Vol. II, p.296.
45. NLS Acc. 11353. (This letter was recently discovered in a commonplace book by Dr Iain Gordon Brown of the National Library of Scotland, who has published it, in context, in 'Hume in Paris', pp.6–9, *Folio*, Vol. 6, 2003.)
46. Boswell, James, *Edinburgh Journals*, p.220, *Op. Cit.*
47. *Letters*, II, p. 310.
48. Gibbon, Edward, *The Decline and Fall of the Roman Empire*, Vol. II, p.92, Folio Society 1984.
49. *Ibid.*, p.200.
50. *Letters*, Vol. II, p.310.
51. Boswell, James, *Edinburgh Journals*, pp.193/194, *Op. Cit.*
52. *Ibid.*, p.311/312.
53. *My Own Life.*
54. Home, John, *Works*, ed. Mackenzie, Vol. I, pp.167/158, Edinburgh 1822.
55. *Ibid.*, pp.168/169.
56. *Ibid.*, p.170.
57. *Some Unpublished Letters*, p.17, *Op. Cit.*
58. Hume, John, *Works*, ed. Mackenzie, p.174, *Op. Cit.*
59. *Letters*, II, p.320.
60. Carlyle, *Autobiography*, p.560, *Op. Cit.*
61. *Letters*, Vol. II, p318.
62. Hume, David, *Some Unpublished Letters*, p.27, *Op. Cit.*
63. *Letters*, Vol. II, p. 325.
64. *Ibid.*, pp.328/329.

65. Doig, Andrew, *Dr Black, a remarkable Physician,* p.38, Royal Scottish Museum, Edinburgh 1982.

66. Wilkinson, J., 'The Last Illness of David Hume', p.77, *Proceedings of the Royal College of Physicians of Edinburgh,* Vol.18, 1988.

67. Hume, David, *Some Unpublished Letters,* pp.33/34, *Op. Cit.*

68. NLS MS 23159, p.24.

69. Hume, John, *Works,* ed. Mackenzie, p.164, *Op. Cit.*

70. www.scottishdocuments.com. Consult under Famous Scotsmen/David Hume.

71. *Letters,* Vol. II, p.323.

72. *Ibid.,* p.453.

73. Boswell, James, *Edinburgh Journals,* pp.256–258, *Op. Cit.*

74. *Letters,* p.330.

75. Hume, David, *Some Unpublished Letters,* p.36, *Op. Cit.*

76. *Letters,* Vol. II, p.335.

77. *Caldwell Papers,* I, pp.39/40, *Op. Cit.*

78. *Letters,* Vol. II p.451.

79. *Ibid.,* p.449.

80. *Scots Magazine,* Vol. 37, p.435, 1776.

81. Several designs by Adam are in the Soane Museum AV 19/78.

82. Brown, Iain Gordon, 'David Hume's Tomb', *Proceedings of the Society of Antiquaries of Scotland,* 121, (1991), pp.391–422.

CHAPTER FOURTEEN

1. *Letters,* II, p.453.

2. NLS, MS 23153, p.51.

3. *Letters,* I, p.380.

4. *Essays,* p.577.

5. *Ibid.,* p.583.

6. *Ibid.,* p.588.

7. *Ibid.,* p.588.

8. *Ibid.,* p.590.

9. *Ibid.,* p.598.

10. Hume, David, *Essays on Suicide and the Immortality of the Soul ascribed to the late David Hume, never before published with remarks intended as an Antidote to the poisons contained in their Performances,* p.39, London 1783.

11. *Ibid.,* p.38.

12. *Ibid.,* pp.41/42.

13. *Ibid.,* pp.46, 50.

14. *Ibid.,* p.51.

15. *Ibid.,* p.52.

16. *Ibid.,* p.56.

17. Hume, David, *Principal writings on religion including Dialogues Concerning Natural Religion,* ed. J.C.A. Gaskin, p.29, Oxford 1993. (All quotations from the *Dialogues* are from this edition.)

18. Mossner, E.C., *David Hume, Bicentenary Papers*, ed. George Morice, p.1, Edinburgh 1977.

19. Hendel, Charles, *Studies in the Philosophy of David Hume*, p.309, Boobs-Merrill, 1963.

20. Mossner, *Bicentenary Papers*, p.18, *Op. Cit.*

21. Pehelhum, Terence, *Hume*, p.163, London 1975.

22. Capitan, William H., *Part X of Hume's Dialogues*, in *Modern Studies in Philosophy*, p.384, ed. V.C.Chappell, University of Notre Dame 1968.

23. *Ibid.*, pp.18/19.

24. Penelhum, pp.169/195, *Op. Cit.*

25. Wollheim, Richard, *Hume on Religion*, p.15, Collins 1963.

26. *Letters*, Vol. I, p.439.

27. Wollheim, p. 16, *Op. Cit.*

28. Noxon, James, *David Hume, Many Sided Genius*, p. 81, University of Oklahoma 1976.

29. *Ibid.*, p.62.

30. *Natural History*, p.154.

31. Bayle, Pierre, *Pensées diverses*, Rotterdam 1704.

32. *Natural History*, p.178.

33. *Ibid.*, p.184.

34. *Essays*, p.80.

35. Hendel, Charles, pp.22/24/27, *Op. Cit.*

36. *Ibid.*, p.11.

37. Noxon, p.82, *Op. Cit.*

38. *Of Miracles*, p.86, *Op. Cit.*

39. Capaldi, Nicholas, *David Hume, the Newtonian Philosopher*, p. 197, Twayne Publishers, Boston 1975.

40. *Ibid.*, p.189.

41. Hendel, Charles, p.309 *Op. Cit.*

42. *Letters*, Vol. II, p.452

Works Consulted

The Internet bookseller Amazon has 584 listings of David Hume – including a namesake of the historian writing on Marquetry – but there is no standard edition of his collected works. They are simply too many and they are too diverse. But the works by Hume I have consulted are as follows:

Hume, David, *An Abstract of a Treatise of Human Nature, 1740*, ed. J.M. Keynes and P. Sraffa, Thoemmes, Bristol 1990

Hume, David, *A Concise and Genuine account of the dispute between Mr Hume and M. Rousseau*, London 1766

Hume, David, *Dialogues Concerning Natural Religion*, ed. Norman Kemp Smith, Edinburgh 1947.

Hume, David, *An Enquiry concerning Human Understanding*, ed. Antony Flew, Chicago 1988

Hume, David, *Essays*, Indianapolis 1985

Hume David, Essay on Chivalry and Modern Honour, National Library of Scotland, Hume MSS 23159 Vol. IX

Hume, David, *Essays on Suicide and the Immortality of the Soul ascribed to the late David Hume, never before published with remarks intended as an Antidote to the poisons contained in their Performances*, London 1783

Hume, David, *Essays and Treatises*, Vol. II, pp.124/125, Oxford 1962

Hume, David, *Four Dissertations*, Thoemmes Press, 1995 (reprint of the 1757 edition)

Hume, David, *Historical Memoranda* (a forgery), NLS MSS732/734

Hume, David, *History of England*, Edinburgh 1754 and 1757

Hume, David, Letters, National Library of Scotland, Hume MSS 23152 Vol. II

Hume, David, *Letters*, ed J.Y.T Greig, Oxford 1932

Hume, David, My Own Life, National Library of Scotland, Hume MSS 23159, Vol. IX

Hume, David, *New Letters*, ed. Klibansky and Mossner, Oxford 1954

Hume, David, *Some Unpublished Letters*, ed. Geoffrey B.B. Hunter, Leeds 1958

Hume, David, *Principal writings on religion including Dialogues Concerning Natural Religion*, ed. J.C.A. Gaskin, Oxford 1993

Hume, David, *A Treatise of Human Nature*, ed. L.A. Selby-Bigge, Oxford 1978

Hume, David, *A True account of the Behaviour and Conduct of Archibald Stewart, Esq., Late Lord Provost of Edinburgh*, London 1748

The relevant Hume manuscripts in the National Library of Scotland are:

MSS 509, 732–4, 786, 1703,2619, 5722, 23152–9, 25688, 25163

Acc 10805, 11353

And in the British Library:
Add MS 36638

Printed Books:

Adam, William, *Sequel to the Gift of a Grandfather*, Blair Adam Press, 1836
Adams, William, *An Essay on Mr Hume's essay on Miracles*, London 1752
Anderson, George, *An Estimate of the Profit and Loss of Religion*, Edinburgh 1753
Anderson, George, *A reinforcement of the reasons proving that the stage is an unchristian diversion*, Edinburgh 1733
Annual Register for 1776, London 1777
Arnot, Hugo, *The History of Edinburgh*, Edinburgh 1998
Ayer, A.J., *Hume*, Oxford 1980
Balfour, Sir Andrew, *Letters writ to a Friend*, Edinburgh 1700
Barker, Felix & Jackson, Peter, *London, 2000 years of a city and Its people*, 1974
Bayle, Pierre, *The Dictionary, Historical and Critical*, London 1738
Bayle, Pierre, *Pensées diverses*, Rotterdam, 1704
Bazin, Hippolyte, *Une Vieille Cité de France*, Vol. II, Reims 1900
Beattie, James, *An Essay on the Nature and Immutability of Truth*, New York 1983
Beattie, James, *London Diary*, ed. Ralph Walker, Aberdeen 1956
Bennet, Nolan J., *Benjamin Franklin in Scotland and Ireland*, Pennyslvania 1938
Berlin, Isaiah, *The Age of Enlightenment*, Oxford 1979
Biographical Dictionary of Eminent Scotsmen, see Chambers, Robert
Blair, Hugh, *Observations on a pamphlet*, Edinburgh 1755
Bondar, John, *An analysis of the moral and religious sentiments contained in the writings of Sopho and David Hume esq.*, Edinburgh 1755
Book of the Old Edinburgh Club, Vol. III, Edinburgh 1910
Boswell, James, *Edinburgh Journals*, Edinburgh 2001
Boswell, James, *Private Papers from Malahide Castle*, privately printed, 1932
Boswell, James, *Boswell on the Grand Tour*, London 1955
Boswelliana, Grampian Club
Brown, John, *An Estimate of the Manners and Morals of the Times*, 2 Vols., London 1757
Buchan, William, *Domestic Medicine*, Edinburgh 1769
Burt, Edward, *Letters from the North of Scotland*, Vol. I, London 1815
Bussy-Rabutin, Roger Comte de, *L'Histoire Amoureuse des Galles*, Liège 1725
Capaldi, Nicholas, *David Hume, the Newtonian Philosopher*, Boston 1975

Capitan William H., *Part X of Hume's Dialogues*, in *Modern Studies in Philosophy*, ed. V.C. Chappell, University of Notre Dame 1968

Carlyle, Alexander, *Autobiography*, London 1910

Catalogues de Bibliothèques Jésuites, Bibliothèque Patrimoine de Reims, MSS 2007/2008

Cave, C.H., *A History of Banking in Bristol*, Bristol 1899

Chambers, Robert, *Domestic Annals*, Vol. II & Vol. III, Edinburgh

Chambers, Robert, *A Biographical Dictionary of Eminent Scotsmen*, London 1875

Cheyne, George, *The English Malady*, London 1733

Clarke, Samuel, *A Demonstration of the being and attributes of God*, ed. Enzio Valiati, Cambridge 1998

Cobban, Alfred, *A History of Modern France*, Vol. I, Penguin 1965

Cobban, Alfred, *In Search of Humanity*, 1960

Cockburn, Alison, *Letters and a Memoir*, ed. T. Craig Brown, Edinburgh 1899

Coke, Lady Mary, *Letters and Journals of Lady Mary Coke*, ed. J.A. Home, Vol. II, Bath 1970

Common Sense or the Englishman's Journal, London 1740

Cosh, Mary, *Edinburgh, The Golden Age*, Edinburgh 2003

Craig, Maurice James, *The Volunteer Earl*, London 1948

Crébillon fils, *L'Écumoire*, ed. Sturm, Paris 1976

Dalziel, Andrew, *History of the University of Edinburgh*, Vol. II, Edinburgh 1862

Desgraves, Louis, *Revue Française de l'Histoire de la Livre*, No. 55, June 1987

Dictionnaire Biographique Française

Disraeli, Isaac, *Calamities of Authors*, London 1812

Doig, Andrew, *Dr Black, a Remarkable Physician*, Royal Scottish Museum, Edinburgh 1982

Drummond, Henry, *Histories of Noble British Families*, Vol. II, London 1846

Du Bos, Abbé, tr. Thomas Nugent, *Critical Reflections on Poetry, Paining and Music*, Vols. 1&2 London 1748

Du Deffand, Marie, *Correspondence Complète*, Paris 1865

Edinburgh Magazine, 1802

Edinburgh Evening Courant, 1767

Sir Gilbert Elliot of Minto, *Convention of Royal Burghs*, 8th July 1752

Epinay, Mme de, *Mémoires et Correspondence*, Paris 1818

Erickson, Carolly, *Bonnie Prince Charlie*, Robson Books 2001

Feiling, Keith, *A History of England*, London 1950

Fénelon, Francois de Salignac de la Mothe. *Instructions et avis sur divers points de la morale at de la perfection Chrétienne*. Trans. London 1750

Fénelon, Francois de Salignac de la Mothe, *Five pieces on the evidence of the existence of God* including *The Difference between a philosopher and a Christian*. Supposedly translated by Bishop Barclay, London 1779

Fortescue, J.W., *A Side-show of the Eighteenth Century*, p.332, *Blackwood's Magazine*, Edinburgh 1933

Fraser, Antonia, *Marie Antoinette*, London 2001

Freeman, Charles, *The Closing of the Western Mind*, London 2003

Glotz et Maire, *Salons du XVIIIe Siècle*, Paris 1949

Gossman, Lionel, *French Society and Culture*, New Jersey, 1972

Graham, Henry Grey, *Scottish Men of Letters*, London 1901

Graham, Henry Grey, *Social Life in Scotland in the Eighteenth Century*, London 1928

Graham, Roderick, *John Knox – Democrat*, London 2001

Grant, Sir Alexander, *The Story of the University of Edinburgh*, Vols. I&II, London 1884

Gresset, J.B.L., *Vert Vert*, tr. M.Montagu, 1840

Hancock, P.D., *A Short History of Edinburgh University Library*, Edinburgh 1980

Hardy, Francis, *Memoirs of James Caulfield, Earl of Charlemont*, London 1812

Harrison, John, *Oure Townis Colledge*, Edinburgh 1884

Hendel, Charles, *Studies in the Philosophy of David Hume*, Boobs-Merrill, 1963

Henderson, G.D., *Chevalier Ramsay*, Edinburgh 1952

Herman, Arthur, *The Scottish Enlightenment*, London 2002

Hilson, J., *An Early Account of David Hume, Hume Studies*, pp. 78/80, Vol. I, University of Western Ontario, 1975

History of the works of the Learned, Nov./Dec. 1739

Hog, James, *A letter to a gentleman detecting the gangrene of some errors vented at this time*, Edinburgh 1716

Home, John, *Works*, ed. Mackenzie, Vol. I, Edinburgh 1822

Horn, D.B., *A Short History of the University of Edinburgh*, Edinburgh 1967

Houston, R.A., *Social Change in the Age of Enlightenment*, Oxford 1994

Hyde, H. Montgomery, *John Law*, 1948

Jesse, John H., *George Selwyn and his contemporaries*, London 1882

Journal of the History of Philosophy, Vol. IV, University of California 1966

Klibansky, R. and Mossner, E.C., *New letters of David Hume*, Oxford 1954

Kincaid, Alexander, *The History of Edinburgh*, Edinburgh 1737

La Fontaine, Jean, *Contes et Nouvelles*, Paris 1873

Larousse Gastronomique, London 1976

Latimer, John, *Annals of Bristol in the 18th Century*, Bristol 1893

Lauder, Sir John of Fountainhall, *Journals*, ed. D. Crawford, Edinburgh 1900

Law, Alexander, *Education in Edinburgh in the Eighteenth Century*, London 1965

Leechman, William, *Some account of the life of Francis Hutcheson*, Foreword to Hutcheson, Francis, *A system of Moral Philosophy*, Glasgow 1755

Lehmann, W. C., *Henry Home and the Scottish Enlightenment*, The Hague, 1971

Lehrer, Keith, *Thomas Reid*, London 1989

Lenman, Bruce P, *From the Union to the Franchise Reform of 1832*, New Penguin History of Scotland, London 2002

Little, Bryan, *The City and County of Bristol*, London 1954

Locke, John, *An Essay Concerning Human Understanding*, Wordsworth Classics, 1998

London Chronicle, November 5/7, 1776, p.44

The London Stage, ed. A.H. Scouten, Illinois 1941

Loriquet, Ch., *Lecture sur la vie de L'Abbé Pluche*, Reims

Lough, John, *An Introduction to 18th century France*, London 1960

Lough, John, *Encyclopédie, Selected Articles*, Cambridge 1954

McElroy, David D., A Century of Scottish Clubs, (unpublished thesis) Edinburgh 1969.

Mackenzie, Henry, *Anecdotes and Egotisms*, Oxford 1927

MacQueen, Daniel, *Letters on Mr Hume's History of Great Britain*, Edinburgh 1756

Mansell, Philip, *Prince of Europe*, London 2003

Maxwell, Constantia, *The English Traveller in France, 1698–1815*, 1932

Meyer, P.H., Hume in 18th Century France, Ph.D. thesis, Columbia University, 1954

Minute Book of the faculty of Advocates, Vol. 3, Stair Society, Edinburgh 1998

Montagu, Lady Mary Wortley, *Selected Letters*, ed. Robert Halsband, 1970

Moore, *View of Society and Manners in France*, London 1779

Morgan, Kenneth, *Bristol and the Atlantic Trade in the 18th century*, Cambridge 1993

Morris, Constance Lily, *Maria Theresa*, London 1938

Morrisoe, Michael, 'Did Hume read Barclay?', *Philological Quarterly*, No. 53, University of Iowa 1973

Mossner, E.C., *The Continental Reception of Hume's Treatise, Mind*, Vol. LVI , Edinburgh 1947

Mossner, E.C., *David Hume, Bicentenary Papers*, ed. George Morice, Edinburgh 1977

Mossner, E.C.. *The Forgotten Hume*, New York 1943

Mossner, E.C., *The Life of David Hume*, Oxford 1980

Mossner, E.C. 'David Hume's Essay on "Chivalry and Modern Honour"', *Modern Philology*, Vol. 45, Chicago 1947

Mossner, E.C., *David Hume, Bicentenary papers*, ed. George Morice, Edinburgh 1977

Murray, Thomas, *Letters of David Hume*, Edinburgh 1841

Nolan, J. Bennet, *Benjamin Franklin in Scotland and Ireland*, University of Pennsylvania 1938

Norton, David Fate, 'More Evidence that Hume wrote the Abstract', *Hume Studies*, Vol. XIX, University of Utah 1993

Nouvelle Biographie Générale, Paris 1857

Noxon, James, *David Hume, Many Sided Genius*, University of Oklahoma 1976

Parochial registers, County of Edinburgh, B.1704/1714, Vol. 685

Pehelhum, Terence, *Hume*, London 1975

Percy, Elizabeth, Duchess of Northumberland, *Extracts from her diaries*, p.61, ed. Greig, J., London 1926

Plant, Marjorie, *The Domestic Life of Scotland in the Eighteenth Century*, Edinburgh 1952

Ramsay of Ochtertyre, John, *Scotland and Scotsmen in the Eighteenth Century*, Thoemmes Press 1996

Richmond, H.W., *The Navy in the war of 1739–48*, Cambridge 1920

Ross, I.S., *Lord Kames*, Oxford 1972

Scotch Haggis, Edinburgh 1822

Scots Magazine, Vol. III, Edinburgh 1741

Shackleton, Robert, *The Enlightenment*, in *The Eighteenth Century*, 1969

Schazmann, Paul Emile, *La Comtesse de Boufflers*, Lausanne 1933

Sheridan, Thomas, *A Course of Lectures on Elocution*, London 1762, reprint Scolar Press 1968

Simson, John, *The Case of Mr John Simson*, Edinburgh 1715

Smith, Adam, *The Wealth of Nations*, ed. J.R. McCulloch, Edinburgh 1872

Stewart Dugald, *Biographical Memoirs of Adam Smith, William Robertson, and Thomas Reid*, Edinburgh 1811

Stewart, M.A. and Wright, J. P., *Hume and Hume's connexions*, Edinburgh 1995

Strathern, Paul, *Hume in 90 minutes*, London 1996

Strathern, Paul, *Locke in 90 minutes*, London 1996

Stroud, Barry, *David Hume*, London 1999

Stryienski, Casimir, *The Eighteenth Century*, London 1916

Temple, Launcelot, *Sketches on Various Subjects*, London 1758

Texte, Joseph, *Jean-Jacques Rousseau and the cosmopolitan spirit*, London 1899

Tilley, John and Gaselee, Stephen, *The Foreign Office*, London 1933

Topham, Edward, *Letters from Edinburgh, 1774/5*, Edinburgh 1971

Transactions of the Royal Society of Edinburgh, Vol. I, Edinburgh 1788

Tuchman, Barbara, *Bible and Sword*, Papermac 1982

Wain, John, *Samuel Johnson*, London 1974

Walpole, Horace, *Letters*, Vol. VI, ed. Paget, Oxford 1903

Weekly Magazine or Edinburgh Amusement, Vol. VIII, Edinburgh 1771

Wexler, Victor G., *David Hume and the History of England*, American Philosophical Society, 1979

Whatley, Christopher A., *Scottish Society, 1707–1830*, Manchester 2000

Wilkinson, J., 'The Last Illness of David Hume', *Proceedings of the Royal College of Physicians of Edinburgh*, Vol. 18, 1988

Wokler, Robert, *Rousseau*, Oxford 1995

Wollheim, Richard, *Hume on Religion*, Collins 1963

Wood, *Peerage of Scotland*, Vol. I

Williams, Basil, *The Whig Supremacy, 1714–1760*, Oxford 1949

Young, Arthur, *Letters concerning the present state of the French nation*, London 1769

Index

Note: DH stands for David Hume; page numbers suffixed 'n' refer to footnotes.